To Dad,

1992

nth

THE HISTORY OF

NOTTINGHAMSHIRE
COUNTY
CRICKET CLUB

THE CHRISTOPHER HELM
COUNTY CRICKET HISTORIES

Series Editors:
Peter Arnold and Peter Wynne-Thomas

DERBYSHIRE
John Shawcroft, with a personal view by Bob Taylor

GLAMORGAN
Andrew Hignell, with a personal view by Tony Lewis

GLOUCESTERSHIRE
David Green, with a personal view by B. D. Wells

LEICESTERSHIRE
Dennis Lambert, with a personal view by Mike Turner

MIDDLESEX
David Lemmon, with a personal view by Denis Compton

SURREY
David Lemmon, with a personal view by Peter May

WARWICKSHIRE
Jack Bannister, with a personal view by M. J. K. Smith

WORCESTERSHIRE
David Lemmon, with a personal view by Basil D'Oliveira

YORKSHIRE
Anthony Woodhouse, with a personal view by Sir Leonard Hutton

THE HISTORY OF

NOTTINGHAMSHIRE
COUNTY
CRICKET CLUB

Peter Wynne-Thomas

With a personal view by
DEREK RANDALL

CHRISTOPHER HELM

London

© 1992 Peter Wynne-Thomas and Derek Randall
Christopher Helm (Publishers) Ltd, a subsidiary of
A & C Black (Publishers) Ltd, 35 Bedford Row,
London WC1R 4JH

ISBN 0-7136-8087-3

A CIP catalogue record for this book is available
from the British Library

Typeset by Rowland Phototypesetting Ltd, Bury St Edmunds, Suffolk
Printed and bound in Great Britain by Biddles Ltd, Guildford and King's Lynn

CONTENTS

A PERSONAL VIEW
Derek Randall

I JOINED THE PLAYING staff at Trent Bridge in April 1971, with two other local Nottinghamshire hopefuls, Dusty Hare and Phil Wilkinson, plus the fast bowler, Bill Taylor, who had had experience as a part-time pro with Leek in the North Staffs League.

Apart from us, there were only twelve professionals on the books – Richard Bielby, Brian Bolus, Graham Frost, Pasty Harris, Basher Hassan, Peter Plummer, Dave Pullan, Mike Smedley, Gary Sobers, Barry Stead, Mike Taylor and Bob White. Unlike 1991 when 24 full-time professionals are fighting to get a place in the first team, or fighting to retain a place! In 1971 the team chose itself; the only question was who acted as twelfth man.

Until I arrived at Trent Bridge most of my cricket had been in the north of the county, playing in the Bassetlaw League for my home town of Retford. Mike Hall, the Retford captain and former county cricketer, recommended me to the County Club and my first match for the second team was in July 1969 on the Steetley Works ground, against Derbyshire – I was out without scoring.

The following summer I played for the seconds on the Retford ground and, for those who like records, took a wicket with the first ball I bowled in the Second Eleven Competition. The match was against Warwickshire and bowling for the opposition was a certain Eddie Hemmings. He did not get me out. In the return game, at Bedworth, I scored my first fifty and Eddie scored 51.

Although I turned out in six second team games during 1970, not one was played at Trent Bridge and since nearly all the players in the seconds were local club cricketers like myself, there were few opportunities to rub shoulders with the county players themselves. In fact the only match I played at Trent Bridge in 1970 was for the Club & Ground against the RAF. I regret to say I was stumped before scoring a run.

Jack Baddiley, the former captain of Worksop Cricket Club, and a farmer on the northern border with Yorkshire, was the Chairman of the County Club in 1971. He was a great enthusiast for Notts cricket and especially keen that some of the players from his part of the world were given a chance in county cricket. Much of his time was spent watching the second eleven games. The County coach was the old Notts player, Frank Woodhead, who originally came from Edwinstowe. This meant that two of the most important people in the life of someone coming on to the staff actually spoke my language.

The County team of the 1960s and early 1970s was not a world-beating side. We had the great Gary Sobers, but the bowling was moderate and the eleven never looked like challenging for the Championship, or indeed the two one-day competitions. My first chance in the first team came when Graham Frost was injured on the Saturday of the three-day game against Yorkshire, so that left the side a batsman short for the Sunday League match, which was arranged to be played on John Player's own ground, off the Nottingham ring road.

The opponents were Surrey and Notts, batting first, had to contend with a trio of England seamers – Geoff Arnold, Robin Jackman and Bob Willis – while Pat Pocock was the main spinner. Even Gary Sobers found runs hard to score and the total gradually built up to 123 for three. When the fourth wicket fell Barry Stead was sent in to speed the run rate and though he failed, the 40 overs were complete before I could get in. We lost by three wickets.

I thought I might have a second chance in the next three-day game, since our opposition was Cambridge University, but an additional bowler, Peter Plummer, was preferred – in those days counties usually played strong sides against Oxford and Cambridge, another part of cricket that has altered over the last 20 years.

So it was back to either duties as 12th man or in the seconds, and not until the following summer did I first appear in Championship cricket.

Looking back it seems odd how often I managed to avoid playing at Trent Bridge itself. Not only were virtually all the second team matches arranged for club grounds around the county, but that Sunday League game at the Player ground was one of the very few that Notts have staged away from headquarters. The same thing happened when I made my first-class debut. The game was played at the RHP Ground at Newark. Notts had signed a young batsman from Trinidad for the 1972 season – he had had a trial in 1971 and batted well in the seconds. Richard Bielby had left at the end of 1971 and Nirmal Nanan was given his place in the first team for the opening games of 1972, but he didn't manage a decent score and at the end of May I was substituted for him in the Essex match. Essex batted first and as the Notts innings began late in the day, Dave Pullan was drafted in as night-watchman, so though I was down to bat at number seven, I actually went in at number eight. I scored 78, kept my place for the rest of the season and the rest, as they say, is history.

For those who have only known Trent Bridge and Nottinghamshire County Cricket Club for the last few summers, it is difficult to realise how much has changed during my playing career.

Of course most of the players who were in that team against Essex in 1972 are seen still at Trent Bridge in one guise or another. Mike Harris, who coaches at Stowe, comes to offer advice in his holidays and helps with some of the young batsmen of the 1990s; Bob White umpires county matches; Dave Pullan works across the road with Nottingham Forest Football Club; Mike Smedley still plays cricket for Kiveton Park and captained our Old Players Team in 1991. Gary Sobers flies from one continent to another; Mike Taylor is the Marketing Manager with Hampshire and Basher Hassan performs the same duties at Trent Bridge; Bill Taylor runs a local printing firm. The eleventh player was Barry Stead, who sadly died soon after retiring from first-class cricket.

Of the two youths who started in the same season as myself, Dusty Hare became a world-famous rugby footballer and has now returned to farming, which in fact he never left, and Phil Wilkinson plays in the Yorkshire Leagues.

2

Of the men behind the scenes, 20 years has seen numerous changes, but Ron Allsop still cuts the grass for us. Today there is a marketing office, an accounts office and a squash club and probably other strangenesses about which I know little in and around the old Trent Bridge Pavilion. In 1971 things were much quieter. Ron Poulton, the Secretary, seemed to have been in his office with the enormous desk since it was built – a kindly balding man with a pipe. Mrs Woodhead, the wife of the coach, sat in the outer office, answered the phone and dealt with those who stood on the other side of the counter. If you were thought important you were ushered into the inner sanctum. Above the Secretary's office was Frank Wood-head's abode, where among the ledgers and sundry items of cricket equipment the groundstaff spent a deal of time when not in the indoor nets or out on the field.

The great scoreboard was still in existence, requiring four or five men to make it work. There was nothing like it in England and to this day no club has tried to build such a comprehensive edifice – the names of all 22 players on permanent display and a light going up against your name each time you fielded the ball. The spectators could sort out the identity of poor fielders much quicker; perhaps it was one such unfortunate that had the board done away with. Too embarrassing!

The ground itself was an acre or more bigger than it is today. No great office block peered over the grass, and on what is now the office car park were the row of practice nets. The TBI (Trent Bridge Inn to the unfamiliar) was the one place to go after the game – unless it was to the Eddie Marshall bar behind the pavilion. This was a pre-cast concrete shed against the Hound Road Wall, which was used by the Supporters' Club.

Where the squash club now stands were the remains of what had been a rather pleasant outside tea bar with chairs and tables – somewhat continental in its atmosphere. A local artist painted a picture of the scene as it had been, I suppose, sometime in the 1930s and it could almost be a street scene in Paris.

The bricks and mortar of the pavilion itself remain largely unchanged, though more and more of the front is painted white each year and generation succeeds generation complaining of the lack of a scoreboard at the pavilion end. I think the record score by one batsman in a single day, some 345 runs by a certain Charlie Macartney, was made at Trent Bridge, even before the first coat of white paint disguised the red bricks of the pavilion. Young players today don't eat carrots the way we used to.

The Long Room bar and the Long Room itself in 1971 had scarcely altered since it was built. A sound solid Victorian public bar type of place for those with hob nailed boots and none of your fancy ways. It was around this time, I think, that women were allowed in the Long Room for the first time and permitted to sit on the long green benches in front of the pavilion itself. The dressing rooms as well had scarcely changed in 50 years, though before my time the professionals were confined to the semi-basement.

In a way the Pavilion and indeed the stands which surrounded the ground accommodating well over 20,000 spectators were a monument to the long gone great days of Nottinghamshire cricket. The old codgers in the long bar muttered

3

about Larwood and Voce and bemoaned there was still no one to equal the batting of old George Gunn. The County hadn't won anything since 1929 and the team was still associated with the miners who had come from Kirkby and its nearby villages. By the 1960s Nottinghamshire-born county cricketers were an almost extinct breed, but the tide was beginning to move the other way and in 1972 I was a member, at least for part of the season, of a Notts team which did come out on top. The Notts seconds won the Second Eleven Championship. Phil Wilkinson took 52 wickets at 16 runs each, and Peter Plummer took 36 at 20 runs each – both were born and bred in the county. My major contribution was an unbeaten hundred in the final match against Leicestershire at Loughborough and winning this game gave us the trophy.

The flow of local talent into the Notts first team has gathered momentum during my time with the club. Whereas it was unusual to find at most two Notts-bred

(Patrick Eager)

4

players in the first team the reverse is now almost the case. When I was lucky enough to gain my first Test cap for England in 1976–77, I was the first Notts-bred cricketer to do so since Cyril Poole 25 years before. Now Tim Robinson and Bruce French have followed me and both Andy Pick and Paul Johnson are on the fringes.

Whilst emphasising the improvement of the quality of our local players, I cannot overestimate the part played by the cricketers who have come to the club from outside. We were very fortunate to have both Richard Hadlee and Clive Rice and then Franklyn Stephenson as our overseas players – their records speak for themselves. Coming from not so far away, we have had Eddie Hemmings, Mike Bore and Chris Broad, and two of those three have gained England caps whilst at Trent Bridge.

We have won the County Championship twice and also won all three of the major limited-overs competitions, but the memory which remains with me is that of the NatWest Final at Lord's in 1985. For once both Rice and Hadlee failed to make a great impact with bat or ball. Essex made 280 and Gooch and Hardie had added 202 before Pick at last bowled Gooch and one run later Hardie was run out.

Tim Robinson and Chris Broad gave us a great start with a stand worth 143, but then three wickets went down for 30 runs. Richard Hadlee and I added 41 for the fourth wicket, before Richard was bowled by Ian Pont – the player Notts had rejected a year or two before. That left us needing 67. Young Duncan Martindale came to the wicket, in what was really his first match of major importance. The runs came and by the time Derek Pringle ran up to bowl the first ball of the last over we needed just 18. The sequence of scoring shots in that final over were 2, 4, 2, 4, 4. Two runs were wanted from the last ball. Fatally I hit the ball into the hands of Prichard. The match was lost by one run. Two years later however we won the same trophy against even greater odds: such a game is cricket and I am one of those fortunate few who have been lucky enough to play it at county level for 20 years and also lucky enough to have Trent bridge as my home ground.

ON THE FOREST

CRICKET IN ITS MARCH northwards from the cradle of south-eastern England arrived in the Midland counties during the reign of George II. Historians have compiled a careful list which proclaims the dates on which cricket is first found in the various counties and from which one deduces that the game arrived in Northamptonshire in 1741. Ten years later it had hopped a few counties and come to Yorkshire. In 1757 Derbyshire was embraced; Nottinghamshire joins in 1771 and five years later, following this curious pattern, Leicestershire springs to cricketing life.

It is a timetable which in reality conceals everything and unveils little. The dates are the first known newspaper references to the sport in the given counties. The occasional private letters and diaries which have survived from the first half of the 18th century show that cricket was a great deal more common than the newspapers would have one believe. It is unfortunate for Nottinghamshire that no private papers have yet been discovered concerning 18th century cricket in the county. Until the last few years of the century the researcher is forced to rely on the scattering of press reports.

Although Nottinghamshire apparently does not feature as a cricketing county until 1771, an inspection of the files of the *Nottingham Journal* for the year make it more than clear that cricket must have played an important part in the recreational life of the county for many summers before, otherwise the Editor of the *Journal* would hardly fill half of a column with the following letter:

> Sir: Being one of the numerous spectators who attended on Monday and Tuesday, the 26th and 27th inst. to see the great Cricket Match (on the forest of Sherwood) between the Gentlemen of Nottingham and the Gentlemen of Sheffield, and apprehending that some circumstances relative to the dispute which happened on Tuesday morning might be set in a wrong light, I thought a particular account thereof would not only be agreeable to many of your readers, but would likewise be a means of preventing the unprejudiced part of mankind from rashly determining which of the two parties were in the wrong. First, the game began on Monday, and was to consist of three goings in on each side; the Sheffielders went in first, and the number of notches got that day is as follows:

Sheffield	first going in was	81		
do.	the second going in	62	}	228
do.	the third going in	105		
Nottingham	first going in was	76	}	188
do.	the second going in	112		

So stood the account on Monday Evening, when the Sheffielders had seven men out; but as the fee was set, it was agreed to finish the game the next day. At nine on Tuesday morning the game was resumed, and one of the Sheffield party was knock'd out the very first ball; the last man but one now coming in, got five notches more, and at the next bowl struck the ball again, by which he got one notch, and in running for another, he ran against his partner and push'd him against one of the adversaries men; but he being too late was knock'd out. Having now but one man to come in and only 60 notches a head, against the whole of the Nottingham party who was yet to come in for a third time (and who was much superior in point of play) they (the Sheffielders) according to their usual custom, when the game is going against them, raised a dispute about the man being out: The Umpire for the Nottingham Gentlemen was positive that the man was fairly out, the other hesitated and would not say it was so or not; but said he believed the man could not have got in, if no accident had happened; Upon this accident alone some time was spent without coming to any determination, during which time, some of the Sheffield Gentlemen stole out at the back part of the tent that was pitched for their accommodation and got off in carriages and on horses with all secrecy imaginable; having previously packed up their clothes etc to be ready for flight: This seems to me to have all the appearance of a design to get off their betts (as they had many depending and the game greatly against them). However they posted away, but the driver of the chaise not being well acquainted with the road, they were set fast before they had got 400 yards from the place: upon which they alighted and ran away on foot, but were pursued and brought back to Nottingham with intent to put an end to the game some way or other; but they were resolved to play no more, upon which their Umpire declared he was ashamed of them; in the evening they stole away once more, and got to Red-hill, the place of rendezvous, where they quarreled amongst themselves and blamed each other for their past conduct to the Gentlemen Cricket-players at Nottingham: On the road they invented a plausible tale to tell on their arrival at Sheffield; for a just account of their behaviour would make them appear ridiculous after so much boasting and puffing. I could relate many other things with equal truth, but as a recital of every circumstance would be tedious, I shall only say the general opinion is, that, the two men ran against each other on purpose to raise a dispute in order to prevent their playing the game out and save their betts.

I am your's &c

A SPECTATOR

P.S. The eleven Nottingham Players (have since) challenged the same eleven Sheffielders for any sum they shall chuse (*sic*) to mention, and meet them half way; but they declined it. The Nottingham party still continue in the same opinion: It is very remarkable that the Gentlemen of Sheffield sent three different times to have their challenge confirm'd, before the Nottingham Gentlemen would accept the challenge.

The whole tenor of the letter indicates that Nottingham folk were well versed in cricket by the date of this match. A regular coach service had been operating between Sheffield and Nottingham since 1760 – though the journey occupied the best part of a day – and it is very probable that previous matches, of which the details are now lost, had been played between the two 'societies' as the clubs were termed at that time. The surnames of this Nottingham team have survived, but without initials so it is difficult to identify them. They deserve to be recorded here: Huthwayte, Turner, Loughman, Coleman, Roe, Spurr, Stocks, Collishaw, Troop, Mew, Rawson.

The venue of this match was The Forest. Today The Forest is a rectangular area bounded on all sides by bricks and mortar, but in the 17th century it was a vast tract of scrubland which separated Nottingham from the wooded area of Sherwood Forest itself. In 1650 a race-course some four miles in length was laid out on The Forest and somewhere in this vicinity the 1771 match was played. What remains of 'The Forest' is one mile north of the Nottingham Market Place.

One feature which distinguishes this Nottingham against Sheffield match from a similar contest staged in London or the South East in the 18th century is the total lack of any patron to finance and support the opposing parties. The equivalent match in the home counties would be styled perhaps 'The Earl of Tankerville's Team against The Duke of Dorset's Team', with The Earl selecting the Surrey players and the Duke the Kent players. The aristocracy and landed gentry organised virtually all the major cricket matches which involved many hours travelling and staying overnight, for the cost of travel before the age of the train was beyond the pockets of ordinary people – especially so if the travel was purely for pleasure.

This basic difference between the great matches of Nottingham, Sheffield and to a lesser extent Leicester and one or two other towns of the Midlands and the North and the matches in the South of England was to produce the cricketing North–South divide which has remained such a salient factor in the game over the years.

Although it is not possible to discover details regarding the occupations and social standing of the 1771 Notts cricketers, by the turn of the century this information begins to be known. The cricketers, who themselves largely financed their own matches, were mainly lower-middle class, like shopkeepers or publicans, or the better-off lower class of tradesmen, like framework knitters, or in the building industry.

The quarrel between Nottingham and Sheffield was mended by the following season, when Nottingham went up to Sheffield and on a terrible wicket were completely outplayed, giving up the match. There was no enmity this time and the report notes: 'The two parties supped together very amicably.'

There seems to be no further record of Nottingham playing Sheffield until 1800, but in the interim, the local cricketers were not idle. Leicester were met for the first time in 1781 and once more the conclusion of the match was unsatisfactory: 'At the conclusion of the first day's play, the Leicester Club went in against 50 notches only. The Nottingham Club then began to bowl what are called Sheffield Bowls, which every lover of the game have complained of as unmanly in the extreme . . .'

In other words, Nottingham bowled wides, which at that time were not scored. Later the Nottingham umpire gave one of the Leicester batsmen out to a ball that was 'a yard and a half' outside the wicket (presumably leg before wicket!) the batsman refused to go, the Nottingham bowler refused to bowl and that finished the game.

There were various attempts to play a second match in 1782, but the Leicester players asked for their money for the 1781 match and as Nottingham declined to pay plans came to nothing.

The next opponent of the Nottingham Club was Melton Mowbray and for the first time the detailed score was published. The first game was staged near Melton, and the return 'in a close, near Trent Bridge'. The venue was probably chosen because it was that much nearer Melton Mowbray and reduced the journey for the Melton players – it would be a good two miles further to The Forest.

It would be nice to believe that this game was played on the site of the present Trent Bridge Cricket Ground, but it might just as easily have taken place on the north side of the bridge. 'An incredible number of spectators were present, who conducted themselves with becoming propriety and, to the honour of both parties, the utmost harmony prevailed.' Nottingham won both matches and the report noted that the Nottingham players were dressed in green jackets, and the Melton players in white.

'The Cricket Players of the Town of Nottingham' in 1784 challenged any team within 50 miles for any sum of money. The challenge was not taken up, so evidently Nottingham was the strongest cricket side in the Midlands. Four years later, the Leicester Cricket Society issued a similar challenge except that it was limited to 25 guineas and that if Nottingham accepted the challenge the match must be played in Leicester. Nottingham said that they would play only if matches home and away were arranged, or the venue was half way between the two towns.

This latter arrangement was eventually agreed to for the following year, the venue being Loughborough. Nottingham won the first match by an innings but the second has gone down in history as 'The Odd Notch Match'. The reason for this can be seen by the accompanying score.

The leading Nottingham bowler in this match and at this time was Richard Warsop. Warsop was one of four cricketing brothers – William, Samuel and Thomas were the other three – who all played for Nottingham for a period of almost forty years.

The narrow defeat of Nottingham did not deter the players and they were further encouraged when, two years later, Colonel Churchill, who was stationed in Nottingham with his regiment, offered to put up a challenge against the newly formed Mary-le-bone Cricket Club, on behalf of the Nottingham players. The MCC accepted the challenge and came to Nottingham. The match was advertised as for 1,000 guineas, but this was no more than newspaper puff, according to J. F. Sutton in his 'Nottingham Cricket Matches 1771 to 1853'. The MCC was captained by the Hon Col Lennox and included the Earl of Winchilsea, Lord William Bentinck and the Hon E. Bligh. The visitors stayed at the White Lion and Blackamoor's Head and a piece of ground in Upper King's Meadow was roped off for the contest. It was the first time the MCC had ever sent a team outside the London area. A crowd of 10,000 spectators came to watch the match, which MCC won by ten wickets. A second game when Nottingham fielded 22 men against 11 was also won. Sutton commented: 'The match witnessed the introduction into this locality of a new style of play. Old science had to contend with new science, and, as is generally the case in the march of intelligence, the improved style bore off the palm.'

Sutton interviewed 60 years later two of the Nottingham players, who said that the bowling of Thomas Lord and Capt Cumberland was faster than any they had ever faced and their antiquated batting style was hopeless against it.

The next year the Nottingham players were invited to Burley Park near Oakham, the seat of the Earl of Winchilsea, and played the MCC again, but despite having 22 men, still lost easily. Directly after that match Nottingham opposed a combined Rutland and Leicestershire team and lost again, but Joseph Gilbert, the Nottingham captain, hit 51, the first half-century for Nottingham.

The Napoleonic Wars and civil unrest in England caused cricket, at least so far as major matches were concerned, to be less frequently played during the next two decades. There was, however, a flurry of activity on the part of the Nottingham Club in 1800. On the evidence of the results of the three matches played by the Nottingham Club that season, the local cricketers had learnt the new scientific method of play which had so astonished them when the 1791 MCC team travelled to the town.

Meeting Leicester at St Margaret's Pasture in Leicester, Nottingham bowled out Leicester for 15, scored 61 and then dismissed Leicester a second time for just 8 runs. The matches with Sheffield were resumed the same year. Playing at Mansfield, Nottingham dismissed Sheffield for 24 and 22, winning by 123 runs; a month later the teams met again, at Worksop, and despite Sheffield having 22 men, Nottingham won by an even larger margin – 133 runs. The success seems to have been due to the bowling of William Chapman and the youngest of the Warsop brothers, Thomas. He was an under-arm bowler whose style was later copied by William Clarke. In 1800 he was aged about 21.

Thomas Warsop later captained Nottingham. He was a very affable and well-spoken man and, unlike most of his contemporaries, honest and not given to double-dealing. Cricket and gambling went hand in hand at this period; the players made what money they could by side bets and it was not unknown for players to place money on their own side losing and then assist in the matter by missing catches, or generally playing a poor game. The only other trustworthy Nottingham player (at least according to an old report) was Humphrey Hopkin, who was born at

LEICESTER *v* NOTTINGHAM

Played at Loughborough, 5, 6 October and 2 November 1789

LEICESTER WON BY ONE RUN

LEICESTER	**FIRST INNINGS**		**SECOND INNINGS**	
J. Needham	c E. Stevenson	8	st R. Warsop	11
W. Clarke	b R. Warsop	0	b J. Stevenson	1
W. Barsby	run out	4	b J. Stevenson	0
M. Graham	c E. Stevenson	6	c E. Stevenson	9
C. Wilkinson	b R. Warsop	9	c S. Hedderley	2
R. Stringer	b J. Stevenson	2	c R. Warsop	0
T. Nutt	b R. Warsop	7	b R. Warsop	1
J. Rowell	b J. Stevenson	5	b R. Warsop	4
T. Fielding	not out	11	c J. Gilbert	4
R. Black	c E. Stevenson	9	b R. Warsop	0
T. Watts	c J. Stevenson	2	not out	0
Extras		0		0
Total		63		32

NOTTINGHAM				
E. Stevenson	b Graham	1	c Watts	18
S. Hedderley	b Rowell	0	b Graham	3
W. Barker	c Needham	16	b Graham	2
S. Willow	run out	1	b Nutt	5
J. Gilbert	b Graham	0	b Rowell	10
S. Mugglestone	b Graham	1	b Graham	6
W. Warsop	run out	10	st Graham	3
G. Harrison	b Rowell	6	c Graham	2
J. Carter	not out	0	b Graham	1
J. Stevenson	run out	2	not out	4
R. Warsop	b Rowell	2	b Graham	0
Extras		0	bye	1
Total		39		55

The reason why there was a break of nearly a month between the start and finish of the match was that the Leicester umpire insisted that the Nottingham team, being 24 behind on the first innings, should follow on, but the Nottingham umpire disagreeed. The dispute was amicably settled and the match resumed on Monday 2 November. Nottingham proceeded to bowl out Leicester for only 32 and therefore required 57 in the final innings. When the total reached 55 with two wickets remaining, 'there was exhibited a scene of anxiety in both parties much easier conceived than described: for on a single stroke depended the whole match involving the fate of every person who was interested in the event.'

Graham, the Leicester bowler, then dismissed the last two men with successive deliveries and Leicester won by one run.

the White Hart, Old Lenton, in 1774. Hopkin paid a price for his honesty, for being fonder of cricket than of work and making little money at the former, he ended his days in the poor house.

Joseph Dennis made his debut for Nottingham in the 1800 matches and became famous as the most celebrated wicketkeeper of his day. He was also an excellent batsmen and his career lasted some 30 years. He kept various public houses in Nottingham and latterly The Eclipse in Chapel Bar, but in 1829 he suffered a paralytic stroke and a further stroke, in the Bell Inn two years later, was the end of him. Dennis was not above altering his style of play to suit his pocket. Another of that ilk was Peter Bramley. He kept the Old Spot, in Arnold, for some time, but later moved to The Forest, living at the end of the racecourse. Bramley was shunned by many Nottingham people due to his reputation as a blackleg, but after he died, in 1838, it was discovered that he was not quite as black as he was painted.

A series of matches which require a brief mention were those played in Yorkshire in 1798 between various teams of Militia. On 1 and 2 October, the Nottingham Militia, with three other officers including General Lennox, beat 'All Yorkshire' by 58 runs at Wetherby, having already won an earlier match at Beverley by five runs. Chapman, who performed well in these matches, is perhaps the William Chapman to which reference has already been made.

In 1803, Nottingham players appeared at Lord's for the first time – the famous London ground had been laid out in 1787 and by the turn of the century was considered the headquarters of cricket. The circumstances surrounding this important event in Nottingham cricket history appear to be lost. Major Morgan of Leicester put up the money for a combined Nottingham and Leicester team, with Lord Frederick Beauclerk as its captain, to oppose Hampshire – the remnants of the old Hambledon Club. Thomas Warsop and William Chapman as well as Joe Dennis were among the eight Nottingham players in the team, Morgan and Stringer being the sole Leicester representatives. Hampshire won by an innings and 20 runs and none of the Nottingham players distinguished himself.

Nothing more is heard of Nottingham in the cricketing sense until 1813, when the game is revived – the war and inflation meant that people had more important matters to attend to.

In September 1813 a match was played between the Town of Nottingham and the County. It is the first recorded such match, but the meetings between these two sides were to become common over the next 30 years. As a result of this game it was decided to challenge 22 of Leicestershire. The match was arranged for Loughborough and the result was embarrassing; only Dennis of the Nottingham players reached double figures in either innings and Nottingham lost by an innings.

The defeat did not dim the enthusiasm of the Nottingham cricketers and after two lesser matches were won – against Barrow on Soar at Bunny by 58 runs and against Rutland at Burley Park by an innings – the Nottingham Club in 1815 challenged XV of Barrow and Mountsorrel and won by four wickets.

In the same year one of the Nottingham players set a trap which he successfully sprang two years later. Dennis and Hopkin challenged Osbaldeston, one of the leading MCC cricketers, to a single wicket match and were overwhelmed. Hopkin made 11 and 3, Dennis 1 and 2, whilst in his single innings Osbaldeston was undefeated with 84. Dennis then helped to arrange a match between an England Eleven organised by Osbaldeston and 22 of Nottingham in 1817. Because of the way Osbaldeston had beaten the two best Nottingham batsmen in 1815, the odds were in favour of an England win and Dennis also got a good price for a bet in which he wagered he would outscore Osbaldeston.

The match was played on The Forest and some 12,000 spectators attended. Nottingham won by 30 runs; Osbaldeston failed to score in either innings, whilst Dennis made 3 and 4.

Dennis was not the only one with money on the game, as E. H. Budd, one of the major England amateurs, commented: 'In common with others I lost my money, and was greatly disappointed at the termination. One paid player (W. Lambert) was accused of selling (the match), and never employed after.' William Lambert was the Surrey professional. He was barred from Lord's for the rest of his life.

Almost all the cricketers playing for the Nottingham Old Club – the Nottingham Club was now so described – were professionals. It must be said that the leading cricketers of the day had gained a dubious reputation. An old cricketer commented 50 years later: 'The leading professionals were stigmatised as blacklegs, and so men fond of the game preferred to participate in the second-class matches, which were always fair and aboveboard, rather than be mixed up in the questionable transactions connected with county matches.'

A return match with England was arranged in the following year, the agreement – £150 a side, with Nottingham paying £40 towards the cost of the England Eleven travelling from London –

was signed by George Osbaldeston and Joseph Dennis. The London players duly arrived, only to discover that Osbaldeston was in Scotland shooting. Osbaldeston had not sent any money for the stake. There was a great deal of anger on the part of the Nottingham players, but eventually it was agreed to play the match without any money attached and the Nottingham people gave the Londoners £30 to pay for their journey home. About 20,000 spectators watched the game, which was played on The Forest and won by Nottingham by 14 wickets – Nottingham fielded 22, as in the previous year.

No matches were played by the Nottingham Old Club in 1819 or 1820. Perhaps the win against England had put off possible opponents, or the manner in which Osbaldeston had failed to produce the stake money had deterred the Nottingham people from arranging any games. In 1821, however, Nottingham found an opponent in the Holt Club of Norfolk. The terms must have been favourable, because Nottingham travelled to Norfolk for the match – the furthest from home they had played. Holt at this time had three of the Pilch family playing for them, including the famous Fuller Pilch, although at this time he had not built up his reputation.

The Nottingham players not only backed themselves to win, but put up an extra £100 that they would win by an innings. When in Holt's second innings the last man appeared, Holt needed one to avoid an innings defeat. The Nottingham captain placed the best fieldsman, James Britain, in the deep at long on and fed the batsman with an easy delivery. The ball was lofted and was falling about three yards in front of Britain, who, according to his own description, felt as if he was glued to the spot – the thought of so much money resting on his single action was too much for him. It is not recorded what the Nottingham players said, but the match was won by ten wickets. Britain later became one of the best known Nottingham umpires.

Becoming even more ambitious Nottingham challenged 16 of Leicester and suffered the size of defeat they had wished to inflict on Holt, being dismissed in their first innings for 24.

In 1821 Thomas Barker first appeared for the Old Club. He was a fast bowler with a very ungainly action and played in virtually every Nottingham match from his debut until 1843, when he broke his leg whilst jumping out of a runaway cab crossing between railway stations in London on the way to Southampton. Well known for his joviality and good-fellowship, Barker was also renowned for his 'whisper'. He was engaged as a professional at Lord's in the 1830s and 1840s and the following story is told of him reporting to the Lord's proprietor, James Dark, at the beginning of one season.

'How do you do, Mr D.' said Barker in his whisper.

'Ah, Barker', was the reply, 'I heard you get out of the train at Euston half an hour ago.'

Like many of his Nottingham contemporaries, Barker worked as a stockinger during the winter. It was in fact the framework knitting trade that helped to give Nottinghamshire the edge over so many of its rival counties when it came to cricket. Many of the framework knitters worked in their own homes doing piecework and, unlike farm labourers and factory hands, they could choose the times when they worked and could take time off to play cricket or take cricket engagements during the summer, knowing they could come back to their trade as they wished. In contrast the agricultural worker slaved from dawn to dusk, especially through the harvest times, and the factory worker was governed by the factory hooter.

A second player who came out in 1821 was George Jarvis. A stylish batsman, he excelled at the cut, but was unlucky in having his hand injured on numerous occasions whilst batting. He was one of the first Nottingham players (with Barker) to be recognised outside his native county and played both for England and the Players. He was originally a gardener, but took up lacemaking and then in his old age resumed gardening. When interviewed in 1873 (aged 73) he issued a challenge for £200 to play any cricketer in England of the same age as himself at single wicket.

In 1822, the Holt Club came to Nottingham, but were beaten by 105 runs. Nottingham then challenged 15 of Sheffield to two matches, both of which were won with ease. In the first William Hewitt scored 50 for Nottingham (15 of Sheffield were all out for 41). Hewitt was given to fits of madness and generally kept in an asylum, but was released to play for Nottingham. After his success in this particular match, he suggested that the Old Club should include more madmen in the team and they would win more matches. His brother, John, also played occasionally for Nottingham but emigrated to France, where, in the Calais region, there were many Nottingham people involved in the lace trade. John died in Calais in 1842.

Thomas Warsop was now something of a veteran and suffered much from gout – he had travelled to Holt in 1821 for the match, but owing to his afflication was unable to play. In the return with Sheffield in 1822 it was noted 'Warsop's running was defective owing to gout' and he was given out for stopping the ball with his bat when it was thrown in. Warsop's career finished in 1823 and he died in 1845, his death certificate giving 'gout of the brain' as the cause.

Nottingham played, and beat, 14 of Leicester in 1823. Joe Dennis scored 50 not out in this match. After another blank year in 1824, Nottingham ventured further afield in 1825 to play Bury St Edmunds in Suffolk. Fuller Pilch had now moved on to that club. The match was arranged for 200 sovereigns but when the Nottingham team arrived at Bury, it was discovered that the home club had engaged two or three outside players and after a discussion the stake was reduced to 20 sovereigns. Nottingham lost by 33 runs.

The most remarkable match of this decade was played on the Darnell Ground at Sheffield in 1826, when Nottingham challenged a combined Sheffield and Leicester Eleven. The result was a resounding defeat for Nottingham by an innings and 203 runs and the cause of this disaster was the batting of Thomas Marsden, a 21-year-old Sheffield man who scored 227, batting over eight hours. One verse from a long poem on the match goes:

Oh, Marsden, at Cricket, is nature's perfection,
For hitting the ball in any direction;
He ne'er fears his Wicket, so safely he strikes,
And he does with the Bat and the Ball what he likes.

Marsden was destined to have a brilliant career, though he never repeated his incredible 227, though he did score 125 against Nottingham in 1828.

In the latter part of the 1820s, the Bell Inn, in Nottingham's Market Square, became the headquarters of Nottingham cricket and consequently of the Old Club. The landlord of the Bell was William Clarke, who had been born in 1798 and for the best part of 30 years was to control Nottingham cricket. Clarke it would seem moved into the Bell about 1819.

Honours were even between Nottingham and Sheffield in 1827, each team winning at home. In the match on The Forest there was a prolonged dispute regarding the fairness of action of the Sheffield bowlers and on the last day, with the umpires unable to agree on the no-balling of the Sheffield players, the umpires were changed, the new men being William Charlton and Major Taylor, both Nottingham men. A note in the Sheffield scorebook states: 'a most disgraceful match, as the Nottingham umpire called no-ball whenever a straight ball was bowled, and it is regretted that Sheffield was foolish enough to continue the game in which such an unfair advantage was taken.'

Sheffield issued a challenge to the Old Club in 1828 and Clarke replied that they would play either on the same terms as last year,

WILLIAM CLARKE

Although there have been many famous Nottinghamshire cricketers, none had such an influence over the development of the game as William Clarke. His scheme, begun in 1846, to form a team containing the best players in England and tour the country giving what were in effect exhibition matches, was the instrument by which the game changed from one of parochial interest to one of national pride. The All England Eleven was founded by Clarke in 1846 and remained a major attraction for some 25 years, though Clarke himself died in 1856.

Clarke was a natural cricketer, for he made his debut in Nottingham Old Club matches in 1816 aged 17, and for some years played mainly as a batsman. Some time in the mid-1820s he lost the sight of an eye whilst playing fives, and this clearly affected his batting and probably made him decide to concentrate on bowling. His slow under-arm delivery was based on the style of Tom Warsop but his main principle was made plain when he was asked 'What is a good length ball', and replied 'One which the batsman is not expecting.' In his capacity as bowler and as captain, he would spend the hour or so before each match studying the style of the opposing batsmen and at a time when field placing was not the fine art it is today, Clarke would surprise in-coming batsmen by adjusting the field as soon as the new man took guard.

William Clarke, one of the men who most helped to spread the game of cricket in the 19th century. Among other pioneering acts, he set out the Trent Bridge ground. (NCCC)

Having made his public house the headquarters of Nottingham cricket, he became captain of the Old Club in about 1826 and from then onwards he acted as secretary and organiser of Old Club matches. In 1838 he set out Trent Bridge Cricket Ground, having married the landlady of the Trent Bridge Inn, but he moved to London in 1846 and from then until his death arranged many of the leading fixtures in addition to the All England matches against local clubs. He thus controlled the future of many major professional players. His dictatorial manner meant that he was unpopular with many of his brother professionals and as the *Sporting Life* noted: 'The professionals were by no means sorry to crump his bowling when opposed to him, though they generally found out that they had to get up very early in the morning to circumvent Clarke's insidious twisters.'

Clarke led Nottinghamshire in what is regarded as the shire's first genuine inter-county fixture, *v* Sussex in 1835, but although he remained in the county team until 1855 (at 56 he is the oldest player to represent Notts) he played in only a handful of inter-county games because his All England Eleven took away all the best players and made county cricket only of peripheral interest for his last ten seasons.

or at a venue midway between the two towns, or at Lord's. The matches would be played for £500.

The matches were in fact played on the same terms as in 1827, but this time the Old Club lost both games. Thomas Heath appeared for Nottingham in these matches and proved a useful batsman, but was best known as a brilliant fieldsman, both catching the ball and throwing in. He was the first Sutton-in-Ashfield born man to appear for the Old Club, though he moved to Nottingham as a young man. In 1839, due to a slump in the lace trade he emigrated to Calais. When he came back he had grown so stout as to be hardly recognisable. In his later years he acted as a gateman at Trent Bridge; by then he was not only very deaf, but somewhat eccentric. On a visit to his brother in 1872 in Sutton, he was seized with a fit and lay unconscious for a week before dying. Emanuel Vincent made two appearances for Nottingham in 1828 and his career is of interest because it shows that even then there were rules regarding the qualification of players. Vincent had moved from Sheffield to Nottingham before the 1827 season, but the newspapers pointed out that he was barred from playing for Nottingham in 1827 as he had not lived there long enough.

In between the two Nottingham *v* Sheffield matches of 1828, the proprietor of the Sheffield ground organised what might be described as the first North *v* South match, though the actual title was Yorkshire, Leicestershire and Nottinghamshire *v* England. Jarvis, Clarke, Vincent and Barker were the Nottingham representatives, but England won by 242 runs. The cricketing strength of England would not move northwards for some years yet.

The Old Club played home and away matches with both Sheffield and Leicester in 1829, Nottingham winning all four contests. Sam Redgate made his debut for the Old Club on his 19th birthday – 27 July 1829 – *v* Leicester. He soon gained a reputation as the fastest bowler, and the most deadly, in England. His most notable feat was in 1839 when in a single four-ball over he dismissed Stearman, Alfred Mynn and Fuller Pilch, this being in the match between England and Kent at Town Malling. He was reported to have consumed a glass of brandy after each of these wickets and it is not therefore surprising that he died of drink at the age of 40, his bowling being described as 'slow and feeble' towards the end of his career. He left a widow and seven young children with no means of support.

Only three major Old Club matches took place in the three seasons 1830, 1831 and 1832. All three were played on the Hyde Park Ground at Sheffield. Why no matches were arranged for

Nottingham is not clear, but presumably it was to do with the financial arrangements. Sheffield won the first, Nottingham the next two. Included among the professionals who first appeared for the Old Club in these matches were 'Billy' Good and William Garrat. Unlike the previous players noted neither was born in Nottingham. Good came from the Lincolnshire town of Market Rasen, whilst Garrat hailed from Shrewsbury, though his family moved to Nottingham when he was six.

Good was left-handed both as a batsman and bowler and being engaged at Lord's from 1836 he played fairly frequently in the major matches of the day. His powerful build was deceptive, for he had a delicate constitution and this was not helped by his winter job as a conductor on the Paddington omnibus. He died in London of consumption in 1848, aged only 36.

Garrat, a defensive opening batsman, played for Nottingham until the 1840s, but by this time he had moved to Peterborough, where he set up a jewellery and watchmaking business. Un-usually the Old Club included an amateur in their 1832 match, George Rothera. He was notable as a fieldsman, but ill-health cut short his career and he died in Nottingham in 1841 aged 31.

In 1833, the Old Club arranged a match at Ripon against 20 picked from clubs within 30 miles of that city. One wonders if this match placed in Clarke's mind the germ of the idea to create the England Eleven? The Nottingham Eleven made 76, Ripon made 52, then Nottingham 51 in their second innings. Ripon were five wickets down for 12 at the close of the second day. Overnight several Yorkshire supporters disputed a run out deci-sion in the Ripon second innings and in the morning some of the local side refused to play on and the match was abandoned.

When the Nottingham team returned home they met with further discord, as a number of the local cricketers argued that the Nottingham team was not the strongest available – the dictatorial hand of Clarke was probably being questioned. A match was therefore set up between the Eleven which went to Ripon and the Next 22. The match, on The Forest, lasted four days and ended in victory for the 22 by two wickets. The best batting for the winners was by William Nix of the Rancliffe Arms Club, who made 30. He moved later to Derby, as professional for the South Derbyshire Club. Another successful batsman was William Woodward, who reached double figures in both innings. He was to play for Nottingham in most of their major matches until 1839. He emigrated to America.

Turning southwards, Nottingham took on the Cambridge Town Club in two matches in 1834. The Town Club were overwhelmed – by 152 runs and an innings and 114 runs. Later in the year Sheffield were also beaten by an innings. John Oscroft senior made one of his intermittent appearances in this Sheffield game. He was one of three cricketing brothers from Arnold and he was regarded as a very stylish batsman – his nephew William was later to captain Notts.

Having comprehensively beaten Sheffield and Cambridge (Leicester were no longer regarded as a leading cricketing power), Nottingham sent a challenge of £50 a match to Sussex. Sussex and Kent were the only two county teams of any consequence in the 1820s and early 1830s. It was between the two as to which was the 'Champion' county and when not opposed to each other they played against the Rest of England and were quite capable of beating that combination.

In the past Hampshire, Surrey and occasionally Middlesex had fielded county sides against Kent and Sussex, but these Southern shires had never been challenged by any sides in the Midlands or the North. The Nottingham Club was thus breaking completely new ground.

Sussex accepted the challenge. This is the moment when Nottingham Old Club suddenly becomes 'Nottinghamshire'. Those who are keen on hard historical data are anxious to pinpoint the date on which 'Nottinghamshire County Cricket Club' was established. Unfortunately for those zealots, Nottinghamshire county cricket developed in the same manner as cricket itself – it was part of a slow evolution rather than a sudden explosive force.

The first book on Nottingham cricket is entitled 'A Correct Account of all the Cricket Matches played by the Nottingham Old Cricket Club'. It was published in 1830 and the compiler, William North, dedicates it to 'The Gentlemen of the Nottingham Old Cricket Club'. On the face of it this is a definite proof of the existence of a major Cricket Club in Nottingham in 1830 and dating back at least until 1813, if not 1771. Several of William Clarke's letters and notices printed in the newspapers are signed: 'For the Nottingham Old Cricket Club, William Clarke.' In 1825 the Old Club is reported to have a membership of about 100, but no meetings of this Club seem to have been reported and no evidence of any specific officers, or committee, has survived, or at least has been found. In view of this lack of information one is drawn to the conclusion that the Old Club was run single-handed by a succession of inn-keepers, who controlled the finances and the selection of the teams. The same state of affairs possibly reigned in Brighton for the 1835 Nottingham challenge was directed to George Brown of the Hanover Arms in Brighton. He also controlled the main cricket ground in Brighton.

Nottinghamshire beat Sussex by two wickets in the first match and by three wickets in the second, played on The Forest. William Howitt, in 'Rural Life in England' describes the home match and his final paragraph runs:

> There were said to be twenty thousand people, all hushed as death, except when some exploit of the players produced a thunder of applause. The playing was beautiful. Mr Ward, later member of Parliament for London, a great cricket player, came from the Isle of Wight to see the game, and declared himself highly delighted. But nothing was so beautiful as the sudden shout, the rush, the beating up of the crowd, when the decisive notch was gained. To see the bat of Bart. Good, the batsman on whom the fate of the game depended, spinning up in the air, where he had sent it in the ecstacy of the moment; and the crowd, that before was fixed and silent as the world itself, spreading all over the green space where the white figures of the players had till then been so gravely and, apparently, calmly contending – spreading with a murmur as of the sea; and over their heads, amid the deafening clamour and confusion, the carrier pigeon, with a red ribbon tied to its tail, the signal of loss, beating round and round to ascertain its precise position, and then flying off to bear the tidings to Brighton – it was a beautiful sight, and one that the most sedate person must have delighted to see,

The Nottingham team for these matches contained one notable newcomer, Butler Parr. Although born in Lincolnshire, he came to Radcliffe on Trent as a very young child and it was in that village that he set up a business as a brewer. Although relatively well-to-do, he played as a professional and the *Sporting Life* commented: 'A paid cricketer of a good social standing raises the tone of his calling, and it would be unfair to defraud the professional element of their due in this respect.' Later Butler Parr was a member of the Committee of the County Cricket Club. He usually kept wicket, but was to lose his place when Charley Brown came on the scene.

The 1836 season was very much occupied with two matches between the North and the South. The first of these matches took place at Lord's, when Notts had six representatives in the Northern eleven – Clarke, Barker, Jarvis, Good, Redgate and a young fast bowler, Charles Creswell. The North won by six wickets and not only did Barker and Redgate make the highest scores for their side, but the Nottingham men took all the opposition wickets.

It was then announced that the return would be staged at William Barker's (no relation to the Notts Barker) Ground at Leicester. This arrangement happened because Captain Cheslyn of Leicester had been one of the main backers of the Northern side at Lord's. The people of Nottingham, however, felt they had been slighted and a public meeting chaired by the Mayor was organised as a protest. A petition was drawn up, setting out the reasons why the match should be played on The Forest and this was sent to Lord's. It did no good, the MCC Secretary simply replying that he could not break the promise he made to have the match at Leicester, though The Forest might be considered at some future time.

Hundreds of spectators walked from Nottingham to Leicester for the match and then had to walk to Loughborough to get overnight accommodation. The South won by 218 runs, with Alfred Mynn making a century, though he suffered such a battering from the fast bowling of Redgate that he was unable to play for a good while afterwards.

A minor, but interesting point during 1836 was an obituary in the Nottingham papers for George Petty, aged 67. In the brief notice it stated 'perhaps he scored in more matches in Notts and neighbouring counties than any other person.' He is therefore the first in the list of Nottinghamshire scorers.

In 1837, Nottinghamshire arranged to travel to Brighton and play Sussex and then move on to Town Malling to play Kent. Clarke did not go on this tour and his name is also missing from other representative matches during the year. Either he had taken umbrage over the 1836 North v South match being staged at Leicester, or perhaps he did not feel able to move from Nottingham due to the illness of his wife – she died on 5 September. Clarke's absence seriously weakened Nottinghamshire and they lost to Sussex by three wickets and to Kent by nine wickets. Henry Crook of Bingham played in place of Clarke and though he batted well in local matches, the bowlers in county cricket were too good for him. The amateur George Galloway also appeared for the county in these two games, and as with Crook they were his only two appearances. He was a lace manufacturer and he helped to finance the team.

Sussex came up to Nottingham in late August and inflicted a second defeat on Nottinghamshire, even though Clarke played. A much more important cricketer than Galloway or Crook first appeared for the county in 1837 – Joe Guy. Aged 23, Guy quickly built up a reputation as a scientific batsman. He excelled in forward defensive play and was soon rated second only to Fuller Pilch. The following year he was chosen for the Gentlemen *v* Players fixture and played regularly for the Players until 1852. Clarke enrolled him as an original member of the All England Eleven in 1846 and he appeared for that side until 1856. An unassuming man, his smile was childlike and bland. In later life he kept a quiet pub – the Carpenters Arms in Mansfield Road, Nottingham. He died aged 58 after a long illness, perhaps brought about by his occupation.

THE FIRST YEARS AT TRENT BRIDGE

THE DEATH OF JANE CLARKE left William Clarke a widower with five children under the age of 14. Three months after his bereavement Clarke married Mary Chapman (nee Singlehurst) a widow ten years his senior. She was landlady of the Trent Bridge Inn. She had some cricketing connections in that her first husband, Samuel Chapman, had played in local matches in the 1820s and the son of that marriage, John Chapman, now aged 23, was a more than useful player. Clarke moved from the Bell Inn to the hostelry run by his new wife.

In May 1838, the Forest Club played South Nottinghamshire on Clarke's 'new ground at Trent Bridge'. Later in the season he played for Holme Lane, a hamlet a mile or two from Trent Bridge against Bingham and scored 128, the first recorded 100 at Trent Bridge. The newspaper report noted: 'It is but justice to Mr Clarke to say that he has displayed great judgement in laying out the Trent Bridge Ground and the admirable condition in which it is kept renders it a delightful place for this healthiest and most manly of British sports.'

It is thus regarded that 1838 was the year in which the Trent Bridge Ground was founded, but it must be borne in mind that as early as 1783 Nottingham played a match 'near Trent Bridge' and in 1822 West Bridgford (the Trent Bridge Ground is situated in West Bridgford) played Samuel Chapman's XI in 'a field near Trent Bridge'. In the 1830s matches were played in a close of Mrs Chapman's at Trent Bridge'. The exact year in which cricket was first played in the field at the back of the Trent Bridge Inn is therefore open to debate, but it was in 1838 that the field was enclosed as a cricket ground, thus changing from a piece of land on which cricket matches sometimes took place to a site specifically designated as a cricket enclosure.

Nottingham's only match of 1838 was against the Next 22 in September and took place at Trent Bridge. Clarke played for the 22, who won by 194 runs. No matches of note involving Nottingham teams were staged in 1839, but the expertise of the major Nottingham players was now recognised at Lord's and five appeared in the England v MCC match – Jarvis, Guy, Garrat and Redgate for England, Good for MCC. Five Nottingham players also took part in a match between Nottingham and Sussex and England at Lord's.

The year 1839 was another quiet one for the Nottingham Club, the single match of any consequence being against 14 of the Rancliffe Arms Club at Trent Bridge – the Rancliffe Arms being a well-known cricketing inn in Nottingham. John Buttery appeared for the Rancliffe side in this game and subsequently appeared occasionally for Notts. He was an excellent medium-pace bowler. In 1847 he was engaged as a professional with Manchester CC and later for 20 years acted as a coach at Oxford, not giving up that post until he was 56.

For 1840 three inter-county fixtures were arranged exactly as in 1837 – home and away with Sussex and away with Kent. The Nottingham team travelled to Brighton in June and were beaten by Sussex with an innings to spare. Moving from Brighton to Town Malling they then beat Kent by ten wickets, due to the batting of Guy who scored 73 not out. Perhaps owing to the expenses involved in the journey south, the Notts side included several amateurs who had not previously played for the first eleven. T. B. Redgate, who made his debut in the Sussex match, was a 30-year-old solicitor with a practice in Clumber Street, Nottingham. A useful all-round cricketer, he moved to Scarthing Moor and opened offices in Newark and Tuxford in the 1850s. Another debutant was T. B. Charlton of Chilwell Hall, whose father, also a keen cricketer, had been High Sheriff of the County. T. B. Charlton seems to have owed his place in the team more to his financial support than his cricket prowess. Edwin Patchitt was another solicitor who played in the match against Sussex. A fast bowler with a high action, which was pronounced illegal by some umpires, he achieved little in top-class cricket. He was elected Mayor of Nottingham in 1858 and after retiring went to live in Hastings. A fourth new player was Creswell, who has already been noted in 1836 when he represented North *v* South. He seems to have left Nottingham about 1847.

Sussex travelled up to Nottingham for the return in July and this match was the first inter-county game to be staged at Trent Bridge. Clarke appropriately opened the batting and made the highest score in Notts first innings, but it was a modest 17 out of 85. Sussex won by 14 runs. Kent came up to Nottingham for the first time in 1841 – it was the only Notts match of the year. Notts lost by 22 runs, Fuller Pilch, the most famous batsman of the day, scoring 48 for the southerners. Four players made their Notts debut in this game, of whom the most interesting was Thomas Nixon, a spare-built man aged 27. An accurate spin bowler, he had an inventive mind and constructed the 'balista', an automatic bowling machine based on the crossbow and fired from shoulder

height. He patented the idea in 1862. Earlier, in 1853, he introduced cane-handled bats and at various times new styles of pads,
using cane, cork and rubber. Nixon was a most useful bowler,
but his batting and fielding were weak. He appeared for Notts
until 1854, after which he moved to Oxford where he ran a public
house with cricket ground and racquet court attached. In 1861 he
moved to Chelford and ran the Cheshire County Ground in that
town.

A second debutant in this Kent match was George Butler of
Mansfield. Unlike Nixon he was a good batsman and fielder,
usually at long-slip. In 1851 he became the professional at Trent
Bridge for Nottingham Commercial CC, one of the major club
sides in the county, and in that capacity he looked after the Trent
Bridge wicket in his later years, as well as acting as umpire in
many matches. The Rev William Musters made the first of seven
appearances for Notts in the 1841 game, he being the Rector of
West Bridgford. He had played for Oxford against Cambridge in
the 1829 university match. His family lived at Colwick Hall and
were the freehold owners of much land in the district, including
the Trent Bridge Inn and ground.

Just before the start of the 1841 season a notice appeared in the
Nottingham Journal, April 9:

> We understand the coming season at Nottingham promises to
> be of the most brilliant description . . . A few days ago, a
> meeting of gentlemen who support this first of our English
> games was held at the George the Fourth Inn when it was
> unanimously agreed to establish a county club and resolutions
> were passed inviting the gentry of the county to become
> members. T. B. Charlton, Esq., of Chilwell Hall kindly
> accepted the office of Hon. Secretary.

This is the first mention of a Nottinghamshire County Cricket
Club and the present Club dates its foundation from this meeting,
though the continuity between 1841 and the formation of an
elected Committee to run the Club in 1859–60 is at times tenuous.
No documents relating to the Club for the 1840s or 1850s appear
to have survived. A check among the Charlton family papers
revealed no cricket references. The nomenclature of teams representing Nottinghamshire through the 1840s adds to the confusion.
Sutton's 'Nottingham Cricket Matches' published in 1853 almost
invariably gives the team as 'Nottingham' the only two excep-
tions being in 1843 when the side is shown as 'Nottingham Trent
Bridge Club' in one match *v* MCC at Lord's and the 1853 match at
Lord's *v* All England, when the team is entitled (for the only time

in the entire book) 'Nottinghamshire'. When Richards published his 'Fifty Years of Notts Cricket' in 1890, he styled all the local teams 'Notts', even when they were playing Sheffield.

The available evidence indicates that Nottinghamshire County Cricket Club from 1841 was based at Trent Bridge, was run initially by an Honorary Secretary and by the early 1850s by Secretary and Treasurer and mainly operated to help with the cost of sending a Notts team to away matches and playing occasional games at Trent Bridge, not necessarily inter-county ones. It would also seem probable that William Clarke had a great deal to say on selection of teams and fixtures.

There was almost a repeat of 1836 in 1842, with yet another row over the North v South match – though the title was North v MCC in the press. The first game in June at Lord's was won by MCC by 43 runs. Noyes, Garrat, Guy, Barker, Good, S. Redgate and Creswell were the seven Notts players involved. The return was arranged for Leicester and the press in its preview gave the North team as eleven Notts players. MCC objected. Clarke withdrew from the side and issued a challenge for 100 sovereigns to the Rest of England. Fuller Pilch took up the gauntlet. MCC beat the North at Leicester and a week later Pilch arrived at Nottingham with his England team – Notts were beaten by ten wickets, though Clarke made the highest score in both innings (18 out of 122 and 26 out of 110) for his side, and also took seven of the ten wickets. Clarke's stepson, John Chapman, made his Notts debut in this game as did Francis Noyes. Noyes was a wine merchant in Nottingham and his claim to fame is that he was allowed to bat twice in each innings for Notts against Hampshire in 1843, when Barker was unable to play due to injury. He also had a horror of being stumped and in practice used to tether his back leg to a peg in order to prevent himself moving out of his ground to play the ball.

Sheffield were played twice in 1842, but with the rise in strength of the Nottingham players, several Nottingham men were barred by agreement and thus the interest in the matches was reduced.

For the first time since 1791, Nottingham(shire) played MCC on even terms in 1843, there being matches at Lord's and at Trent Bridge. The Lord's match was lost by 58 runs, but at home Notts won by 26 runs. A new departure was matches against Hampshire, a county having a brief revival. Hampshire came to Trent Bridge with ten men and had to co-opt a local amateur, J. Hadden, to make up the side. The visitors lost by an innings. Notts arranged to play in Southampton immediately before their game at Lord's. It was on the initial journey south that Tom Barker lept out of a runaway cab crossing London and broke his leg; in these circumstances Notts had only ten men and, as mentioned above, Noyes batted four times. Notts won this game by 39 runs.

'Charley' Brown began his county career in 1843 – he scored 107 for Nottingham *v* Sheffield in July and this no doubt prompted Clarke to include him in the county side. Brown was best known as a wicketkeeper, though some reporters stated he was a little too sharp in that position, tending to adjust the bails when the ball just missed the wicket. He had an extraordinary knack of delivering the ball from behind his back when bowling and being very accurate with such deliveries. His major defect was his excitability, but he was very popular with the spectators and about 10,000 attended each day of his benefit match in 1855. He acted as Secretary to the County Club in 1852.

Five amateurs turned out for Nottinghamshire in 1843 for the first time; G. M. Kettle played mainly for Burton-on-Trent, but was also a member of MCC. A useful batsman, it would seem that he played in emergency for Abram Bass, who played his only match for Notts at Southampton this year – Kettle's appearance was in the home Hampshire game. A great supporter of cricket in Burton-on-Trent, Bass played for Leicester in 1839, and his connection with Nottingham would appear to be membership of the County Club. The Rev Henry Maltby played in three of the 1843 matches, and according to comments his place in the side was secured solely due to his financial support of the Club, though when he died in 1869 he left only £20. E. S. E. Hartopp, who also played in 1843, but only at Lord's, when Notts had ten men (due to Barker's injury), was much more wealthy and was auditor to the MCC from 1876 to 1894. He was educated at Eton and Cambridge and was in the XI against Oxford in 1841 and 1842. Later he played for Gentlemen *v* Players, his ability being mainly in the field and in particular as long-stop. The fifth 1843 amateur was the mainstay of the Gentlemen of Notts Club based at Southwell, J. B. Warwick. Warwick's cricket career was restricted due to his medical practice, but even so he played local cricket for about 25 years, being a good batsman and excellent wicketkeeper. He died in 1873, having been bedridden for eight years.

The final match of 1843 was against Sussex, Notts winning by an innings, and an unknown from Mansfield, John Gilbert, was mainly responsible with an innings of 91. One of the Sussex team later said that Gilbert played the bowling as easily as shelling peas and quite astonished both the Sussex side – and his own. His 91 stood as a Notts record for 16 years, but Gilbert was not interested in being a professional cricketer and devoted his time to helping with local Mansfield cricket and his occupation as a silk lace hand. This Sussex match was played for the benefit of William Clarke, the first time a Notts match had been organised for the benefit of a single cricketer.

The only match of note in Nottingham in 1844 was Players of Nottingham v Six Gentlemen of Nottingham and Five Players of England. The match goes down in the annals as marking the debut in important cricket of George Parr, the younger brother of Samuel, George was to become the leading batsman of his day and to take over from Clarke as the captain of the County side.

Nottinghamshire played Kent home and away in 1845. On 23 and 24 June the North opposed MCC at Lord's and won by an innings, the whole of the Northern side except Dakin, the Rev Richard Seddon and Philip Williams being Notts men. The identical team (except that Batchelor played for Warwick) moved to Canterbury and represented Notts v Kent – Notts lost by an innings. In the return at Trent Bridge the following month, Dakin and Seddon had gone, but Williams played his second and last match. Notts won this encounter by eight wickets due to Clarke's exceptional bowling – he had nine victims in the first innings and seven in the second. In September 14 of Notts played All England at Trent Bridge, the 14 being all professionals except the Rev William Musters. Samuel Parr made an unbeaten 40 in Notts second innings, winning the match for his side.

Why Kent did not object to Dakin and Seddon playing for Notts is not known. Both were at that time connected with Leicester cricket. Dakin was on the groundstaff at Lord's from 1847 to 1855 and a very useful all-rounder. Seddon was in the Cambridge XI in 1846 and 1847 and was 20 when he played for Notts. He did not play in any major matches after going down.

Chappell Batchelor, who appeared in the Canterbury match, was a keen member of the Gentlemen of Notts Club (it was established in 1844) and was an organist at Southwell Minster. A useful batsman, he played in three matches for Notts and for Notts Gentlemen for eleven years.

There were two other matches of 1845 which have been the cause of some confusion. A few record books still show William Clarke taking all ten wickets for Notts v Leicestershire in 1845. The match in question was Nottingham Amateur Club with Clarke v Leicester and the majority of the Nottingham team at no time played for the County XI. The report of the match in the

Nottingham Review downgrades the feat still further, in that Clarke is credited with only nine wickets in the innings.

The same newspaper on 20 March 1846 printed the following notices 'Mr W. Clarke the celebrated slow bowler has removed from Nottingham and will in future be found on Lord's Ground.'

The move effectively paralysed Nottinghamshire as a cricket team. John Chapman, Clarke's stepson, who had trained as a vet, returned to the Trent Bridge Inn and tried to run the cricket ground. In fact in 1846 no major cricket took place in Nottingham and with the Gentlemen's Club at Southwell flourishing it almost seemed as if Southwell would take the lead as the centre for Notts cricket. It was on the Southwell ground that Clarke arranged a second benefit for himself; 'Five Gentlemen of the Southwell Club and Five Players of Nottinghamshire with Mynn against England'. This was the famous match when Mynn stayed with Parr at Radcliffe on Trent and the pair badly misjudged the time required to travel, via the river, to Southwell, arriving very late and so annoying Clarke that he refused to pick Parr for any matches for the rest of the summer. Parr therefore missed playing in the first three matches involving the All England Eleven.

The All England Eleven was created by Clarke during 1846, his idea being to sign up the best cricketers of the day and tour England with this team playing what amounted to exhibition matches. The fast-growing railway system was allowing cheap and easy travel over most of mainland Britain for the first time and cricket being the only major team sport of the day the leading players were popular heroes, and spectators flocked to see them. Clarke arranged just three All England matches in 1846, at Sheffield, Manchester and Leeds, and all were a great success. Within a year or two Clarke had acquired a full season's fixture list for his team and indeed had more offers of matches than he needed. Generally speaking the England Eleven was opposed by 22 locals and even then Clarke often gave the side a professional bowler to level up the two teams.

Clarke's activities, which increasingly involved Nottingham players, obviously had a detrimental effect on Notts county cricket, but also discouraged other counties, since everyone wanted to see Clarke's famous eleven in preference to the more limited expertise of the local county players. The publicity given to Clarke's team, however, encouraged the development of cricket in general and no lesser figure than W. G. Grace mentioned much later (in his biography) of the interest taken when Clarke's team visited Gloucestershire in the 1850s.

John Chapman organised a match for Thomas Barker's Benefit

GEORGE PARR

'The Lion of the North' was the description given to Parr, for he was the leading batsman from about 1848 to 1860. His most famous shot was the leg sweep and the elm tree on the square leg boundary at Trent Bridge became known as Parr's Tree through the number of times he hit the ball into it (the stand now situated in front of the site of the tree is the Parr Stand). In his younger days he was also a brilliant field at long leg, known for the accuracy and power of his returns to the wicket.

Born in Radcliffe on Trent in 1826, he was the son of a gentleman farmer, but the family lost much of its money and Parr took up cricket as his profession. He made sufficient out of the game to enable him not to work during the winter months. In 1859 he became the first Notts batsman to score a hundred for the County and at the close of that season accomplished another first by leading the first England team to tour overseas – to North America. He refused to lead the first England side to Australia, the monetary reward not being sufficient, but he did captain the second such team in 1863–64.

He seems to have inherited the Notts captaincy in 1856 (rather than being officially appointed) and led the side until 1870, but most of his matches were not for the County, but for the All England Eleven, which he managed from William Clarke's death until he himself retired. In the 1860s he became increasingly involved in the disputes which marred many county matches, his disagreements with Surrey lasting several years, and as he employed many cricketers he could also direct them to refuse to play in matches if he so felt. No Players side was complete without Parr for a period of 20 years, though he declined to play in several matches against the Gentlemen at Lord's and the Oval.

Richard Daft stated that Parr was 'a man under whose banner I am proud to have fought, for a more honest and straightforward cricketer never took hold of a bat.' Some would not perhaps agree with the second half of that statement. Parr died in 1891 and was buried, with a bough of his elm tree, in the cemetery at Radcliffe, where a stone to his memory still stands.

Notts captain George Parr, throughout the 1850s the best batsman in England. (NCCC)

at Trent Bridge in 1847 which was styled Notts *v* England. The dates clashed with MCC *v* Sussex at Brighton; Clarke played for MCC, as did Alfred Mynn, and apart from Fuller Pilch and Martingell the so-called England side was very weak – Notts won by ten wickets. Even so Mr H. Brown deserves much praise for capturing ten wickets in the match on his Notts debut. Brown in fact was Henry Attenburrow, the surgeon at Nottingham Hospital playing under an assumed name – the reputation of cricket as being disreputable clearly had not entirely died. Attenburrow was one of the original Fellows of the Royal College of Surgeons in 1843 and was a slow under-arm bowler. The professional, R. C. Tinley, also played for the County in this match and bowled with success, taking six wickets. He was the youngest of three cricketing brothers from Southwell and was only about 16 or 17 (it has not yet been possible to verify his date of birth). Tinley was the protégé of Abram Bass and engaged by him at Burton on Trent. In his early career he was a fast bowler, but later adopted a slow under-arm style which proved a very effective contrast to the lightning deliveries of Jackson at the other end. A very hard-hitting batsman and an agile fielder at point, Tinley was an all-rounder of distinction and played regularly with the All England Eleven – he went to Australia with Parr's side and captured over 250 wickets at less than five runs each. Tinley represented Notts until 1869 and the All England Eleven until 1874. He retired to keep the Royal Oak in Burton on Trent, dying after some years illness in Burton in 1900. His brother Frank played in a few matches for the county commencing 1845 and the third brother, Vincent, turned out once in 1864.

John Chapman made an effort to bring more matches of note to Trent Bridge in 1848, home and away games being arranged against Sussex and Sheffield, but neither fixture proved of much interest to spectators and Chapman lost money on them. Clarke did not come, the two games at Trent Bridge clashing with his All England fixtures. Notts lost three of the matches, the fourth being drawn as Sussex had arranged to play elsewhere. Three players made their debuts for Notts during the year. William Selby, a professional, was of some interest, as he was the father of the England Test cricketer, John Selby. The Rev Champion de Crespigny made his single Notts appearance *v* Sussex at Trent Bridge. He was a curate at Southwell from 1847 to 1850 and whilst there was a tower of strength to the Notts Gentlemen. Educated at Cambridge he had played one or two matches for the University, but not against Oxford. He also played in a number of matches in Essex at Hill Hall, he being the cousin of Sir W.

Bowyer Smith. A contemporary described him as 'a jolly good fellow and a good cricketer.' The third newcomer of 1848, Mr John Johnson will be referred to later.

Disillusioned by his lack of success, John Chapman did not concern himself with major cricket matches at Trent Bridge in 1849 and 1850 and pigeon-shooting, athletic meetings and other activities were held to bring in some income. Cricket continued to be played but by two local clubs. The Nottingham Amateurs and the Nottingham Commercial both hired Trent Bridge for their home matches.

In 1851 for the third successive year there were no important cricket matches in Nottingham, but William Clarke's nationwide venture did result in his signing an agreement with Mr Houghton, the proprietor of Kennington Oval, for two matches at The Oval. The first was Clarke's North Eleven *v* South and the second Notts *v* Surrey, and they came during a purple patch for Clarke. It began when the North beat Surrey due to the bowling of Clarke, who captured 15 wickets; Clarke then crossed the river and played for England against Kent at Lord's, picking up another eight wickets. The following three-day match was MCC *v* Surrey Club at The Oval, where Clarke managed only six wickets. After a three-day break he was back at Lord's playing for North *v* South, another four wickets as the North won again, and the following day to The Oval for Notts *v* Surrey, when he took five wickets. This was the first match between the two counties and the beginning of a rivalry which was to last for 100 years, and until 1900 to dwarf all other county rivalries.

Alfred Clarke, son of William, made his County debut in the Surrey game. Aged 20, he was a good batsman and excellent outfielder. A regular member of the All England Eleven, Clarke managed the travel arrangements and thereby acquired the nickname of 'Bradshaw'. He went to Australia with Parr's Team in 1863–64.

A much more important debutant of 1851 was James Grundy. He was already 27 and had just joined the groundstaff at Lord's, having previously been, for several years, a professional in Norfolk. An all-rounder, his bowling was fast-medium and very accurate, while as a batsman he was always cool and collected, a player to steady the team and hold one end. He remained at Lord's for 21 years. In his last years he kept the Midland Hotel in Nottingham and this was used as the venue for the County Cricket Club's AGM for several years.

The slumbering County Cricket Club was woken by Charley Brown in 1852. A five-man committee was set up consisting of

Henry Smith, Charles Thornton, John Thornton (Treasurer), Charles Brown (Secretary) and A. N. Other.

The objective of the committee was to gather subscriptions in order to finance home and away matches with Surrey. The original manuscript containing the subscribers is in the Trent Bridge Museum and is the County Club's oldest document. With Clarke taking twelve wickets and Guy hitting 65, Notts won the first game, at The Oval, by an innings. M. J. Ellison played for Notts in this match, being qualified by birth, though he had long been associated with Sheffield. An amateur, he had come to London to play for Gentlemen of North *v* Gentlemen of South, and then found himself co-opted into the Notts side due to the indisposition of William Selby. Ellison, who was the agent for the Duke of Norfolk's extensive Sheffield estates, was largely responsible for the laying out of Bramall Lane and the creation of Yorkshire CCC with Bramall Lane as its main venue. He was President of the Yorkshire Club from 1866 to his death in 1898.

It was the bowling of Grundy which won the return with Surrey at Trent Bridge. He took five wickets in each innings and the visitors were beaten by ten wickets. The double success of Notts in 1852 led to Clarke arranging a fixture at Lord's, Notts opposing the Rest of England in May 1853. Notts beat the strong England side by 27 runs. Curiously there was not another county game until the end of August, when the side went to Brighton and overwhelmed Sussex by an innings. A week later Sussex came up to Trent Bridge and had their revenge, despite lacking one man and co-opting Captain Holden into the side. Holden later became the powerful Honorary Secretary of Notts as well as Chief Constable. When Edwin Browne (the Notts paid secretary) wrote a brief history of the Club in the 1880s, he had a dig at the bellicose captain:

> The gallant Captain was I presume not allowed to bowl, or he would have given a good account of himself as he was very dangerous with the ball in those days. However he caught a man out, and although he was given out leg-before-wicket before scoring, it is generally understood that the decision was a bad one, at least so I have heard the worthy Captain assert on several occasions.

Immediately after the Sussex defeat Notts travelled to London to play Surrey. Notts won by an innings and did not even require William Clarke's bowling, Frank Tinley, Grundy and Bickley taking all the wickets. George Parr had a marvellous record in Notts' matches during the year: 4 and 49, 46, 36 and 28, 55 not out. A double-figure score was considered quite a feat in first-class matches and Parr's scores the equal of anyone in England.

After the success of 1853, Notts arranged home and away fixtures with England and Surrey in 1854, but lost all four games. The antics of Old Clarke in the first fixture – against England at Lord's – made an appropriate beginning for a poor year. Clarke disputed an umpiring decision and left the field to discuss the point with the MCC Committee, thus holding up the game till he returned.

The victories of 1853 had provoked the four games of 1854. Now the losses of the latter year discouraged the promoters from any ambitious matches in 1855, only one Notts game being played and that with the odd title: Notts *v* Kent and All England. The County again lost, though Grundy with 60 made the highest score in the game. It was to be the last time William Clarke appeared for Notts and the first time John Jackson played.

Jackson had been discovered by Clarke when playing in a local match against the All England Eleven. Born in Suffolk he had moved to the small Nottinghamshire village of Wellow when a week old. Clarke engaged his services for the AEE and he remained a member of that side until 1867. Arthur Haygarth's brief biographical note sums up Jackson:

The first Trent Bridge pavilion, which was used until 1872. (NCCC)

For half-a-dozen years, John Jackson, called the 'Demon Bowler', was one of the fastest and most successful in the country. (NCCC)

He was one of the straightest, fastest and best bowlers that has ever appeared and though his speed was so great, he delivered easily to himself, all weathers suiting him. By some he was called 'the demon bowler' and his delivery was unexceptional as to fairness . . . his career, though rather short, must be considered most brilliant.

During the seven seasons when he was at his best, 1857 to 1863, only one batsman managed to score an individual hundred when Jackson was on the fielding side. His most famous match for Notts was the one *v* Kent at Cranbrook in 1863 when he took 13 for 43 and hit exactly 100 in his only innings. He has a small niche in history as the first person to feature in a cricketing cartoon in *Punch*. A bystander addresses a much battered cricketer returning

37

NOTTINGHAMSHIRE *v* KENT AND ALL ENGLAND

Played on the Trent Bridge Ground, Nottingham, 16, 17 and 18 August 1855

KENT AND ALL ENGLAND WON BY SEVEN WICKETS

NOTTINGHAMSHIRE	FIRST INNINGS			SECOND INNINGS	
A. Clarke	c Anderson b Hollands	8	(2)	c and b Diver	1
J. Grundy	b Diver	60	(1)	c and b Diver	1
S. Parr	c Diver b Hollands	5	(5)	c Stephenson b Hollands	39
G. Parr	b Buttress	19		b Hollands	29
E. L. Bateman, Esq	c Fryer b Buttress	4	(3)	b Hollands	0
R. C. Tinley	run out	6		c Stephenson b Hollands	45
J. Jackson	c Bartholomew b Diver	8	(10)	b Willsher	0
J. Bickley	c Diver b Buttress	0		not out	12
†J. S. Need	not out	15		c Buttress b Hollands	6
R. Gibson	run out	8	(7)	c Anderson b Hollands	17
★W. Clarke	c and b Diver	1		b Diver	4
Extras	b 1, lb 2, w 1	4		b 4, lb 3, w 1	8
Total		138			162

BOWLING	O	R	W		O	R	W
Buttress	18	29	3		5	16	0
Willsher	24	32	0		27	34	1
Hollands	20	36	2		29	56	6
Diver	15	36	3		13	48	3

KENT AND ALL ENGLAND	FIRST INNINGS			SECOND INNINGS	
Julius Caesar	c Jackson b W. Clarke	4	(5)	not out	22
T. M. Adams	run out	43	(1)	c S. Parr b Bickley	11
F. Hollands	st Need b W. Clarke	12			
G. Anderson	c Bateman b Clarke	36		not out	21
F. S. Clifford	b Jackson	17			
H. H. Stephenson	c S. Parr b W. Clarke	36			
E. Willsher	b W. Clarke	1	(3)	c Grundy b Tinley	23
A. Bartholomew	b Jackson	2			
A. J. D. Diver	not out	10	(2)	c A. Clarke b W. Clarke	23
W. H. Fryer	b Jackson	0			
W. Buttress	c G. Parr b W. Clarke	5			
Extras	b 16, lb 5, nb 3	24		b 6, lb 1, nb 4	11
Total		190		(3 wkts)	111

BOWLING	O	R	W		O	R	W
Bickley	24	30	0		8	23	1
W. Clarke	68	92	6		12	31	1
Jackson	24	28	3		16	18	0
Grundy	19	15	0		12	19	0
Tinley					2	8	1

Umpires: J. Guy and W. Hillyer
★Captain; †Wicketkeeper

The bowling is incorrect in both Notts analyses.
This match is significant as being the final appearance of William Clarke for the County and the debut of John Jackson. The end of one great career and the beginning of another.

from a match. 'Good match, old fellow?' 'Oh yes; awfully jolly!' 'What did you do?' 'I 'ad a hover of Jackson; the first ball 'it me on the hand, the second 'ad me on the knee, the third was in my eye and the fourth bowled me out.'

He was only 33 when he played his last match for Notts and though he maintained that he was dropped because he was not born in the county, in fact he had burnt himself out. The County gave him a benefit in 1874 and he received about £300, but Jackson was an easy-going individual and he finished his life in the Liverpool Workhouse, destitute save for a small pension provided by some cricketing buffs.

Two other players making their debut in this 1855 match were E. L. Bateman and Robert Gibson. The former was one of three brothers who were sons of the rector of West Leake. E. L. Bateman had played in the University matches of 1854 and 1855. A useful batsman and very good fielder he lived in London for much of his life and was a member of the MCC Committee for many years. This was his only appearance for the County; likewise his brother Augustus only played once, in 1862. Gibson was a medium-fast round-arm bowler, who was a professional at various times in Norfolk and at Oxford. He played in two more Notts games in 1858.

AFTER CLARKE

THE HAND OF CLARKE HAD been controlling Nottingham cricket for about 25 years. He made his last appearance as a player for his All England Eleven against 22 of Whitehaven in June 1856, taking a wicket with the last ball he bowled; a month later he umpired in a match at Melton Mowbray and on 25 August 1856 died at his residence in Wandsworth Road, South London.

During the final ten years of his life he had become increasingly autocratic. In 1852 14 leading professionals signed a manifesto stating that they would refuse to take part in any matches arranged by Clarke and a rival travelling professional eleven was formed, the United All England Eleven. How he became captain of Nottinghamshire is not known, but having taken over the job, Clarke was too strong a character to be dispossessed and though some Nottinghamshire games were organised without him, after his move from Trent Bridge, the County side seemed a little lost in his absence. The fact that he employed the best Notts players from the time he started his England Eleven tied the hands of any Committee formed to stage Notts matches.

What arrangement had been made to carry on the All England Eleven after Clarke's death is unknown. George Parr seems to have 'inherited' the team and with this came also the captaincy of Notts, though the latter job was none too arduous since only one match was played in 1856 and one in 1857. The 1856 game took place just days before Clarke's death and was organised by the All England Eleven, being Notts *v* England at Newark. England, even without those players who refused to have anything to do with Clarke, beat Notts by seven runs. James Chatterton, a local Newark man, made his Notts debut in this game. A professional for over 20 years, he was a useful batsman with a good defence, but played in only six major Notts matches. In his later years he umpired in county cricket. One of George Parr's brothers, Henry, also played for Notts in this match. Aged 18 he was a promising batsman, but died in 1863 aged 25.

George Parr organised the only Notts match of 1857 and this was more in line with an All England game, being against 16 of Sheffield. John Jackson took 18 wickets and Notts won by nine runs, R. C. Tinley and George Parr being the only batsmen to flourish. The Rev R. B. Earle, headmaster of the Grammar School at Southwell and vicar of Edingley, played for the County and turned out once in 1861, his second and last appearance.

Between 1853 and 1869 he was a regular member of the Notts Gentlemen and also a leading player with the Midland Counties Diamonds, a club which played some good class cricket in the 1860s. Earle was a useful all-rounder.

The major event of 1857 took place at Lord's on 1, 2 and 3 June, when the All England Eleven played the break-away United Eleven for The Cricketers' Fund, which was set up that year to help professionals down on their luck. The match put into the field the top 22 professionals of the day. The composition of the teams gives an indication of the relative strengths of the counties – Notts provided six of the 22, Grundy, Parr, Tinley, Clarke, Bickley and Jackson; Surrey had five, Sussex three, Cambridge two and Kent two and the other four came from Lancashire and Yorkshire, neither of whom had county sides on any organised basis.

The Notts players dominated the match, the All England side winning with Parr, undefeated in both innings, making most runs and Jackson taking most wickets. The matches between these two teams continued until 1869 when the United closed down, but in the last few years they played in the north of the country, being composed almost entirely of northern men.

There were several complaints in the Nottingham papers around this time about the lack of a proper County Cricket Club for Nottinghamshire and this state of affairs continued in 1858 when the two Notts matches were set up by the opposition! The Surrey Club paid all the expenses to bring a Notts team to The Oval and a cricket fanatic in Stockton-on-Tees financed a match in that town between Notts and a combined Durham–Yorkshire combination. Parr was totally occupied with running the All England Eleven – the side being involved in 21 three-day matches – and the five principal Notts professionals were signed up with Parr. In addition Grundy played regularly for the United Eleven and when fixtures such as Gentlemen *v* Players, North *v* South and the Canterbury Week were added there were few dates available for Notts matches.

The 1858 Surrey match proved a disappointing game for Notts. Parr had to cry off at the last moment through injury and Bickley, Tinley and Brampton could not obtain leave from their engagements. Alfred Diver was allowed to play for the County in place of Parr – Diver was the Cambridgeshire professional. The Southwell amateur, Batchelor, was co-opted and two other amateurs, A. W. McDougall and Richard Daft, filled the other vacancies. McDougall was a Cambridge student, who lived at Wilford and was a very keen cricketer at club level. This was his only match for Notts. Richard Daft was a young amateur who had been encouraged by George Parr. He was to succeed Parr as the greatest professional batsman of his day.

This weakened Notts side was beaten by nine wickets, though Daft made an unbeaten 44 in Notts second innings. The match at Stockton ended in confusion. With seven wickets in hand and needing just 24 to win Notts suddenly found that the local umpire declared the wicket unfit for further play. John Hogg, the Burton Joyce wicketkeeper, took the place of Charley Brown at Stockton.

Tom Davis, known by his fellow cricketers as 'Oily', also played at Stockton. He was a very fine fielder. Daft stated that he knew no one who put so much energy into fielding and Davis was most upset when he made an error in the field. He ended his days as ground superintendent on The Forest, being employed by the corporation.

It would be wrong to give the impression that, whilst Nottinghamshire, as a cricket club, muddled through on a hand-to-mouth ad hoc basis the other counties were busily organising matches. Cambridgeshire, with one of the best collections of players, rubbed along in the same way until 1870, when what little organisation existed died altogether. Yorkshire did not exist, cricket organisation being split between the major towns in the county. Officially Sussex CCC existed, but its matches were irregular and its side had deteriorated from the 1830s. The same applied to Kent, whose state of affairs was similar to Notts. Only Surrey had a proper Club and an organisation that could be recognised as such.

In contrast the 'County Gentlemen' teams were in much better shape and Notts in particular had a very well-run Club based at Southwell and playing on the ground, which is today used by Southwell CC.

Urged on no doubt by the comments in the press and the example of Surrey, one man decided to sort out the muddle surrounding the almost clandestine Notts County Cricket Club. That man was John Johnson, a solicitor in Nottingham, aged, in 1859, 49. He had been Hon Secretary to the New Forest Club in the 1830s and acted in the same capacity for Nottingham Commercial CC, which club played at Trent Bridge. In his younger days he had been a fair club cricketer, but it is impossible to distinguish between him and another useful local amateur Isaac Johnson, who was two years his senior, who also played for the Commercial Club and was a lace manufacturer. Richard Daft tells the story of meeting someone who had played cricket against Mr

RICHARD DAFT

Apart from his great ability with a cricket bat, two qualities which shine through the fragments of biography and newspaper clippings relating to Richard Daft are his honesty and the trust he placed in his acquaintances. Unlike so many amateurs of the 19th century – W. G. Grace, W. W. Read and A. E. Stoddart being supreme examples – Daft could not abide the hypocrisy which meant that most of the amateurs playing full-time county cricket were paid under the table. He chose to switch from amateur to professional and then late in life, when he did not play regularly, he switched back to amateur status. He ran various business enterprises in Nottingham, the two major ones being a large sports goods shop and a brewery. Unfortunately he put too much trust in his shop managers and though the business did well, he was swindled more than once by his employees.

His cricketing ability is described in Sutton's 'Nottingham Cricket Matches': The style of Richard Daft's batting is perfection itself, and whether in his back or forward play he be noticed, there is such an artistic grace pervades the whole while at the wicket as makes him the 'observed of all observers', indeed we have seen nothing to excel the beauty of his play, or come near it, since the days of Fuller Pilch.

In the 14 seasons between 1864 and 1877, Daft topped the Notts batting table eleven times and no one since has monopolised the County's batting to that extent. Due to his business interests he rarely appeared in major matches outside the county programme, except for representing the Players *v* Gentlemen at Lord's and The Oval. He also declined to tour overseas, except with the 1879 North American side.

Daft succeeded Parr as captain of Notts and though he officially retired in 1880 from county cricket, so good was his form in local matches that in 1891 he was persuaded, at the age of 55, to turn out for Notts when Shrewsbury was injured. His brother Charles played for the County, as did his two sons H. B. and R. P. Daft. A keen footballer, he was involved in the early days of Notts County FC. Daft died in 1900 and a suitably inscribed stone was placed over his grave in Radcliffe on Trent, but in 1990 the inscription was almost illegible.

Richard Daft, for a while the best professional batsman in England, topped the Notts averages in eleven seasons. (NCCC)

Johnson, but after a long conversation Daft was still unable to discover which Mr Johnson was involved as both wore glasses and had similar hair styles and were of similar build. The possible newspaper confusion over the initials I and J complete the difficulty.

Just like all the other gatherings to organise Notts players and matches up to this date, there seems to be no record of John Johnson formally calling an official meeting and getting a committee elected to run the County Cricket Club. The first extant notice of a meeting is not until October 1861. However in the winter of 1858–59, Mr Wildey, who had taken over as tenant of the Trent Bridge Inn and Cricket Ground from John Chapman about 1850, retired and Joseph Hickling became the new tenant. Unlike Mr Wildey, Mr Hickling was keen on cricket and one can assume that Hickling and Johnson combined forces to promote the interests of County cricket.

Joseph Hickling does not appear in local cricket scores. He did, however, accompany Sir Robert Clifton's Nottingham team to Paris in 1864 and according to Daft's reminiscences the French were amazed at his corpulence and thought he wore padded clothes. Hickling was thoroughly fed up with France, especially the frugal meals that were served up and he missed the large joints of beef he had at home.

One of the first moves of the Johnson–Hickling combination was the building of a brick pavilion at the back of the Trent Bridge Inn. Presumably the players used a tent or the Inn itself for changing until this first pavilion was erected. The exact date of the new pavilion is not known, though it is described in an account of a match in 1863. A single-storey building with a series of French doors filling the whole of the frontage on to the ground, it was simply one large room and served both as an eating place and dressing room.

The only County match of 1859 was against Surrey at The Oval. The Surrey Club arranged the match with George Parr. Unlike 1858, Parr was able to play and marked the occasion by scoring the first century for Nottinghamshire (130) despite a ricked back which forced him to use a runner for the latter part of the innings. Notts batted all the first day for 329; Surrey had to follow on and victory was achieved by eight wickets.

In the autumn George Parr captained the England team to North America, the first such overseas tour. The 12 players on the tour were composed of six All England men and six United. Three Notts players, Parr, Grundy and Jackson, made the voyage (also Diver, who had been a given man for Notts). The side were away from England from 7 September to 11 November and each received £90 after all expenses had been paid. Admirers and well-wishers also gave them generous presents.

In 1860, after a gap of five years, an inter-county match was arranged for Trent Bridge. Caffyn, the Surrey cricketer comments in his autobiography:

> What enthusiasm there was at Nottingham in those days, to be sure! A huge crowd collected each day on the Trent Bridge. Their cheering and clapping of hands for every bit of good play I can hear now. There was no hotel one could go into in the evening but cricket, cricket, cricket greeted us at every turn. The whole town seemed to have gone mad on the game.

There were in fact three matches in 1860 of which this Surrey match was the last – no doubt vividly recalled by Caffyn because he hit 91 and took eight wickets, to bring Surrey success by just 20 runs, after Notts had had a lead of 87 on the first innings. Ill health prevented Parr from playing, which made all the difference, Lord Stanhope taking his place.

Lord Stanhope was a great patron of cricket and organised matches at his country seat, Bretby Hall near Burton on Trent. He was MP for South Nottinghamshire until 1866 when he became the 7th Earl of Chesterfield. He died aged 40 of typhoid in 1871.

The first match of 1860 was at Bramall Lane, where Notts drew with 16 of Sheffield, and direct from that town they went to The Oval, where they beat Surrey by 16 runs in a low-scoring game, John Jackson taking nine for 49 in the final innings.

The rejuvenated Nottinghamshire County Cricket Club took a great step forward in the spring of 1861 by announcing that a match would be played between Nottinghamshire and 22 Colts who had never played for the County, Easter Monday and Tuesday being the dates set aside for this innovation. The County completely overwhelmed the Colts, who were dismissed for 56 and 55 – the eleven made 158 in their single innings – but there were several colts who would make their mark in subsequent years including Alfred Shaw, Bignall and Biddulph.

The inter-county programme consisted of home and away with Surrey. The Surrey side was at the zenith of its power in the first years of the 1860s and Notts were beaten by 103 runs at The Oval and eight wickets at Trent Bridge.

A major change in the Notts side of 1861 was the disappearance of John Bickley and the arrival of George Wootton as his replacement. Wootton, from Clifton, was already 27. He was a left-arm fast bowler and it is claimed did not come forward earlier because of his shy and retiring disposition. He was persuaded to play by Alfred Clarke and immediately secured a permanent place in the County side. For ten seasons he was a mainstay of the side and also secured a post at Lord's until 1873. As a batsman he was at first useless, and failed to score a single run in his first four innings, but later 'often made a slow match cheerful through his aggressive tendencies'. He became an umpire when his playing days were over. 'It is a very thankless office', he said, 'and I soon gave it up. I liked umpiring very well, but if you make a mistake everyone is digging at you. I could not stand that sort of thing.'

A Cambridge University student, William Bury, son of the vicar of Radcliffe on Trent, made the first of three appearances for Notts in 1861. An elegant batsman he was noted as well in the field. One commentator states: 'He was a very peculiar runner, but extremely fast between the wickets.' Like R. B. Earle he was a prominent member of the Midland Counties Diamonds, so-called because of their diamond patterned shirts. In 1862 at Trent Bridge he had the odd experience (especially as three-figure innings were rare) of hitting 121 twice, first for the Gentlemen of the North and second for the Diamonds.

Henry Slater, who had played for the North v Surrey in 1860, made a single appearance for Notts against the Colts in 1861. He played for Newark for over 20 years, being Secretary of the club in the 1870s.

The season of 1861 ended with a Benefit Match for George Butler at Trent Bridge, when the County XI played the Next 22. Butler had now been a professional to local clubs playing at Trent Bridge for ten years – he was to have a second benefit 20 years later.

The Annual General Meeting of the County Club was held in November at Samuel Parr's inn, Long Row, Nottingham. The Secretary was given as John Johnson and the committee for 1862: 'Lord Stanhope, Lord Edwin Hill, Sir H. Bromley, Capt Holden, F. Wright Esq, and others.' The accounts have not apparently survived, but the newspaper report noted a balance in hand of £165.13s.3d.

The two matches against Surrey and what was to be the annual Colts match were arranged for 1862; in addition fresh ground was pioneered with home and away matches against Cambridgeshire (though Cambridge Town Club had been opposed in 1834).

The two away matches of 1862 took place first. Cambridge-shire, despite the presence of their famous trio, Hayward, Carpenter and Tarrant, were beaten by three wickets, Wootton being the most successful bowler, and Richard Daft scoring most runs. The Surrey match at The Oval was drawn due to rain, though Notts had a 64-run lead on first innings – George Parr was unable to play in either match. Horsley and Smith of Gotham played for Notts in these games. William Horsley of Southwell had gained selection after winning the batting prize in the Colts match. Nearly all his cricket was played in the Southwell area, where he followed the occupation of a tailor. John Smith of Gotham (to distinguish him from John Smith of Ruddington) was a useful all-

Richard Daft (left) and George Parr in 1862, two great batsmen who followed each other as Notts captains. (NCCC)

47

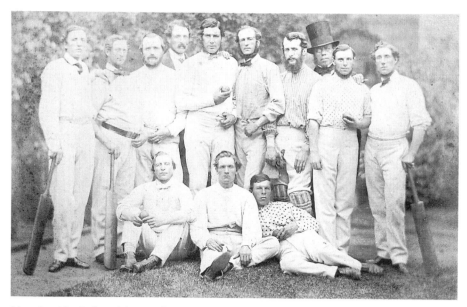

Notts in 1862. Left to right, standing: R. Daft, J. Grundy, G. Parr, G. Anderson (umpire), J. Jackson, C. Brampton, A. Bateman, J. Johnson (Hon. Sec.), G. Wootton, A. Clarke. Front: R. C. Tinley, C. F. Daft, S. Biddulph. (NCCC)

TRENT BRIDGE CRICKET GROUNDS, NOTTINGHAM.—THE COLTS' MATCH.
(From a sketch by Mr. John Hooper.)

The Colts match at Trent Bridge in 1862 from a sketch by John Hooper. (NCCC)

round cricketer. He played three first-class matches for Notts, but about 1866 moved to Bradford and from then on it becomes impossible to locate him with any accuracy.

The two Notts home matches were both victories. R. C. Tinley took 15 wickets to beat Cambridgeshire by an innings, and after Wootton bowled out Surrey for 133, Bateman and Grundy added over 100 for Notts second wicket and the home side gained such an advantage on first innings that they eventually won by five wickets. Bateman was the younger brother of E. L. Bateman and he scored 63 in this, the first innings of his only game for the County. Another player to represent Notts in 1862 for the only time was Frank Moore. He acted as wicketkeeper. He was already 34 and had been a professional with various local clubs, whilst in the winter he acted as an attendant at football matches. The earliest surviving Notts team photograph was taken during the Surrey game at Trent Bridge and apart from the eleven players, John Johnson and the umpire George Anderson are also featured.

Frank Moore did not have an opportunity of extending his County career, because the County had discovered a much younger wicketkeeper, Sam Biddulph.

Sutton in his Nottingham book commented: 'For quickness of sight, execution and indomitable courage, perhaps (Biddulph) stands second to but few in the cricketing world. He receives the ball from the field most masterly and no matter at what speed if well put in, and the chance is there, he is safe of putting down the stumps with an effect the most electric.' Other commentators were not so generous, but it has to be remembered that wicketkeeping gloves were rudimentary, and keeping to Jackson, the fastest bowler of the day, soon caused damaged hands. He held the position of Notts keeper until 1875, in fact until he died, for illness meant that he missed the later matches in 1875 and his death occurred of a disease of the kidneys on 7 March 1876, aged 35. He was also engaged at Lord's from 1863 to his death. Charles Daft, Richard's elder brother, also made the first of several appearances, in 1862. A defensive batsman, he played for the Commercial Club for about 30 years.

Notts and Surrey being acknowledged as the strongest counties it was a pity that a misunderstanding led to the fixture not being played in 1863. It was the first of a number of 'misunderstandings' between the two counties during the decade, usually inter-related with quarrels between the All England Eleven and the ground management at The Oval and/or Lord's.

John Johnson replaced the Surrey fixture by games with Kent and Yorkshire. As Surrey had improved, so Kent had declined and they were no match for Notts. At Trent Bridge Kent, with four second innings wickets standing, needed well over 200 to win; at Cranbrook Notts won by an innings with John Jackson performing (on paper) the best feat of his career. He bowled unchanged through both innings, in the first of which he took six for 23 as Kent were dismissed for 58. When Notts tumbled to 61 for six, Jackson came in and hit exactly 100. Notts reached 280; Kent were bowled out on the second afternoon for 45, Jackson, with Grundy, being unplayable and taking his match analysis to 12 for 43. The Yorkshire matches might be regarded as the first bona fide contests between the two counties. Notts lost at Bradford, but evened the score at Trent Bridge, in spite of being forced to follow on. Yorkshire needed only 101 in the final innings, but Grundy, who had a collection made for him, returned the splendid analysis of 23–16–13–5, and Notts won by six runs.

An unusual match was staged at Trent Bridge at the end of the season for Frank Tinley's Benefit. The County opposed 14 Free Foresters – the amateur club had been established a few years and earlier in the season, with the same odds, had beaten Surrey by five wickets. They looked like inflicting a defeat on Notts, for the County still required 63 to win when the last man, Wootton, arrived at the crease to partner Biddulph. The two Free Forester bowlers were the fast left-hander, David Buchanan, and the slow under-arm spinner, T. C. Goodrich. Gradually Biddulph and Wootton reduced the deficit until the scores were levelled, then Biddulph moved out to one from Goodrich, anxious to make the winning run, and played the ball with his legs rather than the bat. He was given out leg before and the match was tied. W. G. Armitstead gives a detailed description of the game in 'Annals of the Free Foresters' and closes his passage with: 'The Trent Bridge ground was then a far more free-and-easy sort of place than, I feel sure, it is in these more highly organised days: the old pavilion combined a bar with its dressing-rooms etc, and both sexes were admitted in it; and dressing seemed to go on in public, varied and enlivened by liquid refreshment.'

Two of the three players to assist Notts for the first time in 1863 were of little more than passing interest. Michael McIntyre, known as 'Smackintyre' owing to the violence with which he approached both batting and bowling, was the first of three cricketing brothers from Eastwood. He took nine for 18 in the first innings of the Free Foresters match, but his second and last game for the County was in the following year. E. Arthur Howsin had made a name for himself playing for Guy's Hospital in 1862, where he was studying medicine. He was born in North

Muskham, near Newark, but he soon moved away from Notts when he qualified, and practised at Newton-le-Willows and later Stroud – both his matches for the County were in 1863.

The third trialist was an opening batsman, Thomas Bignall of Chilwell. He lived most of his adult life in Basford and worked in partnership with Biddulph on a lace machine – in those days the lace machines operated day and night and the two workers did alternate shifts. A sound, defensive batsman Bignall was 21 and he played fairly frequently for the County until 1874 – in middle life he put on a lot of weight and by 1874 was 13 stone, though only 5ft 7in in height. He was brought out of retirement, in emergency, in one match in 1878.

The Notts season ended as it had begun with a Colts Trial. The match was drawn and the Colt making the highest score was James Billyeald, an amateur, who played for the Commercial Club. He was a traveller in the wine and spirits trade and moved to Wirksworth in Derbyshire, later helping that county in its early years.

George Parr captained the England Team to Australia and New Zealand during the winter of 1863–64, taking three Notts colleagues with him: R. C. Tinley, J. Jackson and A. Clarke. They were not due back to England until June (having set sail in October) and for that reason the usual Easter Colts match for 1864 was cancelled.

John Johnson organised a much more ambitious county programme for 1864 – matches against Kent, Yorkshire and Surrey. In addition the North *v* South match at Lord's was cancelled and Notts *v* Cambridgeshire played in its place. This fact is a clear indicator of the standing of Nottinghamshire in the cricket world of 1864 – that the MCC would think that this county match would be of interest to Londoners.

The trippers to Australia landed back in England only on the opening day of the visit of Kent to Trent Bridge and so were unable to play. Despite their absence, Notts won by an innings, a young medium-pace bowler from Burton Joyce taking six second innings wickets for 31 runs. Alfred Shaw, aged 21, was to develop into the greatest medium-slow bowler of his time. Shaw described his success to Old Ebor:

I don't know how I can explain it. I was always active and, if I could help it, I never bowled two balls alike. Then I always bowled for my men in the field. I used, too, to try to find a batsman's weak point, and then keep him there – stick him up, as the saying goes. I was thought to be very good at the

NOTTINGHAMSHIRE *v* 14 FREE FORESTERS

Played on the Trent Bridge Ground, Nottingham, 13, 14, 15 August 1863

MATCH TIED

FREE FORESTERS	FIRST INNINGS		SECOND INNINGS	
W. G. Armitstead, Esq	b Jackson	15	b Wootton	12
C. L. Hornby, Esq	c Bignall b Wootton	9	st Biddulph b Wootton	7
H. E. Bull, Esq	c Tinley b McIntyre	17 (4)	b Jackson	41
E. K. Hornby, Esq	b Wootton	7 (5)	b Wootton	7
R. A. H. Mitchell, Esq	b McIntyre	0 (7)	b Tinley	34
T. Ratcliff, Esq	b McIntyre	1 (10)	b Jackson	8
F. R. Evans, Esq	c Jackson b Wootton	15 (3)	run out	1
F. W. Wright, Esq	b McIntyre	10 (6)	b Jackson	64
W. J. Lyon, Esq	b McIntyre	4	run out	2
H. S. Armitstead, Esq	b McIntyre	18 (8)	lbw b Tinley	5
T. O. Reay, Esq	b McIntyre	0	c Tinley b Jackson	7
W. K. Mott, Esq	c Clarke b McIntyre	3	b Jackson	0
D. Buchanan, Esq	not out	1	not out	3
T. C. Goodrich, Esq	b McIntyre	0	st Biddulph b Tinley	1
Extras	b 7, lb 6, w 1	14	b 14, lb 6	20
Total		114		212

1st inns: 1-17, 2-37, 3-51, 4-53, 5-55, 6-61, 7-76, 8-90, 9-91, 10-93, 11-97, 12-114
2nd inns: 1-17, 2-22, 3-24, 4-54, 5-133, 6-162, 7-173, 8-183, 9-201, 10-203, 11-203, 12-208

BOWLING	O	M	R	W	O	M	R	W
Wootton	33	11	59	3	32	12	48	3
Jackson	12	3	23	1	18	4	38	5
McIntyre	20.1	7	18	9	18	10	33	0
Grundy					15	7	24	0
Tinley					18.2	4	49	3

NOTTINGHAMSHIRE	FIRST INNINGS		SECOND INNINGS	
C. Brampton	b Goodrich	26 (2)	b Buchanan	20
C. F. Daft	run out	16 (1)	c H. S. Armitstead b Reay	23
T. Bignall	c W. G. Armitstead b Evans	3 (8)	st Mitchell b Goodrich	4
R. Daft	not out	26 (3)	c Bull b Goodrich	56
J. Grundy	b Evans	6	c W. G. Armitstead b Goodrich	0
A. Clarke	st Mitchell b Goodrich	9	c W. G. Armitstead b Goodrich	0
J. Jackson	st Mitchell b Goodrich	0	st Mitchell b Goodrich	1
R. C. Tinley	c Ratcliff b Goodrich	7 (4)	b Buchanan	25
Michael McIntyre	c E. K. Hornby b Buchanan	9 (10)	b Goodrich	0
†S. Biddulph	b Goodrich	2 (11)	lbw b Goodrich	33
G. Wootton	b Goodrich	2 (9)	not out	30
Extras	b 8, w 1	9	b 7, lb 9, w 3	19
Total		115		211

1st inns: 1-44, 2-51, 4-58, 5-77, 6-77, 7-91, 8-101, 9-105
2nd inns: 1-32, 2-62, 3-113, 4-118, 5-120, 6-126, 7-133, 8-144, 9-148

dropping ball, which always appeared to be going farther than it really was. The batsman would have a smack at it, and very often he would miss it altogether or send it into a fielder's hands. I could bowl that ball without any apparent change of delivery. I really used to bowl faster than people thought I did, and I could make the ball break both ways, but not much.

It was several years before Shaw cultivated the art of slow bowling to the extent that he could defeat the greatest batsmen, but from 1870 to the middle of the 1880s he captured vast numbers of wickets at a very reasonable cost. Because Notts did not play many games, the majority of his victims in the 1870s came in MCC and representative matches. In 1878 he took 201 first-class wickets, the only time a bowler playing for Notts had reached above 200, and he is the only Notts bowler to take more than 2,000 first-class wickets. He was on the MCC staff from 1865 to 1881, except in 1868 and 1869. From 1883 to 1897 he was engaged by Lord Sheffield in order to coach Sussex cricketers. From 1883 to 1886 he captained Notts, but after 1886 he was discarded by the County as too old. He proved the Notts Committee wrong, for in 1894, aged 51, he turned out for Sussex and headed the Sussex bowling table. In 1897 he made a brief, one match, reappearance for Notts.

In 1880 he opened a cricket goods firm in Nottingham with Arthur Shrewsbury and the firm 'Shaw and Shrewsbury' became noted for the manufacture of cricket bats, continuing to the 1940s.

He toured Australia several times and goes down as the bowler who bowled the first ball in the very first Test. He captained England in 1881–82 in Australia. Of medium height and somewhat portly in middle life, he was a good-humoured man and fairly easy-going, the latter characteristic causing some friction between him and his business partner, Shrewsbury. His brother William played a few matches for Notts, but he was not related to his other contemporary, J. C. Shaw.

Vincent Tinley, the second of the three Southwell brothers,

BOWLING	O	M	R	W	O	M	R	W
Buchanan	18	6	41	1	54	28	69	2
Goodrich	40	16	40	6	58.1	24	79	7
Evans	22.2	10	25	2	16	6	15	0
Reay					7	1	14	1
Ratcliff					3	0	11	0
Mott					2	0	4	0

Umpires: G. Butler and Vincent Tinley
The two Armitsteads and Reay played under assumed names.

made his only Notts appearance in the game against Kent. His only other 'county' matches had been 13 years previously, when he had represented Lancashire against Yorkshire, being engaged at Manchester at the time. He was a lob bowler and useful batsman, but not up to the standard of his freres.

A fortnight after the Kent game, Yorkshire arrived at Trent Bridge and Notts put on a poor show, the batting failing against W. Slinn. The match was lost by 99 runs. This upset was immediately followed by a ten-wicket defeat at The Oval, where Surrey hit a record 468, H. H. Stephenson and T. Lockyer both reaching hundreds. Notts found some small consolation in the return with Kent and then played a most exciting match at Trent Bridge against Surrey.

Apart from Brampton, who made 40 out of the Notts total of 107, the County failed against Griffith. The Notts bowlers put their side back into the game, Grundy and Wootton dismissing Surrey for 127, but Griffith took another six cheap wickets when Notts batted again and Surrey required only 63 in their final innings. The score reached 40 for two, then six wickets went down for eight runs, Grundy taking three in five balls, and in six overs a total of five wickets without conceding a run. Dowson, the number four batsman, survived and when the last man, Shepherd, came to the wicket, five runs were still required. It took six overs to make those final five runs. Notts lost by one wicket.

The season ended with a seven-wicket win over Yorkshire at Bradford, and then a Colts Trial, which the Eleven won by an innings. A curiosity of the Colts innings was that W. Robinson batted at number 22 and made the highest score! The 21st wicket took the total from 47 for 20 to 76 all out.

William Oscroft of Arnold made his debut in 1864 – his uncles John, James and Sam had all been very useful players in their day. William was at first rather bothered by slow bowlers, but he soon mastered this weakness and became, after Parr and Daft, the best batsman in the Notts side. His leg-hitting was regarded as his best asset. George Parr signed him up for the All England Eleven and he took over the control of the famous band of wandering professionals in its final days. Oscroft went overseas with Grace's 1873–74 side to Australia and Daft's 1879 side to America. After captaining Notts in 1881 and 1882, he retired through ill-health, though he did not die until 1905 when he was 61. His brother John played in 14 first-class matches for the County between 1867 and 1874, but with modest results – he died of cirrhosis of the liver in 1885 aged 41.

Two amateurs made brief appearances for the County in 1864. Alfred Fewkes, the Commercial Club wicketkeeper, played in the Lord's match against Cambridgeshire and the Rev Dodsley-Flamsteed, vicar of Lambley, played against the Colts. He was mainly associated with the Notts Gentlemen, but in 1873 moved to a parish in Bristol. William Williams, a local solicitor from Arnold, had appeared for the Gentlemen of the North v Gentlemen of the South in 1862 and played occasionally for the County from 1864 to 1875. He played mainly for Bestwood Park CC in its early days. Another John Smith, this time from Ruddington, played twice in 1864. He was already 28 and spent most of his cricketing life away from Nottingham, having professional engagements chiefly in Lancashire.

Financially the County Club was flourishing, making a profit of over £50 in 1864 and having a bank balance in excess of £300. Sussex (in place of Kent) Yorkshire and Surrey were the home and away opponents for 1865, with two additional matches, one against 14 Free Foresters and another against Cambridgeshire, the latter being met at Old Trafford. The results were excellent. Sussex were twice beaten by an innings, William Oscroft hitting 107 in the match at Hove; Yorkshire were beaten by an innings at Bradford and 55 runs at Trent Bridge. Surrey lost at Trent Bridge by eight wickets, after Oscroft had batted quite brilliantly to carry out his bat for 53 in a total of 94, but the return at The Oval ended controversially, Surrey again winning by one wicket (as at Trent Bridge in 1864). This time 14 runs were required when Sewell, the last Surrey man, came in. Grundy had dismissed Dowson to take the ninth wicket; Sewell then made two off Grundy's last ball. Stephenson, at the other end, batted out a maiden from Jackson. Sewell hit a four and a single off Grundy's next over and facing Jackson scored two off his second delivery and then made a five, to win the match off his third ball. Notts supporters claimed that Sewell was given 'not out' when he was clearly stumped and earlier Grundy had been given out when the ball hit his arm. Parr refused to play at The Oval, still feeling sore about the controversy of 1862, and the result of the latest controversy was that Notts refused to play Surrey in 1866 or 1867.

The game against Cambridgeshire produced another innings victory and the press announced Nottinghamshire as the 'County Champions'. Oscroft was clearly Notts batsman of the year, averaging over 50, then came Daft, Brampton, Parr and Bignall. The bowlers were Grundy, Jackson, Tinley, Wootton and one newcomer, who in fact took more wickets than anyone (44 at 10.73), J. C. Shaw.

Already 29, Jemmy Shaw was a left-arm fast bowler with an action which was whip-like in that his arm came through very quickly. His career was most unusual in that he played in every important Notts match from his debut until his retirement ten years later. He was especially noted for the number of times he dismissed the great W. G. Grace cheaply (Grace also began his career in 1865). Shaw's other claim to fame was his batting. He was regarded as the worst batsman who ever played regularly for Nottinghamshire. Richard Daft noted: 'When Jemmy finished bowling he had finished altogether, for he was a very indifferent fielder and was about the worst man with a bat I ever came in contact with. In plain words he was never worth 4 runs against any bowling in his life.'

The Mansfield cricketer, John Hilton, played for Notts against Surrey in 1865 substituting for Brampton who had a strained wrist. It is believed that Hilton was the son of John Hilton, who played for Nottingham in 1829. The Hilton of 1865 moved to Staffordshire and died in 1910 of blood poisoning, after cutting his corns with a razor. A third debutant of 1865 was George Paling, an attacking batsman and excellent fielder, who played for the All England Eleven for several years and occasionally for the County.

At loggerheads with Surrey, Notts, for the first time, met Middlesex in 1866, the initial meeting of the two counties providing Middlesex with an innings victory. Rain affected the season and three matches ended as draws – one each *v* Middlesex, Yorkshire and Cambridgeshire, but both Yorkshire and Cambridge were beaten in the return fixtures. After his brilliant batting in 1865, Oscroft fell right away, but Daft scored plenty of runs, with 94 *v* Middlesex in Islington as his best. Jackson's career came to an end – he ruptured a blood vessel in the Yorkshire game and this injury finished his Notts appearances, but Wootton, Grundy, Tinley and J. C. Shaw provided the County with an adequate attack; Alfred Shaw played mainly as a batsman.

The long-established Notts Gentlemen Club at Southwell had finally collapsed and a new, or revived, Club was established by Samuel Watson in Beeston, the ground being adjacent to the station.

The fixture list proved difficult for 1867. Notts were still not on speaking terms with Surrey and internal conflicts had put Yorkshire in a temporary spin, which left only Middlesex and Cambridgeshire – Kent and Sussex were regarded as too weak to be capable of drawing a decent crowd. The Notts Committee therefore 'invented' two new fixtures, one against the North of

England and the second against 20 of Bradford. Of the four genuine county games three were won and the home game with Cambridgeshire lost, when the Notts first innings batting collapsed to Watts and Tarrant – all out 61. George Tarrant also caused problems when Notts faced the North. His fast bowling took ten wickets and none of the Notts batsmen reached 30. The North won by 112 runs.

George Howitt, who had played once in 1866, but neither batted nor bowled, turned out in the two Cambridgeshire matches of 1867. He was the son of Charles Howitt, the Nottingham Old Club cricketer of the 1820s. George was a fast left-arm bowler from Lenton who had moved to London in 1858, aged 15. He played for Middlesex in 1865, but at that time was able to represent both the county of his birth and that in which he resided. He was at his best about 1868, but in the 1870s was handicapped by ill-health, and though Middlesex paid for him to go to Australia in 1880, he died in 1881 aged 38. It was partially due to him that the problem over cricketers representing two counties in the same year was highlighted and in 1873 the regulations forbiding this were introduced.

William Shaw, Alfred's brother, played his single Notts first-class game in 1866, whilst Alfred Sears made a solitary outing in 1867. He failed to score in either innings, but in 1866 he had hit hundreds for both Worksop and Notts Commercial. He died in 1870 aged 23.

There was a complete change of programme in 1868 – neither Cambridgeshire or Middlesex were met; the fixture with Surrey was resumed, as was that with Yorkshire, and Lancashire were played for the first time. A summary of the six encounters produced four wins and two losses. On their first visit to Trent Bridge Lancashire lost by an innings, Wootton taking ten wickets and Daft hitting 94; the return was much closer with Notts having a margin of only 16 runs. Of the Surrey and Yorkshire matches, one each was won and one each lost. This gave Notts four wins and two losses in the season and the County was again acclaimed as the Champions. J. C. Shaw took 41 wickets in the six games and the leading batsman was Richard Daft. No fewer than 19 players were used, seven being in the eleven for the first time. The four who were amateurs all had brief careers in county cricket. J. G. Beevor, a solicitor practising in Worksop, played for Uppingham Rovers and the Free Foresters. A batsman with a sound defence, he was very severe on slow bowlers. P. W. H. Miles, son of the rector of Bingham, was in the Royal Artillery and had been in the eleven at Marlborough in 1865. He was a useful fast-medium bowler. His brother, R. F. Miles, moved to Bristol and in the 1870s was one of the leading figures in Gloucestershire cricket. J. R. Truswell from Farnsfield, where he was a gentleman farmer, played mainly for Newark and South-well. He was an excellent slow bowler, but his appearances for Notts were limited to two, both in 1868. The fourth amateur was Thomas Wright, a dark-complexioned gentleman with Dun-dreary whiskers. He played for the Commercial Club and was employed in a local bank. Although a successful batsman in local matches his technique was not up to county standard.

The three professional trialists were Samuel Sharpe, Frederick Wild (or Wyld), and Martin McIntyre. Sharpe played twice and was the father of the future England bowler; Wild from Eastwood was a fast-scoring batsman, who later became the first Notts player to hit a hundred in a county match at Trent Bridge. He made a name for himself with Squire Walker's team at Eastwood Hall. Engaged by MCC from 1875 to 1887, he played for Notts in 109 matches until 1881. When Biddulph died Wild was made wicketkeeper and this had a very detrimental effect on his batting, which was all the more sad because he was never more than a stop-gap wicketkeeper. A second new player from Eastwood was Martin McIntyre, brother of Michael. A slim, auburn-haired young fellow, he was soon to develop into a bowler regarded as faster than Jackson. In 1870 he went as a professional to America for £5 per week and performed some remarkable feats there; he also went in 1873–74 with Grace's side to Australia. He played for Notts in 45 matches spread over ten seasons and if he had taken care of himself he would have been perhaps the greatest profes-sional all-rounder of his day; as it was his performances were erratic. An illustration of this came in 1872 when he was severely reprimanded by the Notts Committee for indiscipline and drunk-enness. He then played against Surrey, came in with the score 55 for seven and made an undefeated 88. Opening the bowling he took nine for 33 – eight bowled and one caught and bowled!

The Australian Aborigines toured England in 1868 and played at Trent Bridge, but only against Nottingham Commercial. The local club eleven contained seven cricketers who appeared at one time or another for Notts and on first innings the two teams were fairly even, but the Commercial hit over 300 in the second innings and the game was drawn. The museum at Trent Bridge contains an interesting programme of athletics which formed part of the Aborigines visit to Nottingham.

The County retained the title of Champions in 1869, when five out of six matches were won. Richard Daft, who led the side in five matches due to the absence of Parr, had a splendid summer with the bat, averaging 61.17 in inter-county games. J. C. Shaw still dominated the bowling with 43 wickets at 13 runs each, though Daft tried out his lobs against Surrey and nominally topped the bowling table with eight wickets at 9.00.

The most important matches of the year were still those against Surrey, and Notts won at Trent Bridge by nine wickets, Daft making 56, the highest score of the game, and J. C. Shaw taking seven wickets. At The Oval, caution was the order of the day Surrey batted until after 5 o'clock to make only 206; Notts replied with 356, Daft hitting 93 not out in 260 minutes, but Beevor made a quicker 88. Surrey played well in their second innings, so that Notts required 59 in 90 minutes on the last afternoon – not a tall target by today's standards, but the report at the time said it was doubtful whether Notts or time would win. Notts won by six wickets at 6.45 pm.

Kent were beaten twice by an innings. The Notts total of 446 against them at Trent Bridge was a new record for the County, the memorable feature of the innings being the ninth wicket stand of 165 between Wootton and Martin McIntyre's brother, William. William was making only his second appearance for Notts and though he played in county cricket until 1880 he never beat the 99 he made in this innings. In 1870 he took a professional engagement with Bolton and from 1872 played under residential qualification for Lancashire. His bowling proved to be most effective with his adopted county and he returned some remark-able analyses, but in the 1870s Lancashire's opponents were generally not as strong as Nottinghamshire's.

Apart from William McIntyre, two other cricketers were seen in the County side for the first time; Henry Enfield was a nephew of the former town clerk of Nottingham, having the same name. He had had a brilliant season in 1868 in the Brighton College Eleven and in April 1869 had hit 115 not out in a match at Bestwood Park. He played for Notts against Yorkshire at Trent Bridge but made only two runs in both innings. Enfield re-appeared in the same fixture in 1872, again without success and that was the extent of his first-class career. Originally he was studying for the bar, but in 1876 was reported to be an artist living in France. However he came back later to Nottingham.

Walter Price from Ruddington had joined the Lord's staff in 1868 and apart from two years as coach at Rugby remained at Lord's until his death in 1894. He played four first-class games for Notts, but was seen in quite a number of MCC matches over the years, being a useful batsman and fast round-arm bowler. His three sons, William, Frederick and Alfred, were all professionals of some note, but only the last-named played for Notts.

The 1870 season will always bring to mind the name of George Summers. Summers had first played for Notts in 1867, the second day of his debut match being his 23rd birthday. From then on he missed only one game and was a sound and steadily improving batsman. As such he batted at number three in the second Notts match of 1870, against MCC at Lord's. In the first innings, Summers made 41. In the second innings the first ball he received, from Platts, rose suddenly and struck Summers on the head. He was carried back to the pavilion and though he felt well enough to travel back to Nottingham, he died four days later. The following inscription appears on his gravestone in the Nottingham General Cemetery:

> This tablet is erected to the memory of George Summers by the Marylebone Cricket Club, to mark their sense of his qualities as a Cricketer, and to testify their regret at the untimely accident on Lord's Ground which cut short a career so full of promise, June 19th, 1870, in the 26th year of his age.

Notts went on to win the match by one wicket, Daft scoring 117 and 53, J. C. Shaw taking 12 wickets. The first match of the season had been a victory over Surrey at The Oval, with Daft (55 and 80) and J. C. Shaw (8 wickets) the principal architects.

The third game was against Yorkshire and Notts were weakened by the fact that MCC refused to release Biddulph and Wootton, and in addition Wild was absent through illness. Notts brought in Howitt and two men who, as it turned out, never played for the county again, Richard Housley of Mansfield Woodhouse, a fair batsman, and G. N. Martin, a local wicketkeeper – both these players appeared as professionals, but were mainly amateurs. Yorkshire won the game by two runs, and this really decided the destiny of the Championship in favour of Yorkshire.

Notts were much too good for Kent, beaten by an innings both at Trent Bridge and the Crystal Palace. The return with Yorkshire was fought out with grim determination on both sides. The scoring rate was under two runs per over in all four innings, over 200 maiden overs being delivered. Notts made 146, Yorkshire 147. Notts second innings amounted to 142 and Yorkshire had what in the end amounted to 92 overs in which to make 142. They managed only 107 for six and the game was drawn.

The final game of 1870 was against Surrey at Trent Bridge. Daft had broken a tendon in his leg and was unable to play. The lack of the best batsman proved decisive and Surrey won by 53 runs. The County averages give ample proof of the hole Daft left – his average was 61, while the next player in the list averaged 17.

Aside from Housley and Martin two other players represented Notts for the first time. John Selby was a talented batsman, who held his place in the side until 1887, though his best summer was 1878. He appeared for England in the first Test match and went to Australia with the touring sides of 1876–77 and 1881–82. Apart from his cricket ability he was a professional sprinter and was twice placed in the Sheffield Handicap. His expertise on the track made him very agile in the field and he was outstanding at long on or cover point. A manuscript note on Selby contains the cryptic comment: 'A brilliant cricketer but a blackguard.' His financial dealings were on the dubious side and the cause of much rumour during the 1881–2 tour to Australia. The official receiver wrote to the County Club in 1887 when Selby had his benefit, ordering the Club not to pay any monies over to Selby, and in 1893 he was acquitted of criminal charges relating to various financial transactions.

George Parr's nephew, Robert Butler, turned out a few times for the County, commencing in 1870. An orphan, he had the misfortune to lose both parents within a few days of each other and at the time of his Notts debut he was only 18. He was a good batsman, but business soon took him away from Nottingham and thus from county cricket.

Mention has been made of Squire Walker, who employed the McIntyres at Eastwood. Walker lived at Eastwood Hall and was a partner in the Barber, Walker colliery company. He had his own ground laid out at the Hall and in 1870 arranged a match between Notts and England at Eastwood. The remarkable feature of this game was that J. C. Shaw took 10 for 20 in England's first innings, but as Notts fielded 16, the game is not included as 'first-class'. To make up the 16 Walker included three players who never appeared in a bona fide county match, the Rev F. A. Charles, a local Baptist minister who played for Trinity United in Nottingham, William Shelton, who had hit a tremendous century in local cricket in 1869, and later made an impression in the 1872 Colts match, and Thomas Walker himself, who sadly died six months after the match aged only 26.

The match ended in victory by Notts by 142 runs.

RICHARD DAFT'S DECADE

NOTTINGHAMSHIRE WERE ACCLAIMED County Champions in six of the ten seasons between 1871 and 1880. The three Southern counties with whom Notts had wrestled for the premier position, Surrey, Kent and Sussex, had all, in turn, had their day and fallen by the wayside. The vigorous brand of professionalism which Nottinghamshire had fostered through having, in Clarke and Parr, the two outstanding player-managers had encouraged Nottinghamshire lads to take up cricket as a supplement to their earnings as framework knitters and the dozens of semi-professionals thus bred improved the standard of cricket in the county. So much so that most other counties, as well as local clubs and schools, were keen to employ Nottinghamshire coaches and groundsmen who also acted as ground bowlers. There was a growing interest in the competition to be County Champion, but the way the 'Champion' was chosen remained, by modern standards, rather too subjective. In stating a county to be Champions the press took into account the quality of the opposition. Although it was great to go through an entire season undefeated, this was of little value if the two or three counties opposed were the weakest in the country – the strongest counties tended to play each other, because of the increased gate receipts, and usually might consider playing a weak county only if it was near at hand. Notts therefore tried to arrange home and away matches with the three strongest teams and then a match against neighbouring Derbyshire, by way of friendship, but would not feel inclined to offer matches to the struggling Hampshire side.

The only county not to follow this general pattern was Surrey. Employing a full-time staff of professionals, that county took on all comers – in this first year of 1870, Surrey played 14 matches, whereas no other county played more than eight matches. The other counties had few, if any, full-time employees.

Since John Johnson put some semblance of order into the cricket club in 1859 the organisation had moved onward. In 1868, Johnson retired as Secretary and was replaced by G. B. Davy. Davy was educated at Eton and Cambridge where he seems to have gained the reputation of being the best concertina player in England. His father made a fortune in the guano trade and bought Colston Bassett Hall, where the family have a cricket ground. G. B. Davy played for the Gentlemen of Notts and was a useful batsman.

In 1869 the Club decided to create the post of President and elected Sir Henry Bromley of Stoke Hall. Sir Henry is reported as 6ft 8in tall and 18 stone – certainly he was a commanding figure as Deputy-Lieutenant of the County and a former captain in the 48th Foot. Like Davy, he played for the Notts Gentlemen and organised his own side, playing at East Stoke.

The 1871 season saw the close of George Parr's career. He played in the Easter Colts game and then in a match Notts *v* 14 County Gentlemen at Trent Bridge on 29, 30, 31 May. In this he scored 32 not out and 53 (only Bignall scored more in the match). It was Parr's farewell performance. As far as can be discovered he had played his last match for the All England Eleven the week before. Parr remained Secretary of the AEE until 1875, but Daft later stated that he himself did most of the business transactions: 'Parr used to care a great deal more about walking about with his gun than letter-writing.'

Notts arranged fixtures in 1871 against the recently reformed Gloucestershire Club. W. G. Grace had developed into the biggest draw of the day and when the Western county, led by Grace, came to Trent Bridge in August 1871 record crowds gathered – 8,000 on the first day and 12,000 on the second. The young maestro did not disappoint: he made 79 out of 147 in the first innings and 116 out of 217 in the second. This 116 was the first hundred ever made in inter-county cricket at Trent Bridge, but he could not prevent Notts winning by ten wickets, J. C. Shaw taking 13 wickets. Tom Bignall actually hit 96 in Notts first innings. The other Gloucestershire game, at Clifton College, was drawn. J. C. Shaw's bowling was also too much for Surrey – beaten at Trent Bridge by an innings (Shaw 13 for 58) and at The Oval by ten wickets (Shaw eight for 123). The other county matches were home and away with Yorkshire, each side winning at home. The press designated Nottinghamshire Champion County – Yorkshire won only two games and Surrey did not record a single victory, but the two up and coming counties, Lancashire and Gloucestershire, had records second to Notts and were clearly the teams which would challenge Notts during the decade.

Of the half dozen new recruits used by the county in 1871, F. Randon and T. F. King played only against the 14 Notts Gentlemen. King had made the highest score for the Colts in the Easter Trial, he was to have a long career in Nottingham club cricket and score many runs. Randon, though born in Notts was brought up in Hathern. About 1875 he was regarded as one of the most promising 'youngsters' in England on account of his accurate fast-medium bowling, this impression being based on his excellent figures – eleven for 89 and nine for 95 – for Leicestershire *v* MCC in the two fixtures of 1873. Nottinghamshire had so much talent that he was not required and unfortunately Leicestershire were not well organised, so he never had much opportunity in county cricket. He was on the staff at Lord's from 1874 to 1880 when a serious accident ended his cricket and led to his death in 1883. His brother Charles and his son both represented Leicestershire.

Another debutant of 1871 whose talent deserved more recognition on the county scene was Frank Farrands (or Farrand) of Sutton in Ashfield. In 1870, before his County debut, he had been drafted into the Players side *v* Gentlemen at Lord's as a last-minute replacement and took ten for 88. He played only twice for Notts, both matches *v* Yorkshire in 1871, but despite having 80 wickets at 14 runs each in first-class matches in 1871 – mainly games connected with MCC, he being on the Lord's staff from 1868 to 1908 – Notts simply did not require his services. He later became one of the leading umpires in England and stood in several Tests. Like Randon he was a fast bowler somewhat in the style of Martin McIntyre.

William Elliott of Bulwell was tried for Notts at Clifton College in 1871. The rumour was that he was chosen because he was the professional at Clifton and it therefore saved Notts the expenses of sending another man from Nottingham. He was given a second chance in the following match (*v* Surrey) but achieved nothing and was not seen again. The two amateurs who began in 1871 were G. M. Royle and Robert Tolley. Captain of the Commercial Club in the 1880s, Tolley was a very useful batsman; the son of a silk manufacturer, he appeared occasionally for the County until 1878 as a sound defensive batsman. Royle was another captain of the Commercial Club and one of the best amateurs in the county, but his business commitments in the lace trade meant that he played in only three first-class matches for Notts, though from 1894 to his death in 1910 he was a member of the County Committee.

Rain upset the 1872 programme, Notts being unfortunate in that two of the three major home matches – *v* Surrey and Gloucestershire were drawn through bad weather. The third home game, *v* Yorkshire, was won by 50 runs, J. C. Shaw taking seven cheap wickets in the first innings and his namesake Alfred six in the second. The three away fixtures were also drawn, due to relatively high, though slow batting. An extra match was played at the Prince's Ground in Chelsea. The organisers had announced an England *v* Combined Notts and Yorkshire match, but unable to secure a reasonable England side, had switched the fixture to Notts *v* Yorkshire. Notts won by six runs. The Notts record for 1872 thus ended with two wins and five draws. However modest this seems on paper, *Lillywhite's Annual* announced: 'Notts fairly holds the championship of the season.'

From the point of view of records, the Gloucestershire game at Trent Bridge was remarkable; Notts scored a record 489. Wild, with 104, became the first Notts player to score a century in a county match at Trent Bridge and Selby then carried out his bat for 128.

The discovery of the year was Fred Morley, the fast left-arm bowler from Sutton in Ashfield. Aged 21, Morley had bowled impressively for the All England Eleven in 1871 and was given a permanent place in the AEE side for the following year. This led quickly to a place in the Notts team and so rapid was his development that by 1875 he was described as the best fast bowler in England. In 1874 he took a place on the staff at Lord's and returned some remarkable figures for the MCC. In 1878 he became the first bowler to capture 100 wickets in a season for the County. In all first-class matches in 1882 he took 109 wickets at 11 runs each, but in the winter of that year he had a serious accident on the boat taking the England side to Australia and despite the best medical advice when he returned to England his health gradually went and he died in 1884 of congestion and dropsy.

Fred Morley, an outstanding fast bowler whose career was cut short by a tragic accident on the boat taking the touring team to Australia. (NCCC)

Morley was a very poor batsman, though not quite as weak as J. C. Shaw.

The *Sporting Life* evidently did not think much of the other 1872 Notts debutants, for writing of Morley, it notes: 'He is a very civil fellow, and not at all conceited, in which respect he differs from the other aspirants for their County in the season he came out.'

Of the other aspirants, Henry Reynolds of Ollerton, a batsman, played in six Notts matches in 1872 but with little success. He was not tried again until 1875, when he did much better, but effectively that was the end of his county career. For six seasons he was professional with Middlesbrough and from 1880 to his death in 1894 with Burnley. Thomas Barnes, a very powerfully built man, looked a promising batsman, but died of typhoid in 1873 aged 24. John Seaton, a very civil-spoken young cricketer, was engaged at Grantham in 1872 and hit 57 for that club against the United North. As a result he was tried for the County, but his Notts matches were confined to four, all in 1872, perhaps due to his subsequent engagement at Werneth, where he remained until 1892.

The continued success of Nottinghamshire encouraged new members and the number rose to 400. The Committee decided on the erection of a new pavilion on the opposite side of the ground

The Trent Bridge pavilion built by S. Dutton Walker in 1872 and demolished in 1886.
(NCCC)

to the Trent Bridge Inn. Designed by Dutton Walker the building was ready for use at the Easter 1873 Colts Match, when the number of spectators were 8,000 on the Monday and 6,000 on the Tuesday. The regulations preventing players from appearing for two counties in any single season were agreed early in the 1873 season, the first official regulations governing specifically county cricket and applying to all counties, not merely the handful who constituted the 'first-class' variety.

The feature of the Easter Colts game was the batting of a young hopeful, Arthur Shrewsbury, who scored 35, easily the top score for a colt, but he was not to make his County debut until 1875. The first inter-county match saw Yorkshire at Trent Bridge and an outstanding innings by Richard Daft. His 161 was both the highest score made at Trent Bridge and the highest for Notts, who won the game with an innings to spare. The two matches with Surrey followed, in both of which Notts proved successful. J. C. Shaw took 11 wickets in the first match and Martin McIntyre ten in the second, though the great feat at The Oval was the batting of Jupp for Surrey. In the first innings he opened the batting and was ninth out for 53 out of 102, and again opening in the second he finished undefeated with 51 out of 113. The fixtures with Sussex were renewed after a break of seven years, but the Southerners were defeated by nine wickets at Trent Bridge and ten at Hove, when they were dismissed for 19, Alfred Shaw returning figures of 10.2-5-8-6. The return with Yorkshire was drawn due to rain on the third day. Thus Notts played six and won five.

A dispute between W. G. Grace and Notts meant that the County did not play Gloucestershire and the home fixture that had been arranged was changed to Notts v Next 15. Grace had double-booked himself (arranging to play for both Gloucester v Notts and for a benefit match on the same three days). He insisted on playing in the benefit game and asked Notts to re-arrange the county game. Notts refused. In most summers this would have been of little moment except to the two counties, but in 1873 Notts and Gloucestershire were regarded as having the best season's records and thus the press hailed them as joint-champions. If they had played each other then this tie might have been resolved.

To complicate matters still further, Richard Daft arranged a match between Notts and Yorkshire at Huddersfield (i.e. a third meeting between the counties that year) and Notts were thoroughly beaten when forced to bat on a wicket made very tricky by rain. This however was not quite the end of the Notts' season, for the young Derbyshire Club arranged a match with Notts at Wirksworth. Notts rather disdainfully agreed to play if Derbyshire fielded 16 against the Notts Eleven. Notts then found themselves bowled out for 14, Flint taking six for 7 and Mycroft four for 6 – the innings lasted 32 overs of which 22 were maidens. Alfred Shaw and Biddulph couldn't play for Notts but this could hardly have altered the situation. Notts lost by an innings and eight runs.

None of the three 1873 debutants made more than a passing impression on the county scene. Charles Clifton, son-in-law of James Grundy, was a sound batsman with Notts Commercial and appeared in nine Notts matches between 1873 and 1876. He had been pavilion clerk at Lord's (due to the influence of Grundy) from 1868 to 1872, but then set up a wine and spirits business in Nottingham. E. Mitford Riddell was an amateur who played only for Notts v Next 15. He was a batsman with Notts Gentlemen. John Wheeler was already 28 and had been a professional with various clubs since 1863. He played only v Yorkshire and then re-appeared in the same fixture in 1877, but his county cricket was mostly for Leicestershire, as he lived for sometime in Loughborough. A useful batsman, he could also keep wicket and was on the staff at Lord's from 1878 to 1908, being an excellent umpire in later years.

After several winters with little football at Trent Bridge, Notts County used the ground for their matches during 1873–74. The ground was otherwise used for all kinds of sporting activities, anything which might attract a fair audience. The new pavilion cost £1,432.2s.11d and this drained the Club's finances to a stage where the balance in the bank was £44.13s.8d.

The 1874 programme began with a match against Derbyshire, when again the Notts Eleven played against 16 and moreover, because of the North v South match at Lord's, Notts were missing five of the regular team. The result: defeat by 14 wickets, Flint and Mycroft repeating their brilliant bowling of 1873. Notts went then to Lord's and were beaten by MCC, so that genuine county matches did not start until mid-June, against Yorkshire. Notts were outbowled by Hill and Emmett of Yorkshire and lost by an innings. Three defeats in three successive games was the worst beginning Notts had had to a season for many years. Happily the defeats were followed by five successive wins. Surrey and Sussex were taken apart at Trent Bridge, Daft making the highest scores in both matches. The Middlesex game at Prince's was much closer, but was won due to the all-round cricket of Alfred Shaw, who made 60 in the first innings and took nine wickets in the match. A match against MCC at Trent Bridge – the first visit of MCC since 1843 – was organised for John Jackson's benefit (Jackson received about £250) and Notts won by nine wickets in two days.

Due to rain the match against Surrey at The Oval was played throughout on a difficult wicket. Surrey made 100 and 56, Notts 44 and were 100 for nine, needing 13 when J. C. Shaw went in. Shaw, for once, held up an end whilst Biddulph knocked off the runs, victory being by one wicket. The wet weather continued when Notts went to Hove and Sussex proved too good. James Lillywhite, who later captained England in the first-ever Test, captured eleven Notts wickets, bowling unchanged with Fillery through the match.

The season ended with a victory over Middlesex and defeat at the hands of Yorkshire; the season had been one of great contrast. Notts won five, but lost three bona fide county games. The press decided that Gloucestershire's four wins in six matches deserved the accolade of Champion County and Notts were mentioned as runners-up.

William Clarke of Old Basford, who claimed to be the nephew of Notts old captain of the same name, was a medium-pace round-arm bowler aged 27 in 1874. He took five wickets for 19 in the Derbyshire match and subsequently played in 13 first-class Notts matches spread over three seasons. He was engaged by the West of Scotland Club and had a cricket shop in Partick, which reduced his opportunities for Nottinghamshire. In 1878 he went as coach to Harrow School and qualified by residence for Middlesex, appearing for that county from 1880 to 1884. The three other players who played for Notts for the first time in 1874, aside from Shrewsbury, who appeared against the Colts and then through ill-health missed the rest of the summer, were James Lindley from Sutton in Ashfield and John Orange from Woodborough, who only played against Derbyshire, and R. P. Smith, the Derbyshire batsman, who played in a minor game against 18 of Birmingham. None of these three represented the County in a first-class match.

Athletics meetings were a feature of Trent Bridge at this time and a cinder track was laid around the perimeter of the grass; this was also used for cycling events.

The fixtures for 1875 saw some changes on the previous year or two. Derbyshire, following their successes, were granted home and away matches, eleven-a-side, and the quarrel with Gloucestershire was patched up. Yorkshire, Surrey and Middlesex were the other opponents. Derbyshire were beaten twice.

The other four counties were each beaten once. The weather interrupted several matches and there were three draws, Notts losing only one inter-county game – the final fixture against Yorkshire at Trent Bridge, when Armitage came on with his occasional lobs and returned in the last innings figures of 4.1-2-8-5. These figures were bettered when Notts played MCC, for Alfred Shaw's efforts resulted in the following comment: 'Such marvellous bowling as this to such high class batsmen has no equal in the history of the game.' Shaw's analysis was 41.2-36-7-7, but MCC still made 98 and Notts lost by 62 runs. Shaw took 82 wickets for Notts in the season at less than eight runs each.

Notts' six victories and one county defeat enabled them to regain the title of Champions, though Yorkshire with six wins and three defeats ran them close. Arthur Shrewsbury finally obtained a regular place in the County side and won much praise, though he averaged only 17 runs per innings. Arthur's brother William also played for the County. He was a good batsman in

Notts in 1875, Champions for the sixth time in eight years. Left to right, standing: W. Shrewsbury, S. Biddulph, T. Nixon (umpire), Martin McIntyre, R. Daft, J. West (umpire), J. C. Shaw, W. Oscroft. Seated: A. Shaw, J. Selby, F. Wild. On ground: F. Morley, A. Shrewsbury. (NCCC)

club cricket, but appeared in only nine Notts first-class matches. Two others who need only a line were Alfred Anthony, a wicketkeeper from Arnold, who took Biddulph's place in three matches, and John Mills of Wollaton, who played odd matches until 1881, and was an attractive batsman and the brother of the better known Edwin Mills.

The other two players who began in the same year were of different moulds. William Scotton, a school fellow of the Shrewsburys at People's College, began as an attacking batsman – one of his hits went into the pavilion balcony at Trent Bridge, a rare event – but from 1883 he became a very dour player and on at least two occasions batted for an hour without scoring a run. A left-handed opener he held fast whilst Shrewsbury and later Gunn scored the runs, and his painfully slow innings in the third Test of 1886 was the subject of a poem in *Punch*. He played for Notts until 1890 and appeared in 15 Tests, touring Australia three times, but once he lost his place in the County team he went sadly downhill and in 1893 committed suicide in his lodgings in London, being still on the staff at Lord's.

A much more cheerful companion was Billy Barnes from Sutton in Ashfield. In 1875 he was the professional to Notts Amateurs and some good innings for them resulted in a place in the Notts team, a position he then retained until 1894. Although he had a rather ungainly stance, Barnes was a brilliant executor of the off-drive and until Shrewsbury matured he was the leading Notts batsman for several seasons, topping the county averages in 1880, 1882 and 1883. In 1877 he was asked to bowl, almost as a last resort, when Alfred Shaw was away injured, and to the surprise of many he not only performed well but his medium-pace deliveries soon became an integral part of the Notts attack. He played in 21 Tests for England and like Scotton toured Australia three times.

Barnes was an independent fellow and not one keen on self-discipline; as a result he fell out with his captain on various occasions, most famously in the third Test of 1884–85 when he refused to bowl after being requested to by Shrewsbury. Once or twice he turned up for Notts matches the worse for drink and warnings from the Committee had only a temporary effect, so as soon as his form dipped the Committee excluded him from the County side and a press campaign in 1895 failed to get him reinstated. He remained on the MCC staff until he died in March 1899.

There was a change of control at Trent Bridge for 1875 in that G. B. Davy left as Honorary Secretary, being replaced by Henry

ARTHUR SHREWSBURY

Technically the outstanding batsman of the late 19th century, Shrewsbury's career lasted from 1875 until his death in the spring of 1903, when he committed suicide, due, in the opinion of some, to the fact that he was unable to play cricket any more for Notts.

Dedication and a devotion to practice were the factors on which his batsmanship were founded. His runs were scored not by dramatic shots, but by carefully executed cuts and glances. His defence relied on playing back, giving himself as much time as possible to see the ball's movement.

He was the first batsman to hit a double century for Notts (in 1882) and four times increased the highest score by a Notts player. In addition he was the first player to hit 1,000 runs in Test cricket. He made his first visit to Australia in 1881–82 and then made three further tours, which he financed and organised in conjunction with his team-mate Shaw and Lillywhite of Sussex. The final tour of 1887–88 proved a disaster because a rival England team went out at the same time, so Shrewsbury lost all the money he had made on the previous trips. He stayed behind in Australia, thus missing the English 1888 season, in order to manage a football tour, but this was also financially unsound.

In 1887 he topped the English first-class averages with the highest average ever recorded up to that time – 78.71. He was the leading batsman in England in 1885, 1886, 1887, 1890, 1891, 1892 and in his final summer of 1902.

He captained England in the five Tests of 1884–85 and again in the two Tests of 1886–87, but he declined the captaincy of Nottinghamshire.

Born in New Lenton, about a mile or so from the centre of Nottingham, he was educated at the People's College in the same year as W. H. Scotton, so it was rather odd that both these great cricketers should end their own lives, though in different circumstances. Shrewsbury was the main partner of the sports goods firm set up by himself and Alfred Shaw. The firm continued until the Second World War.

Arthur Shrewsbury, perhaps Notts' greatest batsman, and W. G. Grace's preferred opening partner. (NCCC)

Holden, the Chief Constable, whose authoritarian mood was to cause some unpleasant scenes in the early 1880s.

The one weakness in the eleven of 1876 was behind the wicket. Biddulph was gone, Anthony had been tried but not proved satisfactory in 1875 and a young man from Cinderhill, Mordecai Sherwin, was drafted in when Fred Wild's hands gave out. Although he was a much better keeper than Wild, the Committee demoted Sherwin as soon as Wild's injuries permitted, and it was not until 1880 that Sherwin finally secured the position on a permanent basis. A man of good humour, whose only fault was that he sometimes played to the gallery, Sherwin was regarded as equal to any wicketkeeper in England in the second half of the 1880s. He represented the Players *v* Gentlemen in eleven successive matches at Lord's commencing 1883, and this gives a good indication of his ability, though he played only once in a Test in England. He toured Australia in 1886–87.

He captained Notts in 1887 and 1888, being succeeded by J. A. Dixon, and continued as the County's principal wicketkeeper until 1893. His weight was then about 17 stone and even so he was still nimble on his feet. From 1896 to 1901 he was a first-class umpire and officiated in a Test in 1899.

Season 1876 was a poor summer for the County, as Gloucestershire (the Champions), Yorkshire and Lancashire all returned better results. Only four matches ended in victory – both Surrey games and the two away fixtures with Lancashire and Yorkshire. On the other hand Gloucestershire performed the double over Notts, W. G. Grace making the highest score in both matches. The Middlesex match at Prince's was stopped when Tom Box, the former Sussex cricketer and scoreboard attendant at Prince's, suddenly dropped down dead on the third day. Notts required just 54 to win with nine second innings wickets remaining.

Daft and Shrewsbury had excellent batting figures and were well supported by Oscroft and Barnes. Seven players appeared in every Notts match, but the other four places were uncertain and no less than eleven cricketers, apart from Sherwin, were given trials for the first time, but none lasted long. The oddest was Dr Power, who had played for Notts Amateurs in 1875 and happened to be at Trent Bridge on the first day of the Surrey match when Tolley fractured a finger attempting a catch. The Surrey captain sportingly allowed Power to come on as substitute and bat in place of Tolley. Another Notts Amateur was A. T. Ashwell, who had been in the Rugby XI of 1870 and was a local solicitor. Ashwell had the misfortune to bat in four innings for

Notts and he dismissed without scoring four times. A. W. Cursham, also a member of a legal family, was one of the leading soccer players of the day and captained England *v* Scotland. He was a brilliant fielder and appeared 12 times for Notts over three seasons before moving to Derbyshire in 1879. He emigrated to Florida under a cloud in 1884 and died there the same year of yellow fever.

John Tye and William Clarke of Kirkby were the two most notable debutants among those not yet mentioned. Tye, a tearaway fast bowler, had appeared for Derbyshire in 1874, but was born in Bulwell. He took 28 wickets for Notts in 1876, but only ten in 1877. In 1880 he moved to Brighouse as professional and lived there the rest of his life. William Clarke of Kirkby (easily confused with William Clarke of Basford) played in six Notts matches without achieving much. In 1877 he became professional to the Royal Artillery at Woolwich, remaining there until 1892.

John Taylor of Beeston, John Kesteven of Sutton in Ashfield and William Padley of Moorgreen made fleeting appearances, the last named another wicketkeeper. Alonzo Smith and George Freeman turned out only in the match for the benefit of Biddulph's widow and children, when Notts opposed 12 MCC Groundmen (a team which included seven Notts men), whilst Samuel Birmingham's solitary outing was for Notts *v* 22 of Stapleford.

The major match of the season at Trent bridge was Daft's Benefit, in which North opposed South. About 16,000 attended over the three days and almost inevitably W. G. Grace hit the highest score, an unbeaten 114 in the second innings which won the match for the South. Daft received £750, which was reported to be a record for a Notts player up to that date. (Another account gives £650.)

In the close season of 1876–77, Alfred Shaw and Selby accompanied Lillywhite's team to Australia and both appeared in March in the first Test ever against Australia. Selby kept wicket in the absence of Pooley (detained on criminal charges in New Zealand) in the historic Test.

An innovation of 1876 was a match between Notts Colts and Yorkshire Colts. This was the start of a fairly regular series, Notts picking the best of those young players from the Easter Colts game. Apart from an innings of 45 by William Shrewsbury, the Notts Colts did not distinguish themselves, Yorkshire winning by an innings.

W. E. Tinley, who had acted as Notts paid Secretary for about ten years died in February 1877 at the early age of 33 and Edwin

Browne was engaged. He also acted in the same capacity for Notts County FC. Browne was to write a brief history of Notts cricket in 1887 and he accompanied Daft's Team to America in 1879.

The record for 1877 was not as good as the modest record of the previous summer. The confusion over the wicketkeeping post continued, but the main cause of the decline was not that, it was the severe illness which struck Alfred Shaw just as he returned home from the match at Canterbury in mid-June. He was unable to play again during the season. Up to this point Notts had won both their matches – by 45 runs against Lancashire at home and by 239 runs at Canterbury.

Notts in fact won their third match but by only 22 runs, with Martin McIntyre taking Shaw's place and capturing seven for 77. The second half of the season however was one of misfortune. Gloucestershire won at Trent Bridge by an innings, despite W. G. being out for three – he retaliated by capturing six for 23 in Notts second innings. In the return Notts again lost by an innings and rain saved the County from an innings defeat against Middlesex at home. There followed defeat by an innings at the hands of Kent. Rain caused a draw in the final game at Bramall Lane.

Gloucestershire, Kent, Lancashire and Surrey all had better returns than Notts, whose final results included five wins, five losses and two draws.

Daft was the only batsman to average above 20; Morley took 60 wickets, Barnes 28, Shaw 16 and Daft, coming on in desperation with lobs, 13. No one else had more than a dozen victims. Of the three new players, two need only a passing reference. Samuel Hind of Calverton had played for the Colts of England v MCC and batted with success, but though tried in five county games in 1877 could make a highest core of only 22. A. J. Brooks was the professional at Holbeck. He took eight wickets in the 1877 match against Yorkshire Colts, being a fast-medium bowler, but turned out in only two first-class matches for Notts. He played four games for Somerset in 1880, whilst being a professional in that county, and later was a professional in Liverpool.

One 1877 player went on to greater fame. Wilfred Flowers, a native of Calverton, resided in Sutton in Ashfield from early childhood. Like Brooks he had good figures against Yorkshire Colts and this produced a trial with the County First Eleven. By 1878 he had secured a permanent place in the side as an all-rounder. An accurate medium-pace bowler, who moved the ball off the wicket, he was a hard-hitting batsman. In 1878 he was engaged at Lord's and remained on the staff there until 1899. He took many wickets for MCC and played regularly for the Players *v* Gentlemen at Lord's. Like Sherwin he played only once for England in England, being selected in 1893 as a late replacement for W. W. Read at Lord's, but he toured Australia with Shaw and Shrewsbury's sides in 1884–85 and 1886–87 and played in all the Tests on both trips.

In 1883 he had the distinction of being the first professional to achieve the 'double' of 1,000 runs and 100 wickets. His final match for Notts was in 1896. A most popular and likeable man,

Alfred Shaw, whose bowling figures are unexcelled. He and Morley bowled unchanged to dismiss Australia for 63 and 76 in 1878, Notts winning by an innings. (NCCC)

he was very unlucky with his benefit matches. The one given him by Notts was over in two days and when MCC granted him Middlesex *v* Somerset in 1899 it was over in a day.

All the talk of 1878 centred on the visit of the Australians – discounting the 1868 Aborigines, the first Australian team to tour England. Their first match was arranged for Trent Bridge and 8,000 spectators came to see the first day's play. The Australians won the toss, decided to bat and were bowled out by Alfred Shaw and Morley for 63. The County obtained a first innings lead of 90 and Shaw and Morley then repeated their first innings success, Notts winning by an innings. After the match, the County Club entertained the Australians to a dinner at the George Hotel and the Australian captain praised the hospitality of Nottinghamshire.

The Notts inter-county programme for 1878 was the largest yet arranged with 16 matches. For the first time Leicestershire were met, and were totally outplayed, but these two victories did not count in assessing the Championship. Notts were defeated by Yorkshire, Gloucestershire and Lancashire, but claimed seven wins, in addition to those against Leicestershire and the Australians. The bowling of Shaw and Morley was the outstanding feature of the season – they captured over 200 wickets between them, bowling through four completed matches unchanged. Selby topped the batting and hit the only Notts hundred of the season, his 107 at Bramall Lane being made in 225 minutes.

The North met the South in a benefit match for George Parr at Trent Bridge in June; W. G. Grace bowled out the North, who were forced to follow on, and the South won by ten wickets.

Morley's 126 wickets in Notts first-class matches created a new record for the County, the first time more than 100 wickets had been taken in a season and it was not until 1902 that his record was overtaken. Curiously Alfred Shaw, though just failing to reach 100 wickets for Notts, took 201 in all first-class matches, and this remains a record for a Nottinghamshire bowler.

The dispute over which County won the 1878 Championship remains to this day and modern record books show 1878 as 'undecided'. Middlesex had some claim to the title, being unbeaten, but they played only six matches and won three. Notts record of seven wins in 14 and three defeats persuaded some journalists to award Notts the crown.

The season was played under a new President. Sir Henry Bromley, who had been Notts' first and only President to date, resigned after the 1877 season and changing the rules Notts decided to elect a new President each year, Earl Manvers being the first of the annual rotation.

NOTTINGHAMSHIRE *v* AUSTRALIANS

Played on the Trent Bridge Ground, Nottingham, 20, 21, 22 May 1878

NOTTINGHAMSHIRE WON BY AN INNINGS AND 14 RUNS

AUSTRALIANS	FIRST INNINGS		SECOND INNINGS	
C. Bannerman	c Flowers b Shaw	9	c Barnes b Morley	13
A. C. Bannerman	b Morley	7 (4)	lbw b Shaw	4
Mr T. P. Horan	c and b Shaw	2	c Wild b Morley	2
Mr F. R. Spofforth	b Shaw	7 (5)	b Morley	2
W. E. Midwinter	c Tolley b Morley	13 (2)	not out	16
*Mr D. W. Gregory	b Morley	0 (9)	b Morley	0
Mr W. L. Murdoch	run out	0 (7)	b Shaw	0
Mr T. W. Garrett	c Daft b Shaw	20 (6)	c Oscroft b Shaw	21
†Mr J. M. Blackham	b Morley	1 (10)	c Wild b Shaw	1
Mr G. H. Bailey	b Shaw	3 (11)	c Oscroft b Shaw	0
Mr F. E. Allan	not out	0 (8)	c Flowers b Shaw	6
Extras	b	1	b 9, lb 2	11
Total		63		76

1st inns: 1-9, 2-19, 3-20, 4-26, 5-27, 6-30, 7-54, 8-60, 9-60
2nd inns: 1-16, 2-20, 3-27, 4-34, 5-65, 6-65, 7-75, 8-75, 9-76

BOWLING	O	M	R	W	O	M	R	W
A. Shaw	36.3	25	20	5	58	40	35	6
Morley	36	17	42	4	57	39	30	4

NOTTINGHAMSHIRE	FIRST INNINGS	
*R. Daft	lbw b Allan	3
W. Oscroft	c Horan b Allan	6
A. Shrewsbury	b Allan	8
J. Selby	c C. Bannerman b Horan	66
Mr R. Tolley	c Blackham b Midwinter	7
†F. Wild	c Murdoch b Horan	28
Mr A. W. Cursham	c A. C. Bannerman b Horan	7
W. Barnes	not out	5
W. Flowers	b Horan	0
Alfred Shaw	b Spofforth	11
F. Morley	c Midwinter b Horan	3
Extras	b 4, lb 5	9
Total		153

1st inns: 1-10, 2-10, 3-21, 4-40, 5-110, 6-135, 7-135, 8-135, 9-150

BOWLING	O	M	R	W
Allan	41	23	43	3
Spofforth	28	12	39	1
Midwinter	18	9	17	1
Horan	17.2	5	30	5
Garrett	17	10	15	0

Umpires: Mr P. S. Waddy and R. P. Carpenter
*Captain; †wicketkeeper

Midwinter batted three hours for 16 in the second innings

Nottinghamshire shared the Championship title of 1879 with Lancashire, both counties having five wins and one loss. Notts' reverse occurred at the hands of Yorkshire at Bramall Lane, when the batting failed twice. Rain ruined many matches including both games with Lancashire. Shaw and Morley had splendid figures for the season, though they were enhanced by cheap wickets in the two Derbyshire fixtures – Morley took 26 wickets for 88 runs in the games. Outside the county programme Notts played MCC at Lord's and on a terrible wicket not one of the four innings realised 100, MCC winning by 16 runs. Three other games took place involving the County. A match was arranged at Bestwood Park against I Zingari but when half their team failed to put in an appearance, a scratch MCC side was assembled; in addition Richard Daft organised matches against Wakefield in June and Keighley in July, both towns being allowed 18 men.

In the two seasons of 1878 and 1879 twelve newcomers found their way into the County side, but only one made much of a name for himself. Walter Wright from Hucknall Torkard, who was a professional with Mote Park CC in Kent, performed brilliantly in the 1879 Colts trial, dismissing the first five Notts batsmen for 11 runs and being the only colt to reach double figures in both innings. He was almost at once drafted into the County team and though he did not thoroughly establish himself until 1883, he then turned in some excellent figures both as a left-arm fast-medium bowler and as a defensive batsman, coming in about number eight. In 1886 he fell out with the Notts Committee when he demanded extra payment in the match that year against the Australians. The Committee refused to give way and Wright, who was qualified by residence for Kent, moved to that county and played until 1899. In his youth he was a well-known athlete and twice won the Sheffield Handicap.

Edwin Mills, brother of John, was the best of the other debutants. He played on and off until 1884 and then, failing to retain a place in the side, moved to Surrey, playing for three seasons in occasional matches for that county; he was not helped by an increasing weight problem. Looking briefly at the other trialists, Edward Anthony, Morton Handley and A. M. Wood did not appear in a first-class match for the County; the last-named was Derbyshire-born, played a few games for his native county, then emigrated to the United States and eventually returned to England with the Philadelphian tourists. He was one of the best batsmen in America for about two decades. Apart from Wood, four other amateurs came and went. The Rev Christopher Harrison was a curate at Edwinstowe and had been in the XI at Shrewsbury; B. F. Blackburn was a notable figure in club cricket and football in Nottingham and also a member of the Nottingham Rowing Club; G. S. Foljambe of Osberton, an Old Etonian, did little for Notts, but played frequently for MCC as a batsman; W. F. Story was a military man, educated at Repton, who played in six first-class matches for Notts as a wicketkeeper; he was later on the Notts Committee, but much better known in racing circles.

The other two hopefuls were Henry Bembridge of Bulwell and Sam Widdowson, the Nottingham Forest and England foot-baller, both of whom played in one first-class game.

Nottinghamshire won the Championship outright in 1880. They were defeated only once, on a difficult wicket at Bramall Lane, when Bates bowled Notts out twice, taking ten for 68. The Yorkshire game at Trent Bridge was another low-scoring affair. This time Bates took 11 wickets, but Morley picked up 13 and in intense excitement Notts won by two wickets. Lancashire were beaten twice and Shaw and Morley bowled out Surrey at The Oval for 16, Morley's figures reading 19.2-12-9-7, and this in reply to a Notts total of 266. William Barnes hit the highest score of the summer, 143 in 5 hours 45 minutes against Gloucestershire at Cheltenham; for once the Grace family failed (all three brothers played) and the draw was very much in Notts' favour.

The Australian tour to England of 1880 was a muddle in that no definite decision on a tour was made until after the inter-county fixture list had been arranged. Most of the Australian matches were therefore against local towns playing odds. Notts managed to set up a fixture late in September when it was agreed that the Australians should have half the receipts, with the other half, after expenses, being divided between the Notts players and the Club. Alfred Shaw and five other players refused to agree and de-manded £20 per man. The Committee had no time in which to negotiate and were forced to agree, though by way of protest they paid the other five Notts players £21 each.

The game itself was described by Edwin Browne as the most exciting he ever witnessed at Trent Bridge. Notts needed 131 to win in the final innings. With two needed Alfred Shaw, Notts last man, joined Shrewsbury, who was not out 66. A thunderous cheer arose as Shaw sent the ball through the slips and made the winning runs. Sherwin and Morley rushed out and seized Shrewsbury who was carried shoulder high into the pavilion.

William Gunn, the founder of the Gunn & Moore company, made his debut for the County in 1880. The tall, right-hand batsman scored 70 against the Yorkshire Colts in May and was chosen for all 12 of Notts fixtures of 1880. He averaged only 10 with the bat, but his promise was obvious and he quickly became associated with Shrewsbury as one of the leading batsmen in county cricket. He became a great exponent of 'pad-play' and was much criticised, but his technique was very successful and he played in 11 Tests, including the first ever staged at Trent Bridge.

Mordecai Sherwin, who kept goal for Notts County and kept wicket for Notts and England. (NCCC)

Because of his footballing and then business commitments he toured Australia only once, in 1886–87. Following a brief flirtation with Nottingham Forest he joined Notts County and played once for England, thus being a member of the very exclusive band of Double Internationals. He originally worked for Richard Daft in his sports outfitters, but founded his own firm in 1885 and became a very wealthy businessman. His two nephews, George and John Gunn, later played for Notts and England, but fell out with their uncle and did not have much to do with the family business.

H. A. Cursham, brother of A. W. Cursham, another soccer player, appeared against Surrey as wicketkeeper, but had the odd experience of not re-appearing for Notts until 1904 – 23 seasons separating his two matches. He was a member of the Notts Committee from 1896 to 1933. The wicketkeeping problem was still causing a headache but as the 1880 season progressed, the Committee finally took the decision they ought to have taken two or three years before and installed Sherwin as the permanent man behind the stumps.

William Marriott, who had been a professional with Huyton CC near Liverpool since 1873, played once in 1880 and made a second appearance in 1881. A useful all-rounder, he was a great success with Huyton, remaining until his death in 1887. J. H. Hogg played once, in emergency, when his brother-in-law, John Selby, had to stand down at the last moment.

The 1880 season marked the end of an era for Richard Daft announced his retirement. He was aged 44 and had had two modest summers with the bat. His authority was to be missed and as Sir Henry Bromley commented: 'Richard Daft has been tried in the fire and has not been found wanting. Both in the cricket field and in social life he is alike esteemed and respected, and whenever Notts plays away he invariably makes many friends through his urbanity and good conduct.'

TROUBLE, BUT A PLEASANT AFTERMATH

THE TWO AUSTRALIAN VISITS to England had netted those fortunate tourists a handsome profit which had been divided among the players, after the organiser had taken his profit. The English professionals viewed the spoils with envious eyes. The division between amateur and professional in England had been sharply drawn, but the Australians broke down the barrier, being treated as amateurs yet paid liberally.

The Notts *v* Australians match of September 1880 was an occasion when the English professionals struck back. Why should half the players involved in a particular match receive twice as much money as the other half?

The authorities running the Park Avenue Ground at Bradford had ambitions to build a reputation to equal Bramall Lane. In 1880 they organised an Australian fixture with success and in 1881 they asked Alfred Shaw to bring a Notts team there to play Yorkshire. Captain Holden, the Notts Secretary, on learning of this plan wrote to Shaw objecting, taking the view that Notts teams should only play under the auspices of the County Committee. Shaw replied reminding him that Daft had arranged a similar match some years before without the Committee objecting. Shaw and his partner, Shrewsbury, were invited to meet the Notts Committee to discuss the matter and refused. They would only have a meeting if Captain Holden was not present.

When the Committee sent out the usual letters to the leading Notts players asking them to agree to be available for Notts matches at a fee of £5 lose or draw and £6 for a win, seven of the principal players, Shaw, Morley, Shrewsbury, Selby, Barnes, Scotton and Flowers, countered with the following three point ultimatum:

1. That the match between Nottinghamshire and Yorkshire at Bradford should be allowed to take place under that title.
2. That every player should be guaranteed a Benefit after 10 years.
3. That the seven players named above should be engaged by the County Club for all the County matches of 1881 and not on a match by match basis.

The Committee declined the first two points, but agreed to

engage five of the seven for all matches, Scotton and Flowers being excluded.

The first match of the season took place with the seven playing, Sussex being beaten by an innings. Oscroft, who kept out of the controversy, was appointed captain in place of the retired Daft; Sherwin, Fred Butler and William Gunn made up the eleven. The seven still refused to enter any discussion with Captain Holden. So the Committee took a firm line, omitted all seven from the second match and brought back Daft and Wild plus five colts.

The national press and the cricketing public at large were now taking interest in the dispute. Each side refused to move, though the Committee line was only held in place by Captain Holden. The MCC were brought in to mediate in July and persuaded the players to offer themselves for selection with no strings attached. Captain Holden then selected five for the next match, leaving out Shrewsbury and Flowers. The five refused to play.

For the first match of August, Flowers broke ranks; he played against Gloucestershire and won the match almost single-handed, taking eight for 23 in the first innings. Selby and Barnes turned out in the next game and in the following match, Scotton and Morley appeared. By now of course the Yorkshire v Notts game at Bradford had taken place. It was given in some versions as Shaw's Eleven v Emmett's Eleven. As many as 5,000 spectators came on the first day, so presumably it was financially viable.

Shaw and Shrewsbury were the only strikers to remain aloof, but they did have other irons in the fire, being busy organising a tour to Australia for the winter.

The Notts team in the circumstances had a moderate season and were named 'Holden's Marionettes' by some wag. The two young players who saved the Committee were William Gunn, who scored most runs, and William Attewell, who took most wickets. The former has previously been noted, but Attewell of Keyworth, in his second game, took five for 45, enabling the 'Marionettes' to beat Surrey, and as an accurate medium-pace bowler he was to have a regular place in the side for nearly 20 years. In fact so dominating was he in the Notts side that from 1886 to 1898, except for one year, he took most wickets. He was on the Lord's staff for 22 seasons and played in ten Tests, going to Australia on three tours, those of 1884–85, 1887–88 and 1891–92. As a batsman he made some useful runs, but only once reached a century and that in 1897, very late in his career.

In their efforts to fill the eleven, Notts called upon seven other new faces, of whom Fred Butler was the best known. A nephew of George Parr, he played in 45 first-class matches for the County as a neat batsman, but like Attewell he scored only one three-figure innings, 171 against Sussex in 1890, his final summer. He qualified for Durham and played a few matches for that county, but later emigrated to New York and appeared in club cricket there.

Thomas Brown from Bingham was rather old for a first trial, being 32, and coach at Rugby School; his four appearances were all in 1881. George Lane of Kimberley was a left-hand bat and left-arm medium-pace bowler. He played in three matches in 1881, but moved in 1882 to the United States and for ten years was one of the leading professionals in America, also having a sports

The autocratic Notts Secretary Captain Henry Holden, JP, whose ways helped bring about a players' strike in 1881. (NCCC)

outfitters at Haverford. Thomas Shooter, whose local cricket was with Bestwood Park, did little in his two games, whilst William Underwood was best known as a professional at Dartmouth and played for Devon. Charles Shore, after ten matches for Notts, moved to Lancashire and in 1889 to Norfolk, having a distinguished career with that county as a slow left-arm bowler. W. C. Oates was at Sandhurst when he played for Notts as a batsman; his claim to fame was his innings of 313 not out in Ireland in 1895 when he and F. Fitzgerald created a world record second-wicket partnership of 623 – the match was described as little more than a farce. His father later became the Notts Honorary Secretary.

Whilst 1881 was a dramatic year for Notts cricketers, there were important developments off the field. William Wright, a member of the Committee and a surveyor, successfully negotiated a 99-year lease of the ground and inn from the Musters family. This lease enabled the Committee to plan for the improvement of the ground.

Shaw and Shrewsbury returned from a very lucrative winter in Australia and immediately made their peace with the Committee, though it would appear that Captain Holden's days in control were numbered. Twelve inter-county matches were arranged for 1882, of which only one, at Bramall Lane, was lost and that because Morley sprained his ankle and could only bowl eight overs in the first innings.

Against Surrey at The Oval, Shrewsbury hit the first double hundred for the County and with Barnes added 289 for the second wicket, a new record. Shrewsbury batted in all six hours and 35 minutes and Notts totalled over 500 for the first time. With Alfred Shaw taking nine wickets and Flowers ten Notts won by an innings and 189 runs. Gloucestershire and Middlesex were also defeated by an innings and Sussex by ten wickets. Shaw and Morley remained the backbone of the attack, but Flowers took 44 wickets and Walter Wright 25, so there was now more variety. Barnes was the leading batsman, followed by Arthur Shrewsbury, though his average owed a great deal to the double century against Surrey. The Cambridge blue, C. W. Wright, who was the son of William Wright, came into the side for some matches after going down and hit 99 when opening the batting against Sussex in the absence of Shrewsbury. Although he continued to play intermittently for the County until 1899, he never scored a century. He was also employed as a wicketkeeper, but was not up to the standard of Sherwin. Wright went on four overseas tours, visiting the USA in 1891 and 1894, India in 1892–93 and South

Africa in 1895–96. On the last named trip he played in the three matches which were later designated Test matches. A batsman with a very strong defence, he had a weakness against slow bowling.

He proved very popular, especially on tour when he used his gift as a mimic to the full. In 1904 he lost the sight of his right eye in a shooting accident and latterly, when one of the leading members of the Notts Committee, he was a rather formidable figure.

Like Notts, Lancashire lost only one match in 1882 and the general opinion was that the title of County Champion should be shared by the two clubs, though the results of the two matches between the counties was a victory for Notts at Trent Bridge and an even draw at Liverpool.

Apart from C. W. Wright, the only other debutant was J. A. Dixon, later the captain of the County, but at this time a very nervous batsman, whose appearances were not on a regular basis until the late 1880s.

Apart from the inter-county matches, Notts played the Australians twice in 1882. In the first game Captain Holden 'forgot' to order any lunch for the Australians and when brought to book maintained that the Club never provided lunch for 'amateurs'. William Wright tried to make amends by inviting the Australians to dinner on the second evening, but Murdoch, the Australian captain, declined the offer. On the field Murdoch clashed with Holden over the use of the heavy roller between innings. Murdoch said Holden had no right on the field, but the Chief Constable claimed he could give orders as he liked to the groundsmen. It was all rather petty and not designed to smooth international relations. Not that Holden reserved his displeasure for the tourists. When Lancashire came to Trent Bridge another dispute over the use of the roller erupted, this time between Holden and the Lancashire captain, A. N. Hornby.

What exactly occurred behind the scenes is not known, but the rest of the Committee had clearly had enough of the imperious Captain Holden and he tendered his resignation at the AGM in January 1883; Mr Henry Bromley, son of the former President, took over the position.

Ill-health forced William Oscroft to retire at the close of the 1882 season and Alfred Shaw was selected as the new captain – though the minute book of the period, which details the players selected for each match, fails to make mention of the captaincy.

The major alteration in the composition of the team for 1883 was the absence of Fred Morley. The injury he received when on

JOHN AUGUR DIXON

John Dixon is commemorated at Trent Bridge by the main entrance gates to the ground, which were erected a year or so after his death in 1931. There are three aspects to Dixon's cricketing connections with Nottinghamshire. His early days were as an occasional amateur playing as a batsman, when he was a major figure in local club cricket with Forest Amateurs. Next came his period of 11 years as captain of the County team. Finally, there were his 40 years on the Notts Committee – in 1910 he was elected the first honorary life member of the Committee.

It was probably in the last role that he played the most important part. From what information is extant it would seem that he was the major figure in the decision on the engagement of young players and thus such names as Larwood, Voce, Hardstaff and so on were signed on the staff after having been vetted by Dixon. It may be only a coincidence that soon after he died the Club went into slow decline on the field of play.

J. A. Dixon (NCCC)

His captaincy on the other hand was not very inspiring, though it could be argued that he inherited an ageing side in 1889 and one which contained mainly defensive bowlers.

As a batsman he has one great claim to fame in that he hit 268 not out against Sussex at Trent Bridge in 1897, the highest individual score for the County up to that date, but in 235 matches for Notts he made only 13 hundreds. Although he never toured overseas, due in some measure to his flourishing business in Nottingham, he did play fairly regularly for the Gentlemen *v* Players at Lord's during the 1890s.

Like several other Notts cricketers of his generation, Dixon was a talented soccer player and was capped by England in 1885.

He was the first Notts man to be appointed as a Test Selector and was on various committees at Lord's. The commemorative plaque at Trent Bridge ends as follows: 'Apart from cricket, at which he excelled as a batsman, as fieldsman, as bowler and as a vigilant commander, he was a sagacious man of affairs, a faithful citizen, a philanthropist, a wise magistrate and a true friend.'

shipboard bound for Australia in the autumn of 1882 proved more serious than anticipated and he played only once and he died the following year aged only 33. Walter Wright therefore was chosen to open the bowling with Shaw for nearly every match and more use was made of Barnes and Attewell; the latter, after his impressive start in 1881, had been rather in the shadows during the previous season.

The season began with an innings victory over Surrey, when Shaw took nine for 35, but defeats against MCC and Lancashire followed. The Lancashire game was marred by the public reception given to Jack Crossland, the Lancashire fast bowler. He had been accused in many circles as a 'thrower', and despite Lord Harris's determined efforts to remove bowlers with doubtful actions from county cricket, Lancashire stood loyally by their player – he had never been no-balled for throwing.

The matter was not quite that simple because Crossland was a native of Sutton in Ashfield and apparently lived in Lancashire only during the cricket season – therefore he was not qualified for that county. The regulations stated a player could appear only for the county of his birth or that in which he resided and were in those days paramount, at least for professionals. Notts sent evidence to MCC to the effect that Crossland was unqualified for Lancashire, but the MCC found the case not proven.

After being defeated twice, Notts just saved the game against Yorkshire at Bramall Lane, but then came a change of fortune and the last nine matches were played without defeat and included a nine-wicket win over Yorkshire and two innings victories. The title of Champion County was retained, though this time not shared with Lancashire. However, in a final match against MCC Notts batting fell to pieces, the County being dismissed for 23, amidst laughter and derisive cheers from the spectators – in fact the first five wickets went down for three runs.

The three new players of 1883 were J. G. Pearson, F. J. Shacklock and A. P. Smith. Pearson of Worksop played only against Surrey and was a good batsman in local cricket; put on to bowl as a last resort in his one county game he took three wickets for one run, a statistic that amazed even his Worksop colleagues, for he rarely bowled for that club. Frank Shacklock made his debut in the final match of the year against MCC, but the following year decided to play for Derbyshire under his birth qualification. A right-arm fast bowler with a slinging action he remained with Derbyshire for three years and then switched back to Notts, much to the disgust of Derbyshire supporters. In 1893 he became the first Notts bowler to capture four wickets in four balls for the County, but later the same year was suspended for indiscipline and not selected again. In rather murky circumstances he emigrated to New Zealand the following year, but clearly changed his attitude in his new country and became a respected coach for Otago, appearing in a few first-class matches for that province.

A. P. Smith of Ruddington was the professional for Nottingham Commercial in 1883 and was brought into the Notts side for a couple of games as a batsman, but in 1884 he moved to Rochdale and in 1886 to Oldham, when he qualified by residence for Lancashire, and played in that county side on and off until 1894.

It is worthy of note that in 1883 in all first-class matches Wilfred Flowers became the first professional to perform the 'double' of 1,000 runs and 100 wickets, many of his appearances being for MCC.

In the winter of 1883–84, the Notts Committee decided to back Lord Harris's campaign against 'throwing' and therefore refused to renew fixtures with Lancashire for 1884 – there was some caustic correspondence between the two clubs during the winter and the matter of Crossland's qualification as well as the success John Briggs (another native of Sutton in Ashfield) was enjoying with Lancashire did nothing to soothe the fevered brows.

The season of 1884 proved to be one of outstanding success for the County and rather than detail one particular victory it would seem appropriate to give the brief scores of the ten inter-county matches played. The outstanding batsman was Shrewsbury, who for the second time created a new individual record, scoring 209 against Sussex at Hove, batting six and a half hours. Shrewsbury found much support from Scotton, Barnes and Gunn. Attewell overtook Shaw as the leading Notts wicket-taker of the season, though by only three victims and the pair had Flowers, Barnes and Walter Wright to support them. No fewer than eight of the side, Scotton, Barnes, Gunn, Flowers, Wright, Shaw, Sherwin and Attewell played in every match, whilst Shrewsbury and Selby missed one each, so a regular eleven gave Notts a certain advantage.

Success on the field made the Committee ambitious to improve the facilities at Trent Bridge. William Wright set about the task and it was decided to obtain an extra piece of land behind the pavilion, build a new pavilion there and demolish the old one. A new wall was built along the Radcliffe Road (then known as Gamston Road) amid plans to demolish the Trent Bridge Inn and build afresh. The flourishing financial state of the club enabled

THE MATCHES OF 1884

At Trent Bridge, 15, 16 May: Notts 271 (W. Barnes 98, J. Juniper 6-79, W. Tester 4-65) beat Sussex 76 (A. Shaw 6-22, W. Wright 4-51) and 44 (W. Attewell 8-22) by an innings and 151 runs.

At Lord's, 26, 27, 28 May: Middlesex 235 (G. F. Vernon 50) and 113 (W. Attewell 7-21) lost to Notts 164 (A. Shrewsbury 70, J. Robertson 5-51) and 186-4 (W. H. Scotton 104 not out, W. Barnes 55) by 6 wickets.

At Trent Bridge, 2, 3, 4 June: Notts 287 (W. Barnes 78, W. H. Scotton 71, J. Selby 54) and 84-3 beat Surrey 171 (W. W. Read 70) and 199 (M. P. Bowden 56, A. Shaw 6-30) by 7 wickets.

At Bramall Lane, 16, 17 June: Yorkshire 129 (W. Wright 5-41, A. Shaw 4-46) and 40 (A. Shaw 6-15) lost to Notts 117 (T. Emmett 4-18) and 54-7 (E. Peate 4-16) by 3 wickets.

At Hove, 26, 27, 28 June: Sussex 128 (W. Attewell 5-31, W. Barnes 4-16) and 302 (W. Newham 85, G. N. Wyatt 59, R. T. Ellis 51, W. Barnes 4-57) lost to Notts 458 (A. Shrewsbury 209, W. Gunn 122, A. B. Hide 4-56) by an innings and 28 runs.

At Gloucester, 14, 15, 16 July: Gloucestershire 201 (E. J. Painter 58, W. Attewell 4-56) and 79 (A. Shaw 8-28) lost to Notts 204 (W. G. Grace 5-54, W. A. Woof 4-100) and 77-4 by 6 wickets.

At Trent Bridge, 17, 18, 19 July: Yorkshire 95 (W. Flowers 5-23), W. Attewell 5-44) and 199 (W. Bates 116, W. Attewell 5-55) lost to Notts 114 and 181-3 (A. Shrewsbury 61, W. Flowers 53 not out) by 7 wickets.

At Trent Bridge, 31 July, 1 August: Gloucestershire 49 (A. Shaw 8-29) and 63 (A. Shaw 6-36, W. Attewell 4-27) lost to Notts 105 (W. Flowers 50, W. R. Gilbert 5-32, W. A. Woof 4-35) and 9-0 by 10 wickets.

At The Oval, 4, 5, 6 August: Notts 216 (W. Wright 50 not out, E. Barratt 5-81) and 334 (A. Shrewsbury 127, W. Barnes 72) drew with Surrey 243 (W. Attewell 4-92) and 155-7.

At Trent Bridge, 14, 15, 16 August: Middlesex 211 (I. D. Walker 80, W. Attewell 4-75) and 105 (A. Shaw 5-23) lost to Notts 407 (W. Gunn 138, W. Attewell 84, W. H. Scotton 66, J. Robertson 5-127, G. Burton 4-88) by an innings and 91 runs.

Summary: Played 10; Won 9; Drawn 1.

Note: In the Gloucestershire match at Trent Bridge, Alfred Shaw performed a hat-trick in each innings and took 3 wickets in 4 balls. This combination constituted a new record in first-class cricket.

these radical changes to be made during the next two years. The club had over £1,000 in hand and this would at least cover the cost of the new Inn.

The single 1884 debutant was Henry Morley of Edwinstowe, a fast bowler whose action was compared to Crossland's and, possibly for this reason, he played just once. His brother Herbert Morley was also a noted local cricketer and in North Notts matches there is much confusion between the two.

Outside the county programme Notts played two matches against the Australians, losing the first by three wickets, but drawing the second when needing 134 to win in 35 minutes – Alfred Shaw was injured whilst fielding on the first day, otherwise the result might have been different. A total of 27,589 people passed through the turnstiles for this second match, which was perhaps a new record for the ground.

The ramshackled Trent Bridge Inn came down in the autumn and the annual advertisement for the Inn changed from 'The Trent Bridge Ground and Inn, Nottingham. Luncheons from 1 pm to 3 pm daily at each Pavilion on County Match days, also at any other time on the shortest possible notice. Wines, Spirits and Cigars of the Best Quality' to 'The Trent Bridge Cricket Ground and New Hotel, Nottingham. Luncheons on County Match

The Nottinghamshire side which won nine of their ten Championship matches in 1884, drawing the other to take the title easily. Left to right standing: G. Street (umpire), J. A. Dixon, H. Coxon (scorer), W. Flowers, E. Mills, E. Henty (umpire). Seated: W. Barnes, A. Shrewsbury, A. Shaw (captain), W. Gunn, W. Attewell. On ground: Walter Wright, M. Sherwin, W. H. Scotton. (NCCC)

Days and by arrangement. Wines, Spirits and Cigars. Billiards. N. B. Single and Double Bed-rooms.'

As a result of winning the Championship in 1884, Notts arranged a match against the Rest of England in 1885. Such a game had not been played since 1856. Unfortunately, as Surrey were playing Gloucestershire, the England side was not at full strength, but eight of the eleven played Test cricket at some time and the other three, Louis Hall, H. W. Bainbridge and J. B. Hide were very prominent county players. Nottinghamshire won the match by an innings, all the players making an important contribution – five bowlers took wickets and the lowest individual innings was nine, and that by Barnes who took nine wickets.

The inter-county matches showed Notts in equally good form, save for the Yorkshire visit to Trent Bridge when, due to poor fielding the visitors won by an innings. It was Notts' only Championship defeat and in contrast four of the six victories were by an innings. Against Middlesex Shrewsbury carried out his bat for 224 in seven hours 50 minutes, but his total creating a new Notts record. He was not only Notts' leading batsman, but, for the first time, headed the national averages, being the only player scoring 1,000 runs and averaging over 50. With Shaw not bowling so much, Barnes was the leading wicket-taker and returned the lowest average.

Nottinghamshire retained the Championship title; Yorkshire also won six matches, but suffered two defeats, and came second. The competition was now developing into a 'League', with the press placing the counties in a definitive order, rather than proclaiming a single Champion County. The curious statistic of the summer was Flowers' bowling against Sussex, when he returned figures of 35-29-8-3, including 18 successive maidens! Sussex were dismissed for 73, but survived 127 overs (or in modern terms 84.4 six-ball overs).

The continued success of the eleven meant there were few opportunities for up-and-coming cricketers. The Committee faced a difficult problem and in the event two notable players were allowed to slip away. George Bean, of Sutton in Ashfield, a promising batsmen, played in five games in 1885, but the following year decided he stood a better chance with Sussex, and being engaged by Lord Sheffield, that county's patron, he qualified by residence, playing for his adopted county until 1898 and also representing England in Australia in 1891–92. A more serious loss than Bean was William Lockwood, who played a handful of matches for Notts in 1886 and 1887, but took a post on the Surrey groundstaff and from 1889 played for that county. Both Pelham

Warner and Ranjitsinhji were of the opinion that Lockwood in the 1890s was the best fast bowler in England and he was no duffer with the bat, performing the 'double' in 1899 and 1900. Lockwood learnt his cricket on the former Notts county ground, The Forest, and played club cricket for Forest Wanderers, both before moving to Surrey and after he retired from first-class matches. The results Nottinghamshire achieved in the 1890s compared to Surrey demonstrate how much Notts missed him – in fact it would be no over-statement to say that if Lockwood had remained at Trent Bridge, then Notts would have taken the Championship several times during the decade of the 1890s.

Harry Daft, the younger son of Richard, made his Notts debut in 1885. Like his father, with whom he worked in the family Sports Outfitters, he began as an amateur, but turned professional. A very defensive batsman, he appeared regularly from 1891 to 1898, but in 190 matches hit only 4,176 runs. He was better known on the soccer field, playing outside-left for Notts County and representing England several times. Two other cricketers made brief appearances in 1885. George Banner of Sutton in Ashfield, a fast right-arm bowler appeared against Gloucestershire. He died aged 26 in 1890. James Barks played only against the 22 Colts in the Easter Trial, the team being a weak one as Shrewsbury, Scotton, Barnes and Flowers were absent.

On 1 August 1885 the Committee convened a Special General Meeting to obtain members' approval for a loan of £3,000 in order to build a new pavilion. The members unanimously approved the motion. H. M. Townshend of Peterborough was appointed as architect and the building was constructed by Messrs Fish and Son. The cost was over £5,000 and the finished result – the pavilion was first used during the Easter Colts Match of 1886 – met with approval all round and was described as the finest pavilion in England. W. H. C. Oates, who was a Committee member and a trustee, took over from Mr Bromley as Honorary Secretary in 1885.

After discussions with Kent, Notts decided to resume fixtures against Lancashire in 1886, Crossland now being banned since, on a further check, it was discovered that he was not properly qualified for Lancashire. The summer proved one of great success, Notts being unbeaten and winning seven out of 14 county matches. An indicator of the changing times came in the first match, *v* Sussex at Hove, which Notts won by seven wickets, but Alfred Shaw did not bowl in either innings, though five bowlers were employed. When Lancashire arrived for the first county home game, Notts beat them by an innings, again without the aid of Shaw's bowling – Walter Wright took ten wickets and Flowers seven. Shrewsbury, for the third successive year, created a new batting record, hitting an unbeaten 227 against Gloucestershire at Moreton in Marsh, when he was at the wicket seven hours and 45 minutes. Shrewsbury again topped both the Notts and the national batting averages; Gunn and Scotton also had excellent returns. Attewell and Flowers were the leading wicket-takers. Shacklock, moving back from Derbyshire (Derbyshire complained in vain to Lord's), gained a regular place in the side, but Walter Wright was omitted after 3 July when he demanded extra money to play against the Australians.

The Championship title again went to Nottinghamshire, though in some quarters voices were raised in favour of Surrey, despite the fact that they lost three matches including the Notts game at The Oval by seven wickets.

Of the three debutants of 1886, Lockwood has been previously noted and the other two need little space; Harry Daft's elder brother, Richard, who managed the family brewery in Radcliffe, played once as a batsman *v* Surrey; William Harris of Kimberley played against Sussex, but in 1887 moved to London and joined the Surrey staff. He played five minor matches for Surrey and then became coach and groundsman to Guy's Hospital. In some publications he is confused with William Harris of Greasborough, who played for Yorkshire. The two are unconnected.

Lord Harris was trying to organise the counties and get the various regulations and rules concerned with county cricket on a more formal basis. At his instigation a County Cricket Council was formed. Captain Holden, who though no longer the power he had been, represented Notts at the formation and reported back to the Notts Committee: 'The Council would do no good to cricket and its objective was to alter the Cricket qualifications for Counties.' The rest of the Committee did not share the Captain's view. The Captain also objected to the new scoreboard introduced to Trent Bridge, saying that it would probably break down. Richard Daft settled the matter by offering to pay for any maintenance or necessary repairs.

The major change for 1887 was that the Committee decided to appoint Sherwin as captain in place of Shaw. Shaw was engaged by Lord Sheffield as a coach for Sussex and it would seem that some misunderstanding arose when Shaw was selected for one Notts match. At any rate he did not appear and his career with Notts (aside from Selby's Benefit and a single match in 1897) was now ended. In retrospect it might seem that the Committee were at fault in retiring Shaw, though he was now 44. Shrewsbury was offered the leadership but refused, and Sherwin took the reins.

The opening match of 1887 was the Whitsun fixture with Surrey. Despite miserable weather large crowds gathered and Notts dismissed the visitors for 115, then themselves collapsed for 89. Surrey reached 264 for four at one o'clock on the last day and a draw seemed certain, but the Surrey captain, Shuter, deliberately hit his own wicket and the remaining five men either let themselves be stumped or gave away their wickets. Such an exhibition had never before been seen in county cricket (declarations were not allowed at this time). Notts' second innings, apart from Gunn, was little more than a procession and Surrey won at Trent Bridge for the first time since 1870. After this reverse, Notts rallied and when they went down to The Oval during August Bank Holiday, they had still lost only the one match. A victory in this return would most probably decide the Championship in Notts' favour.

The public interest was tremendous, a record 51,607 paying admission during the three days. With few police on duty there were some minor problems with the crowd, but it was mostly good humoured horse-play. Notts gained a first innings lead of 36 and in the final innings Surrey required 205. Five wickets fell for 127, but Lohmann and Maurice Read then added 72 and effectively won the game for Surrey. Later Notts lost a third match, against Lancashire at Old Trafford, and so in most tables were shown as third in the Championship behind both Surrey and Lancashire.

Shrewsbury once more created a new Notts batting record, scoring 267 against Middlesex – he batted ten hours and 15 minutes, another record, and the Notts total was 596, yet another high. Shrewsbury topped both Notts and national batting averages and his average of 78.71 was the highest ever recorded to that date. Attewell was Notts leading bowler. No fewer than nine new players were given trials, since Selby, as well as Shaw, was no longer a regular first team man and Scotton missed five matches.

Henry Richardson of Bulwell was introduced into the Notts side in a rather unusual way. An accurate medium-pace bowler he was engaged with Liverpool CC and made his first-class debut for North *v* South at Lord's in May 1887, when neither side was representative. He took nine for 64; he then played for Liverpool and District *v* Yorkshire, taking another nine wickets and hitting 55. Notts then tried him on 30 June and he retained his place for the rest of the season. In 1889 he joined the staff at Lord's and dropped out of the Notts side the following season, having taken 139 wickets at 13.84 – he was aged 32. A popular cricketer, he remained at Lord's until 1919.

Almost as strange was the county career of Jack Carlin, who played twice in 1887. According to tradition he was a left-hand bat, but on learning that Notts did not want a left-hander, he switched hands. In 1888 he joined the Lord's staff and stayed with MCC until 1912. His county career proper did not begin until 1900; in that season and the following he played as a wicketkeeper-batsman, but finished in August 1901. In 1902 he became a first-class umpire and stood in two Tests. In 1924 he was appointed Notts scorer, retiring in 1938.

Two fast bowlers who had trials and made some impression were Richard Hardstaff of Selston and R. J. Mee of Shelford. Hardstaff spent much of his career in Lancashire club cricket with Rawtenstall and Castleton and this restricted his County appearances, his only regular Championship summer being 1896. In 1899 he was no-balled for throwing and this ended his first-class career. Mee was the son of a noted local cricketer and like Hardstaff his county career was sporadic, 1893 being the one year in which he was seen frequently. He moved to Burslem, where he kept a pub and played by residence for Staffordshire in the first years of the 20th century.

There were five other young trialists. A. D. Burrows of Awsworth, an all-rounder, died in 1890 aged 24. Thomas Morley, a cousin of Fred, was a fast bowler who gave excellent service to Norfolk. Alfred Price, son of Walter, was, like Richardson, engaged at Liverpool and actually played a first-class game for Lancashire in 1885. A batsman he had little success in three 1887 Notts games. Joseph Sulley, a professional with Notts Amateurs, was a left-arm medium-pace bowler. He returned some very impressive figures in local cricket in 1887 and was a surprise selection for the 1887 game *v* Surrey at The Oval. On this awesome debut he took six for 106, but as he was already aged 37, he played only in one other Notts match. Finally John White of Bulwell, yet another cricketer with Liverpool CC, played one match as wicketkeeper when Sherwin was absent.

Notts' hopes of regaining the Championship from Surrey in 1888 took a serious knock when Shrewsbury announced that, instead of returning after his winter tour to Australia, he was remaining there to manage a football team. It will be recalled that two English teams went to Australia in 1887–88, one financed by Shaw and Shrewsbury and the other under G. F. Vernon. Shrewsbury lost a large sum of money on the venture and was attempting to recoup his losses by this new scheme – it was to develop into the first-ever England Rugby tour of New Zealand.

Thus 1888 turned out to be the worst season Notts had experienced for many years. Six defeats and only three victories tell the sorry tale. Not a single hundred was scored and in contrast to 1887, with Shrewsbury's batting average of 78, the best 1888 could muster was 27 by Dixon.

Sherwin's captaincy came in for increasing criticism and there were more voices raised in favour of setting up a groundstaff as at The Oval. Sussex were beaten twice, but they were by far the weakest side, now that Derbyshire had been removed from the first-class list. The other success was against Gloucestershire at Cheltenham when Barnes took 13 wickets, though Attewell's figures in the second innings 24-20-5-3 were very odd.

The Australian touring side of 1888 was beaten twice, but the tourists were a moderate combination and in the second game, Notts hit up 441 then dismissed the visitors for 95 and 147. In an attempt to find fresh blood, the Committee introduced eight new players – making 17 in two years. Not one of the hopefuls made a name in county matches. The best known was the amateur J. S. Robinson, who was at Cambridge, where he played just one first-class game for the University. A useful batsman and fair wicket-keeper, he played in some matches in 1891, 1892 and 1894, but suffered from rheumatic gout which affected his hands and was an invalid for sometime prior to his death, the direct result of which was a fall from his horse in 1898 when aged 30. He toured India and the United States with Lord Hawke's sides.

Herbert Emmitt and Tinsley Lindley, who played in two and four games respectively, were both well known soccer players. Emmitt played mainly for Notts County, while Lindley, a barrister in later life, played for Forest and captained England; his brother Leonard Lindley played one or two first-class matches but not for Notts.

Gordon Beves, a good club batsman with Forest Amateurs, played in nine Notts games between 1888 and 1891, but in 1894 emigrated to South Africa and appeared for Transvaal, later becoming Chairman of the South African Cricket Association.

In their desperate search for talent, Joseph Briggs, the 38-year-old brother of the Lancashire all-rounder was tried, but his only success was five for 35 against Gloucestershire. J. Brown of Bingham and W. Kirk of Hyson Green were the other two debutants – neither made any impact.

Not since 1864 had Notts lost more matches than they won – 1888 is best forgotten.

DULL DAYS

THE COMMITTEE'S IMMEDIATE ANSWER to the 1888 results was the appointment of J. A. Dixon as captain. This ended finally (or finally until the 1940s) the county professional as captain. Only two of the counties had had professional captains on any regular basis, Notts and Yorkshire, and in both cases they had developed from the days when Nottingham played Sheffield. Lord Hawke had ended the Yorkshire professional leadership in 1882–83 as a deliberate act of policy to bring more responsibility to Yorkshire cricket and discipline to the county eleven. The Notts switch to amateurs was rather a move of expediency, rather than the rooting out of the easy-going professional. If Shrewsbury had accepted the captaincy in 1887 instead of Sherwin, the course might have altered, but aside from anything else Shrewsbury was too much of an introvert to make a successful captain, though for the occasional match he proved that he had a mastery of the technicalities of cricket on the field.

Sherwin was too easy-going, a man who enjoyed an audience. Apart from the wicketkeeper, the other two senior professionals were Barnes and Flowers. The former was frequently being reprimanded for drinking more than he should and the latter was very much in Sherwin's mould. Scotton was on the way out and his character was not without blemish. It would hardly be politic to choose one of the younger professionals such as Gunn. The two amateurs in the side on a regular basis were Dixon and Harry Daft. Dixon's experience as captain of Forest Amateurs since 1884 as well as his seniority in years swayed the Committee in his favour.

Shrewsbury, after his year in Australia and New Zealand, hit a century in the opening match, against Sussex at Trent Bridge, and Notts went on to an innings victory – this was the first match at Nottingham in which the five-ball over was used. The second county game produced another innings victory when Richardson bowled out Middlesex – he took ten for 44. Then came the Surrey Whitsun game. Notts made 308, with a hundred by Gunn, then Richardson and Shacklock completely routed Surrey, the totals being 98 and 57. Richardson took eight for 69, Shacklock ten for 45. The match was over in two days, but 16,870 passed through the turnstiles and a great crowd assembled outside the pavilion to cheer the victors when the game ended. Success continued with Lancashire beaten by an innings, followed by Sussex. Derbyshire were defeated by ten wickets, then Kent by an innings. At Bramall Lane Yorkshire lost by 36 runs, giving Notts eight successive wins. Innings defeats were inflicted on Derbyshire and Gloucestershire stretching the successive wins to ten.

Notts went to The Oval for August Bank Holiday – 49,935 paid admission, about 2,000 less than the 1887 record. The first innings was very even, Surrey having a lead of 13. When Surrey batted a second time, the former Notts Colt, Lockwood made 83, the highest individual innings of the game and Shuter, the Surrey captain, declared setting Notts 219 in three hours. The wicket drying under a bright sun was very difficult and it was generally thought Notts could only hope for a draw. Lohmann bowled exceptionally well and apart from Shrewsbury Notts gave a poor display, losing by 134 runs.

There followed a draw at Trent Bridge against Middlesex and a win at Clifton College. The matches against Yorkshire and Lancashire were ruined by rain, but under the points system now introduced by the editor of *Wisden*, Notts could take the Championship provided they did not lose their final game – at Beckenham against Kent. The unexpected happened and the Notts batting failed, bowled out for 35 in the second innings: Kent won by four wickets.

According to the Notts Match Scorebook published by C. H. Richards, the table shows Notts as Champions, having lost least matches, but *Wisden* awarded one point for a win and half a point for a draw, which meant Notts had 10½ points, the same as Lancashire and Surrey, producing a triple tie. This unsatisfactory state of affairs led to a meeting of the counties and a revised system to decide the 1890 Championship.

In all Notts matches Attewell took 105 wickets at ten runs each and Richardson 69 at 11, but these figures include the two Derbyshire games, not ranked as first-class. In the batting table Gunn and Shrewsbury came first and second, as they did in the national averages. Attewell actually topped the national bowling figures.

A further eight young players were introduced into the senior side during the summer, but as in 1888 none were to develop into outstanding county players. A fast bowler, Frank Guttridge, played a couple of games, but in 1890 took a professional engagement at Horsham, qualified for Sussex and played for the southern county for three years. In 1896 he re-appeared in the Notts side and held his place until 1900. The other seven debutants have 12 Notts first-class matches between the lot. Richard Lowe, one of three brothers from Kirkby, followed Guttridge to Sussex and moved on to Glamorgan; Jack 'Butcher' Butler, a nephew of George Wootton, was a sound batsman but a very poor field and lacked enthusiasm; Matthew Wright, of Keyworth, moved to Buckinghamshire, being the coach at Eton and was the leading Buckinghamshire all-rounder for about 20 years. W. Foster and H. Robinson were local cricketers who each played once; George Bennett played only against Derbyshire. Walter Marshall was 35 and a long-standing member of Notts Castle CC, he was later to become the grand old man of Trent Bridge and will be mentioned later. He played in the game against Liverpool and District, the first such fixture by the County; another new fixture was a match with Scotland.

The 1890 season opened with another batting record as Shrewsbury and Gunn added 398 for the second wicket, a new high in inter-county cricket and still the best partnership for Notts. Shrewsbury must have been annoyed when he was dismissed for 267, equalling his score in 1887. Gunn reached 196. Sussex fell cheaply twice, with George Bean making the only fifty and taking three wickets.

Interest in the Whitsun match was enormous, with 11,366 paying on the first day. Surrey had no fewer than three Notts born men, Lockwood, Jack Sharpe of Ruddington and Tom Bowley. Notts gained a lead of 78 on first innings and with Shacklock taking ten wickets went on to win by 108 runs. Surrey had their revenge in August, with Lockwood and Sharpe playing the major roles in the defeat of their native shire. Lockwood made the highest score in the match and Sharpe took eleven for 89. Surrey won by seven wickets.

In between times it was a mixed season for the County and five wins balanced five losses, putting Notts in fifth place. Shrewsbury and Gunn were first and second in both national and County averages, but the bowling was becoming more and more reliant on Attewell; in terms of wickets taken Shacklock came second but was expensive, and Richardson's wickets cost over 20 runs each.

A left-arm medium-pace bowler with Notts Commercial was given three matches. Frank Needham of Arnold was, however, already 28 and destined to play in only two more County games. His claim to fame was an analysis of 10-10-0-7 for Nottingham Commercial against Nottingham Forest in 1890. Needham went on the staff at Lord's in 1891 and remained there until his death in 1923.

Two amateurs appeared for the County for the first time during 1890. Oliver Redgate was a good batsman with Notts

Castle and Forest Amateurs, but not up to county standard; F. I. Fox was another Forest Amateur, who batted well in local cricket.

A poor start was made to 1891 (after the formality of victory against Derbyshire). Surrey won the Whitsun game by five wickets, a weak team were beaten by MCC by an innings in a single day, Notts being dismissed for 21, after which Middlesex, despite being forced to follow on, won by 49 runs. It was the first time Notts had been defeated after enforcing the follow-on.

Matters improved in the middle of June – victories over Yorkshire, Derbyshire, Lancashire, Sussex and Yorkshire and Sussex again produced six successive wins. A curiosity of the last Sussex win was that J. S. Robinson went in with seven needed and made all seven off one hit! There were seven matches still to play. Notts, if their latest form held, stood a chance of the Championship – in fact not a single extra win was recorded and the sequence began with an innings defeat by Gloucestershire. The August Bank Holiday arrived, and 25,000 turned up at The Oval. Shrewsbury was unable to play due to injury and Notts invited Richard Daft to return after an absence of ten years.

The return of the great cricketer was an emotional moment, even for the Surrey spectators and the report noted: 'When Mr Richard Daft walked to the wicket he met with a tremendous reception, the spectators rising in their places and cheering him again and again.' The weather was very bad (in spite of it over 10,000 were in the ground) and when Daft reached 12, a great storm broke over The Oval and the game was abandoned for the day. Resuming on the third day, Notts batted on a quagmire and were dismissed for 86, followed on, and were all out for 44 – defeated by an innings. Rain washed out the next four Notts matches, August being one of the wettest on record.

Shrewsbury and Gunn were the only batsmen in England to average over 40, and Barnes and Flowers also had good seasons with the bat. Attewell was the only effective bowler. It irritated Notts supporters to see that Lockwood, Sharpe and Briggs, all Notts-born and rejected by the County, featured in the first ten in the national bowling table.

Five new professionals were tried of whom only the 17-year-old Robert Bagguley of Ruddington survived more than a few matches. A left-arm medium-pace bowler, only 5ft 3½in tall, he produced figures of 8.3-4-5-8 for Notts Second XI v Surrey Second XI in the first ever meeting of these two sides at Whitsun 1891. He was also a useful right-hand bat. He was on the MCC Staff from 1893 for ten seasons, but his county cricket ended in

1896. Two of his brothers were useful players – William played for Derbyshire and Percy had a trial with Notts Colts.

Two Attewells were 1891 debutants. Thomas, brother of William, a right-hand bat, played in seven Notts games, but his best score was only 23. He was on the staff at Lord's from 1893 to 1925. Walter was a cousin of the brothers, William and Thomas. He played once only for Notts, but has found immortality in the writings of Neville Cardus, being the professional at Shrewsbury School, where Cardus acted as his assistant.

George Wharmby, of Sutton in Ashfield, a hard-hitting batsman and medium-pace bowler did little in his four matches for Notts. He moved to Lancashire, but his six games with that county did not produce anything of note. In 1902 he made his debut for Bedfordshire and appeared for that county until 1923.

The odd man of 1891 was John Griffiths. When Notts went to Clifton College in August, Bagguley was taken ill before play began and Dixon telegraphed to Nottingham for a replacement. Griffiths, who worked in Shaw and Shrewsbury's factory, was sent and arrived for the second day's play. He neither batted nor bowled and never was selected again; the only example in Notts first-class cricket of a player with such an unfortunate record. Francis Dixon, a doctor with the colliery company in Eastwood, played for Sherwin's Notts XI *v* Gentlemen of England at Scarborough in the 1891 Festival. Born in Derby, he was a useful batsman in local cricket, played once for his native County and was on the Notts Committee from 1889 until his death in 1943.

The 1892 season opened with a match for Alfred Shaw's benefit at Trent Bridge. Shaw had been manager of Lord Sheffield's team to Australia over the winter and this team played the Rest of England. Rain interrupted play and marred what should have been a very worthwhile game.

In the county matches, Flowers and Shacklock recovered the bowling form that had been absent in 1891 and with Attewell still one of the best bowlers in the country, Notts had a much better summer, challenging Surrey for the title throughout the campaign. In the Whitsun match Attewell and Shacklock began by dismissing Surrey for 97 and from that point the visitors never recovered, Notts winning by seven wickets. The return at The Oval created new attendance records; including members 72,565 attended, with 34,010 on the first day. After the first innings there were only five runs between the two sides and in the final innings Notts required 165. The batting of Barnes and Gunn, who made 58 and 40, won the game for Notts, who thus achieved the double over their rivals. Notts now seemed certain of the title, but for the

SURREY *v* NOTTINGHAMSHIRE

Played at Kennington Oval, 1, 2, 3 August 1892

NOTTINGHAMSHIRE WON BY FOUR WICKETS

SURREY	FIRST INNINGS		SECOND INNINGS	
Mr W. W. Read	c Robinson b Shacklock	5	run out	1
R. Abel	b Shacklock	14	run out	28
G. A. Lohmann	c Shrewsbury b Shacklock	11	c Shrewsbury b Shacklock	0
J. M. Read	b Shacklock	48	c Shrewsbury b Shacklock	10
*Mr J. Shuter	c and b Shacklock	25	c and b Attewell	43
R. Henderson	c Attewell b Shacklock	2	c Jones b Attewell	17
W. H. Lockwood	b Shacklock	0	c Sherwin b Flowers	19
Mr E. C. Streatfeild	c Dixon b Attewell	1	c Dixon b Flowers	7
W. Brockwell	not out	11	c Sherwin b Flowers	14
J. W. Sharpe	b Attewell	2	b Attewell	11
†Mr A. F. Clarke	b Shacklock	2	not out	4
Extras	byes	8	byes	5
Total		129		159

1st inns: 1-9, 2-34, 3-49, 4-100, 5-113, 6-113, 7-114, 8-120, 9-122
2nd inns: 1-1, 2-7, 3-21, 4-63, 5-97, 6-122, 7-128, 8-130, 9-155

BOWLING	O	M	R	W	O	M	R	W
Attewell	32	9	42	2	39.4	23	64	3
Shacklock	33.4	20	59	8	37	24	51	2
Barnes	6	3	12	0	3	0	15	0
Flowers	4	1	8	0	11	3	24	3

NOTTINGHAMSHIRE	FIRST INNINGS			SECOND INNINGS	
A. Shrewsbury	b Lockwood	6		c Abel b Lohmann	10
*Mr J. A. Dixon	run out	12		b Lockwood	0
W. Gunn	b Lockwood	38		c Clarke b Lockwood	58
W. Barnes	c Lohmann b Abel	6		b Lockwood	40
W. Flowers	b Lockwood	27	(6)	b Lohmann	5
F. J. Shacklock	c Clarke b Lockwood	3	(8)	not out	9
W. Attewell	b Lockwood	5	(7)	c Abel b Lohmann	13
Mr J. S. Robinson	c Abel b Lockwood	10			
Mr A. O. Jones	b Lockwood	6			
H. B. Daft	not out	2	(5)	not out	21
†M. Sherwin	c Brockwell b Lockwood	0			
Extras	byes	9		b 7, lb 2	9
Total		124		(6 wickets)	165

1st inns: 1-15, 2-39, 3-61, 4-71, 5-94, 6-102, 7-105, 8-118, 9-124
2nd inns: 1-?, 2-12, 3-106, 4-113, 5-120, 6-142

BOWLING	O	M	R	W	O	M	R	W
Lohmann	17	6	29	0	35.1	17	62	3
Lockwood	26.1	6	67	8	34	10	68	3
Abel	4	1	18	1	2	0	5	0
Sharpe	6	5	1	0	4	0	10	0
Streatfeild					4	0	7	0
W. W. Read					2	0	4	0

Umpires: Jas Lillywhite jun and W. Draper
*Captain; †Wicketkeeper

first time fixtures had been arranged with Somerset, and Notts went down to Taunton in mid-August and were beaten by an innings; worse was to follow, for they then travelled to Old Trafford and another innings defeat. With Surrey not losing any matches save those against Notts, and claiming 13 wins against Notts ten, the title was retained by Surrey. So great, however, was the enthusiasm gendered by Notts defeat of Surrey, that each of the Notts Eleven was presented with a gold medal and £21.

Shrewsbury again topped the national batting averages – for the third successive summer – and was the only batsman with an average over 40. As has been pointed out, Attewell, Shacklock and Barnes all had good bowling figures.

Six cricketers made their County debuts, of whom five soon moved on, but A. O. Jones, the Cambridge student, was to influence the course of Notts cricket through the Edwardian era. Jones was above all else an outstanding fieldsman, usually close to the wicket at short leg. It is impossible to quantify Jones' value to the team as a fieldsman, but the fact that he was awarded his blue and later selected for England more on account of his ability in the field than his other attributes tells its own story. As a batsman he became one of a famous opening partnership with James Iremonger. Normally keen to attack the bowling he was attractive to watch and very strong on the off-side. In 1903 he created a new record for Notts with an innings of 296 and in all hit four double-hundreds for that county.

Jones' enthusiastic fielding went a long way to making him an ideal captain and he led Notts from 1900 to 1914, but missed many matches through ill health in the final two years. He captained England in Australia in 1907–08, but again missed much of the tour through illness. Jones died in December 1914 aged 42. He was also a noted rugby player, appearing for Leicester for ten years.

Of the five professionals first appearing in 1892, Arthur Shrewsbury junior was the nephew of his namesake. Aged 18, he looked like a promising batsman, but did not play after 1892 and was rarely found in local cricket in later years. John Moss played once; he became a well-known umpire and officiated in a number of Tests between 1902 and 1921. Born in Clifton he lived most of his life in Keyworth. Thomas Armstrong was a native of Keyworth, who played six times for Notts as a batsman. He was a

---

The public interest in this match was so great that 72,565 attended, including over 34,000 on the first day and 32,000 on the second – there was not much more than an hour's play on the third day, when Notts required 56 more runs to win, but over 5,000 spectators turned out.

professional with various Lancashire clubs. William Wilkinson of Kimberley was another professional with engagements in Lancashire who was later a successful business man in Nottinghamshire. Outside the normal county programme, Notts arranged a match at Edgbaston against Warwickshire – George Woolley made his only Notts appearance in this game. His cricket was with Lenton United until he emigrated to the United States in 1897 and was coach at Haverford College.

The financial position of the Club was sound, though a loss was made in 1892 due to the weather keeping down receipts through the turnstiles. In broad terms, the members' subscriptions brought in £1,000 and the gate receipts another £1,000 of which about half was taken at the Whitsun Match. The match expenses were about £70 per game and totalled some £1,300 for the season. The Assistant Secretary received £100 per annum and rates, taxes and insurance amounted to about £170. The Ground Account was kept separately. No less than six cricket clubs used Trent Bridge as their home ground – Notts Amateurs, Nottingham Commercial, Forest, Forest Amateurs, Post Office and I and R Morley. In the winter Notts County FC paid £185 for their home games. So the renting out of the ground brought in a total of £315; the groundsmen's wages amounted to £120, the horse cost £25. The leasehold payment per annum was £448, but £425 was then received in rent from the tenant of the Trent Bridge Inn.

There were no players' wages as such, since the players were paid by the match and this money was included in match expenses. In 1892 the Club was still paying off the bank loan for the pavilion and some £450 of building repairs and additions was paid out.

In 1892 the Club had won more matches than they lost; this happy state of affairs was not to occur again until 1900. Of the famous eleven of the 1880s, Shaw, Selby, Scotton had gone; Barnes and Flowers were moving to the veteran stage, as was Sherwin, and the young players, though in some cases looking very promising, could not fully replace those who had gone. Shrewsbury and Gunn remained great batsmen, but with the bowling growing steadily weaker, the famous pair became more defensive and the cries of 'pad-play' grew louder.

The 1893 season began with an innings victory over Sussex, in which Mee took nine for 54 in the first innings. It was a different story against Surrey. Lockwood again embarrassed his native county by hitting the highest individual score, as well as taking five wickets, and Notts lost by seven wickets. In the third Championship match Shacklock performed his feat of dismissing four batsmen in four consecutive deliveries, the unlucky batsmen being Spurway, Newton, Trask and Gibbs. Notts avenged their defeat of the previous year by the large margin of 225 runs. Middlesex proved tougher. Notts were set 331 in four hours on the last day, but could muster only 273, Middlesex winning with ten minutes to spare. The match at Hove in June was perhaps the beginning of the oft-told tale of Notts winning the toss and most of the team going down to the beach whilst Shrewsbury and Gunn spent the day at the crease. The pair added 274 for the second wicket, Shrewsbury making 164 and Gunn 156; the score at stumps on the first day was 376 for two. Barnes also hit a century and Notts amassed 674, the highest total for the County and the second highest, up to that date, in a first-class county match. Notts gained a first innings lead of 453, but Sussex managed to hold out on the last day.

The rest of the Championship matches saw Notts in very variable form. For example, they were beaten by Somerset at Taunton by an innings, Somerset occupying the penultimate position in the table, but inflicted a nine-wicket defeat on second-placed Lancashire. In all five wins contrasted with seven defeats and sixth place.

There was an England v Australia match at Trent Bridge for Shrewsbury's Benefit, England winning by an innings and 153 runs, the Yorkshire left-armer Peel taking eleven for 110 as the match just crept into the third day. Spectators totalled 6,000 on each of the first two days.

In another attempt to unearth talent the Committee arranged a Gentlemen v Players of the County match in mid-August, at which A. R. Bennett, the Notts Castle Amateur, distinguished himself, his fast bowling taking 13 wickets. He played in a handful of county matches, but died in 1899 aged 30. A second amateur who played in that match and made his first-class debut the same year was R. H. Howitt, an opening batsman. He came from Farnsfield and played for many years in club cricket in the Newark area, but was already 29 in 1893. In all he had 28 first-class matches for Notts up to 1901 and served on the Committee until 1934.

The only professional debutant of the season was Silas Hardy, who hit 30 and 50 in the trial mentioned above. His cricket was for Kimberley, though he was a native of Ilkeston. A fast bowler and fair batsman, he achieved very little in his five first-class matches, though he made a name for himself as a professional with Lowerhouse in Lancashire. Silas Hardy should not be confused with Solomon Hardy who appeared for Derbyshire in 1898.

First-class status having been granted to some of the lesser counties in 1894, Notts played 21 first-class matches in the season – the first time 20 or more had been undertaken. The results were unimpressive; four wins against eleven losses. Shrewsbury was unable to play all summer due to illness and in the Championship only Gunn averaged over 20. Shacklock had left and the bowling was almost entirely in the hands of Attewell. He sent down more than 1,100 overs, while no one else delivered 500. Surrey beat Notts twice by an innings. In fact the tone of the season was set in the first match, the first first-class game ever undertaken by Warwickshire – Notts lost by six wickets. J. W. Sharpe, the Ruddington bowler who had done so much for Surrey, turned out for Notts in this match and four others during the year, but scarcely strengthened the bowling. Eight professionals, apart from Sharpe, were given an opportunity in the First Eleven, only one of whom made much impact. He was Arthur Pike, the Keyworth wicketkeeper. The Committee had decided to retire Sherwin and the two amateurs, C. W. Wright and J. S. Robinson, kept wicket in the first matches of 1894, but proved of variable quality and Pike took their place, holding it for the rest of the year. He seemed to be assured of a long career, but midway through 1898 fell ill and though he continued on the MCC staff until 1906, he died the following year aged 44. The rest of the trialists of 1894 were Meshack Chambers of Awsworth, an all-rounder who later played for Northumberland, Thomas Flowers, a cousin of Wilfred and slow-medium bowler, the Church CC professional, who came from Daybrook; and Alick Handford, who was pro at Sefton Park. He made a big impression with his medium-pace bowling and Notts got him a position at Lord's for 1895 so he was readily available for the County, but despite a good number of chances in 1895 he did not live up to his promise and faded away. The brothers Sam and Tom Lowe (their brother Richard had played in 1889) were tried as fast bowlers, but Tom was 35 and Sam 27, so rather elderly for colts. James Turner of Sutton in Ashfield was the Southport professional and a medium-pace bowler and played in two games; Arthur Wilkinson, an attacking batsman and accurate bowler did well in his debut *v* Somerset at Trent Bridge and played regularly in 1895, but then dropped out of the eleven.

The single new amateur of 1894 was P. W. Oscroft, who was a schoolmaster in Newcastle, and coming back to Nottingham in the holidays played in August in 1894 and the two following years; he then moved to Hornsey and later became science master at Uppingham. His son later played for Leicestershire.

Apart from the red faces caused by the continued success of Lockwood and Briggs for Surrey and Lancashire, Notts officials had another uncomfortable jolt in 1894 when Alfred Shaw, aged 52, re-appeared in county cricket, and not only took seven for 34 against Notts, but ended the summer at the top of the Sussex bowling averages – a bowler sacked by Notts at the close of 1886!

Arthur Shrewsbury resumed his place in the Notts side for 1895 and duly headed the batting table by a considerable margin – an average of 48, with Gunn in second place on 33 and Flowers third with 23.

The season had few bright moments. Three wins against ten losses put Notts last but one in the table. One of the wins was against Sussex at Trent Bridge when the County hit up a new record of 726. William Gunn made 219, then lower down the order at numbers seven and eight Howitt hit 119 and Bagguley 110. The total was the highest ever recorded in Championship matches to that date. Howitt and Bagguley added a record 201 for the seventh wicket. After his moment of glory in 1894, Notts made Alfred Shaw pay, as the 53-year-old sent down 100.1 overs and took four for 168. He was easily the most economical of the Sussex attack, but not long afterwards he decided his legs could not stand up to any more such marathons and he retired a second time.

Of the seven 1895 fresh faces, E. C. Weaver and W. Whitlock were two local amateurs who made up the side in an unofficial game against Northants, as did R. G. Bradshaw, the Retford amateur, who made a name for himself in North Notts cricket. Ben Gregory of Digby Colliery was a professional for Notts Amateurs in 1895 and later with various Lancashire clubs. He was a good medium-pace bowler, but not of county standard. He later became landlord of a pub in Worksop and though always using the name 'Ben Gregory' when playing cricket, was actually Benjamin Bridge Simpson. Another miner was Albert Longden, who might have made a name for himself in county cricket, but preferred the security of colliery deputy and worked for the Barber, Walker Co.

Jabez Carter of Ruddington was a useful all-rounder, but moved to the West of Scotland Club and remained there some 20 years. Like Ben Gregory there was some confusion over his name, as Carter was baptised Arthur Gervase.

The last debutant of 1895 was W. G. H. Lowe, who was a member of Notts Castle and played only in emergency when Longden failed to turn up for the match *v* Gloucestershire at Trent

Bridge. He gave a useful account of himself with the bat, but was not asked again and later emigrated to North America.

Behind the scenes there were problems with the Assistant Secretary, Edwin Browne, whose management of the accounts was becoming erratic. He was asked to resign, but refused to do so, or so at least the Minutes of the Committee Meeting on 23 February 1895 stated, but the following meeting announced that his letter of resignation had been overlooked. In April 1895, Henry Turner took over as Assistant Secretary and was to remain in the post until his sudden death after the First World War.

The 1896 season saw a moderate improvement in the playing results. The programme opened with a victory over Derbyshire – William Gunn hit 135 and Attewell took eight wickets – but that was on 20 May, and the next Championship win was not until 1 July, when Kent were beaten by 19 runs, with Brown taking eight wickets. Brown was the same cricketer who had been selected for Notts back in 1883 and whose appearance had been blocked by his club, Stockport. Now, at the age of 39 and with 13 seasons of cricket in the Cheshire County side, he was being recruited by his native county – Cheshire's Club collapsed in 1895. He was to play in 14 first-class games for Notts and take 47 wickets, but only really as a stopgap. Although Notts supporters could not be expected to forecast what was to come, two of the 1896 recruits were to provide the County with many successful days in the long-term future. One was William Gunn's nephew, John Gunn, and the other, Tom Wass of Sutton in Ashfield.

In the public mind John Gunn has now become overshadowed by the reputation of his younger brother, George, whose career began in 1902, but John is the only Notts player to score 20,000 runs and take 1,000 wickets for the County and in four successive years, 1903 to 1906, he achieved the 'double'. Of medium height and cheery disposition he put on weight in his later playing days, so as to appear fairly rotund by the mid-1920s. A left-handed batsman he had a good repertoire of strokes, and though beginning as a defensive batsman soon developed into scoring runs at a fair pace. His weakness was against fast bowling. A slow-medium bowler his successes came in the early part of his career; later he bowled much slower, tossing up the ball, but only in 1921 did he achieve any great number of wickets by this method. His first Championship hundred, in 1903, was a new Notts record as he hit 294 against Leicestershire.

John Gunn toured Australia with the ill-fated 1901–02 side and appeared in all five Tests, but his only Test in England came in 1905 at Trent Bridge. His final match for Notts was in 1925 and then for several seasons he played a high standard of cricket with Julien Cahn's side and was employed by Cahn in his later years.

The final results for 1896 were five wins and five losses, placing Notts in sixth place, but at no time were they challenging for the title. Gunn and Shrewsbury remained the leading batsmen, the former finishing third in the national averages. Attewell was the only bowler to return good figures, though Brown and Hardstaff did as well as expected.

The other cricketers who made their Notts debut in 1896 were G. H. Chambers, the fast left-arm bowler from Digby Colliery; Percy Mason of East Bridgford, an all-rounder who was engaged by Notts Amateurs in 1896, and who played in the Notts side in 43 matches up until 1901 and afterwards for Cheshire; and G. L. Robinson, who lived in Sutton in Ashfield in 1896, but later moved to Denaby near Doncaster, and was a leg-break bowler and fair batsman – his nephew was E. P. Robinson the Yorkshire and Somerset cricketer. Three local club cricketers, W. James, G. Ratcliffe (also of Derbyshire) and S. Thomas, played in sundry non-first-class Notts matches during the season.

The most important decision taken by the Notts Committee in 1896 was to establish a groundstaff of young cricketers. This was a new departure for the Club, although they had given certain assistance to some local clubs, especially those playing at Trent Bridge, by way of payment for the engagement of a professional. The details of the five players who formed the original groundstaff are:

C. E. Dench, paid £2.10s, of Nottingham, an all-rounder aged 24

P. Mason, paid £2.5s, of Gunthorpe, a fast bowler aged 21

F. Hawley, paid £2, of Nottingham, a fast bowler aged 19

T. Oates, paid £2 (plus fare), of Eastwood, a wicketkeeper aged 21

J. Gunn, paid £1.5s, of Nottingham, an all-rounder aged 20

The wages given were for 20 weeks; in addition Walter Marshall, who had played a few matches for the County six or seven years earlier was appointed as coach for 20 weeks at £80. It is not certain when the young players were asked for their ages, but two or three adjusted their ages downwards, a ploy which young trialists had used for many years when applying for the Easter Colts match and one which continued until the Second World War.

In order to give more opportunity to the young groundstaff,

THOMAS GEORGE WASS

Among his contemporaries Tom Wass was a unique bowler. He possessed a natural gift in an ability to bowl medium-fast leg-breaks. Coming to the nets for a trial at Trent Bridge, he astonished everyone by dimissing Shrewsbury several times, a feat rarely achieved, since Shrewsbury batted in practice with the same care and attention he used in match play.

In 1896 and 1897, Wass was engaged by Liverpool CC and meant that he played only in one or two county matches, so his county career effectively began in 1898. He took 100 wickets in a season for the first time in 1900 and from then until 1912 he was one of the best bowlers in England, though he really showed his full talent on soft wickets. In 1907 he and Hallam won the Championship for Notts; on four occasions those two bowlers bowled unchanged through both innings of a match and twice Wass took 16 wickets in a match, the most remarkable being in 1906 at Liverpool, when his 16 wickets all came in one day, his final figures being 16 for 69.

His total of 1,653 wickets remains the record for Notts and 158 times he took five wickets in an innings. Despite his great success, 'Topsy' Wass was picked for only four matches apart from county games – three appearances for the Players and one for an England XI. A plain-spoken man and someone who would make others aware of his disapproval when necessary, he rather 'frightened' the selectors at Lord's. Sir Pelham Warner concluded an obituary of Wass with:

> It is said that the cricket today is somewhat lacking in characters. Wass was certainly one and, if, as I have hinted, he was a 'tough guy' at the start, he mellowed under the influence of such good and true men as J. A. Dixon and others, who realised his heart was in the right place. I do not believe that anyone who played cricket with him will forget him.

He was a bowler, pure and simple, though in 395 innings he did once score fifty; his fielding was also rather weak.

Born in Sutton in Ashfield, where he lived all his life, Wass was employed as a miner at various pits near his home and also as groundsman for some years at the local Grammar School.

home and away matches were arranged with Northants and Staffordshire, in addition to the normal 1897 county programme. The Easter Colts trial was not abandoned and in fact continued for another ten years.

The first-class county matches began with an innings victory over Sussex. Dixon opened the Notts batting and declared the innings closed at 448 for seven, when he reached 268 not out, a new Notts record. He batted on all three days, but in miserably cold weather. There followed seven successive draws, the most interesting of which was the game at Gravesend. Kent hit 406 and then dismissed Notts for 168, enforcing the follow on. After Notts had saved the innings defeat, Attewell came in, scoring 102, his first hundred for the County after 16 years.

The run of draws was broken by a second win over Sussex and then a sentimental match against the Philadelphians, with Alfred Shaw reappearing for his native County after an absence of ten years – he opened the bowling and took three for 75, but A. M. Wood, who had appeared for Notts in 1878, opened the batting for the Americans and scored exactly 100.

The two wins against Sussex remained Notts' only successes in the Championship and with five defeats, they finished well down the table. William Gunn, Shrewsbury and Dixon had excellent batting figures, but the bowling was weaker than ever. Even Attewell's average had crept above 20 and he was easily the best. Guttridge, who had come back to his native county from Sussex in 1896, took second most wickets, but the other veteran recruit of the previous summer, Sam Brown, fell away and dropped out of the side. Three of the new groundstaff made their first-class debuts, Hawley, Dench and Oates. Hawley never played again, but Oates was to have a distinguished career. He secured a regular place as Notts wicketkeeper in 1902 and was nearly 50 when he finally left the side in 1925. From 1899 to 1926 he was on the staff at Lord's and from 1927 to 1938 stood as an umpire in county matches as well as some Tests. Undemonstrative behind the wicket, he coped well with the unorthodox bowling of Wass; as a batsman he hit 15 fifties and was therefore a useful lower-order player.

Dench made a most impressive debut for Notts v MCC, taking nine wickets in the match. A right-arm medium-pace bowler and promising batsman, he remained at Trent Bridge until 1902, but never developed into a worthwhile county cricketer. He moved to Dublin University in 1903 and later became a first-class umpire.

William Henson, a fast-medium bowler, made his debut in

1897 and joined the staff the following year. He bowled usefully in 1898, but early in 1899 was involved in a punch-up outside the pavilion and left Nottinghamshire to be professional with Clydesdale CC. He died in Scotland in 1922. Two amateurs made brief appearances, H. R. N. Ellison, the son of C. C. Ellison, a Lincolnshire cricketer, was a good club cricketer with Free Foresters and Incogniti; he played only against the Philadelphians and later was Hon Secretary to Derbyshire. C. H. Parr of Radcliffe on Trent played one match against Staffordshire and made lots of runs in local cricket.

In February 1897, Trent Bridge had been the venue, for the first time, of an England soccer International, Ireland being beaten 6-0. Notts County's pitch occupied the area on Fox Road which is now filled by an office block and car park, and the football club had stands which were on three sides of the pitch.

Despite the gloomy results on the field, the Notts Committee were still keen to improve the ground and in 1898 the ladies' pavilion was built and also the press box, which incorporated a new scoreboard (the building is now hospitality boxes).

The bowling figures for 1898 were even more depressing than those for the previous season, and of 16 Championship matches only three reached a definite conclusion, a single victory for Notts and two defeats. Because of the points system then in vogue, the County still managed eighth place (out of 14).

Shrewsbury and William Gunn had yet another good summer, both completing 1,000 runs. Both finished in the first ten in the national averages. Critics continued to attack the County for their defensive batting, but in view of the lack of bowling it was difficult to see what alternative the batsmen could have adopted. In a continuing effort to give young players experience two new fixtures were played, *v* Durham and Worcestershire. The three who made their first-class debut in 1898 were Henry Anthony of Arnold, who played in four matches and later turned out for Cheshire, James Riley, who had been on the Oval ground staff, and played twice, and W. B. Goodacre, a local amateur batsman, mainly with Forest Amateurs. The last-named made fairly frequent appearances until 1903 and hit 104 not out against Yorkshire in 1900.

The improvements to the ground, which apart from those noted in the previous season included, during the winter of 1898–99, a continuous semi-cricle of covered seating from the pavilion along the Bridgford Road side, joining up with the new press box and then continuing along Radcliffe Road to join with the football stands. This meant that the ground was now totally enclosed by seating and Trent Bridge was awarded its first Test match when the Australians arrived in 1899. For this game the football pitch was used and the wicket moved over so that the boundaries were 85 yards. The estimated attendance over the three days was 40,000. William Gunn was the only Notts representative. There was good weather on all three days, but the batting on both sides was tame and the match was drawn. It was to prove W. G. Grace's final Test match.

Notts' season was almost as depressing in 1898, with only two wins. Attewell finally faded from the scene and although he bowled 451.2 overs in Championship matches, he took only 19 wickets at 38 runs each. There was, however, some glimpse of a brighter future in the bowling table. Wass had taken 31 wickets at 31 runs each in 1898, but this year the figures were 45 at 23 runs each, and similarly John Gunn's figures moved from 25 at 30 to 56 at 22.

In the batting A. O. Jones, who had been Shrewsbury's regular opening partner for four or five years, helped the veteran create a new first-wicket partnership record, the pair adding 391. Shrewsbury made 146 and Jones hit up 250 in 270 minutes.

No fewer than nine new players appeared for the County of whom one was to be an important figure in Notts cricket for nearly 40 years. James Iremonger, though born in Yorkshire, moved to Wilford in early childhood and first came to public notice as a left full-back for Nottingham Forest. He represented Forest over 300 times and was capped for England. Playing for Notts as a batsman he sprang suddenly to fame in 1901, when he hit four hundreds in four successive matches in early August. A tall man he used his reach to full advantage and hit the ball very hard; he replaced Shrewsbury as the opening partner for A. O. Jones and the pair added a hundred for the first wicket 25 times. His career suddenly took a new turn after 1908. Having bowled only occasionally until then, he was given more opportunity due to the illness of John Gunn and the falling-off of Hallam and in three successive years, 1911 to 1913, took more than 90 wickets – it is an oddity that in 1903 Iremonger topped the Notts batting and in 1912 topped the bowling, whereas John Gunn was the leading bowler of the first year and leading batsman in the second. Iremonger went to Australia with the 1911–12 side, but achieved little and did not play in the Tests. In 1921 he was appointed Notts coach and was responsible for the maturing of such players as Larwood, Voce and young Hardstaff.

Only George Anthony of Arnold, of the other debutants, made any impact. He played until 1905, but ill-health forced his retirement and he died in 1907 aged 31. Daniel Bottom, a Derbyshire cricketer with residential qualification for Notts, and who was already 34, played three games as a slow bowler. G. J. Groves, son of a well known reporter, was born in Notts, but had made a name for himself in London Club cricket. He played in 17 matches in 1899 and 1900 and looked a very useful batsman, but preferred to follow his occupation as a journalist. James Stapleton, a wicketkeeper from Eastwood, played occasionally in Oates' absence until 1911. John Atkinson, also from the Eastwood area, was a left-arm slow bowler, who was on the staff at Trent Bridge from 1898 to 1901 and then became professional with Todmorden. John Drury was also on the Notts staff in 1898 as a bowler, but took up a professional engagement in 1901 in Scotland. Percy Harrison of Mansfield Woodhouse, played once as a batsman; F. J. Hingley, born in Nottingham, but living in Chesterfield, played only against Worcestershire in 1899, in a match not considered first-class.

WITH A SPRING IN HIS WALK

IN 1900 NOTTINGHAMSHIRE PRODUCED better results than at any time in the last seven years. Seven matches were won and four lost, an aggregate which put the County in fifth place and in fact their record was very similar to the counties occupying third and fourth place.

The reason for the improvement? Wass had a very good season, taking 100 Championship wickets at 18 runs each and being effectively the seventh most successful bowler in the national averages; on the other hand not a single Notts batsman featured in the leading batting averages, only Shrewsbury and William Gunn averaging over 30. The playing eleven was much more settled, with eight of the side taking part in at least 16 of the 18 Championship games. The bowling opened with Wass (fast-medium leg-breaks) and John Gunn (medium-slow left-arm) with the only support being Dixon, Dench and Jones. It was not a very usual combination.

The appointment of A. O. Jones as the captain for the season would seem to outweigh any other factor which went into Notts' upward move. He was the kind of man who inspired the rest of the side to try to emulate him and he gave Notts back a will to win. The caution of Dixon was gone. In most seasons Notts had played an early match at Lord's against MCC, giving a trial to young players and as a consequence often losing. This year it was the first first-class game of the summer and they won in two days by eight wickets, even though William Gunn and Shrewsbury were absent. Successive victories followed against Gloucestershire, Leicestershire and Derbyshire. The Whitsun match brought defeat – Lockwood again being very successful against his native county. The game was awarded to Shrewsbury as his benefit, because the match given to him in 1893 was not a great success. The next Notts defeat was against Lancashire at Trent Bridge, when again it was a Notts-born cricketer, this time Briggs, who was largely responsible for the result.

The much more settled team of 1900 meant that only one new player was seen in Championship matches, Charles Pepper. He originally played for Forest Wanderers and was a promising all-rounder. In 1901 he joined the staff at Trent Bridge, but the following year moved to Bedford and played for that county in 1903. Later he took engagements in Scotland and Burton on Trent, but was killed in action in the First World War. The amateur, J. C. Snaith, played against MCC. He was a talented cricketer with various local sides and briefly became well-known as a novelist, writing in particular 'Willow The King', with cricket as its main theme. Between the wars Snaith was regarded as somewhat eccentric, and living opposite Trent Bridge he was known to harangue passers-by from his bedroom window, especially the crowds queueing to attend the Whitsun match or Test matches. Hubert Twells of Eastwood played only in a trial game against Sutton in Ashfield but with no success; he was a useful all-rounder for Eastwood Colleries CC.

For 1901, Notts strengthened the attack by securing the services of A. W. Hallam. A medium-pace right-arm bowler, Hallam was born in East Leake but moved to Loughborough and began his career in county cricket with Leicestershire in 1889. In 1892 he spent a year at The Oval, but in 1893 moved on to Old Trafford, where he qualified for Lancashire and in 1897 had a brilliant season capturing 100 wickets. Illness then struck and for the next three seasons he was scarcely seen in county cricket. On the advice of Shrewsbury, Notts engaged Hallam for 1901, also finding him a winter job in Nottingham. There were some doubts regarding his fitness, but he played right through the season and took more wickets than anyone save John Gunn. In theory therefore Notts should have continued their upward movement but Wass, unfortunately, was completely out of sorts and only half as effective as he had been in 1900, so the attack was no stronger overall.

The early part of the season brought splendid results, with the old enemy Surrey defeated at Whitsun for the first time since 1892, on one of Wass's rare good days, but in mid-June there came a most embarrassing experience against Yorkshire, Notts being bowled out in 15.5 overs for just 13 runs. Shrewsbury injured his hand whilst fielding on the first morning and retired from the match, but Lord Hawke allowed Notts' substitute to bat in both innings. It was the lowest score to then in Championship cricket and remains Notts' lowest ever. Notts seemed to have recovered from this debacle, beating both Leicestershire and Derbyshire, the latter on the private ground of the Duke of Portland at Welbeck, but in the end there were five Championship wins against six losses and ninth position in the table.

A. O. Jones had his best season so far with the bat and averaged over 50; Iremonger came from nowhere in August and moved to second place in the batting table, so the new groundstaff scheme was now bearing fruit. Apart from Hallam, the other professional to make his debut was Isaac Harrison of Calverton. He had joined

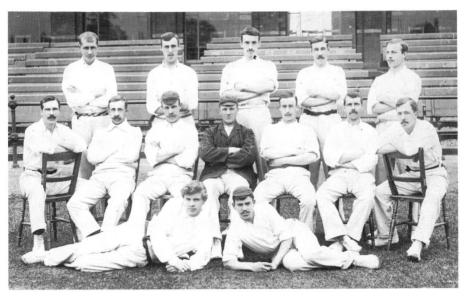

The Trent Bridge groundstaff (ie the professionals) in 1901. The county side began this season well but faded, and Yorkshire dismissed them for 13. Left to right, standing: T. G. Wass, J. Atkinson, J. Iremonger, W. Ross, P. Harrison. Seated: C. Pepper, C. E. Dench, P. Mason, W. Marshall (coach), G. Anthony, A. W. Hallam, J. R. Gunn. On ground: A. Mawer, I. M. Harrison. (NCCC)

the Notts groundstaff in 1901 and played in six first-class matches as a batsman, but in May 1902 was forced to leave the staff due to ill health and died in 1909 aged 28. Three amateurs were also tried. The 18-year-old Etonian, the Hon Mervyn Herbert, son of the Earl of Caernarvon, scored 65 on his debut, but in five later matches did very little. In 1903 he switched to Somerset and played for that county on and off until 1924; he also played a few games for Oxford University, but did not obtain his blue. V. H. Cartwright, another 18-year-old, who was captain of Rugby in 1901, was given some opportunities spread over four seasons, without making any notable scores, though he hit many runs for Notts Amateurs. He was a very capable rugby footballer, gaining his blue at Oxford and going on to captain England. Afterwards he was an England Selector and President of the Rugby Union. The third amateur was another rugby international, A. E. Hind. He obtained blues at Cambridge for both rugby and cricket and though born in Lancashire moved to Notts where he was in the legal profession. His only first-class game for the County was *v* Leicestershire in 1901, when he did not bowl, in spite of playing for the University in that capacity.

119

The County Championship of 1902 was rather a non-event. The Australians, as was now usual when they toured England, stole most of the headlines; the wet weather spoilt many matches and Yorkshire were too far ahead, at least during the climax of the season, to provide any interest in the destiny of the title. However for Nottinghamshire it was a very satisfactory summer. The County moved up to third place, winning six matches and losing three. Tom Wass recovered the form he lost in 1901 and only five bowlers in the country finished with a better record. His 140 wickets cost 15 runs each. Hallam had a second good season, but John Gunn found the wet wickets not to his liking. However it was really Shrewsbury's year. The veteran batsman topped the

Joe Hardstaff senior was only 5ft 6in but a brilliant batsman whose Test matches were all in Australia, where he was called 'Hotstuff'. (NCCC)

national averages and was one of only six men who averaged over 40. Against Gloucestershire at Trent Bridge he had the satisfaction of scoring for the first time a century in each innings of the same match – it was also the first time the feat had been accomplished for the County.

Rather in contrast to 1901, the season began with adverse results, but improved as the summer progressed. In the final game, Lancashire were beaten by an innings, following a brilliant hundred by Jones and then some fine bowling from Wass.

A third member of the Gunn family, John's brother George, made his debut in 1902, as did another batsman who was to play for England, Joe Hardstaff. Hardstaff, a hard-hitting middle-order batsman, was only 5ft 6in tall and looked younger than his age. There are several stories of his being refused admittance to grounds by dubious gatemen, who could not believe he was one of the players. He became a regular member of the Notts first eleven in 1904 and continued so until midway through 1924. He was selected to tour Australia in 1907–08 and batted exceptionally well, being nicknamed 'Hotstuff' by the press Down Under. On the tour he hit 1,360 runs and played in all five Tests. He was never, however, picked for England in England. He was on the MCC staff from 1906 and from 1927 was a first-class umpire, officiating in several Tests until his son was selected for England.

Ben Taylor of Kimberley and later Eastwood was a fast right-arm bowler who played 31 matches for Notts between 1902 and 1909; he was a professional with various Lancashire league sides up to the First World War. John Pennington, another bowler to be given a trial in 1902, was left-arm medium. His main claim to fame is the unfortunate record of conceding 223 runs in a single innings for Notts v South Africans in 1904. He spent most of his life in Newark, being a commission agent.

J. W. White joined the Trent Bridge staff in 1902 as a wicket-keeper and competed with Stapleton for the post of Oates' understudy. He played only three first-class matches for Notts, while being a useful soccer player with Nottingham Forest. Hermon Dexter played ten matches for Notts as a batsman, mainly in 1903 when he was on the Trent Bridge staff; he was chiefly connected with Nottingham Forest CC. Two amateur batsmen, H. H. Goodall and C. R. Morris, each represented Notts in five first-class games. Goodall of Forest Amateurs was an architect by profession and later designed the concrete stands erected between the wars at Trent Bridge as well as the Dixon Gate. Morris of Radcliffe on Trent was a surveyor and after the

Notts in 1902, when they improved to third in the Championship. Shrewsbury became the first Notts player to score a century in each innings of a match, and topped the country's averages, but was to commit suicide at the start of the next season. Left to right, standing: T. G. Wass, W. Gunn, A. Shrewsbury, T. W. Oates. Seated: J. Iremonger, W. B. Goodacre, A. O. Jones (captain), J. A. Dixon. On ground: G. Anthony, J. R. Gunn, A. W. Hallam. (NCCC)

First World War emigrated to South Africa where he lived for about 16 years.

The weather in 1903 was even more inclement than in 1902; six victories and four losses put Notts in fifth place. There was doubt about the appearance of Shrewsbury for Notts when the season began, due to illness. On 19 May, he ended his life by shooting himself in the mouth, and as soon as the news reached Hove, where Notts were playing Sussex, the match was abandoned. The batting was not materially affected by this tragedy, since Jones and Iremonger as the opening pair had excellent records; John Gunn was an effective number four and William Gunn and Dixon continued to be worth a place in the side. Lower in the order, usually at number six, George Gunn was incredibly consistent. Oates had taken over as wicketkeeper in 1902 and the fielding in general was good. Wass had another off season, comparatively speaking, but Hallam and John Gunn had good returns. John Gunn hit his highest score of 294 against Leicestershire, but within weeks Jones bettered it with 296 against

GEORGE GUNN

Although George Gunn cared little for statistics, he remains the only batsman to reach 30,000 first-class runs for the County and is the only player to represent Notts more than 500 times, his figure of 583 being out of reach of any present day player unless the first-class programme is radically altered.

Judged by the description of his batting, he must have possessed a wonderful eye and very fast reflexes, for the one facet of his batting that is still recalled is the ability to walk forward to fast bowling, a very dangerous ploy unless a batsman has the lightening reactions to do it successfully. Not that Gunn was always a batsman attacking the bowling. He was a player of moods – the most famous example of this occurred in the match against Yorkshire at Trent Bridge in 1913. In difficult circumstances he batted six hours for a century in the first innings and came in for some caustic comments from members of the club. These remarks annoyed him to the extent that in the second innings he hit a second hundred, but in 90 minutes.

He is remembered as an opening batsman, but it was not until his 10th summer with Notts that he assumed that role on a permanent basis. His partnership with Whysall commenced in earnest in 1922 and when it was broken by Whysall's death in the winter of 1930, the pair had become one of the most successful in county cricket – in 1928 and 1929 they actually added over 2,000 runs for the first wicket each year. In 1919, Gunn topped the first-class national averages for the first and only time and was still batting well ten years later when he was 50. The Notts Committee then decided to retire him, but the death of Whysall forced them to reconsider and Gunn continued until 1932.

He played in only one Test in England and one can only assume that this lack of recognition was due to the safety-first policy of the selectors who were frightened of a 'character'. He toured Australia with the MCC sides of 1907–08 and 1911–12 and returned with excellent batting figures. His next and final chance came on the West Indies tour of 1929–30, when, aged 50, he again had a good season. George Gunn was the nephew of William, brother of John and father of G.V., and in 1928 he and his son both hit hundreds in the same innings for Notts, a unique feat.

George Gunn, seen with W. W. Keeton, was the third member of the famous family to play for Notts, making his debut in 1902. He was to play 583 matches for Notts, but his eccentric approach meant all but one of his Test matches were overseas. (NCCC)

Gloucestershire, creating a record for Notts that would stand until 1939. In the Leicestershire match the Notts total reached 739 for seven declared, still the best for the County.

Trevor Branston, the Charterhouse all-rounder, was the most talented newcomer. In 1903 he was hailed as the outstanding Public School batsman of the year; in the autumn he went up to Oxford and played in the University matches of 1904, 1905 and 1906. Branston played fairly frequently for Notts in 1907 and 1908, but then business called and he gave up first-class cricket, though making one or two further Notts appearances in emergency. Branston was one of the very few Notts amateurs who deserved a place in the County side but moved away from first-class cricket. Two other new amateurs who began in 1903 and had more than a passing influence at Trent Bridge were R. E. Hemingway and the Rev H. Staunton. Hemingway had moved to Nottingham with his parents, his father being involved in the construction of the Great Central Railway. Two of his brothers represented Gloucestershire and like him were in the Eleven at Uppingham. R. E. Hemingway was a very useful batsman and turned out in 30 matches for Notts up to 1905. The Rev H. Staunton, a very hard-hitting batsman, was not in the XI at Cambridge and was 32 when he made his first-class debut, like Hemingway he appeared only until 1905, though in 1909 and 1910 he captained Notts 2nd XI. Both these cricketers died on active service in the First World War. E. G. Allen, another amateur, was the mainstay of Worksop CC and made two appearances in 1903. J. W. Day was the most promising of the 1903 professionals. He came from Sutton on Trent and joined the Notts staff in 1901 aged 18; an all-rounder he held a regular place in the County side for three years commencing 1904 and his last appearance was in 1907. From 1909 he had a long career with Lincolnshire and then spent five summers as a first-class umpire. The other two newcomers were G. H. Chambers (not to be confused with the 1896 cricketer) and Thomas Simpson. A slow left-arm bowler, Chambers played in four matches, but was to achieve better notice in Scottish cricket, particularly for Forfarshire. Simpson of Keyworth, although only appearing in five Notts matches, flourished as an all-rounder in Lancashire club cricket, especially with Rochdale.

Lancashire had a tremendous season in 1904, being unbeaten, and Notts were among the next six counties competing for second place. They ended fifth with seven wins and four losses – there were still a large percentage of draws, but this was due to the run-making on the hard dry wickets and not to the rain of the previous two summers. The bowlers had a hard time and this found out the support attack, almost everything depending on Wass and John Gunn. Hallam had a poor year and A. O. Jones was the best of the rest. A brief comment in *Wisden* however illustrates what Jones meant in terms of captaincy: 'Admitting that the general result of the season's work fell short of what had been hoped, there was always a pleasant sense of energy about Notts cricket in 1904 – in strong contrast to the lethargy that came over the county in the years immediately following 1893.'

Jones and Iremonger had a brilliant summer opening the Notts batting. Both averaged over 60, which placed them fourth and fifth in the national table. John Gunn completed the 'double' and George Gunn continued to improve, but the old stagers William Gunn and Dixon effectively dropped out of the eleven. During the season Notts volunteered to take part in a three day 'Time Limit' match with Yorkshire. Each innings was limited to 255 minutes batting, but the critics thought the idea a farce and it was not persevered with.

We are now passing through what writers were later to describe as the 'Golden Age of Cricket' and a pause to look at the accounts for the year might be appropriate. Notts had 923 members, who paid a total of £2,091.15.6d, the bulk of them paying one guinea. Match receipts were £1,644.6.0d. The cost of staging matches and paying for away fixtures was £2,227.10.4d, plus talent money of £116.5.0d, and the groundstaff wages of £623.7.4d. Salaries amounted to £200. With sundry other receipts and payments a total of £4,215.0.4d was the turnover, but a separate Trent Bridge Ground account was kept, which basically involved the sub-letting of the ground for both football and cricket teams plus the rent from the TBI, all set against the cost of the groundsmen, caretaker for pavilion, horse and repairs to equipment. The Ground account amounted to £893.11.8d. There was still £3,503.19.6d due to the Bank on the money borrowed for building the pavilion and other stands.

Notts' reliance on Wass became apparent in 1905. The County were reasonably successful up to the end of June, but then Wass injured a finger and did not return to the side until the penultimate game. In that match Wass bowled out Middlesex cheaply but following on they just managed to bat out time. Wass then took ten wickets in the final game, against Derbyshire, to bring an emphatic victory. Whilst Wass was absent, John Gunn and Hallam found life difficult and the County had to settle for tenth place – out of 16 now since Worcestershire and Northants had become first-class. Iremonger, Jones, the two Gunns and Hardstaff provided a relatively youthful and sound batting line-up, but the lower order was somewhat weak.

The Lancashire match at Trent Bridge produced two records, though neither in Notts' favour. The last pair of Lancashire batsmen, J. T. Tyldesley and W. Worsley, added a record 141, and in desperation Notts used all eleven of their players as bowlers.

The first Test was staged at Trent Bridge. A. O. Jones and John Gunn played but neither made much impact with bat or ball, though Jones took a brilliant catch in the slips to remove Layer, throwing himself forward and holding the ball with his left hand. A total of 31,622 paid for admission in the course of the three days. England won by 213 runs.

Wilfred Payton made his debut in 1905 and in batting style, with a strong defence and neat stroke-play, resembled George Gunn. He immediately impressed the Committee and from 1906 until 1930 he was a permanent member of the middle order. Payton could be relied upon to rally the side when the early batsmen failed, most of his runs coming on the leg side. In between the wars he set up a sports outfitters in Beeston. His brother and his son made brief appearances for the County. Three local amateurs turned out for Notts once or twice during the year. Walter Speak was a leg-break bowler from Attenborough; J. D. Barnsdale played for Nottingham Forest CC – and also Nottingham Forest FC – and was a director of the Raleigh Bicycle Company. J. P. Fellows played for Notts Amateurs as an all-rounder; he emigrated to Southern Rhodesia working in the tobacco industry. W. G. Heymann of Notts Amateurs played once.

With the authorities discouraging the overpreparation of wickets and the weather being kind, more matches came to a definite conclusion than for some years. Notts began well and whilst never seriously challenging the three front runners, Kent, Yorkshire and Surrey, were always comfortably placed and finished in fifth position. Wass missed four matches in midseason through injury and George Gunn missed the last five matches due to illness, so the overall results were, in the circumstances, very pleasing. For the first time three Notts bowlers captured over 100 wickets for the County – Wass, Hallam and John Gunn. Wass's great match was at Liverpool, where he bowled unchanged through both innings taking eight wickets in each; Lancashire were all out for 58 and 102, but Notts could muster only 48 and 52. Hallam won much praise for the accuracy of his bowling and so he was complementary to Wass. The fielding was described as brilliant and Oates, who dismissed ten men in the match against Middlesex, was regarded as one of the best wicketkeepers in England.

The Turner brothers, N. V. C. and R. H. T., both made their County debuts. They had gained reputations as batsmen in the Repton XI; R. H. T. was only 17 and still had one more summer of schools' cricket; N. V. C. was 19. The elder played occasionally until 1909 and as goalkeeper won an amateur International cap in 1920. R. H. T. remained involved in Notts cricket for many years and in the 1920s sometimes captained the side in Carr's absence. His final first-class game was in 1927.

Three professionals began their first-class careers in 1906. E. B. Alletson of Welbeck played in 118 matches up to 1914, but is remembered for his hurricane hitting, notably at Hove in 1911, when he made 189, his only Notts hundred. He was also a useful bowler but some doubt as to the legality of his action meant that he was not often used. Albert Iremonger, the very tall Notts County goalkeeper and brother of James was on the Trent Bridge staff from 1906 to 1910, but in 1911 took an engagement with Aberdeen; he was a useful all-rounder. C. C. James had joined the Notts staff in 1904 and remained until 1910 when he moved to Northumberland. A fair right-hand batsman, he played in 20 Notts matches, including one post-war game in 1921.

The combination of players which had been moulded together by Jones since the turn of the century proved irresistible in 1907. The factors that produced the success had an element of luck, in that the side was almost entirely injury-free and the weather produced wickets ideally suited to Wass and Hallam.

The Notts first-class bowling averages of the two bowlers tell much of the story:

	M	Overs	Mdns	Runs	Wkts	Avge
A. W. Hallam	21	857	280	1901	156	12.18
T. G. Wass	22	885	218	2328	163	14.28

Having arranged 20 matches, Notts had their game with Yorkshire at Huddersfield washed out, so of 19 games started 15 were won and the other four drawn. In the long run of success there were two matches which might have caused upsets. On 25 July the County went to Lord's and met Middlesex, who at that stage were the only other unbeaten side. Middlesex required 153 to win in the final innings and the wicket rolled out well, so that 44 was added before the first man was dismissed. Hallam, who bowled throughout the innings, then produced a brilliant spell, taking eight wickets and giving Notts victory by 13 runs. A

MIDDLESEX *v* NOTTINGHAMSHIRE

Played at Lord's, 25, 26, 27 July 1907

NOTTINGHAMSHIRE WON BY 13 RUNS

NOTTINGHAMSHIRE

	FIRST INNINGS		SECOND INNINGS	
★Mr A. O. Jones	lbw b Trott	10	c Trott b Tarrant	19
J. Iremonger	b Mignon	5	c Trott b Tarrant	23
G. Gunn	c MacGregor b Hearne	38	b Trott	37
J. R. Gunn	c Payne b Bosanquet	20	not out	23
J. Hardstaff	c Buxton b Hearne	44	b Tarrant	4
Mr G. T. Branston	c MacGregor b Hearne	46	c Bosanquet b Tarrant	0
Mr N. V. C. Turner	not out	73	st MacGregor b Tarrant	0
W. R. D. Payton	c Buxton b Hearne	28	lbw b Tarrant	0
†J. Stapleton	c Trott b Tarrant	7	c Trott b Tarrant	6
A. W. Hallam	b Tarrant	10	c and b Tarrant	4
T. G. Wass	b Mignon	1	c Trott b Tarrant	1
Extras	b 3, lb 6, w 1	10		0
Total		292		117

1st inns: 1-14, 2-20, 3-61, 4-87, 5-158, 6-181, 7-254, 8-273, 9-291
2nd inns: 1-41, 2-42, 3-90, 4-97, 5-97, 6-99, 7-99, 8-111, 9-115

BOWLING	O	M	R	W	O	M	R	W
Mignon	28.1	8	84	2	4	0	29	0
Trott	19	2	67	1	11	4	17	1
Bosanquet	9	1	38	1				
Tarrant	15	1	53	2	22.1	6	59	9
Hearne	24	11	40	4	14	7	12	0

MIDDLESEX

	FIRST INNINGS			SECOND INNINGS	
Mr P. F. Warner	c Jones b Wass	66		not out	59
Mr M. W. Payne	b Hallam	21	(5)	b Hallam	7
F. A. Tarrant	b Wass	7	(2)	c Stapleton b J. Gunn	24
Mr B. J. T. Bosanquet	c Iremonger b Wass	56	(3)	b Hallam	13
Mr E. S. Litteljohn	b Hallam	36	(4)	lbw b J. Gunn	7
Mr R. V. Buxton	c Jones b Hallam	2		c Branston b Hallam	0
Mr C. C. Page	c Branston b Hallam	31	(8)	c and b Hallam	24
A. E. Trott	b Iremonger	25	(9)	b Hallam	0
★†Mr G. MacGregor	run out	9	(7)	c Branston b Hallam	0
J. T. Hearne	not out	0		c Stapleton b Hallam	0
E. Mignon	c Stapleton b Iremonger	0		c Branston b Hallam	1
Extras	lb 1, nb 3	4		b 3, nb 1	4
Total		257			139

1st inns: 1-26, 2-47, 3-147, 4-155, 5-166, 6-207, 7-244, 8-256, 9-257
2nd inns: 1-44, 2-59, 3-72, 4-85, 5-89, 6-89, 7-123, 8-123, 9-132

BOWLING	O	M	R	W	O	M	R	W
Wass	34	13	91	3	7	2	29	0
Hallam	42	18	80	4	34.3	10	67	8
J. R. Gunn	13	1	47	0	27	11	39	2
Iremonger	8.3	2	26	2				
Jones	1	0	9	0				

Umpires: W. A. J. West and H. Bagshaw
★Captain; †Wicketkeeper

fortnight later Notts went to Gloucester and in a reverse role needed 231 in the final innings, when the three totals thus far had been 198, 151 and 183. Notts got home by two wickets with Payton undefeated on 91. From then on Notts only needed to avoid defeat in their final three games to secure the Championship. As it was all three were easy victories and the margin between Notts and second placed Worcestershire and Yorkshire was therefore large.

Whilst the bowling was left in the hands of two players, the batting was a collective effort. Seven men averaged over 25 in all matches, but the best was George Gunn with just 32.72, and he never made a single hundred. The enthusiasm in the field with few dropped catches, except for Branston who made up for his faults by some brilliant dismissals, and sharp outfielding gave the bowlers added confidence. The Nottingham public responded to the success on the field and a Shilling Fund was started when the title had been secured. This raised the unexpectedly high total of £810.9.6d. This was divided and presented to the players, each of whom was also given a silver cigarette case by the club's President, Sir Francis Ley. A. O. Jones received a silver rose bowl and in acknowledging the gifts he praised the way that all the players had played for the team throughout the season rather than for individual success.

As was now the custom Notts played the Rest of England at The Oval. Unfortunately only three, instead of four, days were allotted to the match and it was drawn. On the last afternoon Notts were set 353 in 210 minutes, which was impossible, though John Gunn cheered spectators by hitting an excellent hundred. The Club made a profit of £237.1s.3d on the year, despite wet weather reducing the Yorkshire home match to 70 minutes. The season signalled the end of an experiment that had proved useful to Notts since 1861, when the final match between the First XI and 22 Colts was staged. It was perhaps significant that none of the Colts, apart from Alletson who was on the groundstaff already, achieved anything. John Gunn took no fewer than 22 wickets in the game. In place of the Colts Trial, the Committee arranged a series of eight District Colts matches, which gave opportunities to many more players, but did not involve any greater expense.

A crucial match in the 1907 Championship campaign, for at the start both sides had yet to be beaten. With Middlesex 123 for six in their second innings, Notts appeared certain of defeat, then Hallam took four wickets for five runs and the game was won.

The Notts side of 1907 which won the Championship without losing a match, winning 15 of their 19 games. Left to right, standing: H. Coxon (scorer), J. W. Day, T. G. Wass, E. B. Alletson, G. Williamson (reporter), T. W. Oates. Seated: J. R. Gunn, J. Iremonger, A. O. Jones (captain), G. T. Branston, A. W. Hallam. On ground: W. R. Payton, J. Hardstaff sen, G. Gunn. (NCCC)

A. O. Jones's brilliant captaincy led to his appointment as captain of the 1907–08 MCC side to Australia and he took with him. J. Hardstaff. It was also agreed that he could use George Gunn on the tour if necessary, Gunn going out to Australia on account of his health. As it turned out, A. O. Jones missed much of the tour due to illness and Gunn, co-opted into the team, was an outstanding success.

After the great season of 1907, the following summer saw Notts drop back into the middle of the pack. Hallam's old problem with rheumatism resurfaced and though he played in all 20 Championship matches his shoulder was affected and the extra bite was lacking from his bowling. Wass bowled as well as the previous year, but Hallam's nagging length was missing from the other end. In view of Hallam's incapacity it was a very serious blow when John Gunn dislocated his thumb in the Whitsun match and missed the next seven games. Iremonger was pressed into service and his record was impressive with 57 wickets at 17 runs each, but he was better as a defensive bowler rather than one who wins matches. A. O. Jones criticised the team's fielding and particularly the number of dropped catches, but this department was only poor in comparison with Jones' very high standard.

The batting was rather patchy. Neither George Gunn or Hardstaff quite produced the form expected of them following their exploits in Australia, Iremonger had a modest summer and the young amateurs, Branston and the Turner brothers, did not contribute much.

The summary of the year was six Championship wins against seven losses. Two new players were tried, but one, the son of William Barnes, a medium-pace bowler appeared only against the Philadelphians. Clifton on the other hand came into the side in July and stayed in the eleven for the rest of the year. A fast-medium bowler from Eastwood, he looked promising without taking many wickets. He spent most of 1909 in the second eleven, but regained a first-team place in 1910; the following season he opted for a league engagement and spent the rest of his career in Lancashire or Merseyside, before dying in Liverpool in 1930.

C. A. L. Sutton, a regular second eleven medium-pace bowler, had played against the MCC in 1907, but most of his cricket was for Forest Amateurs. An architect, he designed the pavilion at Julien Cahn's Loughborough Road Ground in West Bridgford. Another bowler was Ben Taylor, who had first played for Notts in 1902. He played in five matches in 1908, but owing to his league engagement could not appear more frequently.

A wet summer combined with the visit of the Australians diverted the press attention from county cricket for much of 1909. The powers at Lord's preferred Edgbaston to Trent Bridge as a Test venue, so Nottingham was in the shade. The results achieved by the County did little to encourage comment; only six out of 20 Championship games ended in victory, whilst eight were defeats. Surrey were beaten at Whitsun by an innings, Wass taking eight for 64 in the second innings, but in the first innings an unknown slow-medium left-arm bowler, William Riley, returned figures of 9.4-2-27-6; it was Riley's third first-class match. He had joined the Notts groundstaff in 1908 aged 19 and was to remain until the close of 1913. His club cricket was for Newstead Colliery and in 1914 he was a professional with Oldfield CC in Staffordshire. Riley died from wounds received whilst fighting in Belgium in 1917. He is chiefly remembered not as a bowler, but as Alletson's partner in the record last-wicket stand against Sussex in 1911.

Hallam and Wass remained Notts' principal bowlers, but their records were nothing out of the ordinary and the batting was rather uneven. Jones failed to hit a hundred in Championship games and in the later matches dropped himself down the order. George Gunn was the only player to reach 1,000 Championship runs, but when chosen for the Lord's Test he failed and this seemed to upset him. It was expected that Hardstaff would improve; instead it was Payton who showed the way and he and Iremonger looked the best batsmen for much of the year. With Notts finishing tenth in the table, it was a relief when the season ended.

The next season, 1911, saw the County side in better heart. Jones found his batting once more; Wass topped 100 wickets and with few injuries the County were able to field an almost unchanged side for much of the year. Only Hallam failed – he was tried in a few matches and then left out of the eleven. At the end of the summer he opted for the Lancashire leagues, as did Clifton, who played in a dozen Championship games.

The sensation of the summer occurred totally unexpectedly at Hove on 20 May – the second Championship match of the season. Notts were 176 behind on first innings and by lunch on the last day had avoided the follow-on but were nine wickets down and little more than fifty runs ahead. The match was virtually lost and very few spectators hurried through their meal to view the fall of the last Notts wicket. In the next 40 minutes however Notts added 152 runs, 142 of them coming from the bat of Ted Alletson, and included in that were 34 – three sixes and four fours – off a single over bowled by Killick (it included two no-balls). Alletson's innings was made up of eight sixes, 23 fours, four threes, ten twos and 17 singles. It remains the most outstanding piece of fast scoring in the history of Championship cricket. Alletson's score was altogether 189, of which 47 was made before lunch, and the whole innings took 90 minutes. He was selected for the Test Trial which was scheduled for 1 June at Bramall Lane, but scored only 15 and 8. His batting for the rest of the summer was moderate and in fact he was left out of several matches. In 1912 he played in nine Notts games; in 1913 through most of the season; in 1914 a handful of matches. He never again hit a first-class hundred. The First World War brought his county career to an end and he returned to his job as a miner at Manton Colliery. Interest in his famous innings revived when John Arlott wrote a book on Alletson in 1957; a photograph in the book shows him with the bat which scored those 189 runs and made him famous for a day. Ted Alletson died in 1963 aged 79.

Nottinghamshire finished eighth in the Championship with

nine wins from 20 matches – Alletson's game was a draw. The bowling lacked someone with real speed and this was the reason why there was no serious challenge for the title. Herbert Wilson, a 19-year-old fast bowler from Eastwood, joined the staff and made his first-class debut against Sussex at Trent Bridge in July, but was not yet ready for top-class cricket. Ben Hind, a local Nottingham amateur, played once as an all-rounder when Iremonger was absent, but was not seen again. H. A. Hodges, who was in the Oxford rugby XV and had just taken a post as a master at Tonbridge, played against Derbyshire at Blackwell as a batsman. These three were the only new faces. A. W. Carr, the Sherborne amateur, and W. W. Whysall of Mansfield, had both made their debuts as batsmen in 1910 and were afforded further opportunities in 1911, but their careers belong essentially to the period after the war.

The wet summer of 1912 saw no change in the overall results for the County. In a season when so many matches were washed out, their five wins were sufficient to retain eighth place. The attack centred on Wass and Iremonger and the only help they

The Notts side in 1911, when E. B. Alletson played one of the most amazing innings of all time at Hove. From left to right, standing: W. Riley, T. W. Oates, G. M. Lee, J. Stapleton, W. W. Whysall. Seated: J. Hardstaff sen, E. B. Alletson, A. O. Jones (captain), J. Iremonger, W. R. Payton. On ground: G. Gunn, J. R. Gunn. (NCCC)

received came from Riley. The major success of the season was the defeat of the Australians due to some good bowling by Riley and an excellent innings from John Gunn. George Gunn had spent the winter with the MCC in Australia and, as in 1907–08, had had an excellent tour, playing in all five Tests. He was not however selected for any of the Tests in 1912 Triangular Tournament and his highest Championship score of the summer was only 76. Trent Bridge was the venue for one Test – South Africa *v* Australia – but the attendance was poor and this experimental competition between the three countries was deemed a failure.

Two players were given trials in the first eleven. The Warwickshire amateur, A. B. Crawford, who was living in Nottingham, was little more than a hitter and though playing in eleven matches, did little. The other trialist was a groundstaff youngster, Len Richmond, who bowled leg-breaks and googlies; only 5ft 6in tall he was to make his name in the 1920s as a rival to 'Tich' Freeman, the Kent spinner. It was a great pity that Trevor Branston, the Newark amateur, could not spare the time for county cricket, but as he was to say many years later, after his days at Oxford he had to do some work!

Eight wins and fifth place in the Championship table was adequate reward for the side in 1913. Notts were still unable to find a fast bowler of merit so the attack was limited to Wass, Iremonger and Riley. The batting remained strong though the eleven were handicapped by Jones' illness. The captain contracted a severe chill during the Old Trafford match in early May and so serious was his illness that he did not recover until mid-August, managing to play only in the final two fixtures of the season. Branston was persuaded to lead the side for two games and then Iremonger, as senior professional, took over, whilst the Committee searched for a suitable amateur. At the end of June Doctor Gauld, who played for Notts Amateurs, volunteered to fill the gap and appeared in eight consecutive games until Jones recovered. G. O. Gauld was from Aberdeen and had been a very successful fast bowler with his native county at the turn of the century. He had moved to Nottingham in 1909 to take up a medical appointment and was 39 when he made his first-class debut. His fast bowling days were over and he played as a lower-order batsman. Dr Gauld later hit the headlines in the post-bodyline rumpus of 1934–5. He was then Honorary Secretary to the County Club.

George Gunn recovered his batting form and came third behind Mead and Hobbs at the head of the first-class batting table; he was chosen as one of the *Wisden* Cricketers of the Year. No one in England was able to judge the length and speed of the bowling as quickly as Gunn, but his variable form was too much for the England selectors. The other really bright spot in the Notts batting of 1913 was a second-wicket partnership of 333 in about three hours by two young men, A. W. Carr and Garnet Lee. The match was against Leicestershire at Trent Bridge in late August. The pair joined forces with the score 38 for one on a rainy first day, raised the total to 144 for one and then on the second morning Carr went on to 169 in 185 minutes before being leg before. Lee reached 200, at which point Gauld declared. Notts won the game by an innings. It was to be the only hundred made by Carr in pre-war first-class cricket. Lee established himself as George Gunn's partner opening the batting, and completed 1,000 runs for the first time in 1913.

Apart from G. O. Gauld, two debutants in 1913 were Jim Horsley, the Forest Wanderers fast-medium bowler, and Willis Walker, whose father worked on the Wiseton estate in the north of the county. Horsley played just three matches for Notts, then in 1914 switched to Derbyshire, having a birth qualification for that county. He was very successful with Derbyshire, but his career in county cricket was erratic since he preferred to play in the Leagues, where more money was to be found. Willis Walker's career was almost entirely of post-war vintage, when he developed into a very reliable number three batsman for Nottinghamshire. At the time of his death in 1991 he was the oldest county cricketer, being the last survivor of pre-First World War Championship cricket.

Nottinghamshire cricket was a sad affair in 1914. Although clearly unwell A. O. Jones found the willpower to lead the County in the first six matches of the season. *Wisden* noted: 'Sadly wasted and looking wretchedly ill, he was a mere shadow of his old self.' On 10 June the effort became too much for him. He moved to the New Forest and spent the remainder of the summer under medical care. He died from consumption at his brother's home in Dunstable on 21 December 1914. After the war the County Club erected a suitable memorial on his grave in Dunstable.

Once again the Committee were unable to find a regular replacement as captain. Gauld stood in for five matches, Pearson-Gregory for two, Carr for three and Iremonger for the remaining five.

. A fast bowler was discovered — unfortunately Wass had a moderate summer, so the discovery did not overall strengthen the attack in comparison with 1913. The new player was Fred

Willis Walker made his debut for Notts in 1913 and played over 400 matches for the County. He was the last survivor of all pre-First World War cricketers, dying in December 1991. (NCCC)

Barratt, a miner from East Kirkby, aged 20. Although using only a short run-up, he had the height and the body weight to make the ball lift alarmingly. In addition he was a powerful batsman, whose hitting was to bring cheers from the crowds in the 1920s. He made his debut in the first match of 1914, taking eight for 91, the best analysis ever recorded for a Notts bowler in his first game. By the summer's end Barratt had 115 wickets at 21.71 runs each, including five wickets in an innings 10 times. It was the first time a Notts player had captured more than 100 wickets in his debut season. Another fast bowler to be tried for the first time was Wallace Bower of Eastwood. His first match proved to be his last, since he was unable to agree terms to return to Trent Bridge in 1919 and preferred to stay in League cricket.

Nottinghamshire won only five Championship matches and finished in tenth place; the season continued after the outbreak of war, but interest had vanished and several players, including A. W. Carr, found themselves called up in the middle of fixtures.

Financially the final pre-war summers were not a success and the club drifted deeper into debt. Many writers paint a rosy glow over the 'Edwardian' era, i.e. 1900 to 1914, but in terms of first-class county cricket the coffers were empty and the outlook bleak. Several counties were much worse off than Nottinghamshire, an

Notts in 1914, when they were forced to use five captains; Pearson-Gregory was to lead in only two matches. From left to right, standing: F. G. Roberts (umpire), H. Coxon (scorer), T. G. Wass, F. Barratt, W. R. Payton, G. M. Lee, M. Robinson (reporter), R. G. Barlow (umpire). Seated: J. R. Gunn, I. Iremonger, P. J. S. Pearson-Gregory (captain), G. Gunn, T. W. Oates. On ground: W. Walker, J. Hardstaff sen, W. W. Whysall. (NCCC)

extreme example being Worcestershire. The tradition of cricket in Nottinghamshire was however exceedingly strong and the Duke of Portland headed a Special Appeal Committee to make the club solvent. A large sum was raised, several patrons giving £100 or more.

Like all the other county clubs, Nottinghamshire agreed in 1915 not to stage any matches. It was felt that to play cricket when so many were losing their lives would be too frivolous.

Five Nottinghamshire players gave their lives for their country. The Rev Henry Staunton died in Mesopotamia, William Riley, H. A. Hodges, R. E. Hemingway and A. B. Crawford were all killed on the Western Front.

CARR'S MEN

DURING THE WAR THE PAVILION at Trent Bridge served as a military hospital and treated 3,553 wounded servicemen. Hostilities ceased on 11 November 1918. The County Club had been run with a skeleton staff – basically the Secretary and a groundsman, paid by the 600 members who continued to subscribe. The Duke of Portland's Fund raised sufficient money to remove the Club's debts. In the winter of 1918–19 the County Club negotiated with the Musters Family in order to buy the freehold of the cricket ground. The freehold included the Trent Bridge Inn, which the club had sub-let for many years to Messrs Bindley and Co for a rental of £350 per annum. C. W. Wright, as Trustee and Honorary Treasurer, acted for the Club and in a lengthy process which was not completed until the middle of 1919, the Cricket Club bought the freehold, then managed to sell the Trent Bridge Inn to Messrs Ind Coope, making a profit on the deal as a whole. The military hospital itself continued on a reduced scale through much of 1919.

At the instigation of Lancashire, it was decided to play two-day county cricket in 1919. The idea was quickly proved a nonsense and abandoned as soon as the season ended. The first task facing the Nottinghamshire Committee was the appointment of a captain. There were in fact very few candidates and A. W. Carr was the only available suitable one – it was as well that he accepted. Walter Marshall was re-appointed as coach and manager of the ground and took up his residence in the pavilion. Henry Turner remained the Secretary. The first-class programme for 1919 consisted of 15 matches and the County engaged only ten professionals on the groundstaff: George and John Gunn, W. R. D. Payton, G. M. Lee, F. Barratt and T. L. Richmond, all of the 1914 staff, plus the brothers William and Ben Flint, William Holmes and Herbert Wilson. Joe Hardstaff and Tom Oates returned to the Lord's staff, and were available for county matches under their agreement with MCC.

Fortunately the players were untroubled by injury and these 13 proved sufficient to carry out the Championship programme, the only others called upon being Dr Gauld, who played only against the Australian Services, and J. d'E. E. Firth. The latter had been a brilliant leg-break bowler at Winchester and in 1919 was at Oxford. He was tried in two Notts matches, but achieved little and though he had several trials at the university did not obtain his blue.

A. W. Carr took over the captaincy of Notts after the First World War and remained skipper until departing amid controversy in 1934. (NCCC)

Both the Flint brothers made their first-class debuts in 1919. 'Billy' Flint had been a half-back for Notts County since 1908 and was a useful all-round cricketer. He played on and off in the cricket side until 1929. His brother, Ben, a fast bowler, remained at Trent Bridge only two seasons and then moved into League cricket. His son, Derrick, played for Warwickshire and married the famous England lady cricketer, Rachael Heyhoe.

The two-day matches produced a mass of indecisive draws, 56 out of a total of 124. Only one match at Trent Bridge was decided. The system for the Championship table was exceedingly simple, the title being decided on the percentage of wins to matches played. Notts won five out of 14, producing 35.71 per cent and this placed the County third in the competition, but it was really a two-horse race between Yorkshire and Kent and four counties had percentages only marginally less than Notts.

The Notts attack revolved around Barratt, Richmond and Billy Flint. The first two often opened the bowling, a contrast between leg-breaks and fast-medium. George Gunn had an exceptional

W. W. Whysall, whose matches for Notts spanned 21 years from 1910 to 1930. He made over 20,000 first-class runs. (NCCC)

summer, rarely failing. As in the past he would be tedious one day and fast scoring the next. The end of the season found him top of the first-class averages. John Gunn, Payton and Hardstaff all returned good figures. Carr enjoyed driving fast bowling. A natural hitter, he was rewarded with a place in the Gentlemen's teams both against the Players and the Australians.

In August, the Notts Secretary, Henry Turner, was thrown out of his trap whilst crossing Trent Bridge. Aged 76 he did not recover from the accident and died whilst Notts were playing their final match of the summer. 'Wiggy' Turner had been secretary since 1895 and had seen the club develop financially from a rather haphazard organisation, which simply paid players on a match-to-match basis and had no accommodation, save the pavilion, for spectators, into a Test match ground with a groundstaff. His death rather caught the Committee by surprise. C. W. Wright took on the office pro tem. An advertisement was eventually published and some 100 candidates applied. F. S.

Ashley-Cooper, the well-known cricket historian, was appointed. A man of a retiring disposition and somewhat frail, it was soon clear both to Ashley-Cooper and the Committee that he was unsuitable. He resigned after six months and in September 1920, the Committee, as a stop-gap, appointed Captain H. A. Brown, who was Secretary of the local Boys' Brigade, which held their meetings at Trent Bridge. Brown had no knowledge of cricket, but he was a diplomat and efficient organiser – he remained in office for 38 years.

For 1920, the County increased its Championship fixtures from 14 to 20, as well as reviving the MCC fixture. The eleven changed in two major respects. W. W. Whysall returned to the staff. Within a few weeks of the start of the summer he had replaced Garnet Lee as George Gunn's opening partner. Whysall was a well-built man and his defence was solid. His stance was unusual in that he stood square on to the bowler. Though not elegant he put a great deal of power behind his strokes, scoring mainly through pulls and drives. Aged 32, he built up his reputation slowly, but did enough to tour Australia with MCC, and when he tragically died in 1930 still had many runs in him.

The other player to gain a regular place also went on to play for England. Sam Staples came from Newstead Colliery village. He had learnt his cricket with the local colliery side, but in 1919 had been a professional to the West of Scotland club. Tried in one of the 1919 practice matches at Trent Bridge he had bowled so well that he was offered a post on the staff for 1920, although, at 27, he was hardly a colt. He bowled medium-pace off-breaks with a beautiful action, though his run-up was a shuffling jerky affair. One critic described him as dancing a fox-trot as he ran up. By the end of the summer he had taken 44 wickets at 21 runs each and was the chief assistant to Barratt and Richmond, more or less replacing Billy Flint.

Richmond had a marvellous summer. He mixed googlies with his leg-spin and ended with 150 first-class wickets at 19 runs each. His two best matches were against Middlesex at Trent Bridge, when he took eleven for 84 and in the Bank Holiday game at The Oval when he took nine wickets and Notts, after being in arrears by 64 runs, surprised Surrey and won with three wickets in hand. Barratt had some good days, but more often than not he failed to rise above the ordinary.

George Gunn looked in good form when the season opened, but seemed to be troubled by ill-health; his brother John, now 44, topped the batting and hit four centuries. Hardstaff was consistent, but neither Payton nor Carr made runs with any regularity.

Notts were not represented in the MCC side which sailed for Australia in the autumn. Richmond was talked about, but his very poor batting and moderate performance in the field told against him.

Apart from Staples two other cricketers made their debuts. Frank Matthews from Willoughby on the Wolds was a tall right-arm fast bowler. He played in five matches with some success and continued on the fringe of the eleven in the two seasons which followed. His great year was 1923, but two years later he was overshadowed by the up and coming Larwood. Leaving Trent Bridge after the 1928 season he spent the rest of his career coaching in Scotland, for ten years being at Glenalmond School. Finally he retired back to his native village where he had a smallholding.

Lionel Kirk, a leading batsman in local club cricket, turned out in one match. He was appointed as Second XI captain in 1924 and from then until 1929 came into the First XI as captain when Carr was absent. He was a member of the County Cricket Club Committee until he died in 1953 and was President of the Club in 1951. Although born in Sheffield, he had moved to Gunthorpe in boyhood and had played rugby for Nottingham before the war.

Notts finished the season in seventh place having won half their 20 Championship fixtures. In 1921, the County slipped down to

Sam Staples took 100 wickets in a season five times and played 368 matches for Notts between the wars. (NCCC)

eighth and won ten out of 24 Championship games. The lack of young blood was a major concern. The days when clubs and schools through England used young Notts professionals as coaches and ground bowlers were long past. A glance at the details of the eleven who appeared throughout 1921 illustrates the difficulty:

George Gunn	born	1879	debut	1902	age	42
W. W. Whysall		1887		1910		33
John Gunn		1876		1896		45
A. W. Carr		1893		1910		28
J. Hardstaff		1882		1902		38
W. R. Payton		1882		1905		39
G. M. Lee		1887		1910		34
T. W. Oates		1875		1897		45
F. Barratt		1894		1914		27
S. J. Staples		1992		1920		28
T. L. Richmond		1890		1912		31

Barratt was the youngest member of the regular eleven. In June this exact eleven had what is regarded as the most embarrassing experience ever suffered by Nottinghamshire in a first-class match. The Australian tourists formed the opposition – they brought a strong side, only Armstrong missing from their Test eleven. On the Saturday the tourists made 675, even though they lost both openers cheaply. Macartney, coming in at number three, hit 345. The total remains on the record book because it is the most runs scored in a single day by one batsman ever in a first-class match; it is also the highest score made at Trent Bridge and the highest ever against Nottinghamshire. 'He simply did what he liked with the bowling' comments the report. His innings lasted less than four hours and he hit four sixes, one clean out of the ground, and 47 fours. On Sunday the two sides went to Welbeck Abbey for lunch. On Monday the County were bowled out for 58 and 100, the wickets shared by Gregory, McDonald and Mailey. The game was over in two days. Defeat was by an innings and 517 runs. The pitch had not changed over the weekend. There was no logical explanation for the catastrophe.

In general, however, the batting was good enough for county matches. The six main batsmen all had over 1,000 runs each. George Gunn topped the list; John Gunn was not quite as prolific but his bowling, which had been hardly used for ten years or more, was now in demand and he took 51 wickets. The bowling relied too much on Richmond and he suffered in consequence.

Staples had a poor year, and Matthews was very expensive on the few occasions when he was given a chance. Some idea of the lack of youth policy at Trent Bridge is provided by the fact that Charlie James was brought back to fill a vacancy in the side in June – he had not played in county cricket since 1910. T. H. Collins, a 26-year-old fast left-arm bowler, who had been on the ground staff in 1914, played in two games and created a minor sensation by taking a wicket with the first ball he bowled. He went to live in Hampshire in 1926 and in 1935 reappeared in county cricket, playing two matches for Hampshire. A local boy, his parents kept the Trent Bridge Post Office. A second 1921 debutant was Ben Lilley. Born in Kimberley he was a batsman-wicketkeeper with the local side, but directly after the war went to Scotland as a professional at Kirkcaldy. He played a few matches as Oates' deputy until 1925 when he became the regular County wicketkeeper. He was a more than useful batsman and reached 1,000 runs in a season twice, as well as opening the innings in some matches.

The great event at Trent Bridge was the first Test against Australia. This was also the first Test in England since the war. The England selectors included Len Richmond – he was the sole Notts representative and it proved to be his only international appearance. Hobbs and Hearne were unable to play and this weakened the home side, but it was a surprise when Australia won in two days by ten wickets. Interest in the match was tremendous and over 20,000 attended on each day.

The 1921 Derbyshire match was staged at Central Avenue, Worksop – the first time the County had used this ground for a Championship match, though in 1914 the idea of playing matches at Worksop had been mooted. The match proved a success and the venue is still used for county cricket.

Prior to the war the County had introduced a combined benefit scheme for all the players who served on the staff for a long period. This had been wound up and individual benefit matches re-introduced for the first time since 1903. In 1920 Hardstaff was the fortunate player. He received such poor support that the County Club decided to give him an extra £80, making a total of £300. Payton's turn came in 1921. This time receipts from the match did not even cover expenses and the club gave him £300 in compensation.

The Test match gave a boost to the County membership figures and a record 3,764 people joined or renewed their subscriptions. The cost of membership for a person living within ten miles of Nottingham was two guineas (£2.10) and this entitled him to free admission to the ground for all matches for himself, his wife and two ladies, or two sons under the age of 16.

Nottinghamshire confounded the critics in 1922 – fielding the same unchanged side, now twelve months older, they came second to Yorkshire in the table. The most memorable match was at Bramall Lane, where Nottinghamshire outplayed the Champions from start to finish. Yorkshire fell apart on the first morning facing the bowling of Richmond and Barratt. George Gunn and W. W. Whysall took Notts into a first-innings lead before a wicket fell, hitting 158 in 165 minutes. Barratt and Richmond repeated their first-innings effort, though Sam Staples removed the tail, and Notts won in two days by an innings. This was one of 17 Championship victories, many due to the bowling of Richmond, who created a new Nottinghamshire record taking 169 wickets at 13 runs each. His best figures in an innings were nine for 21 against Hampshire. He was well supported by Barratt, who also captured 100 wickets, and Sam Staples.

Hardstaff topped the batting, but mainly due to his large number of unfinished innings. Carr had a great year and gained a place on the MCC winter tour to South Africa as a consequence. Whysall and Payton performed usefully, but the brothers Gunn were not so successful and John Gunn was now beginning to show his 46 years in the field. In contrast to the two previous beneficiaries he was well rewarded and received £992.6.1d.

Two old faces reappeared in the side. R. H. T. Turner, the old Reptonian who had been in the Notts Championship-winning team in 1907, stood in when Carr was absent. Willis Walker, the middle-order batsman last seen in 1914, played in five matches and was invited to rejoin the staff for 1923.

There were in addition two entirely new men, but neither was destined for a long county career. G. N. B. Huskinson of Langar Hall had captained University College, Oxford, in 1921 but failed to obtain a place in the University side itself. His local cricket was mainly for Notts Amateurs and he played in the two opening matches of 1922 as a batsman. This was the extent of his county career, but he became a well-known figure in Country House cricket particularly with the Free Foresters and I Zingari. A good rugby player, he represented both Notts and East Midlands as well as playing for the Harlequins. He served on the Committee of the County Club and then as President. His particular interest was in the literature of cricket and he wrote essays on the game.

Albert Payton, younger brother of Wilfred, joined the Trent Bridge staff in 1921 and remained two years. His single first-class match was against Lancashire at Old Trafford. From 1923 to

1940 he was engaged on the Ind Coope Ground at Burton on Trent.

Although no new players seemed to be breaking into the first eleven, the Committee had made a major change in 1921 by appointing James Iremonger as coach, leaving Marshall to look after the ground. In the course of the next few seasons Iremonger was to pick out some promising youngsters capable of replacing the veterans.

Season 1922 had been without a Test match; in 1923 the West Indies toured England, but interest in their matches was minimal, and as in 1922 the Championship race was of paramount importance. Nottinghamshire continued the form showed the previous summer and it seemed as if the race for the title would be between them and Yorkshire. For the second year running Notts beat their northern neighbours on the latter's home ground, though this time at Headingley rather than Bramall Lane. It was a tight finish, and Yorkshire with five wickets left required 29 to win, but some good bowling by Staples caused the tail to collapse and Notts won by three runs. The batsmen had fought hard for runs throughout the game and on the first day Notts made only 197 runs. This result meant that the two counties were actually level at the head of the table through most of June. Notts, however, faltered whilst nothing deterred the Yorkshire side: that single defeat was their only reverse. Notts' final record was 15 wins and three losses from 26 matches.

The remarkable feature of the summer was the bowling of Matthews. The tall fast bowler had several useful analyses early on in the year, then created a new Notts record in the match against Northants at Trent Bridge. The visitors batted first and were dismissed for 77, Matthews taking eight for 39. Notts made 302 for three, then Carr declared after an hour's play on the second morning. Matthews responded by returning figures of nine for 50 and Notts won in two days by an innings and 109 runs. Matthews' match figures were 30-6-89-17, the best match analysis ever for Nottinghamshire. His complete season's figures were 115 wickets, average 15.30. He stood fifth in the overall bowling averages for 1923. It was curious that he should fail almost completely in 1924 – critics said that the wet wickets were against him, but in 1925 he again did very little. Matthews remains the bowling equivalent of Ted Alletson.

Richmond, Staples and Barratt all had good returns and John Gunn was scarcely used. The veteran however still hit over 1,000 runs, as did Payton, Whysall, George Gunn and Carr.

As in 1922 only two new players turned out for the first eleven and neither was to make a name in county cricket. Jack Bishop, a right-hand opening batsman, had been in the XI at Uppingham before the war and had played for Notts 2nd XI in 1909. He was captain, and the mainspring, of Radcliffe on Trent CC. He played against Derbyshire at Chesterfield, acting as captain in place of Carr, and in 1924 performed a similar role against Essex. His only other first-class game was in 1925. He captained Notts second eleven in 1926. During the Second World War he kept the Radcliffe Club going single-handed. Apart from cricket he was also a good tennis player and golfer. Bertie Marshall from Sutton in Ashfield was a fast bowler with New Hucknall Colliery. He joined the Notts staff in 1923, played once for the first eleven in that summer, then twice in 1924. In 1925 he was engaged to Perthshire and played Scottish County cricket until 1937, returning some remarkable figures: in 1929 he took 56 wickets at 5.6 runs each and this prompted Notts to ask him to play again, when Larwood was absent. He made one appearance only. In 1939 he turned out for Staffordshire, and after the war was for 20 years coach at George Watson's school.

In 1923 was published the first comprehensive history of the County Club. It was written by F. S. Ashley-Cooper and financed by A. W. Shelton, a Notts Committee member who had a great enthusiasm for the history and literature of cricket.

Anxious to encourage young cricketers, Nottinghamshire re-entered the Minor Counties Championship in 1924. In addition to the basic first eleven, there were enough young players on the ground staff, aided by one or two amateurs, to make up a strong second eleven. The pay for colts coming on to the staff was not over-generous, £2 per week, or £3 if you insisted, but in 1923 the Club made a loss, and despite being one of the leading counties, the financial situation was not very rosy.

Season 1924 was Whysall's, but the bowlers rather let him down. The Mansfield batsman finished sixth in the overall batting table with 1,852 runs at 46.30 per innings. The weather was miserable and wet wickets common – only three batsmen managed to average above 50. Whysall's stance, full face to the bowler, came in for much criticism, but he ignored the comments and played in the way which suited him. Carr, by completely different methods, had some brilliant innings; there was no finer driver of the ball in England. He made a brilliant 112 against Surrey at Trent Bridge and 134 in the famous match at the same venue against Middlesex.

In this game Notts hit 462 and then dismissed the opposition for 253. Carr enforced the follow-on and Middlesex's fortunes revived to the extent that they reached 358, J. L. Guise with 100 playing the innings of his life. Notts required 150 to win and the opening pair of Gunn and Whysall took the score to 72. At this point, the relatively unknown 'Gubby' Allen took six for 31 and Notts lost by 27 runs.

In general Notts won matches against the weaker counties, with the exception of the two wins over Kent. Curiously these latter victories were the only matches when Matthews showed anything like the form he had displayed in 1923.

The bowling was mainly in the hands of Barratt, Richmond and Staples, though Flint was employed more often and came second to Barratt in the averages. Richmond was overweight and his bowling did not possess the zip of previous years.

Two of the older batsmen felt their years. Hardstaff failed and was soon dropped from the side, Walker usually filling the gap; John Gunn scored 113 against Middlesex but averaged only 26.93. Oates missed a number of games and Lilley kept wicket adequately in his place. The discovery in the second eleven was Harold Larwood. He topped the bowling table and made his first-class debut against Northants in the third week of August. He was 19 years old.

Another youngster with a future making his debut in 1924 was Sam Staples' brother, Arthur. He had put in some good all-round performances for the second eleven. Young Staples, six years his brother's junior, was to gain a regular first team place in 1928. He was a stock bowler and very useful batsman at number six. Once or twice he was cited as a possible Test cricketer but his only representative cricket was for the Players *v* Gentlemen in 1929. He remained at Trent Bridge until the close of the 1938 season.

No Notts players represented England in the Test series against South Africa and no Test took place at Trent Bridge. Whysall was however chosen to go to Australia with the MCC side of 1924–25 as reserve wicketkeeper. The press were surprised and there ensued letters enquiring as to whether Whysall had ever kept wicket in a first-class match. He had in fact done so once or twice, but was normally found in the slips. He played in three Tests on the tour, but as a batsman.

The wet weather meant that the County Club again lost money. The Committee were anxious to encourage membership throughout the county, rather than just in Nottingham and its surroundings. To further this end the Committee was enlarged by five to allow a member from each parliamentary constituency. Harry Coxon, the long-serving County scorer finally retired. He reputedly scored every run which Arthur Shrewsbury made for the club, his first year as scorer being in the 1860s. Jack Carlin, the former County wicketkeeper, replaced Coxon.

A more important move off the field of play was the election of Julien Cahn to the Committee. Cahn had built up the family furniture business into one of the largest in England with chains of shops as well as manufacturing facilities. He had just established his own cricket team, which within a few years was to achieve first-class standard and, indeed, first-class status in some matches. The financial assistance Cahn gave to the County Club was to transform the arena over the next 15 years. His first donation was for the erection of a new scoreboard adjacent to the Ladies' Pavilion. This was built during the 1925 season. In the winter of 1925–26, Cahn spent £12,000 building his own private cricket ground in Loughborough Road, West Bridgford, a few hundred yards from Trent Bridge. The charming pavilion was designed by C. A. L. Sutton, the former Notts cricketer. Sir Pelham Warner described the ground as 'cricket de luxe'. Not content with one ground, Cahn purchased Stanford Hall on the borders of Leicestershire and laid out a second ground there in 1928 – there had been a rudimentary ground there before, but Cahn employed a professional groundsman and transformed it up to county standard. He was reputed to have spent £100,000 on his improvements to the 18th century hall and the park. This did not include the private theatre which was built some years later.

Yorkshire won the Championship for the fourth successive year in 1925. Notts were somewhere in the middle for much of the summer but then won their last six matches and rose rapidly upwards, too late to catch the front runners, but they finished fourth.

The final burst began on the college ground at Cheltenham. The first day was blank; on the second Richmond found the damp conditions just suited him and the home side were dismissed for 66, the leg-spinner taking seven for 30. Notts also struggled against the spinners – Parker and Mills – but managed 122, thanks to the muscle of Barratt, who coming in at number ten hit 36 in 15 minutes, which turned out to be the highest innings of the match. Richmond was again unplayable in the second innings, taking seven for 53, and thus Notts needed just 36 to win. The match was almost over in a day, only 30 minutes being required on the Friday to finish it off. Larwood played, but did not bowl a ball!

The County then went to Lord's. This time the damage was done by Sam Staples, with five for 28, as Middlesex were dismissed for 175. By the close of the first day Notts needed nine for a first-innings lead with seven wickets in hand. The match was

HAROLD LARWOOD

In post-war cricket, Lindwall, Miller, Thomson, Lillee from Australia, Marshall, Roberts, Holding, Walsh, Garner from West Indies and numerous others have played at Trent Bridge. Fast bowlers have come and gone, but the old stagers in Nottingham look on and comment: 'Fast, but not as fast as Larwood.'

It was his ability to combine speed with accuracy that gained Larwood a reputation which grows with the years. In the popular imagination he is always associated with the titanic struggle against Bradman, which erupted in the 1932–33 'bodyline' series in Australia. Larwood, however, was no nine-day wonder, created during that one torrid winter by Jardine and the English establishment, then conveniently cast aside when the press blew the series out of all proportion. For ten full summers from 1926 to 1936 (excluding 1933), Harold Larwood dominated English county cricket. In those ten years he topped the first-class bowling averages five times. No other 20th century fast bowler can claim such prominence over his contemporaries. Statham, for example, topped the bowling averages twice, Trueman only once, yet in 1927, 1928, 1931, 1932 and 1936 Larwood was England's leading bowler.

His Test career started during his first full season in county cricket, 1926, and in his 21 matches for England he took 78 wickets at an average of 28.41, a record that on paper does not do justice to his ability, but the wickets were by and large all in favour of the batsmen and every bowler had to work hard for his reward.

He never fully recovered from the effort he put into the 1932–33 series. In 1933 he was able to play in only one or two matches and after 1934 he bowled with a reduced run-up. A knee injury prevented him for appearing in many matches in 1938 and at the close of that summer his retirement was announced. In 1949 he emigrated to Australia, where he now lives. At the time of writing he is the senior living English Test cricketer.

won by three wickets, though it should be stated that Middlesex suffered a double disadvantage in the latter stages. Durston was forced to withdraw from the match due to the death of his mother and Allen was so badly bitten by a mosquito that he could neither bat nor bowl in the second innings.

Back at Trent Bridge Notts overwhelmed the weak Northants side. Barratt took seven for 53 in the first innings and Richmond nine for 55 in the second. Young Larwood was called upon to bowl only seven overs in each innings, but he showed unexpected talent with the bat, making 70. The match was over in two days. Notts completed their home programme by beating Gloucestershire. The victory was by six wickets and dropped catches did not help the visitors' cause. The last two games were at Worcester and Swansea. In the former match Larwood's pace was too much for the modest Worcestershire batsmen. He took five for 24 in the first innings and six for 17 in the second. Carr hit the highest score of the game. The pitch suited the bowlers and he simply took chances. The captain made 92 in 100 minutes, but was dropped seven times.

The Swansea wicket was designed for the bowlers. Richmond took five for 18 in the first innings and Larwood five for 33 in the second. The Notts batsmen also found life difficult and only careful innings from George Gunn and Payton enabled enough runs to be made.

Although Richmond (116 wickets, av 17.62), Barratt (94, 18.43) and Staples (101, 23.88) all had excellent figures for the year, the press was in no doubt where the major honours lay:

> The arrival of Harold Larwood, the 20-year-old Nuncargate professional, must constitute one the outstanding features of the season in Notts cricket. This somewhat diminutive recruit for a fast bowler has astonished everybody by his extraordinary pace and accuracy, and the fact that he had taken 73 wickets in the last 20 matches is an eloquent tribute to his ability. The County have not unearthed a more promising bowler since the palmy days of Tom Wass.

The batting prize went to Carr; in all first-class cricket he hit 2,338 runs, average 51.95 and came eighth in the table. His eight hundreds included 206 against Leicestershire at Aylestone Road and 101 for the Gentlemen v Players at Scarborough. He hit two sixes out of the ground and 14 fours, his innings lasting 150 minutes. In case it might be thought he batted against 'Festival' bowling, there was only one other score above fifty in either Gentlemen's innings.

Ben Lilley twice hit 1,000 runs in a season for Notts, as well as claiming 879 victims behind the stumps. (NCCC)

Walker reached 1,000 runs for the first time as did Ben Lilley, who had taken over from Oates. Payton, George Gunn and Whysall also hit 1,000, but John Gunn, having hit 166 against Hampshire at Southampton, seemed at the end of his long career.

The two newcomers to the side were S. H. Richardson and F. W. Shipston. The former had played for his native Warwickshire and had moved to Lowdham in the early 1920s. He was chiefly associated with Notts Amateurs CC and his only county game was against Cambridge University. Shipston joined the Trent Bridge staff at the start of 1925 as an 18-year-old right-hand batsman. He played some good innings for the second eleven and made his debut in the final match against Glamorgan. His county career lasted until 1933 when he decided to join the City Police Force, but in all he played in only 49 matches and scored two centuries. In 1957 he was appointed the Notts coach, a post he held for ten years.

Mindful of the Australian Test match scheduled for Trent Bridge in June 1926, the club began some major building work in the winter. Two new concrete stands were built in the area once reserved for Notts County's football spectators. The first was on Radcliffe Road, accommodating 3,256 spectators, and the second was a curved stand running from the new scoreboard on the Hound Road side to the Fox Road entrance and holding 4,724 spectators. The printing shed next to Parr's Tree was also dismantled and this allowed for some more seating on Bridgford

Road. Sad to relate, although 18,000 people arrived on the Saturday of the Test, there was just fifty minutes play. On Monday and Tuesday no cricket at all took place.

Nottinghamshire's record in the Championship of 1926 was adversely affected by the selection of Carr to captain England. At a time when amateurs were regarded as essential for the purposes of leading county teams, Notts were in the situation where Carr was the only amateur in the side. An amateur from the second eleven therefore had to be promoted in Carr's absence. R. H. T. Turner and Lionel Kirk filled the breach, but neither could inspire the team on the field to the extent that Carr did and the outcricket therefore suffered. Carr, in fact, missed eleven matches. The cause was not helped by the fact that the senior professional, George Gunn, also missed nine games due to a broken finger and that Larwood was selected for representative games and was absent from seven Championship contests.

In these circumstances the County was fairly happy to retain fourth place in the table, winning 13 out of 30 matches and losing seven. Weather ruined both fixtures with rivals Yorkshire, the game at Leeds being totally washed away. The major upsets of the season were the double defeats at the hands of both Lancashire and Kent. On the plus side, Essex were quite outplayed. Notts made 595 for four declared in reply to their opponents' 354 and then bowled Essex out in the second innings for 151. Whysall scored a double century for the first time in his career in this game, batting five hours. Glamorgan were also beaten by an innings when Walker, Payton and Flint all made centuries. Notts won the home Leicestershire match in brilliant style. From 13 for no wicket overnight, Notts required 406 on the last day for victory and hit off the runs in four hours, the last 90 coming from the bats of Payton and Sam Staples in 35 minutes.

Payton, Whysall, George Gunn, Carr and Walker all completed 1,000 runs in Championship matches; Richmond and Staples each picked up 100 wickets, though Larwood, due to the Tests, took only 96. The fast bowler however topped the averages.

In the Tests, England drew the first four games, then in controversial circumstances Arthur Carr was sacked as England's captain, being replaced by A. P. F. Chapman of Kent. The selectors announced: 'Mr Carr, who has not been in good health recently, generously offered to resign his place in the eleven.'

Carr replied with: 'I did not resign because of ill-health, I am as fit as a fiddle.'

England went on to victory in the final Test and took the Ashes

Notts in 1926. A. W. Carr was also England's captain, but was sacked after four draws against Australia. Left to right, standing: G. Gunn, B. Lilley, W. Walker, F. Barratt, A. Staples, H. A. Brown (Secretary). Seated: S. J. Staples, W. A. Flint, H. Larwood, A. W. Carr (captain), T. L. Richmond, W. R. Payton, W. W. Whysall. (NCCC)

for the first time since 1912. Larwood had a major part in England's success, dismissing three of Australia's main batsmen in each innings.

Despite the absences through Test match calls and injury, Notts called upon just one newcomer during the season. Walter Keeton, a 21-year-old opening bat from Mansfield Colliery CC, had joined the staff at the beginning of the summer and made his debut in July against Hampshire. He was however to serve a long apprenticeship before commanding a first team place, his opportunity not coming until 1931, when Whysall's death the previous winter left a gap. Once in the eleven he was very consistent and completed 1,000 runs every year until 1949, except 1935 (due to injury) and of course the war years. He remains the only batsman to score a triple hundred for the County and is for ever associated with Charlie Harris, as Notts opening batsmen each side of the Second World War.

The 1927 Championship battle was one of the most exciting for years. Throughout most of the season, Notts and Lancashire alternated as the leaders. Lancashire took over the premier position from Notts early in August and remained in the lead until 26 August when they were completely outplayed by Sussex – in a remarkable game, Lancashire were dismissed for 99 and 76, struggling against Tate and the Rev F. B. R. Browne; Sussex found few problems and made 371, Holdsworth and A. E. R. Gilligan both hitting hundreds. By a coincidence, in Sussex's previous home game they had played and been beaten by Notts. On 26 August at Trent Bridge Notts beat Glamorgan by 122 runs and this win coupled with Lancashire's defeat put Notts on top of the table.

Notts had two games to play, Lancashire one. The top of the table read:

				1st inns Points				
	P	W	L	W	L	Pos	Obtd	%
Nottinghamshire	26	11	2	8	4	208	144	69.23
Lancashire	27	10	1	10	5	216	149	68.98
Derbyshire	19	8	2	2	3	152	99	65.13

If Notts won their final two games the Championship was theirs, even if Lancashire were successful in their remaining fixture. If Notts and Lancashire lost their fixtures, then Derbyshire would take the title. If Lancashire won and Notts won one and gained first innings lead in the other, the two counties would tie for the top position.

The Notts team went to Ilkeston to play Derbyshire. Lancashire went to Aylestone Road to oppose Leicestershire. About 7,000 spectators turned out for the game on the Rutland Ground on the Saturday. Notts were without Larwood and Carr, but Derbyshire were dismissed for 141 and when bad light stopped play Notts were 78 for three, Payton 29 not out. Payton took his score to 136 on Monday and helped by Barratt and Sam Staples the total reached 353. Derbyshire were 107 for four in their second innings at stumps. By lunch on the last day Derbyshire were 41 runs ahead with one wicket remaining. Sam Staples took the final wicket in the second over after lunch and returned figures for five for 83. George Gunn was bowled first ball of the final innings, but Whysall and Walker knocked off the runs with ease. At Leicester, the home side put up a splendid fight and managed to draw the game with Lancashire. Notts had therefore performed as well as possible and only an outright defeat in the final match at Swansea would lose them the title now.

Larwood and Carr were still absent from the side which travelled to South Wales. On a soft pitch the Notts batsmen found Ryan's bowling tricky and made 233 of which George Gunn scored 68 and Payton 50. Glamorgan were 59 without loss at the close. Bates, the Yorkshire discard, batted very well on the second day, hitting 163 and the Welsh side made 375. The Notts second innings began badly, Mercer, making the ball swing, deceived both George Gunn and Walker, so that Notts went back to the pavilion with the board reading 23 for two, having successfully appealed against the light.

Just before Whysall and Payton went out to bat on the final morning a black crow flew low over the pitch. It was a fateful omen. With only three more runs added Mercer bowled Payton. Whysall followed soon afterwards. The rot set in. Seven wickets were down for 42. At ten past twelve it was all over, Glamorgan winning by an innings and 81 runs. Mercer took six for 31, Ryan four for 14.

The civic reception which was planned in Nottingham to greet the homecoming team was cancelled and the Notts supporters just could not believe the result: it was the only match Glamorgan won all summer. Notts had 12 wins and three losses.

Nottinghamshire were unlucky in that Larwood, when he had taken 91 Championship wickets at 16 runs each, wrenched his knee in the Test Trial at Bristol at the end of July and was effectively out of cricket for almost the remainder of the season; he did play in one later match, but failed to take a wicket and retired hurt. Although Larwood's presence might not have won the final game at Swansea, he would probably have prevented Surrey and Kent making large totals at the beginning of August. Carr's illness did not help Notts, but his batting was nothing like as good as in the previous years. George Gunn, Walker, Whysall and Payton all batted well, as did Lilley, who was regarded as one of the best wicketkeeper-batsmen in England.

The major support for Larwood in the bowling came from Barratt and Sam Staples. Richmond seemed to have lost his skill and was dropped for some matches. Arthur Staples and Flint both bowled usefully at times, but a lot of interest centred on a tall, gangling dark-haired youth who bowled left-arm spin.

The critics were right to keep their eyes on him, for William Voce became, within little more than two years, an England Test player. Voce came from Annesley Woodhouse, the village adjacent to Larwood's birthplace. He joined the Trent Bridge staff in 1926 at the age of 16 and that season had the best bowling record for the second eleven. His opportunity in the senior side came when Larwood was playing in the first Test Trial, and he had an immediate success taking five for 36. Larwood returned, but Voce stayed, being preferred to Richmond.

In 1928 Voce abandoned his slower deliveries in search of pace and swing. The journalists were not happy, but after some teething troubles, the left-arm bowler found success with his new style. He went on the 1929–30 tour to West Indies, and though missing out on the 1930 Ashes series, went abroad with MCC for a second time in 1930–31 to South Africa. He took most wickets in this winter series, but was to make himself a household name in the 'bodyline' series of 1932–33, as Larwood's bowling partner. Unlike Larwood, Voce made his peace with the authorities and returned to Australia in 1936–37, when he was easily England's most feared bowler. The Second World War interrupted his career, though he made a final trip to Australia in 1946–47. After retiring from full time county cricket he was appointed the coach at Trent Bridge and still turned out for the County in emergency until 1952. To outsiders he seemed a rather severe figure, but this impression was a deceiving one and he took a keen interest in cricket coaching and Notts cricket until his death.

Two other debutants of 1927 were A. B. Wheat and G. F. H. Heane. Wheat, a diminutive wicketkeeper who learnt his cricket with Selston Town, had joined the staff in 1923. A very competent performer behind the stumps, he was destined to be ever the blushing bridesmaid, but never the bride. Lilley's career did not finally end until 1937 and by that time Notts had a brilliant amateur batsman-wicketkeeper, C. R. Maxwell. As it happened Maxwell's first allegience was to Julien Cahn's team, so he was not often available for the County. Wheat filled the gaps. After the Second World War he was too old – born in 1898 – and he is now chiefly remembered as the County scorer, a post he occupied from 1947 until he died in 1973.

George Heane was to play a more dominant role than Wheat. He, like Maxwell, was employed by Cahn and then set up as a farmer in Lincolnshire. From 1927 to 1934 he played for Cahn, but only occasionally for Notts. In 1935 he was appointed joint-captain, in the aftermath of Carr's sacking, and from 1936 to 1946 he was sole captain of the side. A very useful all-round cricketer he had captained Retford Grammar School and his hard-hitting left-hand batting and right-arm medium-pace bowling proved effective at all levels of cricket up to first-class. In 1939 he gained a place in the Gentlemen v Players match at Lord's, and this was his best year in county cricket. He had the curious experience of playing in 145 consecutive matches for Notts, every one as captain. His style of leadership was suitable for the 1930s, but after the war was out of place and he therefore retired from first-class cricket rather earlier than expected.

Prospects for 1928 seemed rosy. With the young shoulders of Larwood and Voce to lead the attack and time looking kindly on George Gunn and Payton, allied to the experience of Carr,

Whysall, Walker and Lilley in the batting, plus Sam Staples and Barratt as bowlers, Notts were favourites to secure the title.

They were brought down to earth with the opening match at Trent Bridge. Sussex were the guests. On a beautiful wicket, Tate dismissed Notts for 229. The Notts bowlers were innocuous. Bowley and Parks, opening the Sussex innings, put on 125 before stumps were drawn. On the second day they went on to 226 in 195 minutes. Sussex ended with 516 for eight declared. Notts tumbled to an innings defeat. This match however was nothing to the embarrassment Surrey inflicted during the Whitsun fixture. The Notts innings was exceedingly odd. George Gunn made a century, the rest of the batsmen failed, then Arthur Staples at number nine and Barratt at number ten, both hit 90s. Barratt hit 96 in 85 minutes, including a six which bounced on the top step leading to the pavilion. The total was 457. Hobbs made his 150th first-class century, but aside from the Master, Surrey did little and Notts obtained a lead of 169. Carr then made a crucial error of judgement. In failing light on the second evening he decided to bat again rather than enforce the follow-on. At the close Notts were 15 for four in 30 minutes batting. On the last day Fender and Peach routed the remainder of the side: all out 50. Larwood removed Hobbs for a duck with the second ball of Surrey's final innings but Sandham played sensibly and Surrey won by seven wickets.

At this point Notts were 13th in the table, having played five matches and won one. The rest of the summer saw a praiseworthy recovery, but Notts had begun too low to catch the leaders, Lancashire and Kent, and settled in the end for third place. Creditable enough, but when the County was reaching for the title, not sufficient.

No less than 13 Championship games ended in victory. Notts made no mistake this year against Glamorgan, winning by an innings at Trent Bridge and by ten wickets at Cardiff Arms Park. They turned the tables on Sussex at Hastings, though with only two wickets to spare. Though both matches with Lancashire were drawn, and the other front runners, Kent, were beaten by nine wickets at Trent Bridge. In this match Notts won in two days, George Gunn batting at his best with an undefeated 100 in 95 minutes.

One of the sensations of the summer was the Notts *v* Warwickshire game at Coventry. Short boundaries and weak bowling enabled Notts to score 541 for three on the first day. George Gunn, Whysall and Walker, the first three in the batting order, all made 100s. On the second day the total rose to 600 after, in all, 380 minutes batting. Barratt then went on to score his own 100 in 70 minutes batting. Carr declared at 656 for three. It was the first time in Championship cricket that four batsmen had scored centuries in one innings. Carr received telegrams of congratulation and wired back: 'Time permitting, would have got a thousand!'

Warwickshire batted out the rest of the second day; rain prevented any play on the third.

In all first-class matches no fewer than seven Notts batsmen completed 1,000 runs and 27 hundreds were hit in the Championship alone. Barratt completed the 'double' for the only time in his

Charlie Harris, one of the best-loved and most eccentric of Notts cricketers. His 362 first-class matches were all for the County, for whom he scored nearly 19,000 runs. (NCCC)

career; Larwood was easily top of both the Notts and first-class bowling tables. In the Championship he averaged 14.10 with 116 wickets, the next best was Sam Staples with 23.49 and 91 wickets; in all first-class matches Larwood still averaged 14, the next best in England being 18 by A. P. Freeman of Kent, and no one else averaged less than 19. This gives a clear indication of the margin between Larwood and the rest of the 1928 English bowlers.

The two new players introduced into the Notts side during 1928 were both to play a large part in the cricket of the 1930s. C. B. 'Charlie' Harris was born in Underwood in 1907. His brother George had joined the Trent Bridge staff in 1923 and Charlie followed two years later. George never played for Notts, but left Trent Bridge and joined the police in South Wales. He much later played briefly for Glamorgan. Charlie Harris, a right-hand batsman of extreme moods and, occasionally, a very useful bowler, gained a regular place in the Notts team in 1931 and soon became associated with Walter Keeton, as Notts opening batsman. Robertson-Glasgow paints the picture:

> For Harris is a dreamer. He is a strange addition to Walter Keeton as they walk out to open the innings; Keeton strung up, concentrated, quick-glancing; Harris serenely distrait, revolving idealistic strokes against an attack that will never occur; lagging sometimes a pace or two behind, like a boy with a parent on an unwilling Sunday walk.

Harris was a joker. The stories about him abound and, unlike fishermen's yarns, which grow in the telling, most of those concerning Harris seem to be true: balancing his false teeth on top of the wicket as an added attraction to the bowler; coming out to bat with a lighted candle when he felt the light too poor; putting on a false moustache and posing as a reporter, then conducting an in-depth interview with some poor cricketer making his first-class debut. The crowds loved his batting habit of playing dead bat strokes to a succession of deliveries as if the wicket was treacherous, then for no apparent reason launching into several delightful boundary shots, before going back to his dead bat existence.

His final match was against Hampshire in 1951, but his last season or two was marred by increasing ill-health and he died in August 1954 aged 46, deeply mourned by his admiring public.

The second young debutant was George Gunn's son, usually known as Young George. He was destined to play in his father's shadow. He joined the Trent Bridge staff from Nottingham High School in 1925 at the age of 19 and was a right-hand batsman and leg-break bowler. After some good performances with the second eleven, his chance came against the West Indies at Trent Bridge in July 1928 – during this match King George V and Queen Mary visited the ground and were introduced to both teams. It was the first time since the days of the Dafts that a father and son had played for Notts in the same side. As young George came in to bat the report noted:

> It was an ordeal for the boy, for he had to face Constantine with the new ball, but his responsibilities seemed to rest very lightly upon him. He stayed only ten minutes and made only six, but he was there long enough to show us a nice straight bat, wielded with a sense of touch, an unruffled mien and some of the dear familiar mannerisms of Gunn the elder.

Young George gained a regular place in the County side in 1932 and remained until the outbreak of war. He reached 1,000 runs five times, usually batting at number five, but his leg-breaks tended to be expensive. He did not return to Trent Bridge after the war, save for one game in 1950, and acted as a coach at various schools. He died as the result of a motor-cycle accident in 1957 aged 52. His father said of him: 'If he was half as good as he thought he was, he would have conquered the world.'

Larwood and Sam Staples were chosen to tour Australia with the 1928–29 MCC side; Staples was struck down with muscular rheumatism soon after arriving in Australia and returned home without playing in a match. Larwood began the tour well, but the hard wickets gradually took their toll and against a formidable batting line-up, all the England bowlers worked hard for their wickets. Fortunately the Australian attack was made to work even harder and England won the series. Whysall and Lilley went off to Jamaica with Julien Cahn's side; George Shaw the Trent Bridge dressing room attendant went along as well to look after the baggage. The team were away from England for most of February and all of March and played six games in Jamaica.

Playing an almost unchanged side for the third year running, Notts finally clinched the Championship. The regulations had been altered compared with previous recent summers and in 1929 all counties had to play 28 matches. This eliminated the need for percentages: counties still played more than 28 games if they wished and these extra games were 'friendly first-class matches'. Two defeats were suffered, the first at Lord's in late May and the second at Bramall Lane in mid-June. Derbyshire took an early lead in the table, but Notts came to the front in June and from then on were there or thereabouts. Gloucestershire moved ahead in mid-August; Notts, having a match in hand, soon rectified this and they went to Ilkeston for the final match on 31 August as leaders. The combination was slightly altered from the position before the fatal Glamorgan game of 1927. This time, in addition to Notts having to avoid defeat, Yorkshire had to win their match on the same dates. As it happened Yorkshire were defeated, and the rain forced a draw at Ilkeston, so Notts took the crown.

The Lord Mayor of Nottingham invited the Notts team to come to the Council House straight from the match at Ilkeston and a large crowd gathered in the Market Square as the bus conveying the team arrived. Carr, using a megaphone made an impromptu speech:

> Ladies and Gentlemen, it is most awfully nice of you to come and welcome us like this, and we appreciate it very much. We have tried very hard this year to win the Championship and if you only realised what a great strain it has been, you would not ask me to stand here and speak much longer.

The bowling strength was the reason why Notts won the title, the advance of Voce being the most marked individual factor. He used both styles of bowling according to the circumstances, at times fairly fast, swinging the ball, at others using his height and spin to great effect. His wicket tally in Championship matches nearly doubled compared with 1928 and his average fell by eight runs per wicket. In the overall first-class table Voce came fourth, behind Richard Tyldesley, J. C. White and Goddard. He took 120 wickets at 17 runs each. His best return was 14 for 43 against Northants at Trent Bridge, but he also took ten wickets in a match against Worcestershire and Warwickshire. Larwood felt the effects of his winter in Australia and as he also missed several games due to representative calls, he managed only 80 Championship wickets at 18 runs each. Barratt took over 100 wickets and though he was now fairly bulky he still bowled with pace and made the ball get up alarmingly on occasion. Sam Staples had happily recovered from his winter illness and took 75 Championship wickets at 22 runs each; his brother improved beyond anything he had previously achieved and took 64 wickets at 21 runs each. The County therefore had five bowlers, all with averages below 23. In addition the young Shrewsbury bowler, R. D. F. Bland, was given an opportunity when Larwood was unavailable and looked a useful asset.

Whysall stood at the head of the batting, making over 2,000 runs in Championship cricket at an average of 54. His best innings was 244 against Gloucestershire at Trent Bridge when nearly

NOTTS (Champion County) *v* THE REST OF ENGLAND

Played at The Oval, 14, 16, 17, 18 September 1929

REST OF ENGLAND WON BY EIGHT RUNS

REST OF ENGLAND	FIRST INNINGS		SECOND INNINGS	
J. B. Hobbs	c Larwood b Barratt	2	b Bland	68
A. Sandham	c G. Gunn b Larwood	82	lbw b Larwood	15
F. E. Woolley	b Barratt	106	c Whysall b S. J. Staples	15
J. O'Connor	c Bland b Larwood	6	c G. V. Gunn b Bland	10
*Mr R. E. S. Wyatt	c Barratt b S. J. Staples	85	b Barratt	11
M. Leyland	c Whysall b Bland	17	c and b Bland	75
†L. E. G. Ames	c Whysall b S. J. Staples	15	b Barratt	0
Mr R. W. V. Robins	b Bland	37	st Lilley b S. J. Staples	45
M. W. Tate	c Carr b Bland	32	c Whysall b S. J. Staples	7
T. W. J. Goddard	b Larwood	13	not out	13
E. W. Clark	not out	1	c Lilley b S. J. Staples	16
Extras	b 1, lb 2	3	b 2, lb 5	7
Total		399		282

1st inns: 1-5, 2-159, 3-170, 4-209, 5-244, 6-272, 7-337, 8-383, 9-397
2nd inns: 1-31, 2-77, 3-105, 4-114, 5-135, 6-135, 7-242, 8-246, 9-260

BOWLING	O	M	R	W	O	M	R	W
Larwood	18	3	54	3	15	1	73	1
Barratt	21	1	83	2	18	2	50	2
S. J. Staples	36.1	7	146	2	18.5	2	63	4
Bland	24	2	106	3	13	0	75	3
G. V. Gunn	2	0	7	0	2	0	14	0

NOTTS (CHAMPION COUNTY)	FIRST INNINGS		SECOND INNINGS	
G. Gunn	b Tate	8	b Robins	96
W. W. Whysall	b Clark	97	c O'Connor b Goddard	50
W. Walker	c Tate b Clark	1 (4)	c Sandham b Robins	0
*Mr A. W. Carr	b Woolley	91 (5)	b Goddard	6
W. R. Payton	c Ames b Clark	21 (6)	c Hobbs b Robins	32
†B. Lilley	c Tate b Clark	10 (7)	b Goddard	5
F. Barratt	c Wyatt b Woolley	54 (8)	c Sandham b Clark	45
G. V. Gunn	st Ames b Robins	6 (3)	lbw b Robins	17
S. J. Staples	lbw b Robins	21 not out	18	
H. Larwood	st Ames b Robins	11	c Woolley b Robins	11
Mr R. D. F. Bland	not out	15	c Woolley b Robins	1
Extras	b 17, lb 10, nb 2	29	b 14, lb 13, nb 1	28
Total		364	309	

1st inns: 1-21, 2-35, 3-204, 4-229, 5-256, 6-265, 7-300, 8-336, 9-339
2nd inns: 1-88, 2-114, 3-122, 4-141, 5-200, 6-209, 7-271, 8-279, 9-299

BOWLING	O	M	R	W	O	M	R	W
Clark	25	5	69	4	25	5	73	1
Robins	26.1	6	108	3	27.3	3	89	6
Tate	21	2	64	1	13	4	38	0
Goddard	14	2	52	0	23	5	56	3
Woolley	9	0	42	2	4	0	12	0
Wyatt					4	0	13	0

Umpires: J. Hardstaff and J. Stone

everyone else failed – the total was 396 and Walker the only other player to exceed 50. Payton, now aged 47, missed several matches due to a strained thigh muscle, but came second to Whysall and his 169 against Lancashire, a faultless innings against a strong attack, was the highest of his career.

George Gunn remained remarkable. He celebrated his 50th birthday with an undefeated innings of 164 – it was the 54th hundred of his career and he and Whysall added a century first wicket stand for the 35th time. The match was at Worcester: a week later Worcestershire came to Trent Bridge and George Gunn was formally presented with a variety of gifts from the Lord Mayor, The County Club, his fellow players and the captain. Gunn hit 1,532 Championship runs at an average of 40.31. Walker also completed 1,000 runs.

As was the custom Nottinghamshire went to The Oval at the end of the season to play the Rest of England. It was a great finale to the year, Notts losing by just eight runs.

Bland was the only new player to come into the side. An 18-year-old left-arm medium-pace bowler, he played for Notts Amateurs and was a regular member of the Notts second eleven for several years, but his first-class appearances, apart from one game in 1934, were confined to 1929, 1930 and 1931.

The tourists in 1929 were from South Africa and five Tests were staged, though Edgbaston, rather than Trent Bridge, was the venue for the first. Larwood played in three matches and Carr led England in the last two games.

A SLOW DECLINE

THE AUSTRALIANS TOURED IN 1930. Anxious to maintain the quality of Trent Bridge as a Test match venue, the County Club had made several improvements since the 1926 Test. The new indoor nets, replacing a dilapidated timber structure, had been opened in January 1928, half the cost being borne by Julien Cahn. In the winter of 1929–30, the double-deck West Wing stand was built. The Fox Road stand was also erected and a new Secretary's office with staff room above built. Much of the cost of this work was also borne by Sir Julien Cahn – he was made a baronet in 1929. In the spring of 1930 the double-deck Radcliffe Road stand was also built. The seating capacity was 17,300, but this included forms on the grass for 1,160 spectators. If standing spectators were added the capacity would rise to 25,000.

The Championship of 1930 proved a very close one, only six points separating the first four teams. Notts were in second place for much of June, with Lancashire in the lead. On 27 June Kent went in front, but on 5 July Notts moved ahead, Kent being second and Lancashire third. By mid-August Notts had dropped to third place, Lancashire leading the table from Yorkshire in second place. On 30 August Lancashire completed their programme with victory over Essex and Gloucestershire, Yorkshire and Notts, in that order were second, third and fourth with one match each to play. Notts won their fixture, against Worcestershire at Trent Bridge, inside two days when Larwood finished his Championship season with eight for 33 and Worcestershire were all out for 60. Notts thus moved briefly into second place but on the next day Yorkshire and Gloucestershire both won and therefore overtook Notts.

Larwood was in great form all summer and his 89 Championship wickets cost just 12 runs each. It was unfortunate for Notts that, due to Test match calls and injury, he missed ten matches. Sam Staples bowled as well as in 1929, but Voce and Barratt had comparatively poor seasons and for this reason Notts found dismissing counties twice hard work – 18 matches were drawn, against nine wins and one loss. Both matches with Lancashire as well as those with Yorkshire were drawn; Notts did not play Gloucestershire.

The batting averages were remarkable in that all eleven regular players averaged more than 20; except when Bland substituted for Larwood, therefore, the County had no tail.

The Trent Bridge pavilion in 1930, when many improvements were made to the ground to maintain its Test match status. (NCCC)

Whysall once more headed the table and in all first-class matches reached 2,000 runs, including eight centuries. His success earned him a place in the final Test of the summer. Walker, Payton and George Gunn all had good seasons.

Larwood was the single Notts representative in the Trent Bridge Test. England won by 93 runs and this victory was in some small measure due to a totally unknown Notts cricketer, S. H. Copley. Australia required 429 to win in their final innings. After some early misfortune, McCabe joined Bradman and the pair seemed to master the bowling completely. The total rose to 229, when Copley, who was fielding substitute for Larwood, took a brilliant catch low down at mid-on to dismiss McCabe. The young groundstaff lad dived full length to reach the ball and though rolling over managed to hold on to it. From then on no-one was able to stay with Bradman and the match ended with about an hour to spare.

S. H. Copley made his first-class debut for Notts eight days after the Test. He played against Oxford University, but achieved little. It was to be his only match for the County. Born in Hucknall in 1905 he had joined the Trent Bridge staff in 1924. A useful right-hand batsman and slow left-arm bowler he left Nottingham in 1931 and in 1933 became professional at Cupar. From 1939 until he retired he was coach at King William's

JOSEPH HARDSTAFF junior

In the four Test series in England immediately preceding the Second World War, Hardstaff had a batting average of 67.00, his best series being 1938 with 92.00 and his worst 1936 with 48.00. He was aged 28 when war was declared and the period when batsmen are normally at their most prolific, in their early 30s, was for Hardstaff a complete blank.

Joe Hardstaff junior was frequently called one of the handsomest of batsmen, a description which applied both to his person and the style of his stroke-making. (NCCC)

It might be said that the two other bright stars of the late 1930s also lost six summers, but when play restarted in 1946, both Compton and Hutton were still in their 20s. After the war Hardstaff was not popular with the selectors. He played in bits of four series, averaged 47, but despite several years of press comment headed 'Why Not Hardstaff?' the selectors looked the other way.

For Nottinghamshire only George Gunn, with many more appearances, has scored more runs and no one made run-getting more pleasurable to the onlooker. His cover drive was the stroke most enjoyed, but his neat footwork enabled him to position himself correctly for all the orthodox shots. His double century against India in 1946 is regarded by many as a typical Hardstaff innings. His innings of 126 against Kent in 1937 when he reached a hundred in 51 minutes is equally notable and was not made, as so many fast innings today, against 'joke' bowling.

On a different plane Hardstaff was the last of the line of famous cricketers from the small group of colliery villages just south of Kirkby in Ashfield – Fred Barratt, Sam Staples, Harold Larwood and Bill Voce all preceded him. The Nuncargate Ground where he and his fellows learnt their cricket still exists, with the appropriately named 'Cricketers Arms' guarding the lane to the ground.

College, Isle of Man. His famous catch was no fluke, for he was regarded throughout his cricketing life as a brilliant fieldsman.

Five other cricketers made their debuts for the County during 1930. Joe Hardstaff, the 19-year-old son of the former England cricketer, played late in the season and his potential was quickly recognised. His stylish batting was to grace Trent Bridge for 25 years and he was also to play successfully for England. H. Ramsay Cox was also 19. He came from Radcliffe on Trent and had been in the Uppingham Eleven for two years. Up at Cambridge he played first-class cricket for the university and just missed his blue. In his early years he played for Notts Amateurs, but in 1931 switched to Nottingham Forest and was a tower of strength to that side, as both batsman and bowler for over 25 years. He captained Notts second eleven in the 1950s and between 1930 and 1954 made fleeting appearances, with some success, in the County side.

Another amateur to be tried was S. D. Rhodes, son of a member of the Notts Committee; an opening right-hand batsman he had been in the eleven at Dean Close School for four years and in 1928 had begun a long association with Julien Cahn's XI. He played for Notts twice in 1930 and five times in 1931, but that seemed to be the end of his county career. However in the captaincy crisis of 1934–35 he was appointed joint-captain with Heane for 1935. He played in 12 matches that year without finding his true form. His last first-class game was for Sir Julien's side in Ceylon in 1937. In 1946 he turned out for Hertfordshire, being a member of Harpenden CC.

Jack Reddish played in the same match as Copley and like Copley it proved to be his only first-class game. In the mid-1930s he went to Guernsey, where he was PE master at Elizabeth College until about 1970. He was better known as a soccer player, turning out for both Tottenham Hotspur and Lincoln. The final debutant of the summer was the left-arm spin bowler G. W. Robinson. He played in 21 matches for Notts, but left the staff at the end of the 1933 season. He joined the police force, but in 1936 returned to the County side for a match or two as an amateur and bowled so well that it was thought that the County made a mistake in allowing him to leave.

A serious road accident dealt a fatal blow to Notts' chances of regaining the Championship title in 1931. The accident occurred the day before Notts were scheduled to play a vital Championship game against Yorkshire at Bramall Lane. About 9.30 in the evening young George Gunn was driving a lorry bringing the team's baggage from the match at Leicester. In Loughborough

Road, West Bridgford, only a mile from Trent Bridge, the lorry appeared to skid and collided into Larwood's car. The car overturned; the lorry also finished upside down. In the car with Larwood were Ben Lilley and Sam Staples. Other members of the team in a following car came to the assistance of their dazed colleagues; young Gunn was rushed to hospital, but none of the injuries were very serious. All those involved were clearly badly shaken.

Lilley was well enough to play the following day, but Notts were without Larwood, Sam Staples and young Gunn. Arthur Staples hit an excellent 131 against Yorkshire, but Notts spent nearly all day making 288. Notts made Yorkshire fight for runs on the second day, but the latter gained first-innings points and rain prevented a finish to the game. The five points claimed by Yorkshire for first-innings lead meant that Notts now led the Championship but Yorkshire were only four points behind.

The next two matches were also played without Larwood and Sam Staples. The first, against Gloucestershire, was another draw, so, with Yorkshire winning their fixture on the same days, the Tykes moved to the top of the Championship. The second match was the return with Yorkshire at Trent Bridge. The Notts Committee took a chance by including two youngsters – Charlie Harris, who had not played in a Championship game for two years and Archie Oates, the nephew of the old wicketkeeper and a fast bowler. In addition to the absence of Larwood and Sam Staples, Bill Voce was now unable to play through injury and Arthur Staples, owing to a strain, was unable to bowl. A win for Notts in this match was now crucial, since, if Yorkshire were successful they would take a commanding lead in the table. On the first day Notts were all out for 201, of which Walker made 82. Incredibly Carr opened the bowling when Yorkshire went in and clean bowled Sutcliffe in his second over. Harris then removed Mitchell and Leyland, Robinson had F. E. Greenwood caught behind and Yorkshire went to bed at 80 for four. Holmes, however, was undefeated and made 133 before Yorkshire declared as soon as a first-innings lead was obtained. Batting a second time, Notts fell apart against the 46-year-old Emmott Robinson. The veteran took seven for 27 and Notts were all out for 95. Yorkshire coasted to a nine-wicket victory. Yorkshire, with 17 matches played, were now 21 points ahead of Notts and Gloucestershire had moved into second place.

The Notts match which followed made history, but as it only collected five points for the County as Yorkshire continued on their winning way, the hopes of the title faded. The game was played at Edgbaston and the home side spent the day making 394 for three off Notts' depleted attack. On the second day they batted on, until Carr took a hand – he bowled lobs. Wyatt, the Warwickshire captain, declared after five underhand overs, which in fact conceded only 31 runs. By the close of the second day, Notts were 163 for one, old George Gunn 77 not out, Walker 9 not out. Old George was finally out after seven hours ten minutes for 183, the score then being 383 for seven, and the not out batsman at the other end was young George. Charlie Harris came to the crease and the pair took the total to 512 bringing Notts first innings points at 6.15. The players prepared to leave the field, but Charlie Harris persuaded Wyatt to stay and allow young George to reach 100 – he was 95 not out. Young George made four from the next over and a single off the following one. It was young George's first county hundred and the first time that a father and son had hit hundreds in the same innings of a Championship game.

Young George entered the pavilion and shook hands with his father: 'Well played, dad.' 'Well played, my boy.' The reporter noted: 'with the phlegmatic temperament of the true Englishman, they treated the achievement quite modestly.'

The road accident, allied to other injuries, meant that the rest of the summer – the whole of August – was of little note. Of the eight matches played, Notts won one, lost one and drew six. The bowling, without Voce, Larwood and Sam Staples was moderate. Sam Staples missed 11 matches, Larwood eight and Voce five. In addition Carr and George Gunn both missed six. The almost ever-present teams of previous post-war summers had gone. Notts used 21 players in their 28 Championship fixtures.

By dint of unfinished innings, Charlie Harris topped the batting table, though the real leader was George Gunn senior – he was 15th in the overall first-class averages, not bad for a 52-year-old. Carr had a much better year and came second to Gunn senior, to be followed by young George. In fact the Committee had, at the start of the summer, thought of dropping both George Gunn senior and Payton. They quickly found they could not do without the former and, when the injuries came, Payton reappeared.

Nottinghamshire ended the season in fifth place with nine wins, a disappointment after an excellent start. The bowling weakness in the absence of Larwood, Voce and Staples was obvious; Barratt was really a spent force, though he played in 21 Championship games; Richmond had gone – he was playing for Cahn's XI. The batting was relatively sound and survived the tragic death of Whysall in the winter. He had slipped whilst dancing in a hall in Mansfield and injured his elbow. He thought nothing of the injury, but blood poisoning set in and by the time he realised the seriousness of the situation, it was too late. Thousands attended the funeral in Mansfield, which was believed to be the largest ever to take place in the town. In June 1931 a memorial was erected over his grave and some 15,000 people attended the ceremony. The Club decided to organise a benefit for the widow and children of Whysall in 1931 and £1,377 7s 4d was raised. This was a record for the Club.

Financially the County Club was not doing well. The total indebtedness was now £4,388 6s 1d, losses having occurred both in 1931 and 1930. The membership had dropped by 1,000, but this was due to the fact that 1930 had been a Test match year.

Notts won 13 Championship matches in 1932, four more than the previous summer, but this time they never really challenged for the title, though finishing fourth. Kent and Sussex were the early leaders but Yorkshire, after a moderate first month, played brilliantly later on and went past all the field, ending with 53 more points than second-placed Sussex. The sad part of the season was the final enforced retirement of George Gunn. He opened the

The Notts team of 1932, all of whom had made a first-class century. From left to right, standing: W. W. Keeton, H. Larwood, F. W. Shipston, W. Voce, J. Hardstaff jun, G. V. Gunn. Seated: S. J. Staples, A. Staples, A. W. Carr (captain), B. Lilley, W. Walker. (NCCC)

batting in the first match and hit 67, helping Walter Keeton to add 132 in 100 minutes for the first wicket. The second match was the Whitsun fixture with Surrey. The first ball, a full pitch from the young fast bowler, Gover, hit Gunn on the head causing severe concussion and the ball rebounded on to his wicket. The famous veteran was removed to hospital. He recovered and played one or two games later on, but at 53 he decided the time had come to leave the cricket field. Payton was not seen at all, and thus apart from Walker and the captain, the batting was in the hands of the younger brigade. Of these Keeton made most progress. In his 26 Championship matches he hit six centuries, including an innings of 242 against Glamorgan at Trent Bridge. After Gunn's accident, Harris was promoted to open the innings with Keeton and though the former's highest Championship innings was only 67, he still completed 1,000 runs and averaged 28. Shipston played in ten matches and twice reached three figures, but was inconsistent. Young Joe Hardstaff looked a very good prospect, but batting at number seven had no notable innings to his name. Young George Gunn played almost throughout the summer, but did not score a hundred.

With the ball, Larwood had a quite exceptional year. In Championship games he took 141 wickets at 11 runs each. He was without doubt the best fast bowler in England. Voce also had a splendid record and took 106 Championship wickets. He played for the first time in a Test match in England and captured five wickets for 51. Sam Staples also had an excellent season, taking twice as many wickets as in 1931 and at a cheaper cost. Arthur Staples was the only other effective bowler, though young George Gunn took seven for 44 to dismiss Essex for 98.

Two newcomers were given a trial. Bob Winrow from Manton in North Notts was a 21-year-old left-hander who had joined the staff in 1929. He played in one game and then did not reappear until 1935 when he hit 137 off the bowling of Somerset and created a record eighth wicket stand of 220 with George Heane. He did not, however, remain at Trent Bridge after that summer, but went to Scotland, playing for Drumpellier CC and was picked for Scotland in 1949. R. A. Taylor, a right-hand batsman, like Winrow, hit a single first-class hundred, this being against Sussex in 1934. At the close of the 1935 season he left Trent Bridge and joined the Nottingham City Police. He was a cousin of the England and Lancashire wicketkeeper, George Duckworth.

India were the 1932 tourists, but only one Test was played, that being at Lord's. It was the first time India had been granted a Test in England. The tourists came to Trent Bridge at the beginning of

July to play Notts, and the County won by 224 runs. At the same time as this match was taking place, press interest shifted to the MCC tour to Australia in the winter as an announcement from Lord's stated that Pelham Warner was appointed manager with R. C. N. Palairet and D. R. Jardine was the captain. A week later came one of the most embarrassing matches ever played by Notts, when Hedley Verity, the Yorkshire left-arm spinner, captured all ten Notts wickets for just ten runs, the County being all out for 67. Yorkshire won by ten wickets. Verity's analysis was a world record for first-class cricket. The wicket was described as 'diabolically sensitive to the spinning ball'.

Three days later came the announcement of the first five players to go with Jardine to Australia: Duleepsinhji, Hammond, Sutcliffe, Ames and Duckworth – three batsmen and the two wicketkeepers. At the beginning of the following week was the announcement of 22 names for a Test Trial at Cardiff. Voce, Larwood, Keeton and Arthur Staples were included. When the full list of the touring party was announced the two Notts representatives were Larwood and Voce. At this stage there was no inkling of the storm which was to come.

The story of the 'bodyline' 1932–33 tour has been the subject of many books, articles and also two television programmes. Its repercussions were to be felt at Trent Bridge in 1934–35, after in fact the controversy had been settled at Test match level.

The bowling of Larwood and Voce captured the headlines of the press of the empire as well as the Nottingham press (then two morning and two evening papers). Larwood effectively won the Ashes for England by his bowling, taking 33 wickets at 19 runs each in the five matches. 'In match after match Australian batsmen clearly gave the impression of being overawed,' noted *Wisden*'s reporter.

As the England cricketers made their way home, the press wanted to know whether 'leg-theory' bowling would be used in Championship cricket in 1933. The English press boarded the SS *Orontes*, on which the players were sailing, when it docked in Suez. The headlines in the *Daily Sketch* the following day read: 'Leg Theory bowling this season. Larwood and Carr get their heads together on trip in liner: "To make County Cricket more exciting" says Carr.'

Arthur Carr, the Notts captain, had travelled out to Suez and then travelled with Larwood via Toulon and the French railways to Calais and across to Dover. Thousands of Nottinghamshire well-wishers assembled at midnight at the Midland station to greet the train bringing Larwood from St Pancras.

The press were intent on obtaining Larwood's views on 'bodyline' bowling and eventually, on 7 May, the *Sunday Express* published an interview with the fast bowler and the controversy took the headlines once again.

From Nottinghamshire's viewpoint the main problem was the injury to Larwood's foot. Would he be fit to play for the County? The season began with a visit to Trent Bridge by Worcestershire. The day prior to the game the new entrance gates which had been erected in memory of J. A. Dixon were officially opened by Sir Stanley Jackson. Dixon had died on 8 June 1931 and had been a life-member of the Notts Committee and effectively run the cricketing side of the Committee since he retired from first-class matches.

The Worcestershire game was ruined by rain, only 5½ hours play taking place over the three days and Larwood bowled just two overs. The second game, again at Trent Bridge, was against Glamorgan. The weather remained wet; another draw; Larwood bowled five overs in the first innings and three in the second. He dropped out of the team on the eve of the third match. There was

Notts in 1933. The team has not changed much, but Larwood was absent through injury, and the rumbling on of the previous winter's 'bodyline' argument was to have a profound effect on him, Carr and Notts CCC. From left to right, standing: G. V. Gunn, W. W. Keeton, C. B. Harris, W. Voce, J. Hardstaff jun, H. J. Butler, G. W. Robinson. Seated: A. Staples, S. J. Staples, A. W. Carr (captain), W. Walker, B. Lilley. (NCCC)

clearly something wrong with his left foot and it was later revealed several bones were broken. He did not bowl again for Notts during the summer, though he played in a number of matches as a batsman.

The 'bodyline' controversy still grabbed the headlines. Carr wrote a series of articles for the *Daily Sketch*, claiming that he, rather than Jardine, had devised leg-theory bowling. Both Larwood and Jardine had books published on the subject of the tour during the summer and interest remained at a high level, rather detracting from the actual events in the Championship cricket itself.

During the Surrey Bank Holiday match in June, Larwood and Voce were each presented with £388 and silver salvers. The money was the result of a Shilling Fund run by the Nottingham newspapers. D. R. Jardine made the presentations.

The County dropped to eighth place in the Championship with only seven wins. The virtual absence from the side as a bowler of Larwood for the whole summer and the obvious tiredness of Voce after the Australian visit, though the latter played in 24 Championship matches, meant the attack lacked its two strike bowlers. Sam Staples topped the bowling table and, apart from Voce, the only other man to capture more than fifty wickets was Arthur Staples.

In place of Larwood, Notts introduced a 20-year-old fast bowler from Clifton, Harold Butler. He had joined the staff in 1932 and played his first Championship match in June 1933. He was immediately noted as most promising and played in the second half of the 1933 Championship games, taking 32 wickets at 26 runs each. In 1934 he played in almost every match and was awarded his county cap. It was not until 1937 that he hit the national headlines, capturing eight wickets for 18 in the Whitsun match with Surrey. In 1938 he was one of the leading bowlers in England when he was struck down with appendicitis and missed the remainder of the year. After serving in India during the war, he came back to county cricket in 1946 and was soon regarded as one of the fastest bowlers in Championship cricket. He played in one Test in 1947 and went on the 1947–48 MCC tour to West Indies, but was plagued with injuries. He continued however to be Notts main bowler until 1952 and finally retired on medical advice in 1954.

Ramsay Cox was brought into the side as captain when Carr was away and bowled well against Sussex taking five for 36; George Gunn junior took 41 wickets with his leg breaks, but was expensive; Harris sent down 327.2 overs but was even more expensive.

Few faults could be found with the batting – only three matches were lost. Harris improved and his 234 against Middlesex was the highest Notts score of the season. His unlimited patience was in evidence. Keeton continued on the upward path and completed 2,000 runs for the first time; he was hit on the head by a ball from Bowes and forced to miss two matches in mid-season, but in August could do no wrong, scoring four hundreds in five consecutive innings. His batting was particularly attractive because it was peppered with cuts and off-drives. He was also an excellent fieldsman in the deep. Walker and Carr both averaged 36 and had good summers. Hardstaff junior continued to mature, but Shipston was disappointing. As in the previous year there was very little tail in the batting line-up.

Apart from Butler the other newcomer was Stafford Castledine, a 21-year-old slow left-arm bowler, who had been employed at Rufford Abbey, before joining the Notts staff in 1931. His single game in 1933 was against the West Indians. He played only five first-class matches before moving to Welbeck Colliery and in 1939 he joined the City Police.

At the end of the summer Carr completed 15 years as Notts captain and about 120 members of the County Club wrote a letter to the press praising the way he had led the side during 1933. This letter provoked a most unusual response from the Notts professionals, who sent the following letter to the paper:

> Sir – Having seen the letter in yesterday's *Guardian* to Mr A. W. Carr, which was signed by over one hundred members of the Notts CCC, we, the professionals of the County XI, would like to express our very deepest appreciation and gratitude to our Skipper for the splendid and untiring way he has captained the side this year.
>
> No man could have done more than he has done, and the older members of the side, especially, realise what anxiety and worry this has entailed during what has been a most difficult season – a period of team building.
>
> We all thank Mr Carr from the bottom of our hearts for his guidance, counsel and friendship and hope that he may be spared many years to continue as the county's captain.

This type of tribute is fairly common place on the retirement of a player and as an obituary notice, also when a side has won a trophy, but in the circumstances in which it was written, it would seem to be unique in Notts cricket history. Its significance was to become more apparent when the captaincy crisis blew up 15 months later.

Season 1934 found the Australians in England once more. Larwood, recovered from his foot injury, opened the bowling in Notts first match and took four for 31, starting the game by removing three batsmen for five runs. Rain prevented a finish. In the second match Voce took five for 79 and Notts beat Warwickshire by 24 runs. The first Test was scheduled for Trent Bridge on 8 June. Would Larwood play for England? His foot was still causing problems and he was unfit to play in the Test Trial prior to the Trent Bridge Test. This absence meant that he was very unlikely to be chosen for the international match and so it turned out. There were no Notts representatives in a match now remembered as the 'balloon war'. Photographic rights had been sold to one company and they inflated large balloons, as well as erecting netting on top of various boundary walls, to prevent rivals with long range cameras taking pictures.

Australia won by 238 runs when the England batting collapsed to the spin of O'Reilly. McCabe and Chipperfield were the successful Australian batsmen. England were in difficulties before the match commenced since the appointed captain, Wyatt, withdrew owing to injury. Walters took his place. The England selectors had picked three fast bowlers in their original squad, Farnes, Bowes and Nichols, but only Farnes was chosen for the final eleven. There was a record attendance of over 90,000 for the match, which ended excitingly when Australia managed to take the last England wicket just ten minutes before the official close.

Whilst England were at Trent Bridge, Notts met Sussex at Horsham. Larwood took five for 66. 'Larwood at his best: Pace baffles Sussex' were the headlines. On the Saturday following the Test, Notts played Lancashire. The Sunday newspapers had a field day. *The People* report ran:

> There were two outstanding topics in British sporting circles yesterday – Larwood and the Wightman Cup. Our tennis girls were badly beaten by the American team yesterday. Larwood is the centre of a controversy which grows more heated every day. And to confuse the Test Selectors still more and to ram home his case for playing for England, the Notts express bowler took six Lancashire wickets for 51 runs. And at one time his analysis showed six wickets for one run! Larwood must play (so say many of the experts). Carr his county skipper says: 'So far no invitation has been received by Larwood. When, and if, that invitation does arise, I can say that unless Larwood is allowed a free hand he will not play for England.'

Jardine says the same: 'Larwood must play without bond or fetter if England is to win.'

However in another Sunday paper, the *Dispatch*, Larwood gave an exclusive interview: 'I refuse to play in any more Tests. Politicians are trying to hound me out of cricket. I was fit for the last Test, but they feared I would burst the Empire.' Those were just the bold headlines.

In the Monday morning papers, the headlines read: 'Cabinet Ministers deny Larwood's allegations. Bowler's charge of political interference described as "Extraordinary Moonshine"'.

The press continued on its merry way, but Larwood did not appear in any of the Tests. The furore seemed to be dying away, but then the Australians arrived at Trent Bridge in mid-August to play Notts. Larwood stood down from the match with a diplomatic illness. Carr had had a heart attack at Worcester on 7 July and was ordered not to play again during the season. The Notts team was therefore captained by Ben Lilley, the wicketkeeper.

On the first day Voce, using leg theory, took eight for 66, as the Australians were all out for 237. Notts ended the day 42 for one. Grimmett caused Notts to fail on a damp second day with several stoppages. The County were all out for 183. Australia began their second innings and Voce bowled two overs before bad light ended play.

The team for the final Test had been picked directly after the first day's play. Robertson-Glasgow commented: 'On Saturday, in the match between Nottingham and Australia, Voce, unaided by Larwood, brought off the greatest and most notable bowling performance of the year. He has not been selected for the Oval.'

The other papers had more forthright remarks. This however was nothing in comparison with the press on Wednesday. On Tuesday, the final day of the Notts *v* Australians game with Australia 3-0 overnight, the Notts team went out to field without Voce. Voices in the crowd began to shout: 'Where's Voce?' After persistent enquiries, the Secretary announced over the Tannoy that Voce was suffering from shin trouble and on medical advice would not take the field.

The Australians batted on to 230 for two and then declared. When the tourists took the field a group gathered in front of the pavilion and booed. Adding fuel to the flames, Carr, who was in the pavilion, said that if he had been captain, Voce would have played. Rumours then circulated that several of the Notts Committee had resigned, but this was denied. Further rumours suggested that the Australians had objected to Lord's about Voce's bowling and pressure had been put on Notts to withdraw him from the final day's play.

The season had five matches to go, and two were lost and three drawn. The County Club and the players had been unsettled by the continuous controversial press coverage surrounding Larwood and Voce, coverage which had been now going on for nearly two years. Notts actually won eight matches, but they lost seven and went down to ninth in the table. The bowling was much more expensive than in previous years. Larwood took 78 Championship wickets at 16 runs each, Voce 113 at 23. Very serious was the retirement due to sciatica of Sam Staples. He played in one Championship match. Young George Gunn's leg-breaks were called upon to fill the gap and he took 72 wickets, but at times was very costly. There were no other spin bowlers worth playing.

The batting was considerably weakened by the absence through illness of both Walker (he missed 13 matches) and Carr (he missed 17). Keeton was easily the best run-getter. He hit two double-centuries and gained a place in the Test at Headingley. Harris hit five centuries and averaged 40. Hardstaff improved beyond all recognition. He also averaged 40 and made four centuries. He was also the liveliest of the fielders.

The County tried out two new players, Frank Woodhead and Pat Vaulkhard. Woodhead, born in Edwinstowe, but brought up in London club cricket, was a medium-fast bowler, who gained a regular place in the side in 1936 and remained with the club until 1950, save for 1947 when he was with Todmorden. He was appointed coach at Nottingham High School in 1951 and was responsible for developing several players who later appeared in first-class cricket. In 1970 he became the coach at Trent Bridge, a post he held for ten years, during which time he concentrated on building up youth cricket in the county.

Pat Vaulkhard was one of four brothers who were prominent in local club cricket and through their father were connected with Sir Julien Cahn's side. When Walker was suddenly taken ill, Vaulkhard was drafted into the County side and played with some success in nine matches. In 1946 he turned out for Derbyshire and to the embarrassment of his former colleagues hit the highest score of the season, 264, for Derbyshire against Notts. He captained Derbyshire in 1950.

On 22 December 1934 it was announced that Carr would not captain Notts in 1935, the office would be held jointly by George Heane and Stuart Rhodes, the two young batsmen who, in between occasional county matches, played for Sir Julien Cahn's side.

The upshot of this bombshell was that a petition by members of the Notts Club called for a special general meeting to discuss the attitude of the Committee to the controversy surrounding Voce's retirement on the last day of the Australian match and the aspects surrounding the matter. About 2,500 members turned up to the meeting on 16 January 1935. The leading figure against the Committee was the deputy Lord Mayor of Nottingham, H. Seely Whitby. He obtained a signed statement from Voce stating that he was fit to play on the final day. After a long and heated meeting a vote of 'No Confidence' was passed by a large majority against the Committee. As a result the Hon Secretary of the club, Dr G. O. Gauld, who had announced that Voce was unfit to play on the fatal day, resigned, as did Douglas McCraith who was the spokesman for the Committee. The following day it was announced that the whole Committee had resigned. Both Lancashire and Middlesex announced that they would not renew fixtures with Notts if the County continued to support leg-theory bowling.

When the time came for nominations for the 1935 Committee, it was found that there were 35 candidates for 18 seats – in effect the old Committee was re-standing and the rebels were standing against them.

It was akin to a general election. The candidates standing against the old Committee were: A. C. Adams, Sir Harold Bowden, J. A. O. Briggs, A. W. Carr, B. D. Edwards, G. Green, T. H. Johnson, T. N. Knight, E. Potter, A. Straw, C. A. L. Sutton, J. Wilkinson, H. M. Woolley, H. C. Wright. When the votes had been counted, only A. W. Carr and Sir Harold Bowden among the 'rebels' were elected. All 12 of the old Committee, who re-stood, got in and three others, R. J. de C. Barber, Ald E. Huntsman and H. D. Snook, who supported the old Committee, made up the complement of 17 to serve on the 1935 Committee.

'An unfortunate chapter in the history of Nottinghamshire cricket is now concluded. On behalf of the Committee, I appeal to all lovers of cricket in the County to bury the past and rally to the support of the old Club.' This was the appeal of the new Chairman of the Club, Douglas McCraith, and by and large it was heeded, though A. W. Carr expressed his opinions in his memoirs 'Cricket With The Lid Off' published in 1935.

One important outcome of the winter's machinations was the appointment for the first time of a Committee Chairman on an official basis. Douglas McCraith had acted as the spokesman throughout the winter and was chosen by the Committee as their Chairman.

The appointments of Heane and Rhodes as joint captains remained in place and though Carr stated that he would play if selected, he was not picked for any matches and his county career therefore ceased. The following year – on 20 January 1936 – Carr was presented with a handsome casket, illuminated address and inscribed cricket bat in recognition of his services as player and captain of the County.

There had always been something of the 'rebel' in Carr's make-up. He had been sent to school at Eton, but left before completing his first year. Going on to Sherborne he had been an outstanding games player and it was generally thought that he was the hero fictionalised in Alec Waugh's novel 'The Loom of Youth', which caused quite a stir for its fresh view of Public School life when published in 1917 – Waugh was a contemporary of Carr at Sherborne. Unlike many other amateur cricket captains, Carr identified himself with his players, who worshipped him and understood his little particularities. Carr was fond of the racecourse and was known to disappear from the cricket field to view races and on occasion to arrive somewhat late for matches; he was also not averse to a drink or two. He was a man who knew his own mind and would not suffer fools gladly.

Coming to the performance of the County in 1935, it is pleasant to record that Nottinghamshire had a creditable season. The joint-captains began with a major disadvantage in that Walter Keeton had been severely injured on 19 January, when he was knocked down by a lorry in Mansfield. With several broken ribs and concussion as well as other minor injuries the accident meant he would not be available for at least the first part of the summer – in 1934 he had been Notts' best batsman. As it turned out his first match was on 22 June. Until then the County had to improvise so far as an opening partner for Harris was concerned. More often than not G. V. Gunn took over the position. This however affected the bowling, since Gunn was the only spinner of any consequence in the side. Gunn hit 1,165 runs in Championship matches at an average of 36.40, but he took only 18 wickets and they cost 54 runs each. The batting, despite Keeton's absence, proved strong; no-one had an outstanding season, but nine of the regular players had averages above 25, Hardstaff's 39.42 being the top. The bowling was too dependent on Voce, Larwood and Arthur Staples, though the two younger seam bowlers, Wood-head and Butler, who vied with each other for the final place in the eleven, both had fair records.

Five new players were tried in the course of the summer and, in addition, Bob Winrow was given a further chance and scored a memorable hundred against Somerset. Joe Knowles, a 25-year-old batsman, played several good innings during the year and was a regular member of the side in the three years before the outbreak of the Second World War. In 1938 he completed 1,000 runs. He returned in 1946, but soon dropped out of the eleven and took an appointment as groundsman at the Police Ground in Nottingham. He had in fact been an assistant groundsman at Trent Bridge prior to joining the playing staff – a very unusual circumstance.

David Jones, the Worksop batsman, joined the Notts staff in 1934 and in 1935 had a tremendous season with the second eleven, averaging nearly 60. A fast scorer, he hit 50 in 70 minutes on his first-class debut, when he took Hardstaff's place in the County side. Only in 1938, however, did he play with any frequency in the first team. His county career ended in 1939. Apart from his skill on the cricket field, Jones played League Football for about six seasons with Bury.

Three amateurs who played during 1935 were W. A. Sime, J. B. Hall and W. E. G. Payton. Sime had been captain of Bedford School and had turned out for Bedfordshire in 1928. He went up to Oxford in the autumn of that year and though he played in the Freshmen's and Senior's matches, he played only one first-class game for the University. In 1934 he came to Nottingham setting

Three Notts stalwarts of the 1930s, from the left W. W. Keeton, Arthur Staples and Joe Hardstaff junior. Keeton and Hardstaff continued successfully after the war, but Staples retired in 1938. (NCCC)

up as a barrister in the city. He began to play for Notts Amateurs and made a single first-class appearance for Notts; he did not re-appear until 1939, then playing in two games. In 1947 he was appointed Notts captain and retained the post for four years. He was a hard-hitting batsman and useful change bowler. In 1957 he was created a QC and in 1972 sworn in as a circuit judge. He was President of the County Club from 1975 to 1977. J. B. Hall, a useful medium-pace bowler and member of Julien Cahn's Team, was also captain of Worksop, and appropriately made his Notts debut at Central Avenue against Glamorgan, replacing the in-jured Larwood. In 1939 he played a second game for Notts and then in 1946 turned out in three matches. He was latterly con-nected with Retford CC, as his son still is. His son, Mike Hall, played for Notts in 1958 and 1959 and his grandsons are also very useful cricketers.

W. E. G. Payton, the son of the former professional, was at Cambridge when he played for Notts in his only county game. He gained his blue as an obdurate opening batsman in 1937. After the war he turned out for Derbyshire and the Combined Services, having a commission in the RAF for whom in 1965 he was appointed chaplain in chief.

A summary of results for 1935 show ten wins against three losses and this record put Notts in fifth place in the table. Derbyshire led the field in the early stages, but were then deposed by Yorkshire who soon had a commanding lead. Hardstaff was capped by England, but played in only one Test. He was then chosen for the 1935–36 MCC tour to New Zealand and Australia. Heane looked so promising that he was given a place in the Gentlemen *v* Players team at Lord's.

At the close of the summer it was announced that Walter Marshall, the 80-year-old groundsman, was to retire. He was to continue to live in the pavilion and to act as caretaker. His successor as groundsman was Arthur Widdowson, who had been born in Ruddington and trained under Marshall before going to Old Trafford as chief groundsman.

The Trent Bridge Inn was altered during the 1935–36 winter. The original single-storey brick pavilion at the rear of the Inn, which for many years had been little more than a bottle store, was demolished and a two-storey extension added to the Inn itself.

Financially the County Club was still struggling; 1934 with the Australian Test had brought a profit of £3,440, but 1935 had produced a loss of £395 and there was an anticipated loss of £2,000 in 1936. The new President of the Club, the Earl of Lincoln (son of the Duke of Newcastle) appealed for Nottinghamshire folk to

G. F. H. Heane's career with Notts lasted from 1927 to 1951. He took over the captaincy in 1935 and remained skipper until 1946. (NCCC)

support the County Club, either by attending matches or becoming members.

The opening match of the season was a high-scoring draw against Sussex. Two days afterwards Notts made their first appearance for nearly one hundred years on the old Forest

Ground, where 8,000 turned out to watch a benefit match for Larwood. After the match the teams were entertained at Sam Staples' hostelry, the New Inn, Carrington.

Back with more serious cricket, Notts beat Gloucestershire at Trent Bridge by ten wickets. Harris and Hardstaff hit hundreds, Larwood took five for 56. Having won this match the County kept in the Championship race for three months and at the beginning of July were actually at the head of the table. August proved to be a poor time and, having beaten Surrey in the traditional Bank Holiday fixture, Notts failed to win any of their remaining eight matches. They ended in fifth place, with eight wins and three losses. Most of the 17 drawn matches were rain-affected.

There was a controversial incident in the match at Hove. Notts were bowled out for 74 and Sussex responded with 327 for nine declared, Holmes and Melville both hitting hundreds. At the close of the second day Notts were 100 in arrears with eight second innings wickets standing. On the final day rain continually interrupted play, but in between showers Notts were all out for 261 and this left Sussex five minutes in which to make nine runs. Voce bowled an over which allowed two runs, one leg bye and the final ball going for four more byes. It was now raining heavily. Heane consulted umpire Newman, who pulled up the stumps and the fielders fled to the pavilion. The Sussex captain was not amused. The Sussex Committee sent a strongly worded letter to Notts stating that Heane's conduct was 'a flagrant offence against the spirit of the game'. Sussex went on to say that if Notts did not publicly apologise then Sussex would cancel fixtures with them. The Notts Committee had a suitable apology printed in the press and the matter rested there.

The wet summer did not suit the batsmen; only Hardstaff and Keeton maintained their form. Hardstaff had had a brilliant MCC tour during the winter and was selected for all three 1936 Tests, though injury prevented him appearing in the final match. He hit 94 at Old Trafford. He was selected for the 1936–37 MCC tour to Australia, as indeed was Voce. Keeton had fully recovered from his motor accident and obtained the highest run aggregate for the County. Harris and G. V. Gunn batted well in patches, but Walker fell right away and though afforded plenty of opportunity Knowles averaged only 22.23. Arthur Staples had an even more modest record and the captain rarely made many runs.

Larwood had a fine season with the ball and topped not only the Notts bowling averages but those for the whole country, his 116 wickets in Championship matches costing 12 runs each. Voce also captured over 100 wickets and having made his peace with the authorities appeared in the final Test at The Oval, by which time he had already been picked to go to Australia.

Lilley was not as efficient as before behind the stumps and the County gave a trial to C. R. N. Maxwell. This young cricketer had been the outstanding Public School batsman-wicketkeeper of his generation. He had held a place in the Brighton College side for three seasons, hitting nearly 2,000 runs for the first eleven at an average of 53.72. He appeared in the representative schools' match at Lord's and the following year began playing for Julien Cahn's Team. In 1935 he had created a minor sensation for Cahn's XI in their first-class fixture against Leicestershire, when he hit 268 in 190 minutes, the seventh-wicket partnership with F. C. W. Newman being worth 336. On the strength of that performance he played for the Gentlemen at Lord's; a most unusual honour for someone not connected with either university or county cricket. In 1937 he was chosen for one of the Test Trials, but this was the high point of his career. The last of his 16 first-class matches for Notts was in 1939. In 1946 he played in four matches for Middlesex but in 1948 he moved to Worcestershire and captained their second eleven. His final first-class game was for Worcestershire in 1951.

Notts' final match of the season had been at Gloucester for the benefit of Tom Goddard. Hammond hit 317 in six and a half hours and a record crowd of 7,000 watched his innings during the second day. Notts lost by an innings, making 200 and 215 in reply to Gloucestershire's 485. Directly after the game, the winning captain, D. A. C. Page, was killed in a motor accident as he drove home. He was aged 25. It was a very sad note on which to end the season.

The Ashes series in Australia saw England win the first two Tests largely due to the bowling of Voce, but the other three matches ended in defeat. Hardstaff played in all five matches, but only occasionally showed the form he had displayed 12 months earlier on his other visit to the Antipodes.

Elsewhere, Larwood was engaged as a coach in India, but came home early having found time heavy on his hands. Sir Julien Cahn took his team to Ceylon and Malaya. Among the cricketers on that nine-match tour were S. D. Rhodes, J. B. Hall, C. R. N. Maxwell and T. B. Reddick. The last named was to play for Notts after the war.

During 1936 the death occurred of the old Notts cricketer, C. W. Wright. He was Honorary Treasurer and also the sole Trustee of the County Club. The former post had been a sinecure for some years and he was not replaced. The Westminster Bank took over as Trustees.

The County Club's financial situation was becoming more serious and a special appeal fund campaign was set up in April 1937. The Club required £6,000. J. W. Harding of Parliament Street, who had organised campaigns on behalf of Nottingham General Hospital, was appointed to be in charge of the campaign.

Nottinghamshire did not suffer defeat until the 18th match of the summer when, missing Larwood, Voce and Hardstaff, they were beaten by an innings by Derbyshire at Chesterfield. In the previous 17 matches however they had great difficulty in dismissing the opposition twice and thus obtained, up to then, only five wins. Voce was not only tired from his efforts in Australia, but he was also required for various representative matches and twisted his knee, so that the left-arm bowler made only 14 appearances in Championship matches. Larwood was not fully fit and near the end of the season was suspended for two matches because he failed to attend net practice; he missed ten Championship games. Arthur Staples and young George Gunn played throughout the year, but their bowling skills had deserted them. Gunn's 15 wickets cost 52 runs each and Staples 42 cost 44 runs each. Apart from Larwood and Voce, the only bowler to average less than 30 was Harold Butler; thus when the two England players were away, Butler was the only bowler capable of taking wickets at a reasonable cost.

The captain tried to juggle his resources to make the most of what was available. Nineteen bowlers were used in the course of the 28 matches and unlike the 1980s, the captain did not employ 'joke' bowlers to give the opposition runs.

No fewer than seven completely new players were thrown in at the deep end and failed to swim against the tidal wave of runs. Two 18-year-olds and a 17-year-old were among the cannon fodder, as well as a 32-year-old amateur.

The youngest recruit was the 17-year-old Ron Giles from Chilwell. Giles, a left-arm slow bowler, took two wickets, but they cost 103 runs. He had one famous day as a bowler the following season in the Hampshire match, but thereafter he developed into a very sound batsman and remained at Trent Bridge until 1959, playing in 195 matches for Notts, generally in his later days opening the innings.

The two 18-year-olds were George Walker and 'Steve' Yates. Walker, from West Bridgford, was a right-arm fast-medium bowler. He took one wicket for 176 runs in two matches and at the end of the summer requested his release from the groundstaff.

'Steve' Yates was one of two brothers from Warsop. He played for Welbeck Colliery. His one wicket cost 54 runs, but like Giles he was to develop into a good batsman and scored many runs for Blidworth Colliery in post-war cricket, having left the Trent Bridge ground staff after 1939. His brother Jack was on the staff in 1938 and 1939, but did not play in first-class cricket.

James Bradley from Pleasley Vale was another slow left-arm bowler. He played in five matches and took 12 wickets at 47.16 runs each. He remained on the staff until the war and then appeared for Blidworth Colliery. Joseph Buxton, a fast bowler from Bentinck Colliery, remained on the staff just for 1937 and played in one Championship game, in which his single wicket cost 90 runs. Dennis Watkin, a leg-break bowler with Sandiacre Premier CC, was not on the staff, but was recruited in desperation when Larwood was injured in a car crash. His one wicket cost 113 runs, but he looked very promising and was taken on the playing staff for 1938 and 1939. He was better known as a soccer player for Aston Villa and Reading.

Finally came the amateur, E. A. Marshall. He was employed in the family firm of Marshall Bros, timber merchants, and had been in the eleven at Nottingham High School. His local cricket was for Notts Amateurs and Lenton United. A fast bowler, he took two wickets for 100 in 1937 and played in three matches. Most of his cricket was for the second eleven and he captained that side from 1947 to 1949. After the war he was Chairman of the Notts Supporters Association as well as a Committee member and then President in 1964–65. He died suddenly whilst attending the Annual General Meeting of the County Club in 1970.

These seven new faces therefore did little, in 1937, to improve the bowling strength. Too much was expected of them too soon, and in most cases the outbreak of war prevented them having a chance of becoming established first-class players. Giles was the only exception.

Moving from the bowling to batting, Hardstaff was quite brilliant. His relative failure in Australia was behind him and in 1937 he was, bar Hammond, the best batsman in England. In Championship games he hit 1,802 runs, average 66.74. In the first Test he hit 114 and 64; in the second 58 and 11; in the third 103. In the last innings, the report noted: 'So sure was he in dealing with the bowling that he appeared almost casual, but he drove with skill and grace and often hit on the on-side with splendid power.'

He hit three double hundreds for Notts, against Leicestershire, Middlesex and Somerset, but his 126 at Canterbury was his outstanding county innings. Kent set Notts 310 in 230 minutes.

Notts made their runs in 180 minutes and this was largely due to Hardstaff. He reached 52 out of 68 in 22 minutes and 100 in 51 minutes, his whole innings lasting just 70 minutes with a six and 17 fours. It was the fastest hundred of 1937 and won him the Lawrence Trophy.

Keeton, Harris and Gunn all averaged over 40 in Championship matches. The first named completed 2,000 first-class runs. Arthur Staples also batted well, but Willis Walker lost his place in the side, as did Lilley, who appeared just once. For both it was the end of their first-class careers.

In season 1938 Notts celebrated the centenary of Trent Bridge. The President, Sir Julien Cahn, commissioned E. V. Lucas to prepare a book to mark the occasion and copies were sent free to all members of the County Club. The Special Appeal set up in 1937 had been a success and raised £5,800 4s 0d. This cleared the debt, but unfortunately the accounts for 1937 showed a loss of £860. Sir Julien Cahn continued to subsidise the Club. He paid the first-year membership fee for 800 new members and also paid all the expenses in connection with the captain, George Heane.

Notts began the summer with an eight-wicket win over Northants at Northampton, Butler taking seven for 58 in the match. The first home match saw a complete batting failure. Sussex made 478 for seven declared and Notts were all out for 231 and 176. Another innings defeat followed, this time at Lord's. Bill Edrich hit 245 as Middlesex reached 474. Notts were all out for 291 and 132, of which Hardstaff made 105 and 52 not out. The fourth Championship game was scheduled as the Trent Bridge Centenary Match. Hampshire were visitors to Nottingham and a special exhibition of cricketana, a new centenary flag, a new loudspeaker system so that speeches could be relaid to the crowd and other arrangements were in place. It rained all day and only a handful of bedraggled spectators clustered in the long room. On the second day five hours play took place; on the third day rain again washed out play.

The sun shone for the Whitsun fixture with Surrey. Butler bowled at his best taking five for 18 and dismissing Surrey for 105. Notts replied with 170 of which Hardstaff made 55. Thanks to Fishlock and Gregory Surrey made 339 in their second innings, leaving Notts with 275 to win. Before stumps on the second day Notts reached 41 without loss. Harris went straightaway on the last morning, but Keeton seemed in good form, which was just as well since Hardstaff had injured his hand with a car spanner, tightening up some nuts on the cylinder head.

At lunch Notts seemed in control having six wickets in hand

KENT *v* NOTTINGHAMSHIRE

Played at Canterbury, 4, 5, 6 August 1937

NOTTINGHAMSHIRE WON BY FIVE WICKETS

KENT	FIRST INNINGS		SECOND INNINGS	
W. H. Ashdown	b Woodhead	25	c Harris b Heane	13
P. R. Sunnucks	c Wheat b Staples	16	c Staples b Heane	5
F. E. Woolley	b Woodhead	2	c Bradford b Woodhead	5
L. E. G. Ames	c and b Bradley	93	c Heane b Bradley	44
L. J. Todd	c Harris b Woodhead	135	b Woodhead	72
Mr F. G. H. Chalk	c Butler b Bradley	6	b Woodhead	7
Mr J. G. W. Davies	c Gunn b Butler	17	c Harris b Heane	49
Mr B. H. Valentine	b Woodhead	7	c Wheat b Woodhead	37
D. V. P. Wright	c Wheat b Bradley	22	not out	4
C. G. Cole	st Wheat b Bradley	1	c Hardstaff b Butler	5
C. Lewis	not out	0		
Extras	b 2, lb 5, w 1	8	w 1	1
Total		332	(9 wkts dec)	242

1st inns: 1-37, 2-43, 3-55, 4-179, 5-189, 6-235, 7-256, 8-307, 9-307
2nd inns: 1-11, 2-22, 3-30, 4-90, 5-99, 6-?, 7-?, 8-232, 9-?

BOWLING	O	M	R	W	O	M	R	W
Butler	28	6	89	1	10	1	35	1
Woodhead	31.2	6	60	4	24	6	50	4
Staples	20	5	48	1	14	0	52	0
Bradley	22	0	116	4	10	0	50	1
Harris	6	1	11	0				
Heane					11	0	54	3

NOTTINGHAMSHIRE	FIRST INNINGS		SECOND INNINGS	
W. W. Keeton	b Wright	27	c and b Lewis	51
C. B. Harris	b Wright	21	c Valentine b Todd	8
J. Knowles	lbw b Todd	41	lbw b Davies	84
J. Hardstaff	c Woolley b Davies	97	c Cole b Davies	126
G. V. Gunn	c Woolley b Wright	5	not out	16
A. Staples	c Ashdown b Wright	29	lbw b Wright	0
*Mr G. F. H. Heane	c Ames b Davies	22	not out	12
H. J. Butler	lbw b Wright	2		
F. G. Woodhead	lbw b Wright	0		
†A. B. Wheat	c and b Wright	0		
J. Bradley	not out	5		
Extras	b 1, lb 10, nb 5	16	b 4, lb 8, w 1, nb 1	14
Total		265	(5 wkts)	311

1st inns: 1-41, 2-56, 3-113, 4-128, 5-198, 6-242, 7-253, 8-253, 9-253
2nd inns: 1-9, 2-126, 3-?, 4-270, 5-279

BOWLING	O	M	R	W	O	M	R	W
Todd	21	4	66	1	7	0	44	1
Cole	15	4	41	0	7	1	28	0
Wright	28	1	94	7	25	2	104	1
Davies	12.1	0	41	2	22	3	74	2
Lewis	6	2	7	0	5	0	29	1
Woolley					2	0	18	0

Umpires: W. Bestwick and A. Skelding

In the second innings Hardstaff completed his 100 in only 51 minutes in a dazzling display. Wright took three wickets in four balls in the first innings. The fall of wickets is incomplete in the Notts scorebook.

Notts in 1938, in the Centenary Year of Trent Bridge. From left to right, standing: A. B. Wheat. D. Jones, J. Knowles, H. J. Butler, J. Hardstaff jun, W. W. Keeton, C. B. Harris. Seated: G. V. Gunn, A. Staples, G. F. H. Heane (captain), W. Voce, H. Larwood. (NCCC)

and needing 84 more to win. Gover took the new ball and the batsmen failed one after another. Hardstaff came in at number eleven with 17 runs still required. Five runs were added but, able only to use one hand, Hardstaff was bowled by Gover and the match lost. The injury was most unfortunate for Hardstaff since he had been selected for the first Test against Australia, but was now unfit to play. Almost as disappointed was his father, who would have been picked to umpire in the Test, but was not selected as soon as it was obvious his son would be in the England squad.

The Surrey match marked the retirement of Jack Carlin, the Notts scorer; he had first been connected with Notts as a player 52 years before, and was now aged 75. Sam Staples was appointed as his successor.

With Hardstaff injured and Voce not selected there were no Notts cricketers in the Trent Bridge Test of 1938. It was a match of vast scores. Australia, batting second, made 411, but this was still not enough to avoid the follow on, as England reached 658 for eight declared. Four players hit hundreds for the home side: Hutton, Barnett, Paynter and Compton. Australia batted out the last day, making 427 for six, with Bradman scoring 144 not out and Brown 133. McCabe made 232 in Australia's first innings. McCabe's batting was regarded by many as the best ever seen at Trent Bridge, and his final 72 came in 28 minutes.

Returning to county cricket, Notts beat Sussex, Kent and Northants in the middle of June and moved into eighth place in the table, but after that nothing went right and the slide downwards gathered momentum. On 13 August they dropped to 16th, and only Northants, who had not won a match since 1935, were below them.

The Notts supporters were near despair; the County had not fared so badly since 1895. On 24 August Worcestershire came to Trent Bridge for the final Notts home match of the summer. Woodhead took seven for 24, dismissing the visitors for 73. In spite of the absence of Hardstaff – playing for England in the famous match at The Oval – Notts replied with 364. Worcestershire recovered in their second innings, making 399. This left Notts needing 109. Victory was achieved by six wickets. Notts then travelled to Bournemouth. Hampshire on the last day needed 243 in 150 minutes, and the match seemed to be heading for a draw. However eight wickets went for 58, before Mackenzie and Knott came together and appeared to be holding out. Giles was put on to bowl the final over and ended by taking the last two wickets with the fifth and sixth deliveries of that over.

Notts moved along the coast to Dover for the last match. This time Voce took seven for 39 and Kent were all out for 84. Notts did somewhat better reaching 133; Voce took another six wickets in the second innings and Notts suddenly made batting look easy by hitting off the 74 for victory without a wicket falling. These three wins pushed Notts into 12th place: modest by the County's inter-war standard, but better than feared three weeks before.

The reason for the decline was mainly the bowling problems. Larwood played in only nine matches, more often than not as a batsman, and took just six wickets all summer. In October he announced his retirement from county cricket. The *Evening News* commented:

> Larwood is the last of the classical fast bowlers. He left the coal face and village cricket to become a professional player, and succeeded to the extent of becoming the most famous bowler in post-Great War days and one of the most talked of cricketers of all time.

Larwood went to the Blackpool Club as professional for 1939 and moved to Blackpool where he lived until his emigration in 1949 to Australia.

Arthur Staples was crippled by sciatica and could play in only 11 matches and Butler was struck down with appendicitis after ten matches and missed the rest of the summer. The bowling

The career of fast bowler Arthur Jepson began in 1938, but he blossomed after the war and opened the bowling until 1959. He also kept goal for several League clubs. (NCCC)

resources were reduced to Voce and whatever could be gathered together from the rest of the groundstaff. Voce was grossly overbowled, sending down 944 overs and taking 96 wickets. Woodhead was his partner for many matches and responded well to the challenge, taking 69 wickets at a reasonable cost. Heane bowled himself much more than in the past and proved fairly steady, taking 49 Championship wickets at 26 runs each. Gunn and Harris were used but were more expensive. A 23-year-old medium-fast bowler from Selston, Arthur Jepson, was brought into the side and bowled well enough to hold his place for the second half of the summer. His career was destined to span 22 years and he was, with Butler, the mainstay of the attack in the immediate post-war era. Jepson also proved a very useful batsman, employing the long handle with great effect. He was also a talented goalkeeper with Port Vale, Stoke City and Lincoln. In 1960 he became a first-class umpire and went on to stand in Test matches.

The batting was satisfactory; Hardstaff stood head and shoulders above the rest, but international matches and injury meant he played in only 16 matches. Harris scored most runs; Heane and Keeton, the latter after a poor start, could be relied upon. Gunn and Knowles completed 1,000 runs. Apart from Jepson two other player made their debuts. Harry Winrow, a younger brother of Bob, was left-handed both as a batsman and bowler. He had batted well for the second eleven in 1937, usually opening the innings. After the war he gained a regular place in the County side and remained on the staff until 1952. He then emigrated to South Africa and died there in 1973. His batting was very orthodox and he had a wide range of strokes; his slow bowling had occasional days of success.

J. S. Hodgkins, the other newcomer, was a 22-year-old from West Bridgford. He was in the XI at Nottingham High School, then played for Notts Forest CC as a very good club all-rounder. His county appearances were limited to three, one in 1938, one in 1946 and the last in 1951, though he played regularly during the war. He was also a very good footballer and golfer.

At the end of the 1938 season came the death of A. W. Shelton. He had been a passionate supporter of Notts cricket from an early age. From 1902 he had been a member of the County Committee, and after 1924 when a severe illness restricted his business activities, he devoted nearly all his time to the County Club. He presented many books to the Club and organised the collection of pictures and other cricketana which adorned the pavilion.

Sir Julien Cahn was seriously concerned at the disappointing results of 1938 and determined to solve the lack of success. Jim Iremonger, the coach, was retired and Cahn paid for two world-renowned experts to come and reorganise the coaching of young players at Trent Bridge. The first expert was D. J. Knight, the Oxford University and Surrey batsman, who was a master at Westminster School and a noted authority on coaching young players. The second was the Australian Test cricketer, Alan Fairfax, who had emigrated to London in 1932 and ran a cricket school. He had toured England with the 1930 Australians and played in ten Tests altogether as an all-rounder. Cahn offered to pay for these coaches for three years.

Of course it was not to be expected that the new regime could produce immediate results. Nottinghamshire remained in mid-table right through the summer. The highest they ever rose was ninth and they ended the season in twelfth place with six wins and eight losses out of 27 games. Butler and Voce remained fit all through the campaign and both came out with excellent records.

Butler completed 100 wickets in Championship matches, Voce took 93. Jepson, the third best performer, took 48. The principal defect was the lack of spin bowling. Gunn's 29 wickets cost 40 runs each; Giles was given an extended trial, but his seven wickets cost more than 100 runs each. Voce was therefore used both as a fast and slow bowler as the occasion demanded.

Hardstaff led the batting and played in the Tests *v* West Indies. In all first-class games he hit 2,129 runs and came fourth in the averages behind Hammond, Hutton and Compton. Keeton was in much better form. Against Middlesex at The Oval (Lord's was being used for the Eton *v* Harrow match), Keeton hit 312 not out, the first batsman to make a triple hundred for Nottinghamshire. He was at the crease seven and a quarter hours and hit a five and 28 fours. Notts scored 560 for nine declared and Voce took ten wickets so that Notts won by an innings. As a result of this and other good innings, Keeton played in the final Test at The Oval. Heane had a good summer, scoring over 1,500 runs. Gunn and Harris also completed 1,000. Knowles, however, did not do so well, but Giles put together some useful innings.

Only two new players were tried and both appeared only once, though they were destined to become well-known in post-war cricket. Eric Meads, a 23-year-old wicketkeeper, who played mainly on The Forest with Ellerslie House CC, was the regular second eleven keeper in 1938 and 1939. He took over as first eleven keeper in 1946 and then played in every first-class Notts match bar one for four years. A neat performer behind the wicket he was a very moderate batsman, though twice he hit fifty. He lost his place in the side in 1953 and left the Trent Bridge staff in 1954.

G. L. Willatt, a solid dependable left-hand batsman, was in the eleven at Repton for three years. He went up to Cambridge in the autumn of 1937 and in 1939 played for Notts against Cambridge. After the war he played against Oxford in 1946 and 1947, turning out for Notts in the vacation. He took a teaching post at Edinburgh Academy and in 1948 and 1949 appeared for Scotland. He then moved back to Repton and joined the ranks of Derbyshire, captaining the county from 1951 to 1954. In 1957 he captained Kendal, having accepted the post of headmaster of Heversham Grammar School, but moved later to become head of Pocklington.

War broke out in September 1939, but unlike 1914, the county programme was almost complete. The army requisitioned the Trent Bridge pavilion as an Army Post Office. The cricketers either joined the armed services or were involved in work of national importance, but the Secretary, H. A. Brown, determined to continue with some County matches and, in fact, Nottinghamshire were the only Club to play county games throughout the six wartime summers. Matches were generally one-day affairs, though occasional Bank Holiday fixtures ran to two days. H. A. Brown recruited any notable cricketer who happened to be stationed in the area at the time of a particular match.

In 1940 six games were played. Hardstaff, Keeton and Heane all scored 100s, as did a young Nottingham High School cricketer, R. T. Simpson, who at that time was in the police force. In 1941 Simpson made two centuries and another promising player, C. J. Poole, hit 101 not out against the RAF. Butler was the principal bowler of 1941. Hardstaff and Butler were drafted to India in 1942; Simpson had joined the RAF and Brown had more difficulty in recruiting players. F. C. W. Newman hit the only hundred. J. S. Hodgkins was the most successful bowler.

Hodgkins remained the best bowler in 1943, when C. J. Poole and another player who was to make his name in post-war cricket, F. W. Stocks, played some promising innings. Simpson turned out again in 1944 and hit 133 against Leicestershire, after spending the previous night on flying exercises and only arriving at the ground as the captains tossed up. In 1945, with the war in Europe finishing in May, Notts played ten matches including one against the Australian Services. Voce bowled brilliantly taking eleven for 113, but a young Australian, Keith Miller, hit the highest innings of the match. The two Australian bowlers, Pepper and Cristofani, proved too good for the Notts batsmen – Hardstaff and Simpson were both in India.

So cricket was kept going at Trent Bridge with the reporters' box being used as the dressing rooms. The success of these matches, which were played in aid of various wartime charities, was due to H. A. Brown almost entirely.

A BATSMAN'S PARADISE

NOTTINGHAMSHIRE HAD SUFFERED LESS than most other counties at the hands of Adolf Hitler. Whilst The Oval had been turned into a POW compound and Old Trafford had been badly blitzed, the only major casualty at Trent Bridge had been the Swain Hall, which occupied a site next to the indoor nets, and which was hit by a bomb. The playing area was in near perfect condition and the buildings in general were sound, even if they had been neglected for six years. The membership had dwindled to about 1,000 and in October 1945 the Committee appointed J. L. Lee-Jones as organiser of a campaign to bring the membership up to 6,000. He was to be employed for 30 weeks from 1 January 1946.

The other concern was of course the re-establishment of a playing staff. The following ten players were categorised as 'Class A' and offered two-year contracts: J. Hardstaff, W. W. Keeton, C. B. Harris, E. A. Meads, J. Knowles, F. G. Woodhead, W. Voce, H. J. Butler, A. Jepson and F. W. Stocks. All of these except Stocks had played in 1939.

Stocks, whose father had played for Northants, came from a mining family in Hucknall, but he himself was born in Yorkshire. A sturdy left-hand batsman and useful bowler, he was to make the headlines very early in 1946 by hitting a century on his debut in Championship cricket. Later in another match, he took a wicket with the first ball he bowled in first-class matches, thus performing a unique double. He went on to complete 1,000 runs in a season five times and played regularly for the County for 12 years before retiring.

On the coaching side, the County chose a new approach, engaging the services of T. B. Reddick as 'player-coach' with E. Smethurst as his assistant. Reddick had been born in Shanghai, but had come to England to be educated and had found a job as an assistant coach in the indoor cricket school run in the suburbs of London by the former South African Test player G. A. Faulkner. Reddick had played two matches for Middlesex in 1931, but after Faulkner's suicide had come up to Nottingham and joined Cahn's Team. He was now aged 34. An attractive middle-order right-hand batsman, he was to remain at Trent Bridge for two years before being offered a coaching position in South Africa; Old Trafford briefly tempted him back to England, but he spent most of the rest of his life in Cape Town, dying there in 1982. Wheat and G. V. Gunn were regarded as too old to return to county

REGINALD THOMAS SIMPSON

An all-round sportsman, who played both rugby football and golf to a very high standard, Simpson was one of the greatest performers against fast bowling. When he came into the Nottinghamshire side in 1946 – the war had delayed his first-class county debut by several years, as his fluent innings in one-day wartime games proved time and again – the County possessed an established opening pair in Keeton and Harris. In 1949 however he was promoted to open with Keeton and his Championship record of the season, 1,906 runs, average 68.07, demonstrates the success of this move. It was in the same summer that he made a century on his Test debut in England. He was to play in 28 Test matches, but his outstanding innings was the 156 not out in the fifth Test at Melbourne in 1950–51 – the first time after 14 matches that England beat Australia in post-war cricket.

A batsman with great style, his shots in front of the wicket were always a delight to the eye and his stance a model for any young batsman.

He captained the County between 1951 and 1960, but during his last two or three years he was hampered by a back injury. Happily he recovered, and for several seasons in the early 1960s he played for Notts on a part time basis and made runs as attractively as he had done in his prime. A man of firm views on the ways in which aspiring county cricketers should be guided and the way in which the game should be played, he joined the Committee of the County Club in 1961 and is now its senior member, as well as being the current President.

Reg Simpson, the Club's President from 1991, was one of the most stylish of batsmen for Notts and England in the years following the Second World War. (NCCC)

cricket and were the only two of the 1939 first eleven not re-engaged. Giles was offered terms, but remained playing League cricket in Yorkshire until 1947. Harry Winrow returned to the staff. In May 1946 Isiah Smithurst, a bowler from Eastwood was given a trial and engaged for the season, whilst Charles Morgan, another bowler, was regarded as good enough to play in the second eleven and possibly have a game with the first team. In fact both these cricketers played one first-class match in 1946. Morgan was a notable club cricketer in the north of the county, being a miner at Bilsthorpe Colliery. He later emigrated to the United States.

The 1946 season was very much one of improvisation; travel was difficult and almost everything rationed. To reinforce the dozen or so professionals, the County were able to call upon several amateurs. George Heane was reappointed captain (he had in fact captained the side in many of the wartime matches); R. T. Simpson would be available as soon as he was released from the RAF; G. L. Willatt would be able to play in July and August; J. B. Hall and J. S. Hodgkins, the two pre-war local amateurs, were ready if needed. C. R. Maxwell had moved to the London area and was recruited by Middlesex. Reddick's position nicely illustrates the rather odd position of amateur cricketers in post-war Britain. According to his autobiography, the Notts Committee asked him whether he wished to play as an amateur or professional. He asked which paid the best money and therefore chose to be an amateur.

Sir Julien Cahn had died in September 1944 at his home, Stanford Hall, aged 62. According to Eric Snow's book on Sir Julien's XI, the final match played by his team took place in August 1941, and Sir Julien had played himself even in the last year. He was certainly the most generous patron Nottinghamshire cricket ever possessed. He was much criticised in some quarters and his generosity was balanced by his hard-headed business sense and at times ruthless determination, but cricket benefitted greatly from his interest and many cricketers owed a tremendous debt to him. His cricket grounds, at Stanford Hall and in West Bridgford, are still in use and the Hall itself has been a Co-operative Training College since 1945.

The results in 1946 were even more disappointing than in the last years prior to the war. In June the County were actually bottom of the Championship. The first match, against Kent at Trent Bridge, when Stocks scored his hundred on debut, was won but there followed five defeats and six draws. Voce was unable to play as he was still in the services and only Butler, with some support from Jepson and Woodhead, made much impression on the opposition batsmen. The marl which had been fed into the Trent Bridge square for so many years made spin bowling innocuous. In mid-July Notts gained their second win due to hundreds from Heane and Stocks – Stocks and Meads actually added 110 for the last wicket. The following match at Portsmouth, with Jepson taking nine wickets, provided a victory with one wicket to spare – Stocks hitting the vital winning run. Butler and Jepson bowled Notts to a third successive win, this time over Northants at Trent Bridge and the next game also ended in success, thanks to the same two bowlers. This was a memorable match against Warwickshire at Edgbaston, since Hollies, on the losing side, took all ten Notts wickets in the first innings for 49 runs.

Notts performed the double against Warwickshire two games later, when R. T. Simpson, on leave from the RAF, hit 201 in 245 minutes without giving a chance. These victories pushed Notts up the table with rapidity, but unfortunately not a single success was recorded in eight further Championship fixtures and these included the Trent Bridge game against Derbyshire, when Vaulkhard hit his famous 264 – Derbyshire made 529 for nine declared.

Of the batsmen, Keeton had a splendid summer and in all first-class matches reached 2,000 runs. Harris also batted well, but the form of the middle order was variable. Hardstaff, having played his recent cricket in India, could not adjust to the damp slow wickets and had a very poor summer for the County, though he hit 205 not out in the Lord's Test *v* India and another hundred in the Test Trial at Lord's. Simpson appeared in only 15 of the 26 Championship games. The two other newcomers, Reddick and Stocks, batted usefully but averaged under 30. Willatt topped the Cambridge University batting averages, but in seven matches for Notts his highest innings was only 45. Knowles dropped out of the side after five games; Winrow therefore had more opportunity and batted well in ten matches.

A small profit was made in 1946. The campaign to recruit members had by June brought the total membership to 2,886. Hardstaff and Voce were selected for the 1946–47 MCC tour to Australia. England were overwhelmed on this tour and neither of the Nottinghamshire players made a great impression.

During 1946 a group of members of the Club looked at the possibility of forming a Supporters' Association. A formal meeting was set up in January 1947 with the objective of increasing the membership of the Club and promoting functions to raise funds

for the Club. Cyril Lowater was elected Chairman, F. W. Bee
was Honorary Treasurer, R. M. Poulton, Honorary Secretary
and the remainder of the original committee was: H. R. Cox,
W. L. Miron, T. N. Knight, E. A. Hopkinson, W. H. Sherwin,
E. A. Marshall, H. M. Woolley, R. Forman and E. R. Hardy.
This Association was to grow in size and especially during the
1950s made an enormous contribution to the finances of the
County Club.

In 1946 the Club had finished 13th in the table with six wins and
eight losses; in 1947 there were still six wins, losses were reduced
to six and Notts were 11th equal with Essex and Somerset.
Behind the scenes there had been some adverse comments regarding Heane's captaincy and in April it had been decided that W. A.
Sime should be offered the post. He accepted and was to lead the
team for four summers. Apart from the switch from Heane to
Sime there were no changes in the composition of the first eleven.
Hardstaff, after his lack of success in Australia, was ignored by the
selectors and had a marvellous summer for the County, culminat-
ing in some outstanding innings in August. The wickets at Trent
Bridge were made for batsmen and only three times were a side to
lose 20 wickets in a county match on the ground. Hardstaff hit
2,230 runs in the Championship alone, averaging almost 70, and

The Notts side in 1947, showing five players surviving from the 1938 pre-war eleven. From left to right, standing: H. J. Butler, F. W. Stocks, E. A. Meads, C. B. Harris, A. Jepson, F. H. Winrow. Seated: R. T. Simpson, T. B. Reddick, W. W. Keeton, W. A. Sime (captain), W. Voce, J. Hardstaff jun. (NCCC)

was fifth in the overall averages for the year. Keeton had another good year, but Harris missed 11 Championship games due to illness. Simpson played throughout the summer and completed 1,000 runs for the first time, as did Harry Winrow. Reddick also reached 1,000 runs.

Butler and Jepson were the only bowlers to return reasonable figures. The former bowled so well that he won a place in the fourth Test against the South Africans, as well as a trip to West Indies with the MCC side in the winter.

Willatt, the captain of Cambridge, had another successful season at Fenner's and coming into the Notts side hit two hundreds, against Surrey at The Oval and Northants at Northampton. Voce decided to retire and turned out in only five matches early in the year. Giles rejoined the County but also played in only five matches.

The search for fresh talent continued and the County rejoined the Minor Counties Championship. The outstanding find was Peter Harvey, a leg-break bowler from Linby. Harvey took 21 wickets for the second eleven at 22 runs each and was given a chance in the senior side in August. He played against Somerset, picking up three wickets, and in the following match against Derbyshire, both at Trent Bridge. Notts failed in their first innings and Derbyshire hit 496 for three, gaining a lead of over 300. Notts appeared to be heading for defeat by an innings when Harvey came in at number seven. He hit an undefeated 125 and with Winrow, who made 204, added a record 303 for the sixth wicket.

Harvey was to play for the County for 12 years and was spoken of as a possible England player; his bowling, however, did not develop on the batting wickets at Trent Bridge and when the wickets changed, Dooland and Goonesena had arrived. The only other debutant of 1947 was a student from Nottingham University, Norman Horsley. A right-arm fast bowler he played in three first-class matches, all in 1947. He was born in Leicester and was aged 24.

The hot summer brought the crowds back to cricket. The membership rose to 5,074 and gate receipts for the year were a record £8,277 1s 1d. The Test staged at Trent Bridge was successful with good crowds on all days.

The 1948 summer saw no improvement in the Championship results. The team dropped to 14th, the lowest ever recorded, with five matches won against ten losses.

The season began well with wins over Warwickshire, when Hardstaff made 182 not out, and Surrey, when Hardstaff hit 100

Leg-break bowler Peter Harvey took 332 wickets for Notts between 1947 and 1958. (NCCC)

and 79. According to the press a crowd of 35,000 attended the match on Whit Monday, this being a record for the ground, which still stands. It should be pointed out that members were not counted as they entered the ground and thus the attendance can be only an estimate. Hardstaff made over 350 runs in the first two matches, and his total in Championship games all season was 1,015, so he fell away markedly later in the year. He played in the first Test at Trent Bridge and although making 43 in poor light in the second innings was not selected again. Simpson was selected for this first match, having batted well against the Australians in the game with Notts. He was 12th man in the Test and later gained a place in the MCC side to tour South Africa in 1948–49.

Keeton and Harris remained a reliable opening pair. Sime hit

176 not out against Sussex at Hove and batted six hours – a contrast to his normal batting which was much more robust.

Winrow had a disappointing summer, averaging only 22 with the bat; he had one good match as a bowler, his left-arm slows taking five for 18 in Derbyshire's second innings at Trent Bridge. Derbyshire were all out for 125 and Notts won the match, which was Hardstaff's benefit, in two days. Stocks, the other left-hander, scored runs frequently and came third in the averages behind Hardstaff and Keeton.

Butler was easily the best bowler. He had had a miserable time in the West Indies, suffering injury and also an attack of malaria, and his Test appearances had been limited to one, the second match at Port of Spain. In 1948 Championship games he took 83 wickets at 23 runs each; his partner, Jepson took 88 at 29.22. Peter Harvey's leg-breaks were made frequent use of, and he captured 61 wickets, but at 30 runs each. Woodhead, who had been with Todmorden in 1947 rejoined the staff; he was unable to command a regular place in the side and his 25 wickets cost 45 runs each.

Four players were introduced into the side, two of whom were to have a long-term future in county cricket. Cyril Poole was an aggressive left-hand middle-order batsman aged 27 from Forest Town, near Mansfield. He had first appeared in 1941, but was in

The post-war Trent Bridge ground. This aerial view was taken during the 1948 Test match with Australia. (NCCC)

Cyril Poole, an attacking left-hand batsman who made 18,685 runs for Notts between 1948 and 1962 and briefly made the Test team. (NCCC)

the armed forces until the autumn of 1947 and joined the Trent Bridge staff in 1948. In addition to his batting he was a very agile fielder in the deep and in his later years also kept wicket. A talented soccer player, Poole played for Gillingham and Mansfield Town. John Clay was aged 23 and was born in West Bridgford. A sound right-hand batsman and excellent slip field he played in three matches in 1948 and gained his county cap in 1952, when he usually batted at number three. Later Clay was the regular opening batsman with Simpson. He captained the County in 1961 and after finishing in first-class cricket coached at Trent Bridge and ran the Colts side.

Ted Blagg, a right-arm bowler from Shireoaks, played in one first-class match for the County. He was then aged 30 and had been playing for Shireoaks Colliery since 1933; from 1952 to 1963 he played for Steetley Works, being employed by the company as a sales manager. Like Poole he was a noted soccer player, appearing for Nottingham Forest and Southport. Bill Ellis, the fourth young trialist, was a right-arm fast bowler from Bradford who joined the staff in 1947; he remained at Trent Bridge only two years and later made a name for himself in the Bradford League for Spen Victoria and Baildon.

The playing staff for 1949 consisted of 22 players: Keeton, Harris, Voce (now coach), Hardstaff, Butler, Jepson, Woodhead, Winrow, Stocks and Meads, who were the capped players, plus Giles, Harvey, Poole and Clay, four who had played in the first eleven, then eight who were, as yet purely second eleven players, J. A. Rowbotham, E. J. Rowe, E. J. Martin, J. Kelly, H. Flatters, E. Oscroft, A. Richardson and D. Wood. The only amateurs expected to play at all regularly were Simpson and Sime.

The Trent Bridge wicket was becoming even more benign. Only twice were sides bowled out twice there during 1949. The first occasion was when Kent gambled by putting Notts in first and Ridgway took six for 79, dismissing the home side for 273. In

The Duke of Edinburgh meeting the players at Trent Bridge in 1949. Captain Sime is leading the Duke along the line, and he is shaking hands with wicketkeeper Eric Meads. To Meads' right are Jepson and Winrow, and nearest camera are Woodhead and Stocks. (NCCC)

the second innings Doug Wright's peculiar leg-breaks took seven for 58 and the total was 168. Kent won by seven wickets. On the second occasion Harvey's leg-breaks dismissed Sussex for 137 – he took six for 58 – Butler having removed Sussex in their first innings. Notts won by an innings. The County also won three games in succession at Trent Bridge when the opposition declared setting Notts a target. The first of these was against Northants. Notts required 243 in 155 minutes and won with ten minutes to spare; Hardstaff made a hundred in each innings, both without being dismissed. Surrey set Notts 206 in 120 minutes; the target was reached in 97 minutes, Hardstaff making 74. The most remarkable was the third game. By now opposing captains were becoming wise and Leicestershire left 145 minutes in which Notts had to make 279. Keeton was dismissed with the score at 28, but Poole then joined Simpson and the pair added 251 in 97 minutes. Poole reached his 100 in 60 minutes and made in all 154 not out; Simpson made 102 not out, having hit 143 in the first innings.

That win came on 17 June. After that date only one other county risked setting Notts a target – Hampshire gave Notts 128 minutes to make 225. This time Keeton, the 44-year-old veteran, made 109 and with Hardstaff added 132 in an hour. Notts won with seven minutes to spare. All the other games at Trent Bridge were drawn, as no-one dared set a target. In the Hampshire game a tall fast bowler from Woodbeck in the north of the county, Allen Richardson, made his debut and had a promising analysis of 16-8-25-3. He was to play fairly often for the County for three years, but an injury then finished his cricket altogether.

The first-class batting averages were dominated by Notts. Hardstaff was in first place with 2,251 runs, average 72.61, Simpson was fourth with 2,525, average 63.18, Keeton seventh with 2,049, average 55.37, and Poole was not too far behind. Simpson had made his Test debut in South Africa the previous winter, and then made his debut in England at Old Trafford when he made 103, going from 50 to 103 in 27 minutes; he was caught on the boundary attempting a six.

Whilst the County's batsmen had a glorious summer on hard wickets, the bowlers toiled, and only Butler and Harvey managed averages below 30. Butler, who missed many matches through injury, took 44 wickets at 27 runs each; Harvey took 56 wickets at 28 runs each. Woodhead and Jepson actually bowled most overs, more than 750 each, but their wickets cost about 35 runs apiece.

The County won six matches and lost five, which placed them equal eleventh with Lancashire. Six new players were tried: Richardson has already been noted, the others were Eric Martin,

Arthur Underwood, 'Bill' Notley, Eddie Rowe and B. H. Farr.

Martin, a middle-order right-hand bat played for Gedling Colliery. He joined the staff at Trent Bridge in 1947 and remained until the end of 1959. He played in 125 matches spread over those eleven seasons, but only for two or three years did he command a place in the eleven. After leaving the County he played for Steetley in the Bassetlaw League for nearly 30 years and was immensely successful. Eddie Rowe was also on the staff for exactly the same period. Aged 29, he came from Netherfield and was deputy wicketkeeper until 1953, when he succeeded Meads. His poor batting eventually lost him his county place in 1957. In 1960 he became coach at Ellesmere College and was a pioneer in indoor cricket.

Arthur Underwood, a left-arm medium-pace bowler from Wiseton, looked a very promising player, but was serving in the armed forces. His appearances for Notts spread over five years were very limited and at the end of 1954 he declined a renewal of his contract and left county cricket. Two amateurs who played were 'Bill' Notley, whose club cricket from 1934 to 1962 was with the Casuals – he was an off-break bowler, his first-class cricket limited to one match – and Bryan Farr of Worksop Manor, who had topped the Harrow batting averages in 1942 and the following year played for Cambridge *v* Oxford. He played for the Free Foresters and made six appearances for Nottinghamshire.

In 1950 Notts dropped to 15th place. Only three wins were recorded and two of these near the end of the season just saved the ignominy of the wooden spoon. Not a single victory was at Trent Bridge. The first win was at Ilkeston when Derbyshire set Notts 243 in 145 minutes and victory was by one wicket with three minutes to spare. At Coventry in mid-August Butler took twelve for 84, dismissing Warwickshire for 200 and 89. This brought victory by 178 runs. Finally Kent were beaten at Dover by 51 runs. Notts began this match disastrously. Six wickets went down for 16 runs, before Stocks hit out bravely and, with the aid of Meads at number ten and Butler at number eleven, took the total to 157. Butler took six wickets in Kent's first innings and Jepson six in the second – Kent required only 137 in the last innings but were dismissed for 81.

Simpson had the most outstanding season of his long career. In Championship matches he hit 1,873 runs, average 85.13. He played in three of the four Tests against West Indies – it was the year of Ramadhin and Valentine – and scored 94 in the Test at Trent Bridge, his first wicket stand with Washbrook being worth 212 runs. This Test will be remembered, however, for the brilliant batting of Worrell, who made 261. West Indies won by ten wickets.

Hardstaff had an excellent year, hitting five hundreds for Notts and averaging over 55. Considering the problems the England batsmen had facing the West Indian attack, it was somewhat surprising that Hardstaff was not recalled to the Test side. Rumour had it that he had upset one or two powerful figures at Lord's.

Keeton batted well until he broke a finger and missed quite a number of games; Harris was now normally batting in the middle, but reverted to the opening position when Simpson was on Test duty and on one such occasion against Hampshire played the most remarkable innings of his life. Notts lost four wickets with only a dozen runs on the board. Harris batted right through the day for an unbeaten 169 and on the second day went on to 239 carrying his bat through the completed innings of 401. Winrow made 1,420 Championship runs, but Poole was disappointing.

Towards the end of the year the players suffered numerous injuries and for the Derbyshire match at Trent Bridge both George Gunn and Bill Voce were brought out of retirement. It cannot be recorded that either veteran achieved very much.

Twenty-four players were called upon during the summer and these included four new to county cricket. A. K. Armitage, a Nottingham High School boy, who was at Oxford, was a middle-order right-hand batsman and a wicketkeeper. He failed to obtain his blue, but did play for Oxford in first-class matches. His county cricket was limited to five matches in 1950 and 1951. Fred Stinchcombe was a leg-break bowler from Barnby Moor near Retford. He was taken on the Trent Bridge staff in 1951, but remained only one year. He was for many years a notable figure in club cricket in the north of the county. Eric Oscroft, a promising fast-medium bowler had had a trial at the age of 15 and joined the staff in 1949. He played only in 1950 and 1951 and was rather let down by his fielding. Colin Matthews, a left-arm medium-pace bowler made a big impression. Playing for Firbeck Colliery in the Yorkshire Council in 1950 he returned figures of 7-6-2-10. He played on and off for the County until 1959, being absent on National Service through most of 1955 and all of 1956. With more determination he might well have made a name for himself in county cricket.

Two changes behind the scenes had been the appointment in 1949 of Harry Dalling as Ground Superintendent, taking over the position which his father had occupied since the 1920s. Harry's brother Frank was to become the groundsman and Frank jun is at the present time assistant groundsman to Ron Allsopp. Harry himself retired from his full-time post in 1990 and is still employed on a part-time basis. Arthur Wheat, the pre-war wicketkeeper, succeeded Tom Oates as the Notts scorer in 1947.

The 1950 Test match at Trent Bridge marked the opening of the new 'Australian' style scoreboard, which displayed all 22. It was the gift of Mrs T. Bailey Forman, in memory of her husband, the former proprietor of the *Nottingham Guardian* newspaper.

W. A. Sime announced his retirement from county cricket at the end of the summer and was presented with a silver tea service at the Club's Annual General Meeting. Sir Douglas McCraith was made a life member of the Committee at the same meeting: he continued as the Club's Chairman.

The serious plight of the County Club in terms of results required drastic action and the Committee decided to abandon the unofficial rule which allowed only players born in the county, or with long associations with Notts to play in the eleven. The first cricketer to be engaged following this decision was Ken Smales from Horsforth. An off-break bowler and right-hand batsman, he had made his debut for Yorkshire in 1948 as a 20-year-old and in the three seasons 1948 to 1950 had played in 13 first-class matches for his native county. He was specially registered for Notts for 1951. He was to play for the County for eight seasons;

The famous Trent Bridge scoreboard which was built in 1950, and which displayed the names of all 22 players. It shows the only double-century of H. I. Moore, made against the Indian tourists in 1967. The labour-intensive scoreboard was dismantled in 1974 ground improvements. (NCCC)

Notts in 1951, when the County suffered the humiliation of finishing bottom in the Championship for the first time in their history. Simpson, the new captain, was absent through Test calls. From left to right, standing: E. J. Martin, R. J. Giles, A. Richardson, P. F. Harvey, K. Smales, C. J. Poole. Seated: E. A. Meads, A. Jepson, C. B. Harris, J. Hardstaff jun (captain), H. J. Butler, F. W. Stocks. (NCCC)

in 1955 he took 117 wickets and in 1956 became the first Notts bowler to take all ten wickets in an innings for the County in Championship matches. This was at Stroud against Gloucestershire. After leaving Trent Bridge he was appointed Secretary to Nottingham Forest FC and is the historian for that club.

R. T. Simpson was appointed captain of the team for 1951. He had toured Australia with the 1950–51 MCC side and was one of the few players to return with his reputation more or less unblemished. Simpson came into his own in the final Test of that series scoring a brilliant 156 not out which effectively enabled England to beat Australia for the first time since the Second World War. Simpson also hit 259 at Sydney against New South Wales, a score which was to remain the highest of his first-class career.

The weakness of Notts' bowling allied to the tameness of the Trent Bridge wicket – nine of the home Championship games were drawn – meant that the County had a very poor summer. The single victory came against Hampshire at Trent Bridge. Simpson declared setting Hampshire 289; they failed against the leg-spin of Harvey and were all out for 208. The previous match at home had caused some raised eyebrows. Glamorgan batted first on the Saturday and despite a good wicket were painfully slow – Stocks conceded 31 runs in 30 overs and Harris nine runs in 13 overs. Simpson waited until the Glamorgan captain appeared at number six and then bowled an over of under-arm deliveries at him. This seemed to unnerve the Welshmen and four wickets then fell for 11 runs. On the second day Notts seemed anxious to show the opposition how to play bright cricket, but lost their major batsmen in the process and had to bat even more cautiously to retrieve the situation. Even so the follow-on was enforced. On the last day Poole hit a brilliant 135 in 210 minutes.

Due to Test calls Simpson missed eight Championship games, but still completed 1,000 runs for the County and topped the averages. Second came John Clay, who hit two hundreds and made 851 runs in 14 games. Hardstaff, who missed 12 matches through injury, came third, closely followed by Poole. Stocks also had a good summer, but Harris, clearly unwell, appeared in only eight Championship games.

More serious than Harris's absence was the absence of Butler, who played in eleven Championship games and took only 22 wickets; Jepson was also absent from many matches leaving the bowling threadbare indeed. Altogether 21 bowlers were used during the season and none of the players who sent down more than 100 overs averaged below 30 runs per wicket. Smales, the newcomer from Yorkshire, suffered more than most, his wickets costing 66 runs each. The former captain, Heane, was brought back for four matches but achieved nothing of note. Voce played against Sussex in mid-August and took five for 81, including dismissing both openers, John Langridge and D. S. Sheppard, for single figures. He strained a leg muscle and batted with a runner, hitting 45 in quick time to bring first innings points. Shortly afterwards a freak cloud burst completely flooded the ground.

A number of other old hands were recruited, including H. R. Cox, who had one day of success, taking six for 30 against Derbyshire in the penultimate home match, and J. S. Hodgkins. Of the younger element, Matthews, Oscroft, Underwood and Richardson all had opportunities but fought in vain against the docile wickets. Apart from Smales the only newcomer was Gordon Hayward from Bridlington, who played against Cambridge University. He was a tall fast bowler with an awkward delivery, but this proved to be his only first-class match.

The County finished at the bottom of the Championship for the first time ever. The Committee decided that more drastic steps were needed to improve the results. A sub-committee was set up to examine the best way in which to deal with the pitches. This Committee appointed the Chairman of the Asssociation of Groundsmen, H. Bowles, to inspect the square and write a report. Also during 1951, the Club had discussions with Bruce Dooland to see if he would play county cricket. Dooland, a leg-break bowler from Adelaide, had represented Australia in 1946–47 against Hammond's English team, but had narrowly missed selection for the 1948 Australian tour to England. In 1951 he was playing for East Lancashire in the Lancashire League and had taken his club to the top of the League with the remarkable bowling figures of 83 wickets at 8 runs each; he had also a batting average of 37. Dooland agreed to sign for Notts but he had to qualify by residence and therefore would not be available until 1953.

All that can be said for 1952 is that the County handed over the wooden spoon to Somerset and moved into 16th place. The first third of the summer was a succession of losses and draws. The Committee had had much of the square re-seeded and for the Surrey game took the eccentric measure of not allowing the heavy roller on the wicket for a week prior to the match: Notts were bowled out for 52 in the final innings as the wicket got progressively worse over the three days. It was the lowest total by Notts at Trent Bridge since 1912. Alec Bedser took six for 23. A more balanced pitch was arranged when Lancashire came to the ground at the end of June. Hardstaff made 104 not out; the team totals were 271 and 202, 210 and 216. Notts won by 47 runs, Smales and Butler both benefitting from the conditions. The other two wins of 1952 came in the final two matches. At Bristol, following three declarations, Gloucestershire required 253 at 90 an hour. Emmett and Graveney failed and the rest fell to Harvey's leg-breaks. The western county were all out for 122. The final match was another three-declaration job. This time Notts were set almost the same target as they had given Gloucestershire, but Stocks hit 99 in 75 minutes and the game, against Warwickshire, was won with a quarter of an hour in hand.

The averages told the same story as in 1951. Butler was, however, fit and took 74 wickets at 24 runs each; no one else managed a bowling average less than 36. Simpson and Hardstaff had very similar records as batsmen, both making over 1,500 runs at an average between 45 and 50. Poole had gone to India the previous winter and gained a Test cap, playing in three matches against India. The left-hander scored his runs at a good pace and in 1952 reached over 1,500. His two outstanding innings were both double centuries. The first was 222 not out against the Indians, batting seven and a half hours, the second at Ilkeston was 219 out of 337 when everyone else failed.

Three other batsman completed 1,000 runs: Stocks, Giles and Clay. The last narrowly missed a double-hundred against Hampshire. He made 192 and with Poole added 191 for the fourth wicket. Martin played in 18 Championship matches and had some very useful innings including his maiden century, 122 against Derbyshire at Trent Bridge.

The season saw the last appearances of the two veterans, Walter Keeton and Bill Voce. Both played in one match each. Keeton had played in 382 matches for the Club and scored over 23,000 runs, Voce played in 345, taking 1,312 wickets. Both left the Club at the end of the summer.

Three players made their first-class debuts. Austen Baxter, a local amateur from West Bridgford, was an attractive right-hand batsman. In 1953 he hit 98 in 140 minutes against Essex at Southend and appeared to have a very promising future in county cricket, but business commitments meant that his first-class cricket was confined to 13 matches spread over two summers. Gamini Goonesena was played in the match against the Indians. He was waiting to qualify for the Club by residence. A 21-year-old all-rounder from Ceylon, he had already played for his home country. His original intention when he came to England was to join the RAF – however, his well-flighted leg-breaks and easy batting style caught the eye and his flying career was abandoned. He signed a three-year contract to play for Nottinghamshire. He was a regular member of the County side in 1953, but then changed tack, turned amateur and gained entry to Cambridge. For four years he had a very successful cricket career in the university side and played for the County in the vacation – in 1955 and 1957 he performed the 'double'. In 1958 he resumed county cricket full time, but remained only a single summer. From then until 1964 he played odd matches for the County. He emigrated to Australia and appeared in seven games for New South Wales, also taking part in several minor tours. His final first-class match was for the Free Foresters in 1968.

T. W. Birtle was the third 1952 debutant. A fast-medium bowler from Stockton, he had played for Durham in 1945 and was a professional with Norton in the North Yorkshire and South Durham League. He joined the staff in 1952 and played in seven first-class matches, but at the end of the summer asked to be released and returned to the North East.

The experiments to improve the pitches at Trent Bridge had not produced the desired results. It was decided that the earth was so doped with marl that the only solution was to dig up the square and bring in fresh soil. About 400 tons was removed and replaced with soil from the Eton College playing fields.

The 1952 season was a watershed in other ways. Sir Douglas McCraith, who had run the Club as its Chairman virtually since the 'bodyline' crisis, retired in March 1952 and died within twelve months, as did three other Committee members in the winter of 1952–53, namely Lionel Kirk, the former player, who briefly succeeded McCraith as chairman, Cyril Lowater, whose name is still remembered in the 'Lowater Suite', and W. H. Sherwin, a director of Gunn and Moore's.

A CHANGE OF PACE

WITH A NEW PITCH AND two new bowlers, Dooland and Goonesena, the Notts public were looking forward to 1953. Kent were the first visitors to Trent Bridge and the result was a distinct embarrassment. Kent hit 507 for six before declaring; Arthur Fagg, their veteran opener, made 269 not out, which proved to be the highest innings of the entire season. Dooland's figures were none for 97, Goonesena's one for 121. Simpson responded with two very dashing innings of 84 and 157. Notts were forced to follow on, but Giles with 132 not out and Hardstaff 40 not out prevented any hint of a second innings collapse.

The new look Notts side didn't really settle down until the end of July. On 28 July Yorkshire were beaten by four wickets: Dooland took nine wickets. This was the first of seven wins out of ten matches, the other three being lost. As the two preceding matches had also been lost, it meant that twelve successive Notts games had ended in a positive result; not a single draw recorded. This sequence had not been experienced in over 20 years.

Gloucestershire were beaten by seven wickets, Dooland dismissing nine; Hampshire went down by the same margin, Stocks returning second innings figures of 18.2-12-19-5. Notts went down to Weston and disposed of Somerset in two days. Dooland took ten for 49 in the match and Somerset could manage no more than 94 and 108 in response to Notts' 252. Across to the East Coast and Southend for a second successful seaside match. This time Dooland took eight wickets, but was upstaged by Jepson with nine. Essex were all out for 178 and 145. Notts' batting was only a shade better and the County owed everything to Clay and Baxter with 66 and 98. The last two wins came in the last two matches at Trent Bridge. Dooland was largely to take credit in both, picking up ten wickets for 82 against Leicestershire and twelve for 48 against Somerset.

Nine Championship wins were logged and Notts moved up to eighth place in the table. Dooland captured 152 Championship wickets at 16 runs each – in the overall first-class averages he had 172 wickets, more than any other bowler in England and was fourth in the table, behind Jackson, Lock and Statham. It was the summer in which England at last regained the Ashes, beating Hassett's Australians in the match at The Oval, the other four games being drawn. The press wondered whether Dooland should have played for Australia and if his inclusion would have made any difference to the destiny of the Ashes. Three leg-break bowlers were in the Australian party, Ring, Hill and Benaud. None made much impact in the Tests. Dooland played for Notts against the tourists and hit the highest score, but failed to take any wickets. The match is somewhat of a curiosity since it was designated first-class, though limited to two days. The reason why it was only two days was that the Australian tourists wished to watch the coronation of Queen Elizabeth II, the ceremony taking place on the day after the game.

Goonesena was not as successful as his Australian counterpart, but he played in 19 Championship matches, took 35 wickets and made useful runs batting at number eight. The young Ceylonese cricketer certainly had potential.

Jepson came second to Dooland in the bowling table, Stocks third and Butler fourth – all averaged about 26 runs per wicket. Smales and Harvey found themselves left out of the side and spent the summer in the second eleven. The former was replaced by a newcomer, Jack Kelly, a 22-year-old left-hand batsman and slow left-arm bowler. Born in Conisborough, he lived in Worksop and had joined the staff in 1950 after completing his National Service. He was to play in over 50 matches for the County up to the end of 1957; Kelly then took an engagement in Devon and appeared for that county with great success.

The new bowler-friendly wickets at Trent Bridge meant that the batsmen had to work much harder. Only Simpson averaged above 30. The captain hit 1,815 runs, average 56.71, in 20 matches with five hundreds; he was chosen for three Tests but failed to show his true form and was then dropped by England. The Trent Bridge Test was a great battle. Alec Bedser took 14 wickets, a Test record for the ground; unfortunately rain washed out the fourth day and almost all the fifth and a draw was enivitable.

John Clay, who opened the batting throughout the summer and played in every match, came second to Simpson and hit 1,284 runs. Stocks, another ever-present, reached 1,000 and came third. Hardstaff failed to obtain a four-figure aggregate for the first time since 1934 and most of his runs came late in the season. Poole was also disappointing. Giles hit 132 not out in the opening match, but afterwards did very little and was left out of the side.

Two youngsters made their debuts, apart from Kelly, both surnamed Hill, but not related and as like as chalk and cheese. Maurice Hill, a tall fair-haired elegant batsman in the Hardstaff mould, came from Scunthorpe. He was 17 when he made his debut against Hampshire at Bournemouth. In 1954 he disappeared to do his National Service and reappeared in 1956. The

BRUCE DOOLAND

Dooland was the first in the line of notable overseas players who represented Nottinghamshire. In world terms he was not as well-known as Sobers, Rice or Hadlee, but to those who saw him during the five seasons in the 1950s he was one of the most exciting of cricketers. In the first place he was a leg-break bowler who could confuse top-class batsmen, but he was also a good fielder and a batsman rather after the manner of Hadlee.

He bowled leg-breaks, googlies and the 'flipper', which was a quicker top-spinner. During 1953 and 1954 spectators waited for him to come on and then watched the wickets fall as batsmen played and missed and played and missed again. In 1953 he captured 160 wickets at 16 runs each, in 1954, a record 181 at 14 runs each – the least number he took in his five years was 136 and in that summer he also hit 1,517 runs, thus completing the 'double'.

An abiding memory of Dooland is of his innate cheerfulness. The tantrums associated with many of the more famous sportsmen passed him by. The unusual feature of his career is his very meagre Test record. Born in 1923 he had a brilliant career in school cricket in Adelaide and after leaving school was selected to play for South Australia, but was unable to obtain permission from his employer. He then joined the Commandos and fought in the Pacific. Immediately after the war he played in three Tests, but when he failed to obtain a place in the 1948 Australian side to England, he went into the Lancashire League and in four years helped East Lancashire to the League and Cup double.

Apart from his cricket he was capped by Australia at baseball and was a very fine golfer. Sadly he died in 1980 aged 56.

Bruce Dooland, whose mere three Test appearances in no way reflect his greatness as a leg-break bowler. (NCCC)

following summer he completed 1,000 runs and had a regular place in the side, which he retained more or less until the middle of 1965, but he never made the runs of which he seemed capable. In 1966 he joined Derbyshire, but played just two seasons. In 1970 he turned out for Somerset, but with no great success.

Norman Hill, a month older than Maurice, came from the small Notts village of Holbeck. Like Maurice he missed two years due to National Service and it was 1958 before he secured a permanent place in the side. Dark-haired, a short determined cricketer, he was left-handed and developed into an opening batsman. He twice hit 2,000 runs in a season and in 1966 and 1967 captained the County. He retired at the age of 33 to pursue a business career.

For the 1954 season the staff remained little changed, except that Goonesena had gone up to Cambridge. The season was not many weeks old when Butler dislocated a shoulder when bowling against Sussex at Trent Bridge. After a medical inspection he was advised to retire from the game, otherwise there would be danger of permanent injury. His career therefore came to an abrupt end just at a time when through Dooland and Goonesena he was receiving, for the first time since the war, very strong support from the spinners.

Notts in 1953. From left to right, standing: K. Smales, R. J. Giles, J. D. Clay, B. Dooland, E. J. Martin, F. W. Stocks. Seated: A. Jepson, H. J. Butler, R. T. Simpson (captain), J. Hardstaff jun, C. J. Poole. (NCCC)

Maurice Hill made his debut in 1953 and had his best season in 1964. He later appeared for Derbyshire and Somerset. (NCCC)

Matthews was therefore employed as Jepson's new ball partner, but late in the season Smales, bowling medium-pace, had some success with the new ball. Dooland outshone everyone. He broke the record held by Richmond for the most wickets for the County in a season. Dooland took 181 wickets at 14.96, Richmond, also of course a leg-spinner having taken 169 at 13.48 in 1922. Dooland was easily the leading wicket-taker in England (196 in all matches), with 40 more victims than anyone else: only two others reached the 150 mark. Against Essex at Trent Bridge he captured 16 wickets, eight in each innings. Essex were dismissed for 154 and 117, Notts made 359. On two other occasions he picked up eight wickets in an innings. Added to this his batting was vastly improved on 1953 and with the aid of some other non-Notts first-class games he topped 1,000 runs, thus completing the 'double', even though he did not have an individual hundred to his name. Goonesena took 92 wickets in all first-class matches, but over half of these were for Cambridge. He headed the university bowling table and performed well in the match with Oxford, before rejoining Notts.

Hardstaff was more like his old self, though he missed 12 matches. He scored 856 runs with three hundreds and was the top of the batting table. Simpson began well, but broke a finger and managed only one hundred for the County. He did however hit 101 in the Test at Trent Bridge against Pakistan – England won by an innings. Martin came second to Hardstaff in the averages. He gained a regular place and though he managed just one century, he averaged over 30. Poole did better than in 1953, completing 1,000 runs and generally scoring at a fast rate.

The County won ten Championship matches and this pushed them into fifth place. Badly hit by the weather – only Lancashire had more 'no decisions' matches – Notts might have challenged for the title if the elements had been kinder.

The two debutants of 1954 were Mervyn Winfield and Alan Walker. Winfield, a jovial raconteur from Gainsborough, had joined the staff in 1950, but in August 1951 had been called up and was now back on the staff as a full-time professional. A sound middle-order right-hand batsman, he completed 1,000 runs four times and was to remain at Trent Bridge until 1966. Alan Walker played in 1954 only against Pakistan, when he hit 61 and 33 not out and took four wickets out of the six which fell in Pakistan's first innings. A tall well-built left-arm fast bowler and hard-hitting batsman, Walker was 28. He had made his first-class debut for New South Wales in 1948–49 and the following season toured South Africa with the Australian side. He was also a notable rugby footballer. Walker was currently playing for Rawtenstall in the Lancashire League and like Dooland had to qualify for Notts by residence. He would not be available for Championship games until 1956.

Notts again won ten matches in 1955, but fell to eleventh place in the Championship. Winning two of the first three matches, the County began on a high note. Hampshire were outplayed at Portsmouth, where Smales, bowling well on a moist wicket, removed ten batsmen. Dooland took seven wickets, as well as hitting 91 in the first innings, which gave Notts a lead of 213 and victory came by nine wickets. The second win was unusual. Clay and Stocks completely dominated the first-innings batting making 127 and 92 respectively. Somerset in reply collapsed to 93 for six, then Hilton and Tremlett added 149 for the seventh wicket. Somerset required 286 in 200 minutes to win, but Dooland took seven wickets, making twelve in the match, and Notts won by eight runs with two minutes to spare. These victories put Notts

NOTTINGHAMSHIRE *v* ESSEX

Played at Trent Bridge, Nottingham, 19, 20, 21 May 1954

NOTTS WON BY AN INNINGS AND 88 RUNS

ESSEX	FIRST INNINGS		SECOND INNINGS	
T. C. Dodds	lbw b Jepson	12	lbw b Jepson	15
A. V. Avery	not out	92	lbw b Dooland	13
T. E. Bailey	b Jepson	9	c Clay b Dooland	0
R. Horsfall	b Dooland	3	c Poole b Dooland	9
*D. J. Insole	b Dooland	1	b Dooland	5
F. H. Vigar	c Simpson b Dooland	13	b Dooland	2
W. T. Greensmith	c Jepson b Dooland	0	c Jepson b Dooland	11
R. Smith	c Clay b Dooland	14	b Dooland	26
†B. Taylor	b Dooland	0	c Underwood b Stocks	25
J. A. Bailey	b Dooland	0	b Dooland	3
K. C. Preston	b Dooland	2	not out	4
Extras		8	b 3, lb 1	4
Total		154		117

1st inns: 1-14, 2-46, 3-53, 4-55, 5-79, 6-84, 7-134, 8-140, 9-142, 10-154
2nd inns: 1-21, 2-31, 3-32, 4-56, 5-67, 6-71, 7-82, 8-97, 9-112, 10-117

BOWLING	O	M	R	W	O	M	R	W
Jepson	18	3	50	2	11	3	33	1
Underwood	7	1	17	0	2	0	3	0
Dooland	28.3	9	39	8	19	6	44	8
Stocks	13	5	26	0	9	5	28	1
Kelly	5	1	14	0				
Giles					1	0	5	0

NOTTINGHAMSHIRE	FIRST INNINGS		SECOND INNINGS
*R. T. Simpson	b T. E. Bailey	10	
J. D. Clay	lbw b T. E. Bailey	6	
C. J. Poole	c Taylor b J. A. Bailey	41	
J. Hardstaff	c Insole b Preston	112	
F. W. Stocks	st Taylor b Greensmith	50	
R. J. Giles	c J. A. Bailey b Greensmith	67	
B. Dooland	b J. A. Bailey	14	
A. Jepson	st Taylor b Greensmith	1	
J. Kelly	b T. E. Bailey	22	
A. J. Underwood	c and b Preston	27	
†E. J. Rowe	not out	0	
Extras	b 1, lb 7, nb 1	9	
Total		359	

1st inns: 1-15, 2-36, 3-72, 4-163, 5-253, 6-305, 7-307, 8-312, 9-359, 10-359

BOWLING	O	M	R	W
T. E. Bailey	24	4	61	3
Smith	30	9	65	0
J. A. Bailey	16	3	57	2
Preston	23.2	4	64	2
Greensmith	25	3	94	3
Insole	3	1	9	0

Umpires: J. T. Bartley and T. W. Spencer
*Captain; †Wicketkeeper

up near the top of the table, but five matches, including three defeats, went by before the next success. Notts had been set 276 in 180 minutes by Leicestershire and appeared to be plunging to defeat, seven wickets having gone for 155. Simpson then arrived, batting with a runner due to an injured leg. The captain hit 67 out of 97 added for the next wicket in 50 minutes and Notts won by two wickets. A ten-wicket win over Lancashire followed, with Dooland in irresistible form taking 14 wickets and both Giles and Poole hitting hundreds.

This in and out form continued through the season. Dooland was not so effective as in his first two years, though 142 wickets at 22 runs each is a formidable record by normal standards. Goonesena had a brilliant summer. He took 57 wickets and hit 544 runs for Notts; in all first-class games he had 134 victims and scored 1,360 runs. He almost won the annual Gentlemen v Players bowling the latter out in their second innings for 220, leaving the Gentlemen 201 to win. Unfortunately they made only 180. Smales gave Dooland most support day in day out. He took 117 wickets and five wickets in an innings on eight occasions. Against Lancashire at Trent Bridge he performed the hat-trick.

Midway through the season Hardstaff announced his retirement. He had appeared in 14 matches and scored the last of his 83 first-class centuries against Yorkshire at Trent Bridge. Aged 44 he was only the second Notts batsman to complete more than 30,000 first-class runs and he had played in over 100 fewer matches than the other Notts member of the list, George Gunn.

Giles came out at the head of the batting table but very little separated him from Simpson, Poole and Stocks. All scored 1,000 runs, as did Clay. Martin was disappointing after his good season in 1954.

Four new players were tried in the course of the campaign. Alan Cleveley and Maurice Wood were both right-arm medium-fast bowlers, whose first-class careers were confined to 1955. A 23-year-old from Chaddesden in Derby, Cleveley was a great enthusiast for the game, but was unable to translate this enthusiasm into taking wickets on the field. Wood went on to be coach at Nottingham High School but died tragically young aged 44.

Ken Poole, not related to Cyril, came from a farming family at Thurgarton. His talents were recognised very early, for he came to Trent Bridge at the age of 15 and was offered a post on the staff.

Bruce Dooland's best performance. In this season he took 50 more first-class wickets than any other bowler in the country.

A middle-order batsman and medium-fast bowler, he played in 26 matches for the County in three seasons. Then an accident on his farm resulted in the loss of three fingers and this terminated a promising cricket career. John Springall was a Londoner who had been on the MCC staff. He had moved to Trent Bridge at the start of the 1955 season and remained with the Club until the end of 1963. A sound right-hand batsman, he also bowled useful medium-pace and was known to keep wicket occasionally.

The rains ruined 1956. Notts suffered 17 drawn matches – more than any other side – and this was certainly not due to vast run sprees. Only Simpson of the regular first eleven averaged more than 30 in Championship games and only three other members of the side averaged above 20. Seven matches were won and four lost. This pushed the County three places up in the table. The best win of the year was against Surrey, the County Champions, at Trent Bridge. Lock took eight wickets, dismissing Notts for 220; Smales and Dooland, with five wickets each, struck back and Surrey were all out for 117. Lock and Laker did the damage in Notts' second innings, but the Surrey batting, despite the presence of May and Barrington, was unable to cope with the Notts spinners in the final innings and victory was by 187 runs.

Walker, now qualified, did not bowl as incisively as predicted, but created a record at Grace Road. He dismissed Frith with his final ball in the first innings and began the second innings with a hat-trick, removing Lester, Tompkin and Smithson: four wickets in four balls. Another oddity in this game was that Hallam, the Leicestershire opening batsman, was given out 'run out' by the square-leg umpire after the bowler's umpire had called 'over'. Hallam was brought back. Notts won this game by nine wickets.

Walker was also involved in a century partnership for the last wicket. At Trent Bridge against Somerset, Notts collapsed to 134 for nine. Walker came in as last man and with Dooland raised the total to 257, a partnership of 123 in 120 minutes. Dooland then dismissed Somerset cheaply, taking seven for 41 and a belligerent innings from Clay, which included eight consecutive scoring strokes each worth four, won the match by nine wickets.

Notts had no representatives in the Test series against Australia, but Stocks broke several records when the tourists played Notts. The left-hander hit 171. This was the highest score by a county batsman against the Australians since the war, it was the highest ever by a Notts player against the Australians and it was a personal best for Stocks.

An attempt to solve the lack of runs was made by dropping

wicketkeeper Rowe and putting Cyril Poole behind the stumps. This experiment proved a failure, due to Poole's mistakes, and Rowe had to be reinstated. The search for a wicketkeeper-batsman was, however, instituted and a suitable candidate found the following year.

Dooland took 146 wickets at 19 runs each; his main support came from Jepson, who seemed to find a new lease of life at the age of 41. He took 83 wickets at 21 runs each – in terms of runs per wickets his best year to date. Smales had a famous match at Stroud against Gloucestershire when he became the first player to take all ten wickets in a Championship innings for the County. His final analysis was 41.3-20-66-10 and Gloucestershire were all out for 214. Notts, however, were easily beaten, the batting failing in both innings and the margin of defeat was nine wickets. Smales' total bag for the season was 69 wickets at 22 runs each. The Australian Walker played in every match, opening the bowling with Jepson, but only on two occasions did he capture five wickets in an innings and his 55 wickets cost nearly 30 runs each. Goonesena was available for just five matches, but his 20 wickets at 20 runs each showed how useful he might have been if not at Cambridge – he again topped the university bowling averages.

Simpson, Stocks, Giles and Poole topped 1,000 runs, but only the captain could be proud of his record. No new players were tried during the summer, something that had not occurred since the 1850s.

The 1957 season saw the County fall back to the pre-Dooland position, though Dooland was still playing. The batting record was as poor as in 1956, but the bowlers were much more expensive. Illness and injury were largely to blame. Simpson suffered back trouble. He turned out in ten matches but was clearly unfit to play and the side was led in his absence by Jepson. Stocks broke a finger in pre-season nets practice and was not available for the first month – he played in eleven games in all. Walker went down with mumps during the first match and he played in only half the fixtures.

Dooland failed to find his form early on and not a single match was won in May. The first victory came against Worcestershire on 4 June when Smales took six for 55 and Maurice Hill hit a brilliant 95. The second win was against Middlesex when Notts were set 100 runs an hour and hit 233 with seven minutes to spare. Poole batted in his most attacking form to win this match. Warwickshire were beaten in mid-August thanks to Goonesena and Dooland. The opposition needed 249 in 200 minutes, but

GLOUCESTERSHIRE *v* NOTTINGHAMSHIRE

Played at Stroud, 9, 11, 12 June 1956

GLOUCESTERSHIRE WON BY 9 WICKETS

NOTTINGHAMSHIRE	FIRST INNINGS		SECOND INNINGS	
*R. T. Simpson	run out	5	c Emmett b McHugh	70
R. J. Giles	c Rochford b Wells	30	b Mortimore	18
H. M. Winfield	c Emmett b McHugh	7	c Rochford b McHugh	27
C. J. Poole	c Nicholls b Wells	2	b McHugh	0
F. W. Stocks	b Cook	14	c Milton b McHugh	4
E. J. Martin	lbw b McHugh	24	c Emmett b McHugh	1
B. Dooland	b Mortimore	22	b McHugh	0
A. K. Walker	b Mortimore	1	b Cook	1
K. Smales	not out	8	lbw Wells	8
A. Jepson	c and b Mortimore	0	run out	1
†E. J. Rowe	c Crapp b Mortimore	1	not out	0
Extras	b 4, lb 1, w 1, nb 2	8	b 5, nb 2	7
Total		122		137

1st inns: 1-12, 2-38, 3-51, 4-57, 5-71, 6-112, 7-112, 8-114, 9-114, 10-122
2nd inns: 1-50, 2-111, 3-111, 4-122, 5-123, 6-124, 7-124, 8-127, 9-137, 10-137

BOWLING	O	M	R	W	O	M	R	W
McHugh	22	9	27	2	26.2	11	41	6
Smith	7	0	12	0	2	1	8	0
Wells	18	7	27	2	18	4	33	1
Cook	10	2	27	1	22	10	18	1
Mortimore	10.2	5	21	4	12	4	30	1

GLOUCESTERSHIRE	FIRST INNINGS		SECOND INNINGS	
*G. M. Emmett	b Smales	33	not out	31
W. Knightley-Smith	c Rowe b Smales	34	c Giles b Stocks	8
R. B. Nicholls	c and b Smales	15	not out	6
J. F. Crapp	c Winfield b Smales	0		
C. A. Milton	not out	70		
J. B. Mortimore	c Poole b Smales	45		
D. R. Smith	lbw Smales	0		
†P. Rochford	b Smales	2		
C. Cook	c and b Smales	0		
B. D. Wells	lbw Smales	4		
F. P. McHugh	b Smales	0		
Extras		11		1
Total		214	(1 wkt)	46

1st inns: 1-45, 2-76, 3-76, 4-78, 5-95, 6-198, 7-200, 8-204, 9-206, 10-214
2nd inns: 1-29

BOWLING	O	M	R	W	O	M	R	W
Walker	25	8	50	0	3	0	7	0
Jepson	8	3	20	0	2	0	6	0
Dooland	29	13	67	0				
Smales	41.3	20	66	10	4	2	14	0
Stocks					3.4	0	18	1

Umpires: K. McCanlis and L. H. Gray
*Captain; †Wicketkeeper

were dismissed for 73: Dooland had the curious analysis of 7.1-3-5-4 and Goonesena took four for 30. In this game Norman Hill hit a maiden first-class hundred. Dooland also completed the 'double', the first to achieve this feat in 1957.

The season ended with two exciting games. Notts beat Leicestershire at Trent Bridge by one wicket due to all-round cricket from Dooland in his last home match for the County – he had announced that he would be returning permanently to Australia in the winter. Dooland scored 72 and 51, the highest score in both innings, and took seven wickets.

The final match was at Bristol when again Dooland's batting was to the fore. He hit 58 and 70, the latter in 90 minutes.

These five wins placed Notts in 15th position. Cyril Poole was the leading batsman and the only one to average above 30. In addition to him, Dooland, Maurice Hill and Clay completed 1,000 runs. Dooland and Goonesena were the only bowlers to take wickets at less than 25 runs each. No Notts players featured in the Test series against West Indies, but the Trent Bridge Test was quite outstanding. England made 619 for six, Graveney scoring 258, Peter Richardson (his brother also played) made 126 and May 104. In reply West Indies were saved by a marvellous innings from Worrell who carried his bat right through for an undefeated 191 out of 372. The follow-on was enforced and this time Collie Smith defied the very destructive bowling of Trueman and Statham. Smith made 168. England required 121 in an hour to win, but could make just 64 for one. A total of 61,167 spectators attended the game.

There were four fresh faces in the Notts side in 1957. Geoff Millman, the 22-year-old wicketkeeper from Bedfordshire, joined the staff and became the regular first eleven stumper. He had played for his native county from 1954 and in 1956 had made his first-class debut for Combined Services whilst on National Service. A neat, unobtrusive wicketkeeper, he was considered the most promising in England and he was also a very useful right-hand batsman. Millman was to go on and play for England, captain Notts and then suddenly decide to retire at the age of 30 to devote himself to family business in Bedford.

Two other imported players making their debuts were Tom Atkinson from Cumberland, a useful all-rounder, and Michael Morgan, originally from South Wales, but living in the West

Ken Smales became the only Notts player to take all ten wickets in an innings in an inter-county match.

Midlands. Morgan was an off-break bowler. Atkinson decided to give up county cricket in 1960 and became a professional in Scotland, Morgan finished the following season. The fourth newcomer was Roger Vowles from Grimsby, another useful all-rounder. Vowles had joined the staff in 1954 and played his final first-class match in 1961.

The County had one of the largest playing staffs in the country with 29 players, which did not include the part-time Goonesena or the coach, who was J. H. Parks the former Sussex cricketer. It is worthy of note that the 'office staff' consisted of H. A. Brown, the Secretary, R. M. Poulton as his assistant and one clerk.

Dooland was the major absentee for 1958, but Stocks had also declined to renew his contract and his doughty left-hand batting would be difficult to replace. The County gambled on an extreme measure, starting the season with two completely unknown young bowlers to open the attack, one aged 18 and the other 19. John Cotton from Newstead was a fast right-arm bowler, who had had a trial in the autumn of 1955, and joined the staff as a 15-year-old the following year. Paul Taylor of East Kirkby had had a trial in 1954 and been taken on the staff in 1955. He was a left-arm fast-medium bowler. Both were clearly full of potential but it was somewhat foolhardy to believe that they would make any immediate impact at top level, especially as Dooland was no longer present. The experiment was abandoned after the first few matches. Taylor went to do his National Service and did not return to county cricket. Cotton, a tall young man who was prone to injury, played with some success until 1964 and then moved on to Leicestershire for five seasons. His record in his initial summer was enough to evoke comments in the national press – he took 42 Championship wickets at 24 runs each. In 1958 only Jepson and Smales had better figures for the County. All in all the bowling was better than predicted, but the batting returned probably the worse set of statistics in the 20th century. No one averaged 30. Poole topped the table with 1,230 runs, average 27.33 – he was 50th in the first-class averages. Simpson had still not recovered completely from his back strain and though he played throughout the year did not hit a single hundred – only two were made in Championship matches, one by Poole and one by Maurice Hill.

The County ended bottom of the table with three wins; these were against Hampshire at Trent Bridge, due to the bowling of Smales and Goonesena, against Northants, also at home, when all the bowlers shared the wickets and the opposition collapsed for 94 and 158, and finally in late August at Grace Road when

Goonesena had his best match of the year, taking 13 wickets for 82 runs.

Apart from Cotton and Taylor two other youngsters were given first-class matches. Mike Hall, a stylish right-hand batsman from Retford, was the son of J. B. Hall and therefore for the first time in post-war cricket Notts had both a father and son play for the County. Hall played in 17 matches spread over two seasons, and in many second eleven matches. He was a major figure in Bassetlaw League cricket, playing for Retford for well over 25 years. His two sons are also prominent local club players. Joe Walters, a bespectacled leg-break bowler from Bolsover was 18 years old. Like Hall his county cricket was limited to two seasons.

Financially during this period the County Club was kept afloat by the efforts of the Supporters Association. E. A. Marshall was the Chairman, F. W. Bee the Treasurer and R. M. Poulton the Secretary. In 1958 they gave £19,734 to the Club, and due to this the profit for the year was £502. The most serious item on the 1958 accounts was the drop in membership from 8,057 to 6,389. The early post-war years, when petrol rationing and the lack of alternative sports facilities had made it a boom time for cricket, were over. Unfortunately the county clubs were slow to realise this and the amenities on grounds for the spectator remained the same as in the 1930s.

The prospects for 1959 were described as 'not too promising' in *The Cricketer* preview. As it is normal to predict in this *Spring Annual* that each county looks forward to a better season than the preceding one, this comment was grim indeed. Four players had left the Club. Walker's contract was cancelled and he was paid off. The Club had expected so much from him, mainly due to the tremendous success of Dooland; Walker took just 93 wickets at 32 runs each and averaged under 20 with the bat. Smales left in order to join Nottingham Forest as an administrator; he was only 31 and still had a lot of cricket in him. Harvey, who was 35 and had been mainly a second eleven player over the last few seasons, went to a full-time job with Redmayne and Todd, the sports outfitters. G. Goonesena, who was the greatest loss, had other interests to pursue outside England. In addition the club did not renew the contract of Jim Parks the coach. His place was taken by Frank Shipston, who had been employed as the assistant coach, in March 1958.

A desperate search was made for some immediate replacements. Both Appleyard and Lowson who had retired from Yorkshire were sought in vain. Carlton Forbes, a 22-year-old left-hander playing with Middlesbrough but born in Jamaica, was signed on, but would not be able to play straight away in Championship matches; Ian Davison, a 21-year-old fast bowler, who had topped the Bedfordshire averages (43 wickets, 12.20) in 1958 was also signed up.

The forecast of *The Cricketer* proved accurate. Nottinghamshire finished 1959 at the foot of the table. Not a single bowler had an average under 30. Cotton came out on top with 67 wickets at 30.49 runs each and the only other deliveries to make any impression were the off-breaks of Morgan. He took 81 wickets at 32 runs each. Only four matches were won. The first was a three-declaration job against Leicestershire at Trent Bridge. Notts were set 240 in 140 minutes and won in the final over due to a brilliant innings of 133 not out by Eric Martin, the best he ever played for the County. The second win was when Cotton took five for 32 against Warwickshire at Trent Bridge and in another run-chase Poole hit 78. The only away Championship win was at Southampton. Another three declaration match saw Notts set a target that they reached with three minutes and five wickets to spare. Millman hit 95. The final victory was over Lancashire. The first two innings were completed, Morgan taking five wickets for Notts and Greenhough five for Lancashire. Then Lancashire hit 276 for four before declaring, with Jackie Bond, later to play for Notts, completing a maiden unbeaten hundred. Norman Hill and Mervyn Winfield both hit hundreds as Notts raced to the 305 required for victory. In the process Hill performed the feat of a century in each innings for the first time – as a curiosity he had been dismissed for two ducks in the other match against Lancashire. This win came on 21 July. Notts played 12 more matches during 1959 and failed to notch another win in the Championship.

Both the friendly first-class games did however end in success. The first was against Cambridge University at Trent Bridge. In order to add a little flavour to the match, Keith Miller, the former Australian Test all-rounder, was invited to play for Notts and scored 62 and 102 not out, thereby entering the list of those who had hit centuries on debut for the County. Carlton Forbes also made his first appearance for Notts in this match, but his two wickets cost 100 runs. In addition, the Indian tourists were beaten by eight wickets. Cotton, Matthews and Springall shared the wickets and Simpson hit exactly 100, his final fifty coming in 30 minutes.

In all Notts first-class matches Simpson made 2,033 runs and Norman Hill 2,129. Hill completed six centuries and Simpson five. Simpson was now batting at number five and the openers were generally Norman Hill and Millman. The latter topped 1,000 runs, but did not compile a three-figure innings. Springall, Cyril Poole and Winfield also hit over 1,000 runs but they were not consistent. Maurice Hill had a poor year and was dropped for many matches. Martin and Clay played spasmodically.

Aside from Miller, Davison and Forbes, opportunities were given to three other new players. Peter Forman, a 25-year-old left-arm spinner who had been in the XI at Oakham, played in three Championship games, and was to turn out occasionally until 1962. M. W. Haynes, a middle-order right-hand batsman associated with Lenton United CC, played in nine first-class matches spread over three years. Tony Siddons, a 17-year-old off-break bowler, joined the staff in 1958 and remained until 1961 but never commanded a first-team place.

Season 1959 was that in which the Second Eleven Competition began. Notts competed both in the Minor Counties Competition and the new league, playing ten matches in each. The second eleven was captained by Jack Baddiley, a jovial farmer from the Worksop area whose cricket was mainly in the Bassetlaw League. Many young players were tried out in these 20 games. The old hands Martin, Clay and Giles were the dominant batsmen and Davison and Matthews the best bowlers.

The first Test, against India, was staged at Trent Bridge. Interest was not high and only 32,509 attended over the four days of the match, India being overwhelmed, Statham and Trueman proving much too good for the visitors.

R. M. Poulton succeeded the long serving H. A. Brown as Secretary to the County Club in the spring of 1959. Brown's tenure of office had spanned 39 years, a record which will be difficult to beat. His knowledge of cricket was not great but he had been a quiet diplomat and this, especially during the Second World War, had been invaluable.

The one major recruit for 1960 was 'Bomber' Wells, the Gloucestershire off-break bowler. He had played for his native county since 1951 with much success but had to compete with Allen and Mortimore, both of whom were better batsmen, so in 1959 his cricket had been with the Gloucestershire second eleven. He was only 29 and therefore had several years of county cricket in him. Notts certainly made use of him in his first summer at Trent Bridge. He bowled more overs in first-class cricket than anyone else in the country (1,354.3) and took 120 wickets at 24.25 runs each. Cotton also had a better year, taking 82 wickets at about the same cost. Unfortunately this pair had very little support. Davison bowled with fire but was still somewhat wild.

Morgan did not do so well and was used in only 11 Championship matches. Atkinson was employed as a seam bowler and Springall was often called upon, but neither really worried the top flight batsmen.

As in 1959 Notts could win only four matches, but as Leicestershire managed just two victories, the latter ended with the wooden spoon, Notts moving up one place. After a barren May, Somerset were defeated at Bath, Wells taking eight wickets and Poole playing two excellent innings of 64 and 74 not out. The second victory came at Swansea five weeks later, when Wells returned figures of 11-7-11-5, bowling out Glamorgan for 52 in their second innings, when the Welshmen only needed 120 to win. Northants were beaten at Northampton by six wickets and finally Lancashire were beaten at Southport, when Notts bowled out the home side for 83 – Atkinson took four for 37 and Wells four for 24. Lancashire followed on and Notts required 120 in the final innings, struggling home with three wickets to spare. To more than outbalance the four victories came 16 defeats, and not one of the successes occurred at Trent Bridge.

Poole had a very good season with the bat, scoring 1,622 runs at an average of 41.58. Simpson, Springall and Winfield also completed 1,000 runs, but averaged less than 30. Norman Hill unfortunately broke a bone in his hand and missed nearly half the matches. Maurice Hill scored 109 against Warwickshire at Trent Bridge, but otherwise achieved little. He was such a stylish batsman that it was a great disappointment when he failed so often.

In an effort to improve the playing record, five young cricketers, not including Bomber Wells, made their debut. Alan Gill was a determined middle-order right-hand batsman from Underwood, who had joined the staff the previous season as an 18-year-old. He played in 53 matches finishing in 1965, without making any outstanding scores; Gill also bowled leg-breaks. David Barber played only against Cambridge. A member of the Eton XI in 1956 he went up to Cambridge but failed to obtain a blue. He was the great-nephew of W. D. Barber, who had played for Notts in 1904. Pat Oakden was a fast right-arm bowler from Kirkby in Ashfield. He had joined the staff only at the beginning of the summer and remained two seasons, playing in eight first-class games. Vincent Lindo, a fast bowler from Jamaica, was on the staff just in 1960 and played one first-class match; in 1963 he had one game for Somerset, but his career has mainly been in Staffordshire, where he has been very successful in local club cricket. Lastly, Robin Bilbie, an attractive middle-order right-hand batsman from Nottingham, played in six Championship matches in 1960. He appeared occasionally until 1963 when he left the staff.

There was little interest in the Trent Bridge Test of 1960 against South Africa, the series had been dominated by the controversy surrounding the bowling action of Griffin. England won at Nottingham by eight wickets and a day to spare.

Reg Simpson announced his retirement as captain of the County in the autumn. He had led the Club in difficult circumstances for eleven years and had seen Trent Bridge change from a 'featherbed' to a wicket which opportunities to both batsmen and bowlers. Simpson would still be available to play in a limited number of games in 1961. Although many counties were now abandoning the notion that the leader of a side must be an amateur, Notts decided to import a new amateur. The cricketer who was chosen was Andrew Corran, the Oxford University fast bowler, who played for Norfolk. Norfolk headed the Minor Counties Championship in 1960, but were beaten in the final challenge match. Corran took 46 wickets at 17.02 runs each, and he also topped the Oxford bowling averages.

Corran would not, however, be available for the County until July and therefore Notts appointed John Clay as captain for 1961. As in 1959 and 1960 only four matches were won. Surrey were beaten at Trent Bridge; they required 291 in the final innings and looked like reaching the target until Forbes took three for 12 and victory came by 28 runs. Northants were defeated, also at Trent Bridge, by 127 runs; Winfield made 103 and Millman 99. Forman caused a minor sensation in the Warwickshire match, reappearing in the side after a two-year gap. His left-arm spin picked up eight for 79 and Notts won by 37 runs. The only win away from home was at Yeovil, when Wells took nine wickets in a low-scoring game. No fewer than 20 matches ended in defeat and the County finished bottom of the table.

The County used a new home venue for the match with Sussex, playing on Steetley's ground at Shireoaks (the match score in *Wisden's Almanack* incorrectly gives Worksop). The game, which is the only first-class one ever played at this venue, was most unusual. Norman Hill hit 201 not out and Notts declared at 350 for four; Sussex reached 351 for the loss of three wickets before declaring, their chief scorer being Alan Oakman with 229 not out. Notts then collapsed in their second innings and Sussex cantered home by nine wickets.

Corran made his debut as scheduled after the university term and took 59 wickets, but they cost 34 runs each. Wells was more expensive than in his first years and the attack was weakened by an ankle injury which meant that Cotton missed 15 matches. Forbes in his first full summer captured 50 Championship wickets, but they cost 40 runs each; however he did complete 1,000 first-class runs. Norman Hill topped the batting and in all matches completed 2,000 runs. Simpson appeared in 12 games and came second to Norman Hill. Maurice Hill had a much better summer, hitting three centuries. Poole, Clay and Millman also reached 1,000 runs. Millman was selected to go to Pakistan with the MCC side and there superseded Murray as England's wicketkeeper.

Apart from Corran, two other players made their debut. Billy Rhodes was a wicketkeeper-batsman from Bradford. He stayed on the staff until 1964, when an accident caused him to retire from county cricket; he deputised for Millman behind the stumps and scored some useful runs. His son is the present Worcestershire keeper. Alan Wheelhouse, a fast bowler from Nottingham High School, played in one first-class match. He had gained a blue at Cambridge in 1959. After coming down he joined the legal profession and is a member of the present county cricket club committee.

As David Pratt, the Worcestershire slow left-arm bowler, was the only major recruit to the playing staff for 1962, it could hardly be expected that the County would move very far up the table. Pratt was tried in seven Championship matches, but his bowling proved ineffectual and he was not seen again in first-class cricket. Corran took over the captaincy from Clay, the latter being appointed second eleven captain. It soon became obvious, however, that Corran was not an ideal captain and unfortunately this office weighed so heavily upon him that his bowling fell away. Once more Notts won four matches, but since there were more games drawn due to the weather, the County managed to move up to 15th place.

Glamorgan were beaten in the second match of the season, Winfield scoring a century and Davison bowling well; the second success did not come until the end of June, Lancashire being dismissed at Liverpool for 106 and 124. Cotton, Davison and Corran all bowled well in this game. Lancashire were beaten a second time in mid-August. Simpson hit 79 not out and 82 not out and held the batting together in both innings. The final win was at Northampton. This time, with three declarations, Notts were successful in a run-chase led by Norman Hill and Poole.

Davison had his best season with the ball; in the early stages he actually stood at the head of the bowling averages, but he was very overworked latterly and his final figures were 77 wickets at 27.35 runs each. Cotton took 62 wickets at 28 runs each. Forbes' left-arm medium captured 35 at 33 and Corran 72 at 32. Wells sent down more than 1,000 overs, but was the most expensive of the main bowlers and the only regular spinner. Forman was tried instead of Pratt in some games but did not enjoy the success he had had the previous year.

The batting showed a dramatic decline from 1961; only three players completed 1,000 runs and of those only Norman Hill averaged more than 30. Simpson appeared in ten matches, and when present made a vast difference to the side, rarely failing. Poole was now at the close of his career and was seen in about half the Championship games. He did not play a three-figure innings. Rhodes and Gill had some good days and the latter opened the innings during the second half of the summer, replacing Millman. The wicketkeeper was chosen for the first two Tests against Pakistan, then lost his place to Murray, mainly because he was not fully fit during the second Test – at Lord's – and thus came in for some criticism.

Apart from Pratt three other cricketers made their debut in 1962. Ian Moore from Sleaford, an attractive right-hand batsman, was 21. He had already played for Lincolnshire and was to remain at Trent Bridge until 1969. His best summer was 1965. He later returned to Minor Counties cricket and appeared in representative matches for the Minor Counties. Barry Stead played in the match against Pakistan. It was not until 1966 that he played at all regularly in the first eleven, though he had appeared twice for his native Yorkshire in 1959. A left-arm fast-medium bowler, he was a somewhat carefree character: in 1962 he was supposed to be playing for Essex in a first-class friendly match, but turned out for Notts second eleven on the same date. His best season in first-class cricket was 1972. The fourth debutant was another Yorkshireman, Barry Whittingham. His two 1962 matches were against Pakistan and Cambridge. A left-hand batsman, he played in 77 games for Notts over a five-year period and then moved to Cumberland, appearing for that county for five years.

The weather in 1963 was even more depressing than its predecessor. Notts, however, won six matches and this brought a marked improvement in their standing in the Championship as the County moved up into ninth place. The first month went by without a victory, but on 4 June, Surrey were beaten by 115 runs. The next two games also finished with victories. Lancashire were vanquished by three wickets and Worcestershire by ten wickets.

Later both Lancashire and Worcestershire were beaten again and the last success came against Derbyshire.

The chief factor in the change of fortune was the signing of Brian Bolus from Yorkshire. Bolus had played for Yorkshire since 1956 in 107 matches. In 1961 he had done particularly well, but in 1962 had lost his touch and been dropped from the first eleven. An attacking right-hand batsman, he was determined to prove that Yorkshire had made a mistake. This he most certainly did. He ended the year with 2,190 runs at an average of 41.32. No one in the country scored so many runs and only three batsmen had a better average. He hit five centuries, of which the highest was 202 not out against Glamorgan at Trent Bridge. This was an

Brian Bolus joined Notts from Yorkshire in 1963, soon making his Test debut. He captained Notts in 1972 and made over 15,000 first-class runs for them. (NCCC)

236

astonishing display. The Notts total was 303 for seven declared and he hit five sixes and 21 fours. A month later he was opening the batting for England against West Indies at Headingley in the fourth Test. He retained his place for the fifth Test and was also chosen to go to India with the MCC side.

Notts signed a second ex-Yorkshire player, the slow left-arm spinner Keith Gillhouley. He took 74 wickets at 27 runs each, but was no-balled for throwing in the match against Glamorgan at Ebbw Vale. He was to play for Notts for four seasons but the doubt over the fairness of his delivery placed a shadow on his first-class career.

Davison continued to improve. Obtaining better support than in 1962, he kept an edge on his bowling and took 111 wickets at 21 runs each. Cotton and Wells also had better returns, but Corran appeared in only nine Championship games. Millman captained the side with quiet efficiency, though he was somewhat on the cautious side.

Norman Hill had decided to retire before the season opened, but changed his mind later on and played in 15 matches, coming second to Bolus in the batting table. Gill began the season as Bolus's opening partner, then rather lost his way and Whittingham was promoted. He completed 1,000 runs, as did Maurice Hill. Moore played some useful innings, including 108 against Surrey at Trent Bridge. In contrast not much was seen of Winfield and Springall.

Alec Johnson from Loughborough, a 19-year-old fast bowler played in one Championship game. Though he remained at Trent Bridge until 1966 he had only occasional success. Afterwards he played with Northumberland and Durham and prospered in Minor County cricket.

The 1963 season saw the introduction of the Gillette Cup; Notts had taken part in the pilot scheme organised the previous summer by F. M. Turner, the Leicestershire Secretary. The first Notts one-day match of 1963 took place at Middlesbrough. Bolus appropriately carried his bat through the Notts innings, scoring exactly 100 out of 159. Gillhouley produced bowling figures of 14-6-33-4. The efforts of these two exiles was not, however, sufficient and Yorkshire won by four wickets.

In order to reverse the falling membership roll, the County launched a recruitment drive in 1963 with a full-time campaign director. The scheme increased the number of members by 1,860. The sub-committee which masterminded the operation was chaired by Jack Elliott.

Bolus came back from India a changed man. He had opened the

innings in all five Tests and was remarkably consistent, averaging 48 without the aid of any 'not outs', yet with a highest score of 88. Somewhere on the sub-continent he decided to alter his approach to batting. Gone was the carefree stroke play of 1963, to be replaced by batting much more in the Boycott mould. His average and aggregate both dropped. He was selected for the MCC *v* Australians match at Lord's in May and with Boycott added 124 for the first wicket, but the report curiously notes: 'the longer they stayed together the less convincing they became.' Bolus batted nearly four hours for 72. The England selectors ignored Bolus for the first Test, picking Edrich and Boycott as the opening pair, but in the event Edrich was unfit and Titmus opened. Boycott then fractured a finger when fielding and Dexter and Titmus began England's second innings. In fact Bolus was never chosen for England again.

After their relatively successful year in 1963, Notts sank back to 15th place in 1964. The batting was frail indeed. Only Bolus featured in the top 50 batsmen in the averages and he was about 30th. Second to Bolus in the County table was Maurice Hill, the only other cricketer to reach 1,000 runs. In 29 innings Notts were all out for less than 200.

The season opened with an innings victory over Leicestershire, when Cotton bowled the opposition out for 99; he took five for 38. The follow-on was enforced, even though Notts' total amounted to only 252 for eight. Gillhouley returned figures of 20.5-13-21-5 and Leicestershire were all out for 138. The next 12 Championship games went by without a second win, but in early July Gloucestershire were easily overcome at Trent Bridge. Forbes and Davison were responsible for removing the western county twice and, left 101 to make in the final innings, for once the Notts batting succeeded – victory by nine wickets. There was another barren period – eleven games without a win – then in the closing weeks of the season, Lancashire and Gloucestershire were both beaten. In the first of these, Notts were set about three hours to make 240. Bolus and Ian Moore added 151 for the second wicket and with Maurice Hill hitting a quick 48, the win was by eight wickets. In the Gloucestershire game, Goonesena, who had returned to the County for a brief period, took five for 66, Forbes picked up five for 31 and Notts scraped home by four runs.

The bowling averages showed a bag of mixed fortunes. Cotton and Wells had very disappointing returns and both missed many matches. The fast bowler was released at the end of the year and joined Leicestershire for 1965. Forbes topped the averages with 53 wickets at 17 runs each. Davison took most wickets – 82 at 24 runs each – and Gillhouley had some good returns. The most promising debutant was M. N. S. Taylor, who had played for Buckinghamshire in 1961 and 1962. An all-rounder he appeared in 18 Championship games, scored over 500 runs and took 33 wickets. He was to be one of the mainstays of the side until 1972, after which he moved to Hampshire, finally retiring in 1980. His twin brother represented Surrey and Somerset. Mike Smedley, an attractive right-hand batsman from Maltby, played in seven matches, but achieved little. He was to blossom in 1965 and later captained the Club. The third newcomer was David Baker, the Kent leg-break bowler. He appeared in a handful of games this season and the following one.

The Duke of Edinburgh visited Trent Bridge for the Test, but rain prevented him seeing any cricket. Notts again failed in the Gillette Cup, losing their only match by one wicket to Somerset at Taunton. Maurice Hill hit a brilliant 107 in 118 minutes and gained the Man of The Match Award.

There was no comfort for the Notts supporters in 1965. Three matches were won and the County ended at the foot of the table. The batting was even more suspect than in 1964. Only three Championship hundreds were recorded and Smedley's average of 26.80 with 831 runs placed him at the top of the table. Bolus had a very moderate summer, his confidence apparently deserting him. He did struggle to 1,000 runs, as did Norman Hill and Moore. Maurice Hill found himself left out of the side. Whittingham was the other specialist batsman to play regularly. Corran and Forbes shouldered much of the bowling, both sent down more than 900 overs (no one else delivered 500) and both captured one hundred wickets at about 20 runs each. Michael Taylor provided most support. He performed the hat-trick against Kent at Dover. All three of the County's victories came in the first half of the season, so the second half saw them gently move downwards.

The end of the season saw a quite dramatic change in the playing staff. Millman, the captain and wicketkeeper, resigned; Maurice Hill, Bomber Wells and Alan Gill also departed. Corran decided he had no time to spare for county cricket.

The single bright spot for Trent Bridge spectators was the Test match against South Africa. The visitors won with a day in hand and the sparkling 125 by Graeme Pollock remains a vivid memory for all those present – about 20,000 on each day.

Added to the serious situation on the field of play, Notts had an end of season deficit of £12,544. To save money the second eleven was withdrawn from the Minor Counties Championship and the experimental 'Trent Bridge Cricket Week' which has been inaugurated in 1965, abandoned.

Norman Hill was appointed to succeed Millman as captain in 1966. The County signed Bob White, the Middlesex batsman, and Roy Swetman, the Surrey and England wicketkeeper. Two youngsters from overseas, Basher Hassan from Kenya and Ismail Garda from Pakistan, were also recruited. A third overseas recruit was the Trinidad wicketkeeper-batsman and Cambridge blue, Deryck Murray. He would be available after the university match.

The alarming sign in all this movement was the total lack of new blood from Nottinghamshire itself. In less than 20 years the County had switched from being completely reliant on home grown cricketers to the reverse. What annoyed the ordinary Notts follower was that this total change had taken place without any worthwhile long-term improvement in the results. Notts again finished with the wooden spoon in 1966: they might just as well have played eleven Notts-born players and would have done no worse.

There seemed just one person determined to do something to restore pride in Nottinghamshire cricket and that was the former opening bowler, Frank Woodhead. He had spent much of the 1950s converting Nottingham High School from a mediocre cricketing outfit to one of the strongest in the country. In the 1960s he became involved with the Notts Colts team and youth cricket in the county in general. It was not however until the 1970s that this toil at the grass roots began to show some results at first-class level.

Four batsmen reached 1,000 runs, but none had an average over 30 and Norman Hill, the cares of leadership weighing heavily, averaged 20.89 with 1,003 runs. Murray, who captained Cambridge, topped the batting, but could play in only 12 matches. Swetman kept wicket in every game and scored some useful runs, including 115 against Essex at Trent Bridge. White from Middlesex achieved modest results with the bat, but unexpectedly blossomed as an off-break bowler, which was just as well since the County attack would have been almost entirely seam bowling without him. Forbes headed the bowling and again took over 100 wickets at 22 runs each – appreciably cheaper than the rest of the bowlers. Davison and Taylor both exceeded 50 wickets. The former missed several matches through injury and at the end of the summer retired from first-class cricket at the age of 28. Davison went back to Bedfordshire and played in the

Minor Counties Competition; it was a pity that his first-class career ended so soon.

Apart from Hassan (who played only against Oxford), Murray, Swetman and White, two other fresh faces were John Parkin and John Howarth. Parkin came from Kimberley and was a right-hand batsman. He made many runs in local club cricket, but did not make much impression at first-class level, though playing in 28 matches for the County over three years. Howarth from Stockport was a fast-medium bowler. He took 42 wickets for the second eleven in 1966 and was tried in two games; he had a further trial in 1967 when he seemed quite useful, but was released at the end of that summer.

It was in 1966 that Sunday county cricket took place at Trent Bridge for the first time. The match used for the experiment was against Hampshire in early June – about 4,500 turned out for the Sunday's play. The match ended in a controversial manner. Hampshire were 236 for five in their second innings prior to the last ball being bowled. They required one run to level the scores, or two to win. Henry Horton, the striking batsman, played this last ball from Davison, back along the pitch and started to run. Davison attempted to pick up the ball, but it was kicked from his

The 1966 side which finished bottom in the Championship for the second year in succession. From left to right, standing: R. A. White, M. J. Smedley, B. Stead, D. L. Murray, H. I. Moore. Seated: I. J. Davison, J. B. Bolus, N. W. Hill (captain), R. Swetman, C. Forbes. (NCCC)

grasp by Horton and the run was completed. According to the umpires Notts did not appeal for obstruction and thus the scorers counted the run and the totals were tied. When the players returned to the pavilion it took half an hour of deliberation to decide the result. It was agreed that the scores were level and thus Hampshire received extra points, having lost only five wickets.

The third Test, against the West Indies, was staged at Trent Bridge and the tourists won by 139 runs, Butcher scoring 209. The attendance over the five days was 100,000.

If the last few summers had been miserable ones for Notts supporters, 1967 brought them to the very depths of despair. For the first time in the Club's history, not a single first-class match was won – played 30, drawn 26, lost 4. By some freak of the points system then in vogue, the County did not end at the bottom of the table – Gloucestershire with three wins took the wooden spoon.

The batting produced more runs than in the recent years, hence the large number of draws, but of the bowlers only the left-arm medium-pace of Forbes worried the better opposition batsmen. Taylor was economical and very accurate; Stead, who became a regular member of the side for the first time was lively, but could also be wayward in both length and direction. White found bowling more difficult than in his first year. Peter Watts, the Northants leg-break bowler was signed at the start of the summer. He was 29 and had had nine seasons with Northants. He was included in the Notts side for the first match and played until the end of July in virtually every game, but his 23 Championship wickets cost 50 runs each and he left Trent Bridge at the end of the season. Hassan appeared in 16 Championship games, hitting a maiden hundred against Glamorgan at Trent Bridge. His unorthodox stance brought much comment; despite this he seemed a very promising addition to the side. Another young batsman was tried out against the Indian tourists. Graham Frost headed the second eleven batting table in 1967. A sound opening right-hander, he played for Notts for seven years, scoring over 3,000 runs in 102 matches.

The Test Match at Trent Bridge was ruined by the weather. Financially the Club fell deeper into debt and the Club's Chairman, H. T. Milnes, created a new development sub-committee to look at ways in which the commercial potential of the ground could be exploited. The mastermind behind the research into this aspect was Frank Gregory, an expert in the field of property development and a keen local cricket enthusiast.

MORE OVERSEAS INFLUENCE

ESTABLISHED FIRST-CLASS OVERSEAS cricketers had been taking part in County Championship cricket since the famous occasion when W. G. Grace hijacked Midwinter in the middle of an Australian tour – Midwinter in fact was born in Gloucestershire, so is not a very good example, but Grace later acquired Ferris from Australia, and when Derbyshire took Spofforth there were very serious comments. Overseas players had to serve a period of residential qualification before playing in the Championship; as a result very few of the great names could be tempted by the counties.

In 1967–68 all that changed. Each county would be allowed to play one overseas player, who was not qualified by residence. In addition that player could still appear in Test cricket for his country of origin. The main reason behind the alteration in the rules was to try to bring back spectators to county cricket – the number of people going through the turnstiles in the 1960s was less than half the number of the early 1950s.

The biggest name in overseas cricket in 1967 was Gary Sobers, the West Indian cricketer. He had played over 60 Tests and was already the leading run-scorer for the West Indies with a batting average above 60 – of those who had taken part in regular Test cricket, Bradman alone had better figures. In addition Sobers had captured some 150 Test wickets. He would be 32 years of age in July 1968. He had had three seasons with South Australia in the Sheffield Shield and had transformed the results of that state.

E. A. Marshall, the chairman of the Notts Supporters Association, determined that Notts should capture Sobers despite fierce competition from other counties. Sobers signed a three-year contract in March 1968 on his home island of Barbados when West Indies were playing England.

Sobers was appointed Nottinghamshire's captain, Norman Hill agreeing to act as his deputy. The season opened with the first round of the Gillette Cup, Notts entertaining Lancashire at Trent Bridge. Notts' record in the five years of the Cup had been abysmal – in this initial game under Sobers' leadership Notts won with three wickets and ten overs to spare. Sobers opened the bowling and returned figures of 11.2-3-28-3; Lancashire were dismissed for 168. The West Indian then hit an impressive 75 in murky conditions. He was Man of the Match. The second round of the Cup produced a very similar picture. Notts batted first, Sobers came in at 29 for three. He hit 95 and Notts finished with 226. Sobers' bowling figures were 11-7-15-4 and Worcestershire were beaten by 48 runs. In the quarter-finals, the County met Gloucestershire at Trent Bridge. The visitors made 296 for eight. Sobers joined Smedley with the score 78 for three and the pair added 114 in 21 overs. Unfortunately, both were dismissed at the same score and Notts failed to reach the target.

The relative success in the Gillette Cup did not immediately transfer itself to the Championship. The first six matches were all drawn and it was not until 10 June that the County recorded their first win in the competition since 1966. The venue was Taunton. Sobers took five for 31 and removed Somerset for 128. Notts managed marginally better, than Taylor took six for 53, dismissing Somerset a second time for 148. Only 103 runs were needed for victory. Greg Chappell however caused problems, dismissing Moore, Sobers and Murray cheaply. It was left to Smedley to make 42 and win the match. A week later Notts won their first game at Trent Bridge. Sobers was nursing a groin strain and Murray led the County to victory over Derbyshire by three wickets, after the latter had made a sporting declaration setting Notts 233 in three hours. Frost and Grant hit a quick 89 for the first wicket. Chris Grant was a left-handed batsman for Newark and was brought in for three matches during 1968. The innings of 48 and 32 he scored in this game indicated that he might have played more often in the County side. In 1991 he was elected Town Mayor of Newark, in which town he has a sports outfitters.

Six more matches, including one abandoned, went by before in the second half of July two more wins were recorded. The first, at Southport, was the result of a brilliant recovery. Notts were dismissed for 93; Lancashire made 141, Taylor taking six for 36, then a marvellous partnership between Sobers and Smedley allowed Notts to declare, setting Lancashire 213 in 270 minutes. This seemed generous indeed, but Notts won by 56 runs. The best bowler was Halfyard, with five for 39.

Dave Halfyard had been signed by Notts at the start of the summer. The journalists were baffled by this. He was 37 and had played for Kent from 1956 to 1964 in 185 matches as a fast-medium bowler. Due to injury he had then retired from county cricket and joined the first-class umpires' list. He had been spotted practising in the nets by Reg Simpson, who was now chairman of the cricket sub-committee, and Simpson was convinced that

Sir GARFIELD ST AUBRUN SOBERS

The most talented cricketer of his day and West Indies' greatest all-rounder, Gary Sobers came to Nottinghamshire in 1968 already having made the highest score in Test cricket. His Test batting average up to 1968 was 61.95 – only Bradman had a better record, but Bradman did not take 144 wickets, which was Sobers' total at that time. His final Test record when he retired in 1974 was 8,032 runs and 235 wickets in 93 Tests, and he also took 109 catches.

It was a pipe dream to expect Sobers to reproduce this kind of form, day in, day out, in county cricket, especially as county cricket was just changing from three-day Championship matches to the hurly burly of Sunday League and the two other limited-overs competitions, in addition to the first-class game. Even so Sobers' batting with the County ended with 7,000 runs at an average of 48 (a higher average than any other player). In most matches it was felt he batted too low down the order, but he did have the extra responsibilities of bowling and captaincy. His stint in English cricket came too late in his illustrious career and the spectators looked for too much from him. The County was at a low ebb, Bolus being the only other international player in the side. Notts finished fourth in Sobers' first season, but by 1973 they had sunk back to the foot of the table. His most famous feat was to hit six sixes in an over against Glamorgan in 1968, but oddly he never consistently came off in limited-overs cricket and the County's record whilst he was captain was little better than immediately before or after.

A charming man, unaffected by his fame, he continues to act as a great ambassador for his native Barbados.

Gary Sobers, the world's leading cricketer, joined Notts in 1968 as captain, but even the immediate improvement in results could not be sustained for long. (NCCC)

GLAMORGAN *v* NOTTINGHAMSHIRE

Played at Swansea, 31 August, 1 and 2 September 1968

NOTTINGHAMSHIRE WON BY 166 RUNS

NOTTINGHAMSHIRE	FIRST INNINGS		SECOND INNINGS	
J. B. Bolus	c Sub b Nash	140	run out	3
R. A. White	c Wheatley b B. Lewis	73	b Cordle	1
G. Frost	c A. R. Lewis b Nash	50	b Nash	2
M. J. Smedley	c A. R. Lewis b Nash	27	c Majid b Cordle	24
†D. L. Murray	b Nash	0	c Cordle b Shepherd	13
*G. Sobers	not out	76	b Shepherd	72
J. M. Parkin	not out	15	not out	9
S. R. Bielby				
M. N. S. Taylor				
D. J. Halfyard				
B. Stead				
Extras	b 4, lb 7, nb 2	13	b 1, nb 1	2
Total	(for 5 dec)	394	(for 6 dec)	139

1st inns: 1-126, 2-258, 3-289, 4-289, 5-308
2nd inns: 1-2, 2-7, 3-7, 4-30, 5-70, 6-124

BOWLING	O	M	R	W	O	M	R	W
Wheatley	5	0	22	0				
Nash	21	3	100	4	17	4	53	1
Cordle	3	1	24	0	16	4	41	2
Walker	32	4	109	0				
Shepherd	25	5	82	0	25	10	43	2
B. Lewis	13	1	44	1				

GLAMORGAN	FIRST INNINGS		SECOND INNINGS	
A. Jones	c Murray b Taylor	25	c Parkin b Taylor	1
R. Davis	c Taylor b Stead	0	b Stead	18
Majid J. Khan	c Taylor b Halfyard	41	c Bolus b Taylor	4
P. M. Walker	not out	104	c Sobers b White	16
*A. R. Lewis	c Bielby b Taylor	0	c Bielby b Taylor	52
†E. W. Jones	lbw b Sobers	29	c Stead by Taylor	3
A. E. Cordle	lbw b Halfyard	4	c Smedley b Taylor	4
M. A. Nash	b Sobers	8	b White	5
B. Lewis	run out	38	b Taylor	4
D. J. Shepherd	c Sobers b Halfyard	0	b White	4
O. S. Wheatley	b White	1	not out	0
Extras	lb 3, w 1	4	lb 2	2
Total		254		113

1st inns: 1-0, 2-46, 3-56, 4-78, 5-137, 6-142, 7-179, 8-252, 9-253, 10-254
2nd inns: 1-40, 2-45, 3-49, 4-85, 5-96, 6-100, 7-100, 8-105, 9-113, 10-113

BOWLING	O	M	R	W	O	M	R	W
Sobers	20	6	63	2				
Stead	9	3	27	1	9	1	26	1
Taylor	9	2	23	2	16	6	47	5
Halfyard	31	8	71	3	7	1	29	0
White	23.2	5	66	1	8	5	9	4

Umpires: J. G. Langridge and W. E. Phillipson
*Captain; †Wicketkeeper

Halfyard was still capable of playing at first-class level. He was proved right. Halfyard took 68 Championship wickets at 29 runs each during the season.

An all-round performance by the whole side defeated Derbyshire at Ilkeston by six wickets. Three more wins were logged in August, against Kent, Gloucestershire and finally in the famous match at Swansea against Glamorgan.

In this last game of the summer, Notts had scored 308 for five, Bolus making 140, when Sobers arrived at the wicket. Five overs were bowled before tea, Sobers making 25 and the other not out batsman, Parkin, 2. This took the total to 335. Play resumed after the interval. Shepherd went on to bowl and Sobers hit a single off his first delivery, then Parkin batted out the other five balls. Sobers then hit 2 and 1 off the first two balls of an over from Nash. Parkin made four from the final delivery. The next over produced a single and Nash's following over two scoring shots, another single to Sobers and a four to Parkin. Sobers made two fours and a single from Shepherd's over, thus facing Nash for what was the 99th over of the innings. The West Indian hit six sixes. Two of them went out of the ground. It was the first time in a first-class match that such a feat had been performed and remains unique in English county cricket. As soon as the over ended, Sobers declared. He was 76 not out in about 30 minutes. Glamorgan just avoided the follow-on, but Notts still won by 166 runs, Sobers hitting 72 in the second innings.

With seven victories and only three defeats, the County ended the season in fourth place. Sobers scored 1,570 runs in the Championship at an average of 44.85 and took 83 wickets at 22.67 runs each. Bolus recovered his form and hit 1,580 runs; Smedley scored over 1,000 and did well. Murray played all summer and took over as wicketkeeper, Swetman having disappeared. M. N. S. Taylor topped the bowling table, capturing 99 wickets at 21 runs each. Forbes was not quite so effective, taking 72. Norman Hill dropped out of the side during the season and announced his retirement at the end. His place was taken by Richard Bielby, a right-hand batsman and off-break bowler who had topped both batting and bowling averages at Radley in 1965. He played for Notts in 43 matches until 1971.

The Club revived the 'Festival Week' at Trent Bridge, but the weather was terrible and it proved a disaster. No Notts cricketers

---

Sobers hit Malcolm Nash for six sixes in an over, the first time this feat had ever been achieved in first-class cricket.

went with the MCC side to Pakistan in 1968–69, but Nottinghamshire were represented in the English Women's side to Australia. Mrs Enid Bakewell from Newstead, an opening right-hand bat and slow left-arm bowler, proved to be the outstanding player on the tour – in the six 'Tests', she hit 601 runs at an average of 60.10 and took 26 wickets at 18.34 runs each, obtaining the highest aggregates both in batting and bowling. In all matches on the visit she performed the 'double' of 1,000 runs and 100 wickets and became the first woman to be the subject of a feature article in *Wisden Cricketers' Almanack*. She is undoubtedly the greatest woman cricketer to come from Nottinghamshire and one of the most outstanding in the history of the game.

The West Indies toured England in 1969, sharing the season with New Zealand. Sobers therefore was not available for Notts in the Championship until 26 July. Prior to this Notts had played 16 matches, winning three. They went on to win three more which placed the County eighth in the table. This was the year in which the John Player League was inaugurated, but Notts made little impression, winning five games and ending in 13th place. They did best in the Gillette Cup, going down to Yorkshire in the semi-final. This match at Scarborough was watched by a record

Notts in 1969, when the usual skipper, Sobers, was away playing for the West Indian tourists. Despite his absence for half the season, the County finished eighth, a big improvement on pre-Sobers days. From left to right, standing: A. B. Wheat (scorer), G. Frost, M. J. Harris, D. J. Halfyard, B. Stead, B. Hassan, M. N. S. Taylor. Seated: D. L. Murray, R. A. White, J. B. Bolus (captain), H. I. Moore, M. J. Smedley. (NCCC)

Mike Harris joined Notts from Middlesex, and during his career he hit 1,000 runs in a season eleven times. (NCCC)

crowd of 15,242. Yorkshire were put in by Sobers and scored 191 in 59.4 overs; Sobers bowling figures were 12-8-12-1. Harris and Bolus began Notts' reply with a confident partnership of 40, but apart from a brief flurry by Sobers the rest failed and Yorkshire were on their way to the final.

Mike Harris, who opened with Bolus in the Gillette game, had been signed from Middlesex at the start of the season. Born in Cornwall in 1944, he had played for Middlesex for five seasons, but he seemed to have a weakness on the back foot and in 1968 had struggled for runs before being dropped from the Middlesex team. He was, however, to serve Nottinghamshire well for more then a decade, generally as an opening batsman, but he also kept wicket, more especially in one-day matches, and he sometimes winkled out batsmen with his leg-breaks. He might be described as a professional cricketer of the old school. For Notts in 1969 he completed 1,000 runs at an average of 32.81: with the introduction of Sunday League cricket, the County Championship was reduced to 24 matches. Bolus had another good summer and came second to Sobers in the batting table. Murray and Smedley also enjoyed success. Hassan was now qualified by residence and appeared in every game. Stead was the principal bowler with 71 Championship wickets; Halfyard took 57, Taylor 50 and Forbes 40.

Apart from Harris, two other new players were tried; Peter Plummer, a slow left-arm bowler from Nottingham, made 33 appearances in four seasons and returned two or three impressive analyses. He later played for Buckinghamshire. Bob Kelsall, from Stockport, played only one first-class game, but also played for his native county. He was an off-break bowler and right-hand batsman.

Financially the County was still in serious trouble. The 1969 deficit was £7,540. Less than 10,000 spectators paid to watch home Championship games; the average paying attendance for the new Sunday League was about 1,000 per match, but the number was trebled by members who attended. The Club received a bequest of £22,053 from the estate of Cyril Lowater.

In 1969 Frank Dalling won the annual Groundsman of the Year award. He had been head groundsman at Trent Bridge since 1949, his brother, Harry, having succeeded their father as Ground Superintendent in the same summer. Frank Dalling was forced to retire through ill health in the mid-1970s, but Harry remained in full-time employment until 1990 and is still working at the Club in a part-time capacity, being the announcer on the loudspeaker system. Frank's son, another Frank, is the assistant groundsman to Ron Allsop.

There was a sad opening to 1970 with the death, at the Club's Annual General Meeting, of E. A. Marshall, the driving force behind the Supporters' Association. On a broader front the press was full of the 'Stop The Tour' campaign aimed at preventing the South African cricket side visiting England. Nottinghamshire were closely involved, since a Test match was scheduled for Trent Bridge. In April Jack Baddiley, the new Notts Chairman, was threatened with kidnapping by the protesters. In the end the Cricket Council, under pressure from the government, cancelled the visit.

Instead five matches between England and the Rest of The World were hurriedly planned. For Nottinghamshire the idea was not a happy one – it was announced that Sobers would captain the Rest of the World. Having been without Sobers for two-thirds of 1969, the County would miss him for about half-a-dozen games in 1970, as well as for several Sunday League fixtures.

The summer is best remembered for some brilliant batting displays by Sobers. He appeared in 14 Championship games and hit 1,154 runs at an average of 76.93, compiling five hundreds. Bolus, who captained the team when Sobers was absent, completed 2,000 Championship runs and averaged over 50. Harris, Smedley and Hassan all had excellent batting records. The bowling told a different story. Apart from 17 wickets by Peter Plummer, no bowlers averaged below 25 and the two chief wicket-takers, White and Halfyard, had figures of 65 wickets at 28 runs each and 53 at 39. Taylor's 51 wickets cost 34 runs apiece. The attack was incapable of dismissing the opposition twice. Only four matches were won and in only two of these – both away from home – did Notts manage to remove the opposition twice.

The fielding was one aspect that brought praise from spectators. Hassan was very sharp close in. Smedley, Bolus, Harris and Taylor were also most reliable. There was a change of wicketkeeper. Murray and Swetman both having left, the County signed a 26-year-old Yorkshireman, David Pullan. Pullan played in every first-class match and missed little behind the stumps. The only other player to make his debut was the 19-year-old Nottingham High School all-rounder, Peter Johnson. He had gone up to Cambridge in October and gained his blue in 1970. Johnson had broken all records at school and his final year of 1969 had been a personal triumph. He had hit 1,038 runs, average 54.63, and taken 91 wickets at 11.19 runs each. In the same year he captained the English Schools against the Public Schools at Lord's and the Schools against Combined Services. For some reason Johnson never really made the grade at first-class level, though he played for Nottinghamshire for eight years. In 1978 he joined Lincolnshire and made many runs for that county. His leg-break bowling did not worry county batsmen.

In order to try to save money, Nottinghamshire drastically pruned the playing staff. This consisted of just 13 players plus Sobers. One result was the weakening of the second eleven. No fewer than 56 players turned out in the 12 matches, and with this total lack of continuity there came only a single victory. Hidden in this vast army, there were one or two names with a future – Randall, 'Dusty' Hare and Michael Austin, who is now a well-known cricket correspondent.

The England *v* Rest of the World match at Trent Bridge attracted few – 16,000 in five days. Notts lost £10,540 on the season and the overall deficit was now £30,478.

The development sub-committee had obtained planning permission for a squash club on the corner of Bridgford and Hound Roads, but their master plan for development on the Fox Road frontage had met with criticism and required modification. Frank Gregory was appointed President for 1971 and launched a membership campaign with meetings throughout the county. The meetings were well attended but produced only modest results, with the membership now between 4,500 and 5,000.

The results on the field in 1971 were very disappointing; Sobers played throughout the summer, but the constant cricket was wearing out his talents. His 53 Championship wickets cost 30 runs each and his batting average dropped to 46.40. Harris headed the batting table, topping 2,000 in all matches and scoring nine centuries for Notts, a number which equalled Whysall's record. The batting line-up, with Harris and Bolus opening, or latterly Frost taking Bolus's place and the England man dropping down the order, with Smedley first wicket down and Sobers, White and Taylor to fill the rest of the middle, was very strong.

The bowling let the team down. White was the leading player in terms of both wickets and average, but the latter was 28.72. The County had signed Bill Taylor, a fast bowler from Manchester, to open the bowling with the left-handed Stead. Taylor played in 13 Championship matches, but took only 27 wickets – he proved much more effective in one-day matches.

Three Championship matches were won. Leicestershire were beaten at Trent Bridge, even though Notts were behind on first innings. The County required 203 to win and took a painful five hours to reach their objective, though Sobers hit a bright 49 to bring the closing stages to a swift conclusion. The second victory took place at Worksop. It was an all-round team effort. Notts made 339, with everyone scoring some runs, except Stead, but the highest individual total being 78 by Sobers. Forbes, who was now playing in the Lancashire League, having left the full-time Notts staff at the end of 1970, played and bowled very economically. Notts beat Middlesex by 192 runs. The third success was over Warwickshire at Trent Bridge. Smedley and Bolus added 230 in an unbroken third-wicket stand and Stead, Sobers and Taylor all took cheap wickets. Nottinghamshire finished in 12th place. The County occupied the same position in the Sunday League and failed to make any impression in the Gillette Cup, losing their only match to Hampshire at Portsmouth in a low-scoring game.

One unusual feat during the year occurred in a high-scoring match against Sussex at Trent Bridge, when the first three Notts batsmen all hit centuries – Harris 141, Frost 104 and Smedley 131 not out. Sobers declared with the total 416 for two. It was typical of Notts in 1971 that the bowlers were unable to take any advantage of this batting spree. Sussex made 267 for eight declared and batted out the final day with 241 for five.

Apart from Bill Taylor, three others made their Notts debuts in 1971. Philip Wilkinson, a 19-year-old seam bowler from Hucknall, played for seven years and returned some good analyses, then moved into league cricket in Yorkshire. W. H. 'Dusty' Hare, from a farming family near Newark, became much better known as an outstanding England rugby footballer. If he had chosen to concentrate on cricket, he might well have gained a regular place in the County side. Nirmal Nanan, the fourth debutant, came from Trinidad. A neat right-hand batsman he represented the County in 32 matches, but his appearances were restricted owing to his overseas birth qualification. He returned to Trinidad in 1981.

The end of 1971 saw the retirement of the Secretary, Ron Poulton. He had been at Trent Bridge for 46 years and proved a very good servant to the club. He continued to assist with arrangements for Test matches for several years to come.

A second planning application was submitted for the Fox Road development, but again it was turned down. The Club lost more than £10,000 on the year and the members criticised the inability of the Club to find effective bowlers. There was a major change during the winter behind the scenes. The Committee was cut from 18 to 12 members in an attempt to make it more business-orientated.

A knee injury took Sobers out of the Notts side almost before the 1972 summer had begun – he later managed to play in six Championship games and some of the one-day fixtures, but effectively he was absent for the majority of the year. Sobers had requested as soon as he returned from the West Indies that he be relieved of the captaincy and Bolus took over.

The single Championship win came in the penultimate match at Bristol. Stead took six for 81 and White eight for 101, dismissing Gloucestershire for 201 and 152. The margin of victory was 42 runs. Hassan topped the season's batting averages and was well supported by Bolus, Harris and Smedley. White was the best all-rounder with 788 Championship runs and 43 wickets. Stead headed the bowlers and had the best return of his career, taking 98 wickets at 20.38 runs each – no one in the country captured more and he stood 10th in the overall averages. Bill Taylor came second to Stead, but M. N. S. Taylor had an expensive year.

In the Essex match at Newark, which was drawn due to rain, the *Wisden* report comments: 'Nottinghamshire's reply (to Essex's 119) produced a dazzling display by the 21-year-old Randall from Retford, making his County Championship debut. He showed outstanding maturity in an innings of two hours, twenty minutes, during which he hit five 6s and four 4s in his 78.'

Randall was to become the outstanding Nottinghamshire cricketer of his generation. His fielding, mainly in the covers, has always been way above the ordinary; his individual style of batting has produced runs all over the world. He has played in more Tests for England than any other Notts player, and after 20 years retains much of the youthful zest he showed in his first match.

The other newcomer of 1972 was a second Notts-born batsman, Paul Todd from a village near Southwell. Todd scored eight centuries in his eleven years at Trent Bridge and completed 1,000 runs three times. He usually opened the batting.

Before the summer ended the County took the unusual step of announcing that Bolus and M. N. S. Taylor had both been released and Sobers would resume the leadership in 1973. Bolus was quickly snapped up by Derbyshire and Taylor went to Hampshire where he played conspicuously well for another decade and is now the Marketing Manager of that county.

The introduction of advertising boards to Trent Bridge, begun in 1971, made a difference to the finances and for the first time for several years a surplus was shown on the season's figures. Planning permission was finally gained for a nine-storey office block on the corner of Radcliffe and Fox Roads.

Season 1973 saw Notts drop to the bottom of the Championship. The one success was a rain-affected declaration match against Lancashire at Trent Bridge in June. Notts were given 150 minutes to make 220 and Randall hit 93 in 100 minutes with two 6s and 12 fours; the only help he received came from Smedley and the margin of victory was three wickets.

In the Sunday League the County obtained 13th place, the same as in 1972 and in the Gillette Cup they were knocked out by Middlesex in the second round. Sobers hit 75 not out, but a leg injury prevented him from scoring at his usual pace.

There were some crumbs of comfort in the Benson & Hedges Competition, which had been inaugurated the previous year.

Notts topped their zonal table, winning three matches out of four, but meeting Worcestershire in the quarter-final they were thoroughly outplayed. Worcestershire made 234 for eight; Notts sank to 18 for four and Sobers almost threw away his wicket in a desperate attempt to win the match off his own bat.

Trent Bridge began to take on a new face as the 1973 summer progressed. The famous mammoth scoreboard was demolished and replaced by a smaller one which required less manual labour; the concrete stands on the Fox Road side were removed, in order to provide car parking space for the office block which was in course of construction.

The individual statistics for 1973 make depressing reading in the main. Sobers topped the batting with an average of 45.45 in 15 matches – he also led West Indies in the Tests against England – and averaged 76.00 in that Test series. Harris hit 1,407 Championship runs, including a double-century against Glamorgan. Randall, Hassan and Smedley had reasonable returns. The bowling figures revealed that no one captured 50 Championship wickets – this tells its own story. One of the four debutants, Gordon Edwards, an off-spinner from Nottingham University, had the best average and took 12 wickets in his eight games. He did not however pursue cricket as a career. Dilip Doshi, the Indian spinner, played in the second eleven, picking up 28 wickets at 11 runs each and appeared against the West Indies and Cambridge University, but was not qualified for County matches. His left-arm slow bowling later gained him Test match recognition but he had a very erratic career in English county cricket due to the regulations governing overseas players. He played in 44 matches for Notts and later joined Warwickshire, as well as playing for Northumberland and Hertfordshire.

Two local players making their initial appearances in 1973 were John Birch and Trevor Tunnicliffe. Birch's career as a sound middle-order batsman spanned nearly 20 years. Although his overall figures were not outstanding, he was a very useful cricketer and always full of enthusiasm for the game. He was appointed team manager in the close season of 1990–91. Tunnicliffe captained Malvern in 1969. A middle-order right-hand batsman and medium-pace bowler he played in 65 first-class matches for the County, leaving at the end of 1980, after which he spent several years coaching in South Africa.

Season 1974 saw the Club change course once more. Sobers had one year of his contract to complete. He was again relieved of the captaincy, but instead of appointing the senior member of the side to succeed him, Jack Bond was brought from the Isle of Man.

DEREK WILLIAM RANDALL

There is no more popular cricketer with spectators than Randall. He has the entertainer's gift of being able to establish a rapport with his audience. It was his electric fielding which first drew him to public attention, his spontaneous reactions in the covers when the ball came within hailing distance and the speed with which he returned the ball to the wicket. Even after 20 years his reflexes remain much quicker than most of his colleagues.

As a batsman his nervous mannerisms, the quick tweak at his cap and then the top of his left pad before almost every delivery, makes the onlooker nervous on Randall's behalf, almost praying that he will outwit the bowler, at least for the next ball. He is affected by the occasion and the atmosphere – his most famous innings was Chaplinesque, even down to the somersault he performed in front of the Queen. The brief details of the match are worthy of recall. It was the Centenary Test in Melbourne, March 1977. Randall's Test experience amounted to four matches, all against India. Australia scored 138, England were dismissed for 95 and Australia's second innings amounted to 419 for nine declared. England made 417, of which Randall scored 174. He weaved and ducked his way around the formidable speed of Lillee, who had taken six for 26 in the first innings. Strokes orthodox and unorthodox came from his bat. He won the hearts of the Australians as well as the Man of The Match Award.

Derek Randall has been one of the most popular cricketers in the world since his performance in the Centenary Test in 1977. In 20 years at Notts he has hit well over 20,000 first-class runs for the County. (Patrick Eagar)

Although it is now several years since he played for England, Randall has more England Test caps than any other Notts cricketer and more one-day Internationals. His tally of first-class runs comes above 27,000 – his value as a fielder cannot be measured, but if he has saved half as many runs as he has scored, then his worth to Nottinghamshire is great indeed. In 1990 he was all at sixes and sevens, but in the 1991 summer Randall achieved a better record than ever before. He opened the Notts batting in all but one of the 24 limited-overs matches, yet batted in the middle order in all the Championship games. In all types of cricket he scarcely knew failure: very unusual, but typical of the lad from Retford.

He was appointed captain-manager. Bond, a 41-year-old Bolto-nian, had inspired Lancashire as their captain. They had been in the doldrums when he took over in 1968. Bond had led them to three Gillette Cup titles and two Sunday League titles. At the close of 1972 he had retired and taken a coaching position with King William's School on the Isle of Man.

Nottinghamshire had not tried this type of experiment before, the nearest precedent being the appointment of Reddick as player-coach in 1946. This innovation brought no immediate cure to the problems of the Club. As in 1973 only one Championship game ended in success – a run-chase against Kent at Trent Bridge. Notts did avoid the wooden spoon and finished 15th. However they ended at the foot of the Sunday League and failed in the Benson & Hedges Cup. The members signed a petition calling for an extraordinary general meeting to discuss the standard of cricket, but it was unfair to blame Bond, whose influence could hardly be expected to make itself felt immediately.

Injury problems meant that Sobers played in 15 Championship matches and made 1,110 runs. He hit four centuries, including one in 83 minutes against Derbyshire at Ilkeston. This in fact was the fastest of the summer and gained him the Lawrence Trophy. His bowling fell away and his 29 wickets cost more than 30 runs each.

Harris and Smedley were the mainstays of the batting. The County found it difficult to discover the right opening partner for Harris; Nanan, White, Todd and Hassan were all given the opportunity, but with no overall improvement. Randall was quite outstanding in the field and spoken of as an England prospect; his batting average, however, was very modest and he seemed a little out of sorts. Tunnicliffe played in nine Championship games and seemed to be a good prospect. He had decided to take a course at Loughborough University and therefore would be available only in the vacation in 1975. Bond was scarcely worth his place as a batsman and also missed some matches because of his duties as a Test selector. Smedley led the side in his absence.

White's off-breaks topped the bowling table; he took 73 wickets at 24.06 runs each. The other bowler to obtain 50 victims was Stead, but his wickets cost 28 runs apiece.

Trent Bridge staged its first one-day International in August, Pakistan being England's opponents. About 7,000 spectators watched the game. Financially the Club was plunging further into debt with a deficit of £12,025 on the year. Membership dropped to 3,794 – the lowest since 1946. The new squash club was opened in September by Frank Gregory and would hopefully bring in much-needed revenue. Mr Gregory announced his retirement and the club paid a fulsome tribute to the work he had done over the previous decade. He and his wife, Brenda, had been excellent ambassadors for the Club.

Apart from Jack Bond, the three other players who made their debuts in 1974 were Peter Hacker, Harry Latchman and John Cook. Hacker was a seam bowler from Lenton. He played in 61 matches until 1981 and in 1982 joined Derbyshire, but remained there only one season before appearing for Lincolnshire. He returned some good analyses, but was destined to be in the shadow of Hadlee and Rice. Cook, an off-break bowler from Retford, played once in 1974 and a second time in 1975. A member of the police force, he has appeared with much success in local club cricket. Latchman, from Jamaica, had been a regular member of the Middlesex side, bowling leg-breaks. He played 40 first-class matches for Notts, but left Trent Bridge in 1976. He later played for Cambridgeshire and was coach at Nottingham High School.

Early in the New Year of 1975, Bond resigned as captain-manager. He disagreed with the policy of the Committee. Smedley was appointed as captain in his stead and Harris as vice-captain. In place of Sobers, Notts chose the unknown Clive Rice from Transvaal as their principal overseas player. A free-scoring middle-order batsman and fast-medium bowler, Rice had had success with Transvaal and had been on the verge of the South African Test team, when that country ceased to take part in official Tests. He had come to England in 1974 and had had trials with one or two county clubs and appeared for Robins' XI in a first-class match that summer. Ken Taylor, who was now chairman of the Notts cricket sub-committee, met him at Eastbourne and decided that Rice had the sort of talent Notts required. He was 25 when he arrived at Trent Bridge.

Rice's arrival had an immediate effect on the Sunday League performances of the County. Notts rose from the foot of the table to fifth, winning nine matches. Rice took 22 Sunday wickets and scored 416 runs, being the leader in both averages for Notts. In the Gillette Cup, Rice returned the best bowling figures in the first-round match against Sussex, a feat he repeated in the second round, when he sent Kent reeling by dismissing their first three batsmen for 7, 0 and 0. He also made a fluent 46 in Notts' innings of 247 for eight. Notts went through to the third round and a crowd of 12,000 came to Trent Bridge to watch the game against Derbyshire. Unfortunately for Notts, Hendrick bowled excep-

CLIVE EDWARD BUTLER RICE

Trying to judge the merits of one captain against another is not an easy task, if only because each captain leads a different crew. Assets that are sound for one generation can jar on another's. Rice's positive attitude, his method of taking the battle to the enemy and inspiring his fellow players with confidence as the conflict raged, certainly achieved the desired results for Nottinghamshire during the 1980s. It might be said that he was fortunate to have the talents of Hadlee, Randall, Hemmings and the rest at his disposal, but more than one team of talents has failed and disintegrated due to leadership of the wrong kind. Dressing-room squabbles are an all too familiar feature of county cricket. There again it might be pointed out that Rice had Ken Taylor's expertise to back him, but Taylor could only go so far.

If a specific example of Rice's intelligent judgement of cricket (without outside influence) is required, the single-wicket contests are proof that the best natural cricketing talent can be outwitted by a shrewd brain and talent not quite so outstanding. Rice won the world single-wicket title two or three times by outmanoeuvring his opponents.

These comments should not detract from Rice's cricketing ability. There have been few finer batsmen in English county cricket. If one had to pick a single innings for Nottinghamshire out of the many Rice played, then it must be his 105 against Hampshire in 1981. Notts were put in on a Bournemouth wicket designed for the formidable Marshall. Robinson scored 10 – apart from Rice and Robinson no one else reached double figures – and the all out score was 143. Rice thus claimed 73 per cent of the all-out total, a record without equal in post-war Notts cricket.

Clive Rice took over the Notts captaincy in 1978 and led them to great success in the 1980s. (Patrick Eagar)

tionally well and Derbyshire won by six wickets. The Benson &
Hedges Competition produced only one win.

The results in the Championship were not much improved on
1974, but the County moved up to 13th place and won three
matches. All three victories came at home. Sussex were overcome
by an innings, Harris scoring 110 and Rice 92. Stead did much of
the damage, returning five for 43 in the Sussex first innings. At
Worksop Notts made an astounding recovery against Northants.
The visitors scored 184 and Notts could muster just 67, of which
Rice made 27. Wilkinson then bowled out Northants for 117,
taking five for 20, thus leaving Notts needing 235 to win. Rice
scored an unbeaten 109, his first first-class hundred for the
County, and victory was by five wickets. The third win came in
the last match of the summer. Todd hit 178, the highest score of
his career, and everyone else made runs so the Notts total was 488
for nine declared. White had a second-innings analysis of seven
for 72 and Gloucestershire were beaten by ten wickets.

The batting figures overall showed much improvement on
recent years. Six players, Randall, Harris, Johnson, Rice,
Smedley and Hassan all completed 1,000 runs at an average above
30. The bowling remained the weak point; Rice had the best
Championship return, but even that was only 53 wickets at 25
runs each.

Apart from Rice, Roy Dexter was the single other debutant.
Captain of Nottingham High School in 1973 when he had topped
the batting averages with 796 runs, average 61.23, Dexter made
many runs in the Second Eleven Competition, but rarely
achieved much for the senior county side. He played 22 matches
between 1975 and 1981.

One change at Trent Bridge in 1975 was the retirement of
Frank Dalling as head groundsman and the appointment of his
assistant, Ron Allsop, in his place. The financial problems of the
Club were eased by the first year's profit from the squash club –
nearly £11,000.

In 1976 the successes enjoyed by the county were mainly
confined, as in the previous year, to one-day matches. The
County again did well in the Sunday League and were chasing for
the title until fading in the final month. They finished only four
points behind the winners and were victorious in seven out of the
eight home matches. Hassan, Rice and Randall all flourished in
this league and runs were obtained at the gallop in most matches.
In the Benson & Hedges all four group games ended in victory,
but in the quarter-finals, Notts were beaten by Kent at Canterbury when the batting failed.

The County remained static in the County Championship. Four wins placed them 13th. Rice and Randall, the latter chosen for the England 1976–77 overseas tour, topped the batting. Harris came third; he had dropped down the order, often going in as low as number eight, but averaged over 40, and was now the regular first eleven wicketkeeper, having taken over from Pullan in 1975 in order to bolster the batting strength. Smedley and Hassan also had good returns. Todd played throughout the season, normally opening with either Hassan or Nanan, but his form was variable.

None of the bowlers averaged below 30. Rice suffered niggling injuries and sent down 422.1 overs, taking 39 wickets: in 1975 the same number of overs had brought him much greater success.

The find of the summer was the 18-year-old seamer from Hucknall, Kevin Cooper. Making his debut in midsummer, he appeared in ten matches and came second to Rice in the bowling table. His forte was, and is, line and length, and he has been a great asset to the County Club for 15 years. An even younger debutant was Bruce French, the 16-year-old from Warsop. A member of a large cricketing family, he had kept wicket in the Bassetlaw League for Welbeck from the age of 12. On his first appearance, against Cambridge University in late June, he became the youngest cricketer ever to represent the County in a first-class match. French took over the regular first eleven wicketkeeping place in 1977 and has remained in that post ever since. He went on to keep wicket for England and is still regarded by many as the best keeper in the country, losing his England place only because the selectors preferred a better batsman.

Mark Allbrook, the Cambridge University off-spinner, made his first appearance for the County in 1976. Although playing in the university match for four seasons, he never commanded a first-team place with Notts and retired from first-class cricket at the end of 1980 to join the scholastic profession.

W. K. 'Kenny' Watson appeared for the County in the match against the West Indian tourists and made a great impression, taking four for 23 as the West Indies were dismissed for 81. The West Indies took their revenge in the second innings by scoring 313 for five and winning the game with ease. Watson, then a 21-year-old seam bowler from Port Elizabeth, was on the staff at Trent Bridge for several seasons, but his appearances in first-class cricket were restricted because of the presence of Rice and Hadlee. He has been successful in domestic matches in South Africa, mainly for Eastern Province, and has appeared in unofficial Tests for his home country.

It was a pity that Watson was not available for Championship games in 1976, because Stead was ruled out of nearly the whole summer due to an injury and Latchman, the leg-break bowler, had so little success that he dropped out and left Trent Bridge at the end of the season.

The Test match at Trent Bridge is remembered now for the famous innings of Viv Richards, who hit 232. The match was drawn and the attendance good. Financially the Club was looking sounder than for many years, largely due to the increased revenue from the TCCB and advertising and sponsorship. The capacity of the ground had, of course, been reduced by the demolition of the Fox Road stands.

Derek Randall hit the headlines across the world when he scored his 174 in the Centenary Test at Melbourne in March 1977. His success on the tour was partially responsible for the optimism at Trent Bridge in April 1977. The County had re-engaged Doshi

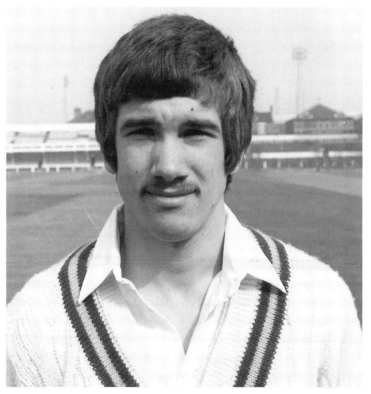

Bruce French is considered by many to be the best wicketkeeper in England. He first appeared for Notts in 1976, and made his Test debut in 1986. (NCCC)

to strengthen the spin department and hoped that Cooper would build on the figures he obtained in 1976. The season, however, turned into one of bitter disappointment. Rice alone could look back with pride. He topped the batting averages with 1,107 runs, average 32.55, and the bowling with 50 wickets, average 21.22. Randall had an exceedingly odd summer. He played in all five Tests and averaged 34.50: for Notts his figures were 375 runs, average 17.04. Even worse was the fate of Harris. He averaged 14.87 and eventually lost his place in the side. Smedley and Hassan were the only batsmen to provide Rice with any reliable support. Johnson and Todd were both erratic. Doshi took 68 wickets, but they cost 31 runs each; White's 38 cost 38.

The single Championship victory came at Worcester in September. That was a three-declaration match which set Worcestershire 240 in 165 minutes. Rice bowled quite exceptionally, returning figures of 11.5-4-16-6 and Worcester were all out for 89. This late win was not sufficient to lift the County from the bottom of the table.

In the Sunday League, where Notts had performed well for the two previous seasons, there was little to bring satisfaction. The County finished 12th with six wins. In the Gillette Cup the County were annihilated. Notts made 215 all out; Hampshire scored 220 without loss; Barry Richards 101, Gordon Greenidge 106. The Benson & Hedges Competition brought two wins, not enough to reach the knock-out section.

One newcomer in 1977 was the Southwell batsman, David Coote. A left-hander, and a relation of the old Yorkshire all-rounder Ted Wainwright, Coote played in one first-class game scoring 20. A great enthusiast in all aspects of the game, he is still very active in Southwell, captaining the local club.

The Test series of 1977 was clouded by the fact that most of the Australians on tour had signed to play for Kerry Packer's World Series, as had Tony Greig the England captain in 1976–77 and several other leading England players. The Australians appeared to have no enthusiasm for the official Tests run by the Board and did not win a single match in the 1977 series. The third Test was staged at Trent Bridge. Her Majesty Queen Elizabeth II came to Nottingham for the first day and the players were presented to her. The notable event of the game was the return, after self-imposed exile, of Geoff Boycott to Test cricket and his running out of Randall.

Nottinghamshire, despite their on-field disasters, made a profit on the year's workings. The squash club flourished and plans were laid to build two additional courts.

After a five-year stint, Group Captain R. G. Wilson announced that he would retire as Notts Secretary in the autumn and Jack Baddiley, Chairman for eight years, also announced that he wished to relinquish the chair, though retaining his place on the Committee. Dick Milnes, the former Chairman, retired from the Committee and in the Spring of 1978 was chosen as the new President, succeeding W. A. Sime, the former County captain.

John Heatley, a former captain of Radcliffe on Trent CC, was to take over as Chairman of the Club. The question was, would these multiple changes behind the scenes make any tangible differences to the playing results and the ground?

SUCCESS AT LAST

AT THE END OF NOVEMBER 1977, the Committee appointed Philip Carling as the 'Chief Executive' of the Club. This was a totally new departure and one more radical than the appointment of Bond in 1974. Carling, 30 years old and from Surrey, had played cricket for Cambridge, gaining a blue in 1968 and 1970. He had played for Surrey second eleven, but not in Championship cricket and had come to the notice of Nottinghamshire through his connections in squash, when he acted as an advisor in the creation of the Trent Bridge Squash Club.

Carling believed that the cricket team would succeed only if run by a full-time manager. The idea of having managers in county cricket was by no means new, but the majority of county clubs were opposed to such an idea, presumably on the grounds that it would bring cricket into line with soccer in this respect. The man chosen to take the post of cricket manager was Ken Taylor, who was chairman of the cricket sub-committee. Taylor, a manager in the electricity industry, had been a professional cricketer with Warwickshire immediately before and for three seasons after the Second World War. The choice was a wise one because Taylor had long experience in management skills and also had a talent for picking out potential county cricketers from the mass of those who aspired to such status.

Taylor, however, had not moved into place when a series of unforeseen events changed the pattern of Notts cricket. Rice's contract had finished at the end of 1977. He signed a fresh contract for three years and at Taylor's instigation, Rice was appointed captain for 1978. The Packer Affair was throwing up all sorts of red herrings and others of a different hue through the autumn of 1977. The Notts Committee ranged itself firmly behind the TCCB, England's governing body, in the anti-Packer camp. In January 1978, Notts joined the chorus of disgust when Sussex appointed Tony Greig, Packer's leading figure in England, as county captain. Sussex bowed to the general feeling and cancelled Greig's appointment.

On 19 April came the announcement that Rice had signed for Packer. The Notts Committee immediately sacked Rice as both captain and player and quickly searched for an overseas replacement. Carling scurried down to London, where the New Zealand Test bowler, Richard Hadlee, was involved in an indoor competition. Events moved swiftly. Hadlee signed a three-year contract;

Rice sought a High Court Injunction to fight the County's decision to sack him; the County consulted lawyers. Peace was made. Rice was reinstated as a player, but not as captain.

The dust settled and the season began. Most of 1978 was spent in the pavilion. The rain seemed never ending. No fewer than five of Notts' Sunday games were washed out, but towards the end of May, when the sun broke through, Notts suddenly won three Championship matches in succession. Derbyshire were beaten by eight wickets. Hadlee surprised everyone, who thought he was a bowler, by hitting 101 not out and straight afterwards taking five for 25 as Notts forced Derbyshire to follow on. The eventual margin of victory was eight wickets. Hadlee took eleven wickets in the next game, against Yorkshire at Worksop, and victory was by a similar margin. Finally Warwickshire were trounced at Trent Bridge, bowled out for 56 and 81. Hadlee picked up eight wickets and Rice six. Victory was by an innings and 169 runs. The match finished in the middle of the second afternoon. Nottinghamshire found themselves at the top of the Championship table on 6 June. A week later Hadlee was contracted to report to the New Zealand team manager for the start of the Kiwi Test tour of England, Pakistan being the visitors for the first half of 1978. Notts did not win another match all summer and had to settle for seventh place in the Championship: this was of course vastly superior to the previous few summers.

In 1978 the counties were permitted two overseas players in any one match. Whilst Hadlee was present there was no difficulty, since he and Rice were automatic choices. When Hadlee left, Notts had two other overseas players on the books – Watson, the seam bowler, and Doshi, the spinner, Doshi usually had preference, but his 49 wickets cost 30 runs each.

The one-day competitions did not bring much joy to the County. They finished 13th in the Sunday League and although winning through to the knock-out section of the Benson & Hedges were disposed of in the quarter-finals.

Rice had an outstanding summer with the bat and headed the first-class averages by a great margin. He hit 1,871 runs at 66.82; Turner of Worcester came second with 1,711 at 55.19. Both Randall and Harris rediscovered themselves and averaged over 40. Todd completed 1,000 runs, and he and Harris generally got the innings off to a reasonable start. Cooper, who normally opened the bowling in the absence of Hadlee, made up the ground he had lost in 1977 and captured 52 wickets at 26.48 runs each.

Hadlee and five others made their first-class debuts during 1978. Richard Hadlee was one of three cricketing sons of the

Sir RICHARD JOHN HADLEE

One of the most intensively competitive cricketers ever to represent the County, Hadlee joined the playing staff at Trent Bridge almost by chance, but then grew so attached that he played as if his very life depended on the outcome of each match and was unable to understand why every member of the side did not possess the intensity of his commitment.

Hadlee put New Zealand cricket on the map and to an extent he achieved this because of the experience he gained playing county cricket. When he came to Notts in 1978 he had been a Test cricketer for six years, but his achievements had been modest. The continual grind of the county circuit forced him to refine his bowling – he reduced his run-up and delivered the ball with more accuracy but less wear and tear on his physique. His batting matured at the same time as his bowling; from being a useful lower-order run-stealer, he ended at the top of the Notts batting table with a double-hundred to his name.

His will-power enabled him to scale whatever peak was in his sights. The 'double' of 1,000 runs and 100 wickets in first-class cricket had not been attained since limited-overs matches had reduced the first-class programme. The pundits said it was impossible. Hadlee proved them wrong in 1984. He motivated the New Zealanders into winning a Test series against both England and against Australia, another task which had seemed impossible. Most outstanding of all, he became the first bowler to capture 400 Test wickets and even if his total of 431 is beaten, it will take a colossus to claim five wickets in a Test innings 36 times and ten wickets in a match as many as nine times.

His 105 wickets in 1981 went a large way towards Notts claiming the Championship and his all-round cricket of 1987 again made Notts' record of that summer possible. The County owes a great debt to the cricketer who arrived by chance!

Richard Hadlee, who has more Test wickets than any player in history, proved himself one of the world's greatest all-rounders with his performances for Notts. (Patrick Eagar)

former New Zealand captain Walter Hadlee. He was 26 when he signed for Notts and had played Test cricket since 1972–73 with some success, but seemed to be prone to injury. He was to become the greatest cricketer New Zealand ever produced, but in 1978 this reputation was still in the future.

The brothers John and Chris Curzon both made their debut in 1978. John, a seam bowler, played in only one first-class match; Chris, a batsman-wicketkeeper, acted as French's deputy, but after seeing little future at Trent Bridge, joined Hampshire in 1981, but then dropped out of first-class cricket. Kevin Mackintosh, a 20-year-old all-rounder from Surrey, played in 13 Championship matches in 1978. He had been on The Oval staff for 1976 and 1977, when he had mainly been employed as an opening batsman. He made only a few appearances for Notts in 1979 and 1980 and then left to rejoin Surrey, making his first-class debut for that county in 1981.

Kevin Saxelby, a fast-medium bowler from the north of the county, appeared in two Championship games in 1978. His career was to stretch until 1990 in the first eleven, after which he was appointed captain and mentor to the second team. His bowling proved especially useful in one-day matches and Sunday games in particular. His brother is now a member of the playing staff. Tim Robinson appeared once for the first eleven in 1978 and made another single appearance in 1979, though batting very well in second eleven and Colts matches – he was studying accountancy at Sheffield University and did not join the playing staff full-time until 1980. An attractive opening batsman, he quickly won a permanent place in the County side and gained his first England cap on the 1984–85 England visit to India. He had a splendid record for England in the Ashes series of 1985, but like the rest of the England batting failed the following winter in West Indies. In 1988 he was appointed captain in succession to Clive Rice and in recent seasons has batted in the middle order. His record in first-class cricket is an excellent one and his batting in the one-day matches, particularly the Benson & Hedges Trophy games, has been very impressive.

During the winter of 1978–79 there were extensive renovations carried out on the Trent Bridge Ground, and these alterations continued for some 12 months. The area on the top of the pavilion was converted into an Executive Members' Suite; the Long Room and entrance to the pavilion was changed, with the main entrance now directly off the Dixon Gate car park; the new library was set up; the old reporters' box was converted into executive boxes and a new press box built over the cricket office.

The cricket manager saw that the principal weakness in the side was the lack of spin bowling to support the seam of Hadlee and Rice; he was fortunate that two experienced cricketers, Eddie Hemmings of Warwickshire and Mike Bore of Yorkshire, were being released from their counties at the end of 1978. Both were keen to join Nottinghamshire and both made their debuts and became regular members of the Notts first eleven in 1978. Hemmings had been a youthful prodigy with his native county, first playing at the age of 17 in 1966 as a medium-pace bowler, but he now mainly bowled off-breaks. He was also a very useful batsman. His career at Edgbaston had been a chequered one and he had never quite fulfilled his early promise. His move to Trent Bridge was to prove very successful and by 1982 he had gained his first Test cap. For over a decade he has been Notts chief spin bowler. Mike Bore bowled left-arm medium-pace. He had made his debut for Yorkshire, being born in Hull, in 1969, but his appearances had been limited – 74 first-class matches in ten years. He was now 31 and had a reputation as a hard-working professional. Bore played for Notts until 1988 and after a spell as second eleven captain he returned to Yorkshire as a coach.

Nottinghamshire made a watery start to 1979. Of the first six Championship games, three were totally washed out – something of a Notts record. In the other three, the initial match consisted of just two hours cricket over three days; the Leicestershire game at Trent Bridge, which featured a charming hundred by Randall, was played between showers and the other game, against Glamorgan at Trent Bridge ended in a six-wicket win, Hadlee returning second-innings figures of seven for 28 and Tunnicliffe scoring 97. Two more wins followed at Bournemouth and Trent Bridge. In the first Notts made 325 for five off 100 overs, Rice 81, Hemmings 85 not out. Rice then dismissed Hampshire for 156. Smedley enforced the follow-on and victory was by six wickets. Hadlee was at this time absent with a hamstring injury and Watson opened the bowling with Rice. The win at Trent Bridge was by seven wickets over Northants. It was Harris's match. He scored 133 not out of 255 in the first innings and 132 in the second when Notts were set 256 in 150 minutes – victory was with three balls to spare, Birch hitting a six and a four to clinch the game.

Thus far the County were flourishing, but there then came a period when matters went awry. Leicestershire beat them at Grace Road and Worcestershire at Trent Bridge, then Essex at Southend. The other Championship game, against Sussex, saw the final Sussex pair thwart the Notts attack and play out for a draw.

269

Gloucestershire came to Nottingham on 14 July. Notts batted first making 368 for nine in 100 overs, Rice 129. Rice then took four for 44 and Hacker four for 46, removing the visitors for 116. The follow-on was enforced and Notts won by eight wickets. On the final day of the match it was announced that Rice would replace Smedley as the County captain. The reason for the timing was that Notts were due to play Warwickshire the following day in the Gillette Cup second round.

The decision to change captains in mid-season was made by the manager, Ken Taylor, and created much discussion at the time. Smedley was naturally shattered by the news and decided to retire from county cricket. His 16 seasons had brought him over 16,000 runs and 28 centuries. Smedley, like his batting, was quietly competent, a player who could be relied upon, both as a batsman and in the field. He returned to Bassetlaw cricket and continues to score runs for Kiveton Park, which club he also captains.

Nottinghamshire won the Gillette Cup game by 79 runs. Todd

Mike Bore joined Notts from Yorkshire in 1979 and played until 1988 when he became second eleven skipper. (NCCC)

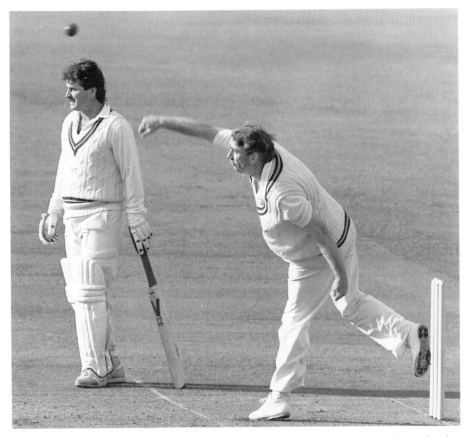

Eddie Hemmings played 13 seasons for Warwickshire before joining Notts in 1979, since when he has become a Test bowler and proved invaluable to the new successful Notts. (Patrick Eagar)

hit his first Gillette hundred and Warwickshire never looked likely to score he 266 set by Notts. Though Randall's 75 gained him the Man of the Match award in the next round of the Cup – against Sussex at Hove – Notts, without Hadlee, lost by six wickets.

No fewer than four Notts matches were abandoned in the Sunday League. The County won all six of their matches in the middle of the season, but failed at the beginning and end, thus finishing in eighth place. In the Benson & Hedges Competition they did not reach the quarter finals.

Returning to the Championship, six matches of the 22 were wins and as Notts fell to ninth place, the overall result was not as good as in 1978. Hadlee was fit to play in ten matches. He easily topped the bowling with 37 wickets at 16 runs each; Rice took 45

The two great fast bowlers of the 1930s, Bill Voce (left) and Harold Larwood (right), with John Heatley, the Notts Chairman, during their last visit together to Trent Bridge in 1980, where they are now commemorated in the Larwood and Voce Bar. (NCCC)

at 21 and the two newcomers, Bore and Hemmings had very similar figures, fifty or so wickets at about 30 runs each. The batting was headed by Randall, but he was still in the England side and thus missed half the county games. Harris had a good summer. He and Todd usually opened the batting, but in the final match Randall was put in first and created a unique record for the County by scoring 209 in the first innings and 146 in the second. No one before had hit a double-century and a century in the same match for Nottinghamshire.

The County Club had decided to enter a team in the Bassetlaw League in 1979 and with Tim Robinson scoring a record breaking 994 runs and Saxelby taking most wickets, the County won the title in its first season.

Off the field of play, Carling brought in David Pullan, the former wicketkeeper, as General Manager to look after the growing sphere of advertising and sponsorship and Brian Robson, the present Secretary, was recruited as the Club's accountant.

The 1980 season saw a marked advance in the Championship table. Notts rose to third place, despite the fact that Hadlee appeared in only seven matches. The leading bowler was Hemmings, who was the only one to capture more than 50 wickets – his 72 in the Championship cost 21 runs each. Hemmings also performed well with the bat, averaging more than 20. In Hadlee's absence Hacker was given more opportunities and took 48 wickets at 20 runs each. Although Rice played in every match and had a splendid batting record, he was unable to bowl as often as in 1979 and took 38 wickets.

Notts first Championship win came at Swansea. Rice, Hemmings and Bore bowled out the Welshmen and victory was by seven wickets. The second win came at The Oval. The first day was rained off; on the second the two first innings were declared and Clarke then removed Notts to leave his side nearly three hours to make 170. Bore and Hemmings dismissed Surrey for 131, the last wicket going down with the last possible delivery. The first home win did not come until 14 July. Cooper took five for 31 and Kent were all out for 67. They never recovered and the game was over in two days. The famous win over Derbyshire at Worksop followed. White, who had not played for two years, took ten for 57 and Notts, who had been well behind on first innings, won by 89 runs. A third successive win was achieved against Leicestershire. Robinson, who had replaced Harris as Notts opening batsman, scored 138 out of 271 all out and good bowling by everyone brought victory with nine wickets in hand.

Following this good period, Notts did not win again until the last home game. They required victory to secure third place in the Championship and simply crushed Hampshire. Hampshire were dismissed for 100 and 58 by Hadlee, Hacker and Rice. The game ended at tea-time on the second day.

Notts never challenged for the Sunday title; their six wins placed them 14th equal with Essex and Yorkshire, only Glamorgan having a poorer record. The quarter-finals of the Benson & Hedges Competition were reached, but the batting failed and Northants were left needing 144, a task they found simple. In the Gillette Cup again the batting let the County down, and Middlesex removed Notts in the second round, Gatting scoring an unbeaten 95.

A total of 50,010 spectators came to watch the first Test against the West Indies at Trent Bridge. The most exciting part of the game was on the last day, when West Indies really struggled against Willis before winning the match – unfortunately only about 1,000 spectators bothered to come to the ground on that day. Late in the season the Australians played Notts – they had come to England to play a celebration centenary game against England and had arranged four county matches as preparation. Watson and Hadlee dismissed the tourists for 207. Notts then hit 465, Rice, Birch and Hadlee all hitting fifties; the Australians failed a second time and Notts won by an innings – the biggest county win against the Australians for nearly a hundred years.

Before the 1980 season began, Jack Elliott, a major figure in club cricket circles in Nottinghamshire, was appointed the new President, but within a few weeks of taking office, tragically died and Dr J. B. Cochrane, another well-known figure in club cricket, was elected in his place. The cricket office, run by Ken Taylor, was reinforced in 1980 by the appointment of John Cope as 'Cricket Development Officer', whose role was to build on the work done by Frank Woodhead and to build up cricket in Nottinghamshire Schools and at club level in order to raise the standard of the game throughout the county. In the last ten years Cope has so invigorated cricket in the county that many other counties have come to seek his advice and more Notts-bred cricketers are reaching county level than at any time in the last 60 years.

In 1981 the players who had been gathered together over the last few seasons were at last free of injury and could bring their talents together throughout the season. The principal eleven were Rice, Randall, Hassan, Birch, Hadlee, Todd, Robinson, French, Cooper, Hemmings and Bore.

The first half of the Championship campaign revealed nothing out of the ordinary. The weather wasn't all that good and by 3 July, Notts had won just two games – against Leicestershire by eight wickets at Trent Bridge and against Gloucestershire, also at Trent Bridge by nine wickets – both matches had been emphatic successes, no phoney declarations. They had also been thrashed by Somerset at Bath and by Middlesex at Trent Bridge. The other six games were drawn and a healthy number of bonus points placed the County fourth in the table, six points behind the leaders but the three front runners had a game in hand.

The next six matches produced four more wins and took the County above the main rivals. As with the earlier successes the wins were by good margins and unaided by sporting declarations. Worcestershire lost by ten wickets, Yorkshire by nine wickets, Lancashire by eight and Surrey by an innings. All four matches were at Trent Bridge. In between Notts were beaten at Hinckley by Leicestershire in a high-scoring game when Leicestershire's first innings totalled 431 for eight. Balderstone, Steele and Davison all hit hundreds. Randall made 76 and 101 and the young colt, Weightman, 105, but the other Notts batsmen gave them little help.

Six matches now remained and Notts were 24 points ahead, but Essex, Surrey and Sussex behind them all had a match in hand and Hampshire in fifth place had three matches to spare.

The 17th match of the campaign was against Worcestershire at Worcester. Rain allowed only four overs on the first day; Notts gained a slender lead on first innings. Randall, Hassan and Birch hit out in the second and Rice declared, setting Worcestershire 239 in a fair time. Hadlee, Hemmings and Bore had the measure of the home batsmen and victory was by 106 runs, pushing Notts' lead to 27 points. Sussex, who were now in second spot, came to Trent Bridge for Notts' 18th fixture. The tension was high and the Notts batsmen were affected by nerves. Sussex made 208, but the Notts team could only muddle their way to 102. Hemmings and Bore opened the bowling in the second innings and Sussex were all out for 144. Notts required 251 and had all the last day to make the runs. The light was poor for much of the time, but a battling innings by Hassan kept Notts in with a chance. The umpires repeatedly offered the light, which the batsmen refused. Hassan fell and after him several wickets. With the total 205 for seven, play stopped for bad light. When the match resumed with 13 overs left, Notts managed to bat out time, the final pair surviving the last few overs.

Both Sussex and Notts had four matches left to play. Both counties won three in succession and thus the destination of the Championship was dependent on the final matches. Notts were opposed to Glamorgan at Trent Bridge; Sussex met Yorkshire at Hove, both matches to begin on 12 September.

Notts were four points ahead of Sussex as these matches started. Notts were in a determined mood and of the team no one more so than Hadlee. On the first morning Glamorgan were bowled out for 60; Hadlee four for 18, Cooper four for 24. That meant four bowling points. The Notts batting was not much better than that of the Welshmen and six wickets were down for 92. Birch and French rallied the side and the total reached 180. Only one batting point was therefore gained. Down at Hove Sussex dismissed Yorkshire for 153, collecting four bowling points and a Sussex total of 250 for five gave them three batting points. Sussex then declared.

On the second day – the Monday – Glamorgan began at 33 for one. They lost two wickets without an addition to the total. Javed Miandad played quite brilliantly, but no one else could master Hadlee or Hemmings and the all-out total was 149, Hadlee four for 38, Hemmings four for 51. Notts won the game between lunch and tea on the second day. Sussex went on to victory, but could not overtake Nottinghamshire, who thus became Champion County for the first time since 1929. There were emotional scenes in front of the pavilion and in the dressing room.

The outstanding figure in the campaign was Hadlee, who took 105 Championship wickets at 14.89 runs each and headed the national averages as well as being the only cricketer to take more than 100 wickets. Rice came seventh in the national bowling table with 65 wickets, average 19.20. The captain also finished in the top ten batting list with 1,462 runs, average 56.23, and was the best all-rounder of 1981.

Hemmings had a splendid bowling return with 84 Championship wickets at 20.71 runs each. Cooper and Bore also performed well and had good figures. Randall came second in the Notts batting table, scoring 1,093 Championship runs. Hassan, Birch, Hadlee and Todd all played important parts in the batting line-up.

The overall results in the one-day competitions were better than in previous years since the quarter-finals were reached in both NatWest (formerly Gillette) and Benson & Hedges Competitions. In the former Derbyshire surprisingly beat Notts by 23 runs when the Notts batting failed; in the latter Surrey always seemed in control. Six matches were won in the Sunday League, which left Notts in mid-table equal on points with three other counties.

Nigel Illingworth, Chris Scott, Neil Weightman and Peter Wood made their debuts in 1981. Wood, who was playing league cricket in Lancashire, was tried only in two Sunday games. Illingworth, a fast-medium bowler, made 15 appearances in first-class matches over three years. He did well at second eleven level, but was expensive in Championship games. Weightman, from Normanton on Trent, a promising opening batsman, played in four matches and as noted scored a century against Leicestershire; he left the staff at the end of 1982. Scott played as deputy wicketkeeper to French. His career continued until the end of 1991 and when required he kept wicket very effectively, being capped in 1988, when French was absent injured for most of the summer. He decided to leave Trent Bridge at the end of 1991 and joined Durham.

Financially the Club had enjoyed three successive years of surpluses, but the overall cost of running the Club had risen dramatically to £543,492, more than double the sum of ten years earlier.

A special Championship dinner was held in the Sherwood Rooms attended by 600 guests in April 1982 and in the same month the team went to Buckingham Palace to receive the Trophy from the Duke of Edinburgh.

The Test match of 1981 was won by the Australians by four

NOTTINGHAMSHIRE *v* GLAMORGAN

Played at Trent Bridge, Nottingham, on 12, 14 September 1981

NOTTINGHAMSHIRE WON BY TEN WICKETS

GLAMORGAN	FIRST INNINGS			SECOND INNINGS	
J. A. Hopkins	b Hadlee	4	(2)	c Randall b Hemmings	11
A. Jones	b Rice	5	(1)	c French b Hadlee	20
R. C. Ontong	c Hassan b Hadlee	11	(4)	lbw b Hadlee	0
Javed Miandad	c Robinson b Cooper	7	(5)	c French b Hadlee	75
N. G. Featherstone	c Birch b Cooper	0	(6)	c Birch b Rice	5
G. C. Holmes	lbw b Hadlee	3	(7)	c Rice b Hemmings	4
A. L. Jones	c Hadlee b Cooper	9	(9)	st French b Hemmings	0
†E. W. Jones	c French b Hadlee	2		b Hadlee	0
B. J. Lloyd	c Randall b Rice	14	(3)	lbw b Hemmings	8
*M. A. Nash	b Cooper	2		run out	10
S. A. B. Daniels	not out	0		not out	0
Extras	nb 3	3		b 8, lb 5, nb 3	16
Total		60			149

1st inns: 1-9, 2-9, 3-25, 4-27, 5-29, 6-34, 7-36, 8-52, 9-60
2nd inns: 1-29, 2-33, 3-33, 4-71, 5-86, 6-101, 7-113, 8-115, 9-145

BOWLING	O	M	R	W	O	M	R	W
Hadlee	12	4	18	4	17	8	38	4
Rice	8.1	1	14	2	15	6	38	1
Hemmings					24	11	51	4
Cooper	10	3	25	4	4	2	6	0
Bore					1	1	0	0

NOTTINGHAMSHIRE	FIRST INNINGS		SECOND INNINGS	
P. A. Todd	c Miandad b Nash	17	not out	18
R. T. Robinson	b Ontong	16	not out	9
D. W. Randall	c Daniels b Ontong	18		
B. Hassan	c E. W. Jones b Nash	18		
*C. E. B. Rice	c E. W. Jones b Daniels	11		
J. D. Birch	b Lloyd	27		
R. J. Hadlee	c Featherstone b Nash	0		
†B. N. French	c Featherstone b Ontong	26		
K. E. Cooper	c A. Jones b Daniels	11		
E. E. Hemmings	b Featherstone b Nash	11		
M. K. Bore	not out	9		
Extras	b 1, lb 8, w 1, nb 6	16	lb 1, nb 2	3
Total		180	(no wkt)	30

1st inns: 1-20, 2-50, 3-55, 4-66, 5-92, 6-92, 7-131, 8-155, 9-155

BOWLING	O	M	R	W	O	M	R	W
Nash	15.1	2	48	4	3.3	0	15	0
Daniels	14	1	58	2	3	0	12	0
Ontong	10	0	47	3				
Lloyd	7	2	11	1				

Umpires: D. O. Oslear and C. T. Spencer
*Captain; †Wicketkeeper

Nottinghamshire clinched the County Championship for the first time in 52 years amid scenes of great jubilation. They won in two days, with the winning run coming from a no-ball bowled by Nash.

wickets. The weather was rather poor and the total attendance over four days was only 38,172.

The season of 1982 began well. Lancashire, Hampshire, Worcestershire and Kent were all convincingly outplayed. Notts had signed Mike Hendrick, the Derbyshire and England seam bowler, during the winter and he opened the bowling in these matches with Hadlee – Rice, suffering a neck injury, was unable to bowl. The rain arrived after the Kent win and the next two matches were abandoned. Hadlee missed several games through injury and five successive defeats were suffered. This dealt a mortal blow to any hopes of retaining the Championship title, especially as Brearley's Middlesex team was playing brilliant cricket and seemed unstoppable. No sooner had Hadlee been put back on his feet than Hendrick retired with a strain, which proved so persistent that he missed the second half of the summer. Victory came in the last two games of the season. Leicestershire were beaten by an innings, in spite of the absence in the bowling line-up of Hadlee, Rice and Hendrick; Cooper, Hemmings and Bore took the wickets. Finally Sussex were overcome by six wickets using the same bowlers. Robinson hit 109 and 79, whilst Randall made a lively 76. These two wins meant fourth place was secured.

Randall headed the batting table, but as he played in all six Tests, he was available for only ten Championship games. Birch had his best year, averaging 36.15. Hassan also batted well, but Rice, handicapped by his injury, was a shadow of his 1981 self. Robinson continued to improve, but Todd fell back. Hadlee was again the leading bowler in England, but missing five matches meant that his victims were not so plentiful. Hendrick bowled well in the nine Championship games he played. Bore, Saxelby, Cooper and Hemmings all had quite respectable figures.

The feature of the season was Notts cricket in the Benson & Hedges Cup. All four matches were won in the group fixtures. The quarter-final was very exciting. Notts made 156 of which Hassan scored 48. Hendrick, Cooper and Bore then bowled with nagging accuracy, not allowing even Gower any freedom, and Leicestershire needed 10 off the final over – they only made seven. The semi-final, like the previous game played at Trent Bridge, was against Lancashire. Hadlee was able to play, but was still not fully fit. Lancashire made 182 and Notts in reply seemed to have lost their way, the scoring rate going beyond eight per over. Hadlee, however, hit 55 in 78 minutes and the match was won by four wickets with nearly two overs remaining. Nottinghamshire went to Lord's for the final, meeting Somerset, who were then armed with Richards, Botham and Garner, all fully fit. The Western county crushed Notts. Garner took three for 13 and Botham two for 19, with Notts all out 130. Somerset lost one wicket in reaching the target.

Sussex ran away with the Sunday League title; Nottinghamshire began poorly but picked up later, won eight games and finished fifth. In the NatWest Trophy Gloucestershire beat Notts with ease in the second round.

The season in retrospect seemed very much like the morning after. Injuries were largely to blame and seriously affected the bowling strength, but too often the batting let the team down.

It was sad to record that Bill Thornley, the Notts first eleven scorer, died during the summer after a few days' illness. He had been in charge since the death of Arthur Wheat in 1973. In his stead Notts appointed Les Tomlinson and Len Beaumont as joint-scorers. Tomlinson had been a notable batsman–wicketkeeper in Nottingham club cricket in the 1930s and 1940s; Beaumont had played professional football for Huddersfield, Portsmouth and Nottingham Forest and had later become a well-known cricket coach in Nottingham and District. His son, David Beaumont, had gained a cricketing blue at Cambridge and played for Notts second eleven.

Financially the County had a very poor year. The firm which organised advertising boards on the ground went into liquidation owing the club about £30,000 and the total deficit for the year was more than double that figure. David Pullan, the commercial manager, had left midway through 1982 and he joined Nottingham Forest in a similar capacity; Philip Carling, the chief executive, left at the end of the year and moved to Glamorgan CCC. Brian Robson, the Club's accountant, was promoted to be the new Secretary. John Heatley, the cheerful Chairman, retired after his five years in office and Jim Ward was appointed in his place. In addition Bob White, the second eleven captain, was released and joined the first-class umpires list.

It was going to be a year of retrenchment in 1983 both on and off the field. Hadlee would be absent, playing for New Zealand, for more than half the summer; Rice was still unable to bowl due to his neck injury; there were five young hopefuls determined to gain a place in the first eleven. Mark Fell from Farndon was an attacking batsman, who had been given some opportunities in 1982 and hit a century against Essex at Trent Bridge. Paul Johnson, who had joined the staff before his 16th birthday had played in four 1982 Championship games. He came from the Balderton Club and was full of natural talent. Peter Such, though born in Helensburgh, had learnt his cricket in East Leake and bowled off-breaks. Ian Pont came from Brentwood and was the brother of the Essex cricketer. He was an all-rounder aged 21. Andy Pick from Thrumpton was a 19-year-old fast bowler and even at this early stage in his career made the ball come sharply off the pitch. Apart from Pick they had all made their first-class debuts in 1982; Pick was to make his during the coming season. With the TCCB now clamping down harder on overseas players in county cricket, much more depended on counties unearthing their native talent and the youth programme at Trent Bridge was now going to show its value.

The County won only three matches in the 1983 Championship. The first revealed just how much Notts were going to miss Hadlee. At Hove in early May he bowled Sussex out for 115, returning figures of 20-11-25-4, then hit 103 and picked up another three wickets as Sussex fell to an innings defeat. The two players mainly responsible for the second success were Birch and Hemmings. Notts were dismissed by Lancashire for 86 at Trent Bridge; the Lancastrians then made 158 and seemed well in control. Birch scored 95 with 13 fours on a difficult wicket, which meant Lancashire required 222 to win. Hemmings took seven for 23 and Notts won by 157 runs. The third win was at Worcester. In this game Cooper had a brilliant spell of five wickets for no runs in 19 deliveries. Worcestershire were all out for 69, Cooper's final figures being seven for 33. Robinson scored a sound 110 and victory was by 215 runs. In between these convincing wins were ten losses and Notts finished 14th in the table.

Robinson had an excellent summer; he topped the batting table with 1,464 runs, average 40.66, and hit 207 off the Warwickshire attack at Trent Bridge. Rice, still incapacitated by his neck injury, just reached 1,000 runs, as did Birch. Johnson hit a maiden hundred against Gloucestershire at Bristol. He played in 15 Championship games and was regarded as most promising. Randall was required by England and rarely performed well for the County.

Hendrick was the best of the bowlers. He played throughout the year and took 66 Championship wickets. Next to him came Saxelby with 47 wickets at 26 runs each. Hemmings sent down most overs and had several good analyses, but could be expensive. Such was given an extended trial and looked a bright prospect. Bore had a disappointing summer, his 19 Championship wickets costing 51 runs each.

Results in the Sunday League were very disappointing, the County finishing bottom of the table with four victories and nine defeats. There was an exciting tied match at Hereford against Worcestershire. Notts made 195 for four, Hassan and Rice both hitting 71. Worcestershire equalled that total with the last two men at the wicket. In the Benson & Hedges Competition two wins meant that the County failed to move into the quarter-finals. The NatWest second round match against Sussex found Imran Khan in brilliant form. He hit 114 not out, taking the Sussex total to 227 for seven. Notts never looked likely to reach that score.

The brightest match of the summer for Notts spectators was the Test against New Zealand. Randall and Botham added 186 for the sixth wicket, Botham making 103 and Randall 83. In the final innings Hadlee hit a scintillating 29 not out and won the Man of the Series Award. Altogether 34,763 spectators watched the game during the five days.

There was better news on the financial front, the Club making a profit of £9,043. The Committee decided to launch an appeal fund for 1984. This was under the chairmanship of Dick Tennant. Unfortunately he died suddenly in April 1984 and the vice-chairman of the central committee Cliff Gillott took over the running of the appeal.

Randall went with the England team to New Zealand and Pakistan in the winter of 1983–84 and had an excellent tour. He

Notts in 1984, when the County finished second in both the Championship and the Sunday League. From left to right, top row: R. A. Pick, D. J. R. Martindale, R. J. Evans, P. M. Such, C. D. Fraser-Darling, K. P. Evans, J. A. Afford, M. Newell. Middle row: C. W. Scott, R. T. Robinson, K. E. Cooper, B. C. Broad, K. Saxelby, M. K. Bore, P. Johnson. Seated: E. E. Hemmings, B. Hassan, R. J. Hadlee, C. E. B. Rice (captain), K. A. Taylor (Manager), J. D. Birch, D. W. Randall, B. N. French. (NCCC)

hit two Test hundreds and in the combined first-class averages came second only to Gower with 624 runs, average 56.72.

The prospects for the County in 1984 looked distinctly bright. Hadlee was to be available all summer; Rice had at last sorted out his neck injury. In addition the County had engaged Chris Broad, the left-hand opening batsman from Bristol.

The first half of the summer was a great contrast to that of 1983. With eleven matches played, Notts had won five games and were third in the Championship. The first Championship game – Broad had scored a century on his Notts debut *v* Oxford a few days before – saw Surrey beaten by 225 runs. Hadlee took eight for 22; Rice, Broad and Birch made the runs. The second win was against the formidable Essex side at Chelmsford. Notts hit 264, with Hadlee's 71 not out the best innings. Essex were dismissed for 93, Saxelby, complete with new beard, taking four for 15. The follow-on was enforced. Gooch hit a very sound hundred, but Notts won by ten wickets. The match at Bournemouth proved a much tighter affair. A century from Hadlee meant the scores were virtually level after the first innings. Hendrick and Hadlee then took five wickets each and Notts required 123 in the last innings. Victory was by two wickets. Glamorgan were outplayed at Trent Bridge, as were Gloucestershire. Broad and Robinson, as Notts opening pair, were proving the best on the county circuit and Broad gained his first England cap in the final week of June. He justified his selection by helping Fowler add 101 for England's first wicket against the West Indies fast bowling, and thus secured his place for the remaining matches in the series.

By the end of July Notts had won three more matches – against Sussex, Worcestershire and Lancashire all at Trent Bridge – and were second to Essex in the table; eight points behind but with a game in hand.

Nottinghamshire's successes continued through August. Middlesex were beaten by an innings at Lord's, when Hadlee scored 210 not out, reaching his hundred in 93 minutes, a century from Randall and 97 from Robinson helped to beat Warwickshire at Trent Bridge and in the final home game Bore was brought into the side for his first game of the year and took nine wickets, Northants being beaten by an innings; Rice hit 103 not out. This placed Notts one point behind Essex with a game in hand. There were two matches still to play. The first of these took place at Hove. Notts' bowlers for once could not make any headway and Sussex compiled 436 for nine. From then on Notts had no hope of winning, though they picked up five bonus points, which meant overtaking Essex in the table.

Down to Taunton for the final fixture. Essex were away to Lancashire. On the first day three hours were lost through rain. Somerset on the second day were bowled out for 274. Notts hit out and Rice declared at 222 for seven of which Broad made 88 and Randall 64. However up at Old Trafford, Essex polished off Lancashire on the second day and secured the maximum 24 points. Notts had six bonus points, but had to beat Somerset to take the title. Botham, the Somerset captain, declared setting Notts 297 in 60 overs. Rice hit 98 off 109 balls with three sixes and nine fours. There were 36 runs required off the last three overs. Bore, coming in at number ten, hit out; he lost Hemmings and with the last pair at the wicket 14 were needed from the last over bowled by Booth. Bore hit two fours and a two. He was then caught right on the boundary by the substitute fielder Ollis and Notts lost by three runs. Essex were Champions. Considering the County had finished 14th in 1983, the improvement to be runners-up was certainly outstanding, but few remember the team that came second!

Chris Broad's career flourished after he left Gloucestershire for Trent Bridge. A free-scoring left-handed opening batsman, he made his debut for Notts in 1984 and immediately made his Test debut. (Patrick Eagar)

Hadlee dominated the season. He hit 1,179 runs and took 117 wickets in the 24 Championship matches completing the 'double', a feat which had not been performed since one-day matches had reduced the three-day programme. Hadlee's batting average was 51.26; four other Notts batsmen averaged over 40 and reached 1,000 runs: Rice, Robinson, Randall and Broad. The last named missed eight matches due to his Test match selection. One name was in fact above Hadlee in the batting – Paul Johnson, but he appeared in only six games. However this certainly reinforced the comments made concerning his batting during 1983.

Second to Hadlee in the bowling came another young hopeful, Peter Such. The off-spinner played in eleven games and captured 28 wickets at 22 runs each. Hemmings had a bag of 86 at 24 runs each and Cooper 47 at 26. Hendrick was fit for only three games and left the County at the season's end.

The County reached the semi-finals in the Benson & Hedges competition before falling to Lancashire at Trent Bridge; in the quarter-final, also at home, Surrey had been overwhelmed by 167 runs. Rice had made 94 and Randall 103 not out. Surrey were all out for 89.

In the NatWest matches, Middlesex beat Notts by five runs in the second round, with Emburey and Edmonds, bowling very tightly, permitting only 52 runs off their 24 overs.

The Sunday League ended in the same way as the Championship: Essex champions, Notts runners-up. However, Essex took the lead from Middlesex in July and slowly built up a margin against the other counties. Notts won five out of the last six of their matches and thus moved rapidly upwards in the last month or so, but were still eight points behind Essex at the end.

Taking the overall results, Notts enjoyed their best season to date since the introduction of one-day cricket, even though they failed to land a trophy.

The Trent Bridge 1984 Appeal raised about £30,000, but on the ordinary account the County lost some £22,000 during the year, so much of the extra 'bonus' money did little more than balance the books.

Apart from Broad, five other players made their debuts during the year. David Fraser-Darling, a 20-year-old well built all-rounder remained on the staff until the end of 1988. Troubled by injury, he played in 11 first-class matches but more frequently in the Sunday League. He took 18 wickets at 25 runs each on Sundays, but his first-class wickets cost twice that. After leaving Trent Bridge he joined the police force. Steven Mee's appearances were confined to a single game against Cambridge University in

1984. Andy Afford, the left-arm spinner from Lincolnshire, had enjoyed great success at junior levels with his native county and made his Notts debut before actually joining the County staff. A philosophical cricketer, he has been a regular member of the first eleven for the last three or four seasons. Kevin Evans, a 19-year-old from Calverton, is a talented all-rounder, bowling somewhat above medium pace and batting in the middle order – he, too, is now a regular member of the first eleven. Mick Newell, an 18-year-old batsman, who occasionally bowls leg-breaks and can keep wicket, forced his way into the first eleven in 1987 and played in many of the matches through the following three years. A determined batsmen he is difficult to dismiss and scores runs more by carefully placing shots between fielders than by great lunges. In 1991 he was very unfortunate to find himself almost entirely confined to second eleven matches.

The batting remained very strong in 1985, but with Hadlee not completing his tour of the West Indies with the New Zealand squad until 8 May and then having to continue straightaway with the county circuit, the sting went out of the bowling. The wickets in general were against the spinners, so young Such and Hemmings had an expensive time. Hendrick, of course, had gone and Rice did not bowl anything like as frequently as in his early days; this thrust a lot of work on to Cooper. The Hucknall seamer came second to Hadlee in the final table and was generally very accurate, but his back-up, Saxelby and Pick, was not lethal. Pick was still a raw recruit, whilst Saxelby seemed to do so much better in the limited-overs games than in the Championship.

Notts success in 1985 came in the NatWest Trophy Competition. Johnson hit a century as Staffordshire were disposed of in the first round; Robinson carried out his bat for 98 and then Cooper took four for 49 as Notts beat Warwickshire in the second round. The quarter-final was played at Bristol. Robinson and Broad began the match with a partnership worth 146; the former went on to make 90 and Notts reached 287 for eight. Gloucestershire fought bravely, but failed to make the 15 runs needed from the final over. Robinson was in brilliant form in the semi-final at Worcester; playing what might be described as the best innings of his career he scored 139 before being run out in the penultimate over. Notts won with four balls unbowled. The final at Lord's was against Essex – Notts' great rivals of 1984. The wicket was perfect for batting and Essex hit 280 for two off their 60 overs, Gooch making 91 and Hardie 110. Robinson and Broad soon had the runs flowing. The opening pair added 143. Matters then turned in Essex's favour when both Rice and Hadlee failed. With the total 214 for four, the unknown Martindale arrived to partner Randall. The score mounted without further loss, but 37 were still needed with three overs to go. Randall played some brilliantly improvised shots and at the start of the last over 18 were needed. Randall scored 16 off five balls. Pringle the bowler sent the final delivery down and Randall, forced back, sent a catch to mid-wicket. Essex won an incredible game by one run.

The other two limited overs competitions did not provide many thrills for the County. They failed to qualify for the Benson & Hedges quarter-finals and in the Sunday League finished 12th with six victories.

In the Championship, with the batting so powerful, and the bowling moderate, 18 of the 24 matches ended as draws. Four games were won and two lost.

In April Somerset were beaten at Taunton by nine wickets, Robinson hitting a century, but the second win did not come until 11 June at Tunbridge Wells. Saxelby took ten for 113 and Robinson held Notts together with an innings of 90. The third win was also away from home. Notts required 246 to win on the last day on a tricky wicket. Randall made a typical 115 and the road to victory seemed easy. The only win at Trent Bridge came at the end of August. Randall, Robinson and Martindale provided the runs, Pick, Such and Hemmings the wickets, the margin of victory being ten wickets.

Robinson, Rice, Randall and Broad all had good summers with

The Trent Bridge pavilion in 1986, two years before the ground's 150th anniversary. (NCCC)

the bat – Robinson and Broad were the best opening pair in the country – Hadlee made his contribution and Johnson was more consistent. Of the bowling we have already spoken.

The only newcomer to the side was Duncan Martindale, an attractive middle-order right-hand batsman, who had played his early cricket in Cheshire, but joined the Notts staff as a student in Nottingham. He hit a maiden hundred in the match at Old Trafford and played very sensibly in the NatWest Final. Although remaining on the Trent Bridge playing staff until the end of 1991 he never commanded a regular place in the first eleven, though scoring heavily with the second eleven. There can be few kinder and more considerate cricketers who have represented the County.

The era of renovating and rebuilding Trent Bridge was by no means over. Under the supervision of the Club's vice-chairman, Maurice Youdell, the Larwood & Voce stand, with its own public house at the rear, was completed in June 1985 and officially opened by two of Harold Larwood's daughters and the widow of Bill Voce. The new building replaced the derelict stand on the Hound Road–Fox Road corner. At the top of the stand a 'Taverners Bar' was built, replacing the old Supporters Club room which had been on the Hound Road frontage. Derek Williams and his wife, who ran the old club, moved into the new building.

In 1986 the County's results overall were excellent, but no trophies were won. The battle for the County Championship during its final stages was between Nottinghamshire and Essex. Gloucestershire, the early leaders, faded away in August and the decisive match in the competition was the meeting of Essex and Notts at Trent Bridge on 10 September, although by then the dice were heavily loaded in Essex's favour. As it was both that game and Notts' final match were drawn and Notts picked up only 11 points.

Broad scored a stubborn hundred in the first innings against Essex, the Notts total being 267; Hadlee took six for 51 dismissing Essex for 139. Rice declared in the second innings, setting Essex 313 off 84 overs. The Essex total slumped to 97 for five, but Fletcher was determined and batted the best part of three hours to save his side. It was the same story in the Northants match. This time Rice set Northants 243 in 43 overs. The stumps were drawn with their total 186 for nine. Broad hit another hundred in this match and Afford was the best of the bowlers with eight wickets.

Notts had to be content with fourth place, one point behind Surrey and twelve behind Gloucestershire. Seven victories were recorded. The first was one in which both sides forfeited an innings – against Leicestershire at Trent Bridge. The second was much more convincing, against Surrey in two days, when Hadlee took ten for 72 and Notts won by an innings. Without Hadlee Notts beat Middlesex by 126 runs also at home, Rice making an unbeaten 156. At Worksop the first three batsmen, Broad, Robinson and Johnson all hit hundreds against Yorkshire. Rice declared at 404 for three. Pick then took nine wickets and Notts won a splendid innings victory. Hadlee was again absent: the New Zealanders were touring England and it was arranged that Hadlee should play for his country in the Test matches and one-day Internationals, but otherwise appear for Notts.

There were three victories in August. Against Lancashire Notts were set 296 in 89 overs. Johnson took the opportunity to hit a hundred and at the same time became the youngest batsmen to reach 1,000 runs in a season for the County. The margin of success was by seven wickets. Kent were quite outplayed at Trent Bridge, Afford taking ten wickets and Robinson hitting 159 not out. Finally Glamorgan were beaten at Cardiff in an exciting finish, Afford and Hemmings being mainly responsible.

In the Sunday League the County were among the front runners all summer, but with ten victories had to be content with third place. Broad hit most runs in the competition in 1986 – a total of 701 – and Rice equalled the record for most wickets in a season – 34. The captain actually took four wickets in a match five times, another League best.

In the Benson & Hedges Competition, Notts came second in their group and then beat Essex in the quarter-finals, Rice taking five for 48 and Hadlee hitting 61 not out. The semi-final draw was against Middlesex at Lord's. Randall and Broad were the only Notts batsmen to cope with Emburey and Edmonds, so the total after 55 overs was 189 for eight. Despite some very keen bowling by Hadlee and Cooper, Middlesex got home with five wickets to spare. Notts reached the quarter-finals of the NatWest Trophy. In this Surrey were met at The Oval. Hadlee returned figures of 12-4-17-5 and Surrey were 204 for nine after their 60 overs. Notts collapsed to 70 for six. Hadlee came to the rescue with a brilliant 55, but, though he was the Man of The Match, it was insufficient to beat Surrey.

The Trent Bridge Test was dominated by Hadlee. He bowled out England twice, taking ten wickets as well as hitting 68, and New Zealand won by eight wickets. The two other Tests were drawn and thus New Zealand won a Test series in England for the first time.

Hadlee came second in the first-class bowling averages and

tenth in the batting table, an exceptional all-round performance. He topped both Notts' sets of averages, but due to Test calls played in only 14 games.

Robinson, Rice, Johnson and Broad all made over 1,000 runs and returned respectable averages; Newell also batted well, averaging 35, but Randall was completely out of sorts. The bowling had plenty of variety with Afford looking very promising and taking 41 Championship wickets. Cooper, Rice, Hemmings and Pick all had good days, the captain a regular member of the attack once more. The one disappointment was Such, who was given limited opportunities and at the end of the season decided to move to Leicestershire. No new players were used during the year.

THE DOUBLE

After the tremendous efforts he had put in during 1986, Hadlee was in two minds as to whether to retire from county cricket. He decided in the end to have one more summer and to finish his career with Nottinghamshire on a high note. Rice also intended to make 1987 his swansong in English county cricket.

The County therefore began 1987 with two highly talented players quite determined to achieve something out of the ordinary. The first two months of the season gave no indication of any major success by Nottinghamshire. On 12 June, the County were 15th in the Championship table without a single win – Lancashire at the top had nearly three times the number of points. In the Sunday League Notts were 12th, with Derbyshire at the top with four wins from five contests. The Benson & Hedges Competition had not brought any joy, though the County were a little unlucky not to obtain a place in the knock-out round, since the final decision depended on run rate, with three teams in their group each winning two matches.

The first really cheerful note was struck on 30 June, when Notts won their first match, beating Kent by ten wickets, this despite Taylor carrying his bat right through the first innings of Kent for 123. Johnson hit 108 for Notts and Hadlee in the second innings took six for 44. The next match was lost – the only defeat Notts suffered in the competition all summer – but after that the machinery of success was unstoppable. Yorkshire and Leicestershire were thoroughly beaten at Trent Bridge. In the Yorkshire game Afford took nine wickets and Rice hit 115; against Leicestershire, Hadlee took nine and Johnson hit a hundred.

Newell made 203 not out against Derbyshire at Derby as the County totalled 433 for seven declared and Derbyshire lost by an innings. Newell was the youngest Notts cricketer ever to make a double-century in Championship cricket.

Following two draws, Warwickshire were beaten by an innings, when Martindale scored 103 and Hemmings took ten wickets – Martindale was playing because both Broad and Robinson were in the England side against Pakistan.

In the next game it was Hadlee's turn to hit a hundred and he also captured 12 wickets – the first Notts cricketer since 1921 to perform this match double at Trent Bridge. Notts beat Somerset by five wickets and moved to the top of the table.

Northants were the next to suffer, being beaten by an innings. Robinson scored 102, Broad, Newell and Rice all made fifties. Hadlee helped himself to another eight wickets and Hemmings also took eight.

A couple of days prior to this fixture Notts had gained a place in the NatWest final. Having overcome Derbyshire at Derby in the quarter-finals by 57 runs – Derbyshire never appeared likely to reach Notts' total of 268 for eight – Notts met Gloucestershire at Bristol. Deciding to bat, Notts had made a modest total of 225 for eight, Broad scoring 65. Pick, however, completely destroyed Gloucestershire. His analysis was 9.1-2-22-5 and the Western county were all out for 82.

Four draws followed the win over Northants and when Sussex came to Trent Bridge on 2 September for the penultimate Championship game Notts had to win to keep their title hopes alive. Hadlee did not give Sussex a chance – at lunch on the first day they were 73 for seven. They were all out for 123, the New Zealander's figures 18-4-20-6. Notts in their turn gave an indifferent batting display and it was fortunate that Broad made 73, for the total amounted to only 133. Hadlee and Saxelby then bowled almost unchanged to dismiss Sussex for 80, the latter taking six for 49 and Notts won by eight wickets.

The following day the County travelled to Lord's for the NatWest final against Northants. It was a miserable day weather-wise. First the start was delayed due to rain and later further showers interrupted the proceedings. Northants batted first making 228 for three, the game being reduced to 50 overs a side. When play ended for the day Notts were looking very sorry for themselves at 57 for four, Rice 20 not out, Birch 9 not out. Birch was bowled with the score 84 and Hadlee then came to the crease. Hadlee was determined, and after one or two half chances went astray the fielding became ragged as Hadlee, now with French, moved the total rapidly towards the target. With five overs left, 51 were required, but this dwindled to eight from the last. French was accidently run out off the first ball of the final over, but Hadlee then hit a six and a four. The match was won, and the small gathering of Notts supporters were jubilant.

That victory came on the Monday; on Wednesday began the final vital Championship game to decide the 1987 winners. Glamorgan were the visitors to Trent Bridge. The Welshmen decided to bat first, but were undone by the spin of Hemmings and were all out for 111. Rice celebrated his final first-class match for the County with an unbeaten 104 and declared at 300 for five. Glamorgan managed to stretch the game into the third day but were defeated by nine wickets, Notts picking up 24 points. This put them exactly 24 points ahead of Lancashire, but Notts' programme was complete and Lancashire had one match left – against Essex. If Lancashire gained the full 24 points in this game they would claim the title, the rule being that if two sides were

Richard Hadlee, whose left-handed batting has sometimes been as useful to Notts as his outstanding bowling, notably in the NatWest Trophy final in 1987. (NCCC)

292

equal on points at the top, the team with most wins takes precedence. Notts could therefore only wait and see. The answer came quickly because Lancashire batted first and collected only two bonus batting points. Notts were therefore the 1987 Champions.

Notts were 'double' Champions. They might have added a third title, but having gone for eleven weeks without defeat in the Sunday League, they lost two matches in late August and thus finished two points behind the leaders, Worcestershire.

The first of these vital games was at Moreton in Marsh on 23 August. The game was reduced by rain to 30 overs and Notts lost by two runs, batting second. The following week the County were at Derby and were simply outplayed by the Derbyshire captain, Barnett, who made a splendid 63 – Derbyshire won by seven wickets with two overs in hand.

When the final set of matches began Notts had a theoretical chance of the title, but not only did they have to beat Surrey, but their rivals Worcestershire had to lose. Notts won by the narrow margin of three wickets and two deliveries unbowled, but Worcestershire, with Botham in good form, overwhelmed Northants. Notts had to settle for second place.

The season's results were a fitting way to crown the county careers of Hadlee and Rice. The New Zealander ended with the most outstanding summer's figures. His 97 wickets at 12 runs each placed him well clear of all rivals of the head of the bowling averages for the country and taking those batsmen who scored at least 1,000 runs, he came third with an average of 52.90, behind Crowe and Gatting. Both he and Rice played in the MCC Bicentenary Match at Lord's, when MCC met the Rest of the World: Broad and French played for the opposition.

Rice came second to Hadlee in the Notts batting table, but Robinson and Broad, who were third and fourth, missed many games due to Test calls. Randall had a much better record than in 1986, but appeared in only 11 Championship matches. Johnson and Newell both completed 1,000 runs. French, also in the England side, was absent frequently and Scott, his deputy, played well, taking part in 12 Championship games.

Hemmings came second to Hadlee in the bowling table, but his fellow-spinner, Afford, did not perform as well as in 1986. Of the three debutants, Addil Somani, the Ugandan resident in New Zealand, played only against Oxford University and Russell Evans only against Pakistan. Evans' elder brother, Kevin, also turned out in this match, the first time a pair of brothers had played in the same eleven for Notts since the 1930s. Russell

NATWEST TROPHY FINAL
NOTTINGHAMSHIRE *v*
NORTHAMPTONSHIRE

Played at Lord's, Saturday 5 and Monday 7 September 1987

NOTTINGHAMSHIRE WON BY THREE WICKETS

NORTHANTS

*G. Cook	c French b Saxelby	26
W. Larkins	lbw b Pick	87
A. J. Lamb	b Rice	41
R. J. Bailey	not out	39
D. J. Capel	not out	29
R. G. Williams		
D. J. Wild		
†D. Ripley		
N. G. B. Cook		
W. W. Davis		
A. Walker		
Extras	b 1, lb 2, nb 3	6
Total	(3 wkts, 50 overs)	228

Fall: 61, 152, 169

BOWLING	O	M	R	W
Hadlee	10	1	29	0
Pick	10	1	36	1
Rice	10	0	45	1
Saxelby	10	0	63	1
Hemmings	10	0	52	0

NOTTINGHAMSHIRE

B. C. Broad	lbw b Davis	3
R. T. Robinson	c Ripley b Davis	2
D. W. Randall	b N. G. B. Cook	10
*C. E. B. Rice	c G. Cook b Williams	63
P. Johnson	lbw b Walker	1
J. D. Birch	b Walker	21
R. J. Hadlee	not out	70
†B. N. French	run out	35
E. E. Hemmings	not out	0
R. A. Pick		
K. Saxelby		
Extras	lb 18, w 8	26
Total	(7 wkts, 49.3 overs)	231

Fall: 11, 12, 31, 38, 84, 146, 221

BOWLING	O	M	R	W
Davis	10	1	45	2
Capel	6.3	1	31	0
Walker	10	0	38	2
N. G. B. Cook	10	2	30	1
Williams	10	0	48	1
Wild	3	0	21	0

Umpires: D. R. Shepherd and A. G. T. Whitehead
*Captain; †Wicketkeeper

Evans, a useful right-hand bat, had only limited opportunities with the first eleven and left the Trent Bridge staff at the end of the 1990 season. The third newcomer, Paul Pollard, had come to the County on a Youth Training Scheme and looked such a promising prospect that he was taken on the full-time playing staff. An opening left-hand batsman he has gained a regular place in the County side and seems certain of a long career in county cricket.

The problem which faced Notts manager, Ken Taylor, for 1988 was discovering an adequate replacement for Hadlee and Rice: an impossible task. All counties were now permitted just one overseas player in the team. The player signed for this formidable task was the Barbadian all-rounder Franklyn Stephenson. Stephenson was aged 29, but his experience in first-class cricket until 1988 was both unusual and limited. In 1981–82 Stephenson, who had toured England with the West Indies Under 19 team of 1978, went to Australia and played for Tasmania, ending up second in the first-class Australian bowling averages. He then returned to Barbados and made his first-class debut for his home island, hitting 165 *v* Leewards Islands. In 1982 and 1983 he appeared briefly in the ranks of Gloucestershire, but injury and other league commitments prevented regular appearances. He had had tremendous success in the Lancashire leagues with Royton and Littleborough. Then he moved to Rawtenstall and later Oldham. In 1983–84 he went with the West Indies rebel team to South Africa and it was here that his potential was spotted by Clive Rice. By 1985 he was playing in the Northern League with Fleetwood and took 94 wickets at 9 runs each as well as averaging 39 with the bat.

Robinson was appointed captain in place of Rice. The season opened with the now traditional rain-ruined match against MCC at Lord's, then the competitive cricket started. The first four Championship matches were all lost. French, who had been the England wicketkeeper on the winter tour to Pakistan and New Zealand, decided on medical advice after three games to have a hand operation which would put him out for virtually the whole of the season. This was a blow to a side feeling its way, but luckily Scott proved a capable stand-in. Results in the early one-day matches were also on the gloomy side, with three out of four Sunday matches lost. The Benson & Hedges Cup offered some

---

Rain reduced the match to 50 overs per side. Even so, the game was not finished on Saturday and Notts were forced to resume at 57 for four on Monday, when rain again delayed the start until 1.30, an early lunch being taken. Hadlee's assault won the match, but he could have been out four times in the 43rd and 44th overs.

comfort. In Group B, Worcestershire, Notts and Northants all had two wins, one loss and one abandoned. Notts' run rate enabled the County to obtain a place in the quarter-finals. Here they met Glamorgan and were outmanoeuvred by Maynard who scored a distinguished 108 off 111 balls; the Welsh county won by six wickets.

The first Championship win came at Trent Bridge on 24 May, Sussex being beaten by 67 runs. Two more defeats occurred at the start of June, the most embarrassing being at Edgbaston when Small, taking seven for 15, removed Notts for 44. Wins however then became more common, Glamorgan, Northants, Middlesex and Worcestershire all being defeated in successive home games. Cooper and Stephenson were the principal architects of success in these games all of which were relatively low scoring. The County moved rapidly up the Championship table. A period of draws was followed by two away wins. Essex were defeated at Colchester when Robinson batted in great form, hitting 134 not out as Notts won by two wickets when set 274 in 69 overs. The match ended with the last possible delivery. Cooper and Stepehenson bowled out Lancashire for 121 at Lytham in a match reduced to one innings per side by rain. The eighth and last win was at Trent Bridge against Derbyshire. In this four-day fixture, Derbyshire made 347 and 226 but still lost by an innings, since Notts made 614, Randall, with 237, hitting the highest score of his career. Newell also made a century.

The last match of the season was also at Trent Bridge, against Yorkshire. At the start of this game Stephenson had captured 114 first-class wickets – Cooper had reached exactly 100 in the Derbyshire match – and scored 790 runs. The Barbadian therefore required 210 runs in this final game to complete the 'double'. As he had not scored a century for Notts all summer, the likelihood of him reaching 1,000 runs was too small to measure. Yorkshire batted first, scoring 380, Stephenson picking up four wickets. Notts batted patchily, but Stephenson coming in at number six, hit 111 in 157 minutes. Notts were 296 all out. Batting a second time Yorkshire made 340 for seven and then declared – all seven wickets fell to Stephenson. Notts had all the fourth day to make 425. Four wickets went down for 83, but once again Stephenson blossomed, hitting 117 in 137 minutes with 20 fours and two sixes. He did not give an actual chance, his lofted hits landing between fieldsmen. It was an incredible feat. Only twice before in English first-class cricket had a player taken ten wickets in a match and scored a century in each innings, the last occasion being in 1906.

Nottinghamshire finished the summer in fifth place in the

Championship, which was a very fair effort. Stephenson, of course, was the player of the year with 1,018 runs, average 29.08, and 125 wickets, average 18.31. Cooper had the best summer of his career with 101 wickets at 21.57 – the next most effective bowler was Hemmings with 42 wickets at 31 runs each.

Randall headed the batting table, but only by a fraction from Robinson. These two and Johnson also reached 1,000 runs. Broad had a modest return. He played in the three one-day Internationals against West Indies and then in the first two Tests, but was afterwards dropped. Newell was not as happy as he had been in 1987, but Pollard hit a maiden Championship hundred and Kevin Evans acted a very utilitarian member of the side, playing in 13 Championship games. Pick was rarely seen due to injury and injury also cut down Saxelby's games.

Apart from Stephenson, three other players made their debuts. Chris Cairns, a 17-year-old all-rounder and son of the New Zealand Test player, appeared in four matches and was but a raw recruit. David Millns, the fast bowler from Clipstone, had a good action and plenty of fire. He took 19 wickets in 11 games. David Callaghan, the South African, played in a non-Championship game against West Indies and took a wicket with the first ball he bowled. He was a lusty batsman and scored 934 runs, average 54.94, in the second eleven, but due to the restrictions on overseas players he was not destined to play Championship cricket for Notts.

The 150th anniversary of the opening of the Trent Bridge Ground fell in 1988. An appeal was launched to raise money for youth cricket and to rebuild the Bridgford Road Stand. Events were held throughout the year with a special Festival Week in July. The chairman of the appeal was Bryan Ford and the director of the appeal was Bob Holland. The target of £150,000 was reached, in spite of the fact that the Festival Week was ruined by rain – just as had happened in 1938.

The Benson & Hedges Competition was won for the first time in 1989. In their group, Notts beat Minor Counties, Derbyshire and Yorkshire, all three with reasonable margins in hand, but lost to Somerset. In the quarter-finals they met Gloucestershire at Bristol. Broad hit a century against his old county and in a tight finish Gloucestershire failed to make the seven runs required from the last over – Notts were handicapped because Stephenson broke down after delivering 3.4 overs. Kent were met in the semi-finals and with Broad, Pollard and Robinson all batting well were easily beaten. Afford, who took four for 38, gained the Man of The Match Award.

NOTTINGHAMSHIRE *v* YORKSHIRE

Played at Trent Bridge, Nottingham, 14, 15, 16 and 17 September 1988

YORKSHIRE WON BY 127 RUNS

YORKSHIRE	FIRST INNINGS		SECOND INNINGS	
M. D. Moxon	c Broad b Cooper	68	c Newell b Stephenson	40
A. A. Metcalfe	c Johnson b Evans	74	b Stephenson	18
D. Byas	c French b Saxelby	26	b Stephenson	12
P. E. Robinson	c Robinson b Evans	98	c French b Stephenson	80
J. D. Love	lbw b Stephenson	6	b Stephenson	38
†D. L. Bairstow	run out	26	not out	94
*P. Carrick	b Stephenson	0	b Stephenson	37
A. Sidebottom	c Saxelby b Stephenson	41	c Evans b Stephenson	5
P. J. Hartley	c Newell b Stephenson	7	not out	3
P. A. Booth	not out	15		
S. D. Fletcher	c French b Evans	1		
Extras	lb 14, nb 4	18	b 4, lb 7, nb 2	13
Total		380	(7 wkts dec)	340

1st inns: 1-123, 2-165, 3-178, 4-193, 5-282, 6-282, 7-341, 8-345, 9-363
2nd inns: 1-29, 2-54, 3-93, 4-193, 5-198, 6-284, 7-318

BOWLING	O	M	R	W	O	M	R	W
Stephenson	37	7	105	4	34	2	117	7
Cooper	22	5	70	1	13	5	37	0
Saxelby	15	1	69	1	14	2	65	0
Evans	18.1	2	62	3	17	2	75	0
Hemmings	29	8	60	0	10	2	35	0

NOTTINGHAMSHIRE	FIRST INNINGS		SECOND INNINGS	
B. C. Broad	lbw b Sidebottom	35	c Bairstow b Sidebottom	10
*R. T. Robinson	c Moxon b Sidebottom	10	c Love b Hartley	14
M. Newell	b Sidebottom	11	c Bairstow b Hartley	23
P. Johnson	c Bairstow b Sidebottom	59	c Sidebottom b Fletcher	22
D. W. Randall	c and b Carrick	7	c Bairstow b Fletcher	59
F. D. Stephenson	c Carrick b Sidebottom	111	lbw b Fletcher	117
K. P. Evans	b Sidebottom	30	c Bairstow b Fletcher	0
†B. N. French	lbw b Sidebottom	11	c Booth b Hartley	28
E. E. Hemmings	lbw b Hartley	6	not out	3
K. E. Cooper	b Hartley	1	b Fletcher	0
K. Saxelby	not out	5	c Sidebottom b Fletcher	4
Extras	lb 2, w 2, nb 6	10	lb 10, nb 7	17
Total	(85.4 overs)	296		297

1st inns: 1-39, 21-59, 3-81, 4-106, 5-166, 6-264, 7-273, 8-285, 9-286
2nd inns: 1-25, 2-29, 3-79, 4-83, 5-188, 6-206, 7-280, 8-293, 9-293

BOWLING	O	M	R	W	O	M	R	W
Hartley	14.4	3	51	2	16	0	85	3
Fletcher	18	3	59	0	18.5	3	74	6
Sidebottom	26	4	89	7	12	2	43	1
Carrick	14	3	53	1	15	2	76	0
Booth	13	3	42	0	4	2	9	0

Umpires: J. C. Balderstone, K. E. Palmer, S. B. Hassan (Hassan took over from Palmer after first day)

*Captain; †Wicketkeeper

The final was against Essex. Essex batted first and were contained by the Notts bowlers, especially Evans and Cooper. Notts, requiring 244, lost both openers for 17 runs. Robinson and Johnson then came to the rescue and took the total to 149. Three wickets fell quickly. Notts ended needing nine from the last over, bowled by Lever. French and Hemmings were the batsmen. When the last ball was due four runs were still required. Hemmings hit a boundary on the off side and the match was won.

Notts had a much more successful summer in the Sunday League and with nine victories finished fourth – they had been bottom in 1988. This meant that they took part in the Refuge Cup which had been started the previous year. Notts met Lancashire at Old Trafford and won by five wickets; in the final they met Essex for a second time, the venue being Edgbaston. Essex made 160 for five off the 40 overs and unbelievably, Notts reached the final over of their innings with three balls left, six runs wanted and Hemmings again taking strike. Hemmings hit a lofted drive – this time it went into the hands of Waugh and Essex won by five runs.

In the NatWest competition the county did not progress further than the second round, being well beaten by Middlesex.

The County Championship table showed six Notts wins and six losses. Notts' first win came at Headingley on 5 May, when Yorkshire were beaten in two days. The home side made 92, Stephenson seven for 38; Notts replied with 86. Stephenson then took six for 37 and Yorkshire were dismissed for 109. The West Indian thus achieved career-best figures. After these three abysmal totals, Notts needed 116 and Broad and Robinson scored the lot without a wicket falling. The pitch was criticised by the press, but not by the umpires. The scores in this match became of greater interest at Trent Bridge in August. Derbyshire were the visitors. Robinson won the toss and decided to bat. Broad made 57, but the total was only 185. Barnett then played an attacking innings of 80, but no one else scored many and Derbyshire were all out for 165. That finished the first day's play. On the second morning the pitch was fairly lively. Broad clearly showed that he felt it was unfit for first-class cricket and as soon as he was out, having made 11, one of the umpires left the field to telephone Lord's for instructions. After a two-hour delay, it was agreed to continue the match on the pitch which had been used a few days

---

In the last Championship match of the season, Franklyn Stephenson became only the third player in English first-class cricket to take ten wickets and score a century in each innings of a match. His performance enabled him to complete the now very rare 'double' of 1,000 runs and 100 wickets in a season.

before for the Test Match. Michael Holding, the Derbyshire pace bowler, disagreed with the decision and refused to take any more part in the game. Curiously the batsmen fared worse on the Test wicket than on the rejected strip. Notts were all out for 114 and finally Derbyshire collapsed to Hemmings, all out 64. D. B. Carr and T. M. Lamb hurried up from Lord's and inspected the wicket. Notts gained 21 points for the actual game and then had 25 deducted for preparing an 'unsatisfactory wicket'.

At the end of the summer the loss of 25 points meant that Notts finished 11th instead of eighth. Essex also had a 25-point penalty, and but for that would have been Champions.

Of the other four Notts Championship wins the first was at Gloucester, when Cooper took ten wickets and Stephenson eight in an innings victory, and the second at Eastbourne against Sussex when, after three declarations, Notts made 287 for seven and hit a necessary 12 from the last over and two home wins. Somerset were beaten by an innings, Robinson making 128 and Pollard 91 and Essex by 115 runs, when that county batted last and Stephenson took eight for 47 dismissing them for 148. The West Indian achieved another personal best with fifteen wickets in the match.

Robinson, Broad and Randall all averaged above 40 and topped 1,000 runs. Kevin Evans, Pollard and Johnson had good batting figures, but Newell and Martindale were disappointing. In the bowling table Stephenson was a long way in front. He took 92 wickets at 18.77 runs each. Cooper came second and Hemmings third, both taking over fifty wickets at about 27 runs each. Kevin Evans bowled well. Afford also impressed and gained a place on the winter tour with England A to Zimbabwe.

Among the three debutants in 1989 was Mark Saxelby, the younger brother of Kevin. A promising all-rounder he was to appear fairly regularly in 1991 and at 23 in 1991 has plenty of time to mature. Greg Mike, another all-rounder, has put in some good performances with the second eleven, but injury has meant that his appearances at the higher level had been limited. Michael Field-Buss, an off-break bowler, played for Essex in 1987, but joined Notts in 1988. As yet his first eleven appearances have been very infrequent.

There were six Tests against Australia in 1989 and the fifth was staged at Trent Bridge. Hemmings was the sole Notts representative in an England side completely outplayed. Marsh and Taylor, the Australian openers, batted right through the first day to reach 301 for no wicket. Marsh was finally dismissed for 138, but Taylor went on to 219. The Australian total was 602 for six declared; England were all out for 255 and 167, Alderman returning the best bowling figures. England's defeat by an innings and 180 runs was the largest they had ever suffered at home. A total of 33,139 spectators attended over the four days.

Financially Nottinghamshire prospered in 1989, having a surplus of £43,071, against a loss of £803 in 1988.

In the winter of 1989–90, three of the Notts Test players, Robinson, Broad and French, agreed to tour South Africa with the England side under Gatting. All the English players who took part in this tour were banned from England Test cricket for five years. When one 'Test' and four one-day Internationals had been played the tour was abandoned.

The 1990 season began well for Notts. Three early County Championship victories – against Leicestershire, when Pick took ten wickets and Randall made 120, against Warwickshire, with a century from Broad and good bowling by everyone, and against Northants, when Martindale and Johnson completed hundreds to enable a target of 344 to be obtained – put the County at the top of the Championship. Three wins in the Benson & Hedges Cup

Former Notts players with the current captain at a Trent Bridge re-union in 1990. They are, left to right, top row: M. J. Harris, J. M. Parkin, C. D. Fraser-Darling, C. J. Cook, G. Frost, J. S. Howarth, J. B. Bolus, F. W. Shipston. Sixth row: M. J. Smedley, A. H. Latchman, A. Wheelhouse, K. J. Poole, A. J. Underwood, H. T. Tunnicliffe, P. A. Wilkinson. Fifth row: C. C. Curzon, A. Richardson, J. D. Clay, S. R. Beilby, A. K. Armitage, K. Smales, unknown. Fourth row: A. R. Bilbie, P. J. Plummer, M. N. S. Taylor, H. I. Moore, G. L. Willatt, M. W. Haynes, A. A. Johnson. Third row: J. A. Walters, P. A. Taylor, C. R. W. Grant, E. A. Meads, M. J. Hall, A. Jepson, H. M. Winfield. Second row: K. Gillhouley, W. E. Rhodes, M. K. Bore, E. J. Martin. C. V. Lindo, W. Taylor, N. B. Whittingham, F. W. Stocks. Front row: T. W. Birtle, R. D. F. Bland, J. Knowles, B. D. Wells, D. L. Murray, R. C. Vowles, R. T. Robinson, J. Kelly. (NCCC)

meant that the quarter-finals had been reached and in the quarter-finals, Essex were thoroughly upset. The bowlers restricted Essex to 216 for eight. Fifties by Robinson and Johnson meant victory by six wickets with overs in hand.

From the beginning of June it was largely downhill. Just one more Championship game ended in success – against Yorkshire at Scarborough in a game with two forfeited innings – and Notts had to settle for 13th place in the final table. In the Benson & Hedges semi-final at Trent Bridge, Notts met Worcestershire. Notts batted first and dawdled; Stephenson arrived and hit a speedy 98, but the total was 230 for six from 55 overs. Worcestershire found no problem in topping this and lost only one wicket in the process. Weston ended with 99 not out. The County went out in the second round of the NatWest Trophy. They were unlucky in that both Broad and Johnson were forced to retire hurt (though both did resume later) and Northants won by 24 runs.

The bright spot through the dismal days came in the Sunday League. Ten matches were won and though the title was never really within their grasp, Notts finished in fourth place and qualified for the Refuge Cup. The semi-final of this Cup was played at Derby on 5 September. The home side made 255 for four. Notts struggled; Robinson batted very well reaching 96 off 90 balls but his only support came from Kevin Evans and Derbyshire won by 22 runs.

The first-class bowling table explains Notts' problems. Bowlers in general had a rough time, whilst batsmen enjoyed hard wickets and a gloriously hot summer, but Pick, the best Notts bowler, took 48 Championship wickets at 31 runs each and Stephenson, in second place, took 53 at 38 runs apiece. No Notts bowlers figured in the top 30 in the overall averages. Neither was a Notts batsman in the top 30 in the overall batting table. Broad hit 2,226 runs at an average of 54.29 – Gooch averaged 101, Hick 90 and Moody 89. Robinson, Johnson and Randall could all point to reasonable figures but nothing outstanding when the general run glut is considered. Kevin Evans, who played in 12 Championship games, continued his all-round improvement. Newell and Martindale both played in about half the matches and had days of success. Pollard, so promising in 1989, was dropped and temporarily lost his way.

The first Test of the season, against the New Zealanders, was staged at Trent Bridge. On the day before the match the new William Clarke Stand, together with the Rushcliffe Suite which housed the new Press Box, was opened officially by Richard Hadlee, who later in the same month received a knighthood. The new stand, which had been masterminded by Maurice Youdell, the club's Vice-chairman, replaced the 1899 Bridgford Road stand and considerably increased the seating capacity. The new Press Box replaced the cramped old box which was above the Secretary's Office. The work could not have been completed without the generous support of the Rushcliffe Borough Council.

Hemmings was Notts sole representative in the England side whilst Hadlee, on his final tour of England, played for New Zealand. The match was ruined by the weather, only 23 minutes' play taking place on the second day. Snedden, the New Zealand batsman, actually batted for a time on the first, second and third days without scoring a single run! Later in the summer Trent Bridge staged a one-day International against India. This brought a capacity crowd and some very exciting batting, especially from the Indian captain Azharuddin, who made 63 not out and won the game for his side. Hemmings was the only England bowler to take more than one wicket.

At the end of the season, Ken Taylor announced his retirement as the cricket manager. He had completed 13 years in the post, years which had brought great success to the County side. Unlike batsmen and bowlers, managers don't have 'averages' with which to measure their worth, but whatever yardstick one employs, Ken Taylor was a great success in a post situated in a minefield. The fact that he survived is proof that not one of the mines exploded, and his judgement in the mix of players on the staff was admired even by those who were opposed to 'managers' in county cricket. As a result of Taylor's retirement – he in fact is retained in a part-time advisory capacity – John Birch was appointed team manager for 1991 and John Cope, whilst continuing his role as cricket development officer, became in addition cricket office manager, with Miss Jo Smith as cricket administrator – Miss Smith had previously been Ken Taylor's secretary.

In the December of 1990, Jack Baddiley, the former chairman and second eleven captain, who had been President since 1985, died. At the Annual General Meeting in February 1991, Reg Simpson, the longest serving member of the Committee and former Test cricketer, was elected as the County Club's new President and handed over the reins of chairman of the cricket sub-committee to Alan Wheelhouse.

The outstanding feature in the 1991 season was the success in the Sunday League. A major decision which had some bearing on this was the promotion of Randall to open the innings with Broad, though Randall remained a middle-order batsman in Championship matches. Randall never failed to reach double figures in the 16 Sunday League matches and averaged 44 for the Sunday season, though his highest was only 83. Broad certainly flourished with Randall as his partner and the nine-wicket victory in the opening match was a foretaste of things to come – Broad hit 100 not out, Randall 49 and the 190 runs required to beat Lancashire came off 37.5 overs. Warwickshire were outgunned in the second Sunday game, losing by 82 runs, Stephenson and Hemmings being the best bowlers. The third match saw Broad score 108 and victory over Glamorgan by four wickets. Essex came to Trent Bridge for the fourth game. Essex seemed likely to obtain the 195 needed for victory, but Stephenson took the final three wickets in six balls, bringing Notts their fourth consecutive win. Randall made an unbeaten 83 as Notts strolled to a five-wicket win at Grace Road. Somerset's batsmen could not quite manage a target of 181 and Notts won this home game by four runs. Rain affected the Sunday match at Gloucester, Notts winning on a faster run rate.

The seven successive wins gave the County a clear six-point lead at the top of the table and thus they were able to afford defeat in the eighth match; when Gatting controlled the game. Randall and Broad added 154 for the first wicket when Notts beat Surrey at The Oval and Randall hit 83 in the victory over Hampshire at Trent Bridge, though success only came off the last ball, Evans being the batsman who struck the winning run.

Defeat in the 11th match meant that Lancashire overtook Notts at the top of the table. The next two matches produced one win and one loss – the same fate was suffered by Lancashire, so two points still separated the teams on 11 August, when Kent came to Trent Bridge. At one point Notts seemed in danger of losing – 66 were required off the last 10 overs, but excellent batting by Pollard brought victory. The penultimate match, against Yorkshire at Scarborough saw another fine Pollard innings accompanying a Notts win: Lancashire lost on the same day and Notts therefore moved two points clear.

The final game was against Derbyshire at Trent Bridge and a record Sunday League crowd of about 7,500 turned out to watch a commanding partnership by, appropriately, Broad and Randall. They put on 134 for the first wicket, with Notts needing only 177. Victory was by nine wickets and the title was secured. The match ended with celebrations, a few brief speeches and the official presentation of the trophy.

Notts therefore competed in the Refuge Knock-Out Cup, but lost in the semi-final to Worcestershire. There was little success in the Benson & Hedges Competition. Notts won two matches, but failed to qualify for the knock-out section. In the NatWest, an easy win over Lincolnshire was followed by an exciting finish to the game against Gloucestershire at Bristol: Hemmings scored the winning run off the final ball in the 60th over. Randall scored 95 in the quarter-final match against Hampshire at Southampton, but Chris Smith made an undefeated 105 to bring his side victory.

In the County Championship a spell of success in July when four matches out of five ended in victory pushed the County into third place in the table, 47 points behind Warwickshire, but with a match in hand. This run of victories began against Glamorgan at Cardiff. Notts were set 274 off 73 overs and a chanceless hundred by Randall combining with 77 from Johnson meant the margin of the win was eight wickets. Lancashire were then beaten by an innings at Trent Bridge, Hemmings taking nine wickets and 145 coming from Pollard, plus another hundred by Randall. Northants were also defeated by an innings due to the bowling of Pick and Stephenson. Stephenson took ten wickets in the match and Pick eight. At Lord's Middlesex set Notts 282 off 66 overs. Johnson took the opportunity to hit 105 off 108 balls and the target was reached with four wickets in hand.

Full bonus points in the drawn game with Sussex at the Saffrons put Notts level with Surrey in second place. Essex came to Trent Bridge in the second week of August. Johnson played his

Notts players in Edwardian costume at Trent Bridge in 1990. From left to right, standing: P. R. Pollard, F. D. Stephenson, D. W. Randall, K. E. Cooper, K. P. Evans, J. A. Afford, S. Brogan, M. Saxelby, D. J. R. Martindale, M. Newell, K. A. Taylor (manager), P. Wynne-Thomas (librarian and author). Seated: C. W. Scott, R. J. Evans, B. N. French, R. T. Robinson (captain), G. W. Mike, E. E. Hemmings, J. D. Birch. On ground: K. Saxelby, C. D. French, R. A. Pick. (NCCC)

best innings of the summer, his 100 coming off 98 balls and with Evans taking five wickets, Notts gained a first-innings lead. Foster, the England fast bowler, then shook Notts by dismissing the first five batsmen cheaply in the second innings and the score fell to 73 for five. Recovery proved impossible and Essex won by three wickets. Notts were now 51 points behind Warwickshire but had two games in hand. Failure to reach the target set by Somerset in the next match – 12 runs were required from the final over – meant that hopes of the title were fading. This draw was followed directly by defeat in a three-declaration game against Derbyshire, when Azharuddin made 129 not out and 72, whilst Randall hit 76 and 143 not out. Hopes of the Championship were now very faint, but victory over Lancashire after being behind by 114 on first innings kept a glimmer of light aglow. The next two matches resulted in one loss – against Middlesex – and one draw – against Derbyshire – and with Essex now roaring ahead of Warwickshire, the best Notts could hope for was fourth place. This they achieved in the last match by beating Worcestershire with an innings to spare. Robinson made 180 and Stephenson, who had effectively announced his departure from Trent Bridge during the game, took seven wickets.

The playing results of the first eleven were therefore most satisfactory and the second eleven added to the Club's laurels by winning the Bain Clarkson Trophy, beating Kent in the final match at The Oval.

The batting was very strong. Randall, who hit 1,567 runs, average 62.68, Robinson and Broad all featured in the top 20 in the first-class table. Johnson and Pollard also hit over 1,000 runs. Stephenson was the leading bowler with 78 wickets, average 25.76, but no one else averaged below 30. Pick and Afford took over 50 wickets each and Evans also bowled well and might have achieved the target if he had not missed several matches due to injury.

Mark Saxelby gained a regular place in the Sunday side and proved an asset, but appeared in only seven first-class games. French was very consistent behind the wicket and therefore Scott was rarely seen – at the end of the season he joined Durham. Martindale and Newell spent virtually the whole summer with the second eleven and the success of that side was largely due to their efforts.

Mark Crawley made his debut in the first game of the summer, against Oxford University, and hit a century. An attractive batsman and accurate medium-pace bowler, he played in about half the County matches, an injury forcing him to rest for some weeks. Aged 23, he had had a brilliant career as a schoolboy at Manchester Grammar School and going up to Oxford had gained a blue and captained the university. Born in Newton le Willows, he had played one first-class match for his native county and had joined Notts at the start of 1991. The only other debutant was Pascal Broadley, a young seam bowler from Edwinstowe. He had played in the penultimate game at Derby.

The third Test of 1991 was staged at Trent Bridge in July. The West Indies won by nine wickets and thus maintained their unbeaten Test record at Nottingham. Ambrose, taking eight wickets, won the Man of the Match award. There were near-capacity crowds on the first two days, but the weather interfered with both Saturday and Monday's cricket and the match finished at lunch on Tuesday.

Tim Robinson, the Club captain in the 1991 season. He made his debut in 1978, and by the end of 1991 had made over 15,000 first-class runs for the County. (Patrick Eagar)

Recorded cricket in Nottinghamshire has now (1992) spanned 221 years and it is 156 years since the playing of the first bona fide inter-county game involving Nottingham. That first historic fixture against Sussex was arranged almost single-handed by William Clarke, who seems to have been the self-appointed manager of the County side. The team had no ground of its own but played on the council owned Forest Racecourse, the players made what money they could from side bets, sometimes augmented by gifts from admirers. Travel was then by stage coach and any fixture more than 20 miles from Nottingham was a major undertaking. The railways were quickly to change all that, but the railway age has come and gone. It is perhaps appropriate to close this history with a brief outline of the County Club as it was in 1991.

The County Club has about 4,700 members who elect a Committee of twelve to run the Club's business. The 12 committee members of 1991 were R. T. Simpson (who is also President of the Club), C. W. Gillott (Chairman), M. A. Youdell (Vice-chairman) and A. Bocking, J. R. Cope, A. B. Ford, S. E. Foster, P. B. Pailing, C. F. Ward, A. Wheelhouse, P. G. Wright and P. Wynne-Thomas.

Six sub-committees operate to deal with the various facets of the club: Cricket (Chairman A. Wheelhouse), Finance (Chairman C. F. Ward), Marketing (Chairman S. E. Foster), House and Test (Chairman M. A. Youdell), Projects (Chairman A. Bocking) and Catering (Chairman J. R. Cope).

The chief full-time official of the Club, whose title is Secretary-General Manager is Brian Robson. His personal assistant is Lynda Miles. The Cricket Office is run by John Cope, with Jo Smith as cricket administrator, and Stewart Burrows, David Terrill and Vicky Chatterton. The Marketing Office consists of Basher Hassan, Colin Slater, John Ellison and Pauline Smith. Ces Garrigan, assisted by Chris Rimmer, looks after the Club's accounts. The membership secretary is Lynn Steel, assisted by Rachel Pullan, and the Club shop, under the management of Mike Sheriston, who also runs the Squash Club, is looked after by Annette Miles and Katharine Hough.

Looking after the playing area is the chief groundsman, Ron Allsop, his assistant Frank Dalling, and two under-groundsmen, Richard Johnson and Richard Marshall. The maintenance staff is Les Kirk and Alan Crofts.

The playing staff in 1991, under the management of John Birch, consisted of R. T. Robinson (captain), P. Johnson (vice-captain) and, with dates of debut, D. W. Randall (1972), K. E.

Cooper (1976), B. N. French (1976), K. Saxelby (1978), E. E. Hemmings (1979), C. W. Scott (1981), R. A. Pick (1983), J. A. Afford (1984), K. P. Evans (1984), M. Newell (1984), B. C. Broad (1984), D. J. R. Martindale (1985), P. R. Pollard (1987), F. D. Stephenson (1988), M. Saxelby (1989), G. W. Mike (1989), M. G. Field-Buss (1989), M. A. Crawley (1991) and the following who have yet to make their first eleven debuts, G. F. Archer, R. T. Bates, S. M. Brogan, W. A. Dessaur.

Ian Seagrave is the ground superintendent, with Kevin Healy as his assistant while Harry Dalling, the former superintendent, continues to assist the Club on a part-time basis. Fred Buxton is the indispensible dressing room attendant. Sheila Ball acts as the Club's physiotherapist. John Lawson and Terry Bowles edit the Club's newspaper and the Boundary Restaurant is run jointly with Lindley Catering Investments Ltd, the manager being Bernice Clark with Joan Pykett as her assistant. The 1991 scorers are Len Beaumont, Gordon Stringfellow and Mike Baylis. Peter Wynne-Thomas is the club's archivist and librarian. This list comprises 74 names and, of course, does not include the stewards who are engaged on a match-by-match basis and some other part-time staff who operate the bars and restaurant on match days. The time when William Clarke ran county cricket single-handed is no more!

STATISTICAL SECTION

BIOGRAPHICAL DETAILS
OF NOTTINGHAMSHIRE PLAYERS

This list contains every cricketer to represent the county in a first-class match since 1835; the list conforms to the Guides published by the Association of Cricket Statisticians.

NAME AND EXTENT OF CAREER	BIRTHPLACE	DATE OF BIRTH	DATE OF DEATH
John Andrew Afford *1984–1991*	Crowland, Lincs	12. 5.1964	
Mark Edward Allbrook *1976–1980*	Frimley, Surrey	15.11.1954	
Ernest George Allen *1903*	Holme, Worksop	24. 6.1880	28. 5.1943
Edwin Boaler Alletson *1906–1914*	Welbeck, Woodhouse	6. 3.1884	5. 7.1963
Alfred Feargus O'Connor Anthony *1875–1876*	Arnold	22. 5.1841	10. 6.1900
George Anthony *1900–1905*	Arnold	25. 6.1875	13. 5.1907
Henry Anthony *1898–1902*	Old Basford	16. 5.1873	
Alan Kenneth Armitage *1950–1951*	Nottingham	25. 1.1930	
Thomas Armstrong *1892–1896*	Keyworth	16. 3.1872	5. 7.1938
Arthur Thomas Ashwell *1876*	Nottingham	8. 2.1853	30. 9.1925
John Atkinson *1899–1901*	Nether Green	7. 6.1878	1951
Thomas Atkinson *1957–1960*	Millom, Cumberld	27. 9.1930	2. 9.1990
Henry Clinton Attenburrow *1847*	Nottingham	1807	25. 9.1881
Thomas Attewell *1891–1894*	Keyworth	7.11.1869	6. 7.1937
Walter Attewell *1891*	Keyworth	29. 1.1865	3. 2.1919
William Attewell *1881–1900*	Keyworth	12. 6.1861	11. 6.1927
Robert Bagguley *1891–1896*	Ruddington	10. 7.1873	8.10.1946
David William Baker *1964–1965*	Hull	26. 7.1935	
George Banner *1885*	Sutton in Ashfield	21. 1.1864	20. 3.1890
Thomas David Barber *1960*	Carlton in Lindrick	18.11.1937	
William Douglas Barber *1904*	Lamb Close, Eastwood	17.10.1881	26. 4.1971
Thomas Barker *1835–1845*	Carlton	15.11.1798	2. 3.1877
James William Barnes *1908–1910*	Sutton in Ashfield	14. 8.1886	9. 9.1963
Thomas Barnes *1872*	Sutton in Ashfield	11. 5.1849	22. 9.1873
William Barnes *1875–1894*	Sutton in Ashfield	27. 5.1852	24. 3.1899
John Davison Barnsdale *1905*	Nottingham	24. 5.1878	5. 8.1960
Fred Barratt *1914–1931*	Annesley	12. 4.1894	29. 1.1947
Chappell Batchelor *1845–1858*	Southwell	1822	11. 1.1884
Augustus Bateman *1862*	West Leake	3. 8.1839	18.12.1922
Edward Louis Bateman *1855*	Mickleover, Derbys	15. 9.1834	25. 1.1909

Arthur John Bates *1878*	New Radford	18. 6.1852	13. 2.1925
Austin Godfrey Baxter *1952–1953*	West Bridgford	21. 9.1931	
George Bean *1885*	Sutton in Ashfield	7. 3.1864	16. 3.1923
John Grosvenor Beevor *1868–1870*	Barnby Moor	1. 1.1845	5. 5.1903
Henry Bembridge *1878*	Bulwell	27. 6.1852	
Arthur Robert Bennett *1893–1896*	Mapperley	16.11.1868	7. 5.1899
Gordon Beves *1888–1891*	Brighton, Sussex	15. 3.1862	22. 3.1927
John Bickley *1847–1860*	Keyworth	16. 1.1819	15.11.1866
Samuel Biddulph *1862–1875*	Hyson Green	23.12.1840	7. 3.1876
Stephen Richard Bielby *1967–1971*	Windsor, Berks	9. 3.1947	
Thomas Bignall *1863–1878*	Chilwell	8. 1.1842	19. 9.1898
Anthony Robin Bilbie *1960–1963*	Nottingham	29. 4.1942	
John Dennis Birch *1973–1988*	Aspley, Nottingham	18. 6.1955	
Thomas William Birtle *1952*	Stockton-on-Tees	28. 3.1926	
John Fillingham Bishop *1923–1925*	Radcliffe on Trent	21.11.1891	14.12.1963
Benjamin Fielding Blackburn *1879*	Meadows, Nottingham	10. 9.1855	6. 5.1907
Edward Arthur Blagg *1948*	Shireoaks	9. 2.1918	28.10.1976
Robert Dennis Fraser Bland *1929–1934*	West Bridgford	16. 5.1911	
John Brian Bolus *1963–1972*	Whitkirk, Yorks	31. 1.1934	
John David Bond *1974*	Kearsley, Lancs	6. 5.1932	
Michael Kenneth Bore *1979–1988*	Hull, Yorks	2. 6.1947	
Daniel Bottom *1899*	Whitwell, Derbys	2.10.1864	16. 2.1937
Wallace Bower *1914*	Eastwood	2. 1.1895	7.1971
James Bradley *1937–1939*	Pleasley Hill	3.10.1913	
Charles Brampton *1854–1867*	Hyson Green	5. 2.1828	12. 6.1895
George Trevor Branston *1903–1913*	Newark	3. 9.1884	12. 8.1969
Joseph (Banner) Briggs *1888*	Sutton in Ashfield	4. 6.1860	1.12.1902
Brian Christopher Broad *1984–1991*	Knowle, Bristol	29. 9.1957	
Vaughan John Pascal Broadley *1991*	Sutton in Ashfield	4. 4.1972	
Alfred James Brooks *1877*	Sutton in Ashfield	24. 3.1848	20.11.1911
Charles Brown *1842–1861*	Nottingham	22. 1.1815	28. 9.1875
John Brown *1888*	Bingham	1862	
Samuel Brown *1896–1897*	Kimberley	26. 2.1857	5. 9.1938
Thomas Brown *1881*	Bingham	14. 6.1848	2. 7.1919
Tom George Buckland *1888*	Sutton in Ashfield	20.11.1860	18. 7.1915
Arthur Dixon Burrows *1887*	Awsworth	2. 7.1865	6. 2.1890
William Bury *1861–1862*	Radcliffe on Trent	14.10.1839	21. 5.1927

313

Name	Place	Born	Died
Frederick Butler *1881–1890*	Radcliffe on Trent	29.12.1857	26. 2.1923
George Butler 1841–1852	Mansfield	20. 2.1810	23. 4.1887
Harold James Butler *1933–1954*	Clifton	12. 3.1913	17. 7.1991
John Butler *1889*	Clifton	29. 8.1863	1945
Robert Butler *1870–1877*	Radcliffe on Trent	8. 3.1852	18.12.1916
John Buttery *1843–1845*	Nottingham	21.12.1814	5.12.1873
Joseph Herbert Buxton *1937*	Kirkby in Ashfield	20.11.1912	10. 2.1992
Christopher Lance Cairns *1988–1989*	Picton, NZ	13. 6.1970	
David James Callaghan *1988*	Queenstown, S. Africa	1. 2.1965	
John Carlin *1887–1901*	New Eastwood	3.11.1861	28.11.1944
Arthur William Carr *1910–1934*	Mickleham, Surrey	21.5.1893	7. 2.1963
Arthur Gervase Carter *1895*	Ruddington	1868	19. 7.1933
Vincent Henry Cartwright *1901–1904*	Nottingham	10. 9.1882	25.11.1965
Stafford William Thomas Castledine *1933–1934*	Bingham	10. 4.1912	6.1988
George Henry Chambers *1896–1899*	Meadows, Nottingham	6.10.1875	
George Henry Chambers *1903–1905*	Kimberley	24. 3.1884	13. 9.1947
Meshach Chambers *1894*	Awsworth	23.12.1867	23. 6.1920
Frederick John Champion de Crespigny *1848*	Camberwell, Surrey	12.12.1822	25. 6.1887
John Chapman *1842–1848*	Nottingham	28.11.1814	14. 4.1896
Thomas Broughton Charlton *1840*	Chilwell	15. 8.1815	20. 1.1886
James Chatterton *1856–1865*	Newark	1. 4.1836	13. 2.1891
Alfred Clarke *1851–1863*	Nottingham	16. 2.1831	23.10.1878
William Clarke *1835–1855*	Nottingham	24.12.1798	25. 8.1856
William (Benjamin) Clarke *1874–1876*	Old Basford	5.11.1846	18. 8.1902
William Clarke *1876–1877*	Kirkby in Ashfield	17. 3.1849	29. 5.1935
John Desmond Clay *1948–1961*	West Bridgford	25.10.1924	
Alan Barnard Cleveley *1955*	Chaddesden, Dbys	5. 1.1932	
Charles Clifton *1873–1876*	Ruddington	13. 1.1846	
Cecil Cooper Clifton *1908–1910*	Eastwood	8.12.1885	12. 3.1930
Thomas Hugh Collins *1921*	Nottingham	4. 3.1895	19. 5.1964
Charles John Cook *1974–1975*	Retford	5. 6.1946	
Kevin Edwin Cooper *1976–1991*	Sutton in Ashfield	27.12.1957	
David Edward Coote *1977*	Winkburn	8. 4.1955	
Sydney Herbert Copley *1930*	Hucknall Torkard	1.11.1905	1. 4.1986
Andrew John Corran *1960–1965*	Eaton, Norwich	25.11.1936	
John Cotton *1958–1964*	Newstead	7.11.1940	
Henry Ramsay Cox *1930–1954*	Radcliffe on Trent	19. 5.1911	
Alexander Basil Crawford *1912*	Coleshill, Warw	24. 5.1891	10. 5.1916

Name	Place	Born	Died
Mark Andrew Crawley *1991*	Newton le Willows	16.12.1967	
Charles Creswell *1840–1843*	Radford	10. 3.1813	
Henry Crook *1837*	Bingham	1802	17. 8.1886
Arthur William Cursham *1876–1878*	Nottingham	14. 3.1853	24.12.1884
Henry Alfred Cursham *1880–1904*	Wilford	27.11.1859	6. 8.1941
Christopher Colin Curzon *1978–1980*	Lenton	22.12.1958	
John Timothy Curzon *1978*	Lenton	4. 6.1954	
Charles Frederick Daft *1862–1864*	Nottingham	8. 6.1830	9. 3.1915
Harry Butler Daft *1885–1899*	Radcliffe on Trent	5. 4.1866	12. 1.1945
Richard Daft *1858–1891*	Nottingham	2.11.1835	18. 7.1900
Richard Parr Daft *1886*	Radcliffe on Trent	25.10.1863	27. 3.1934
Samuel Dakin *1845*	Sileby, Leics	12. 4.1808	27.12.1876
Thomas Davis *1854–1865*	Nottingham	27.11.1827	29. 5.1898
Ian Joseph Davison *1959–1966*	Hemel Hempstead	4.10.1937	
John Day *1835*	Nottingham	5. 3.1812	
John William Day *1903–1907*	Sutton on Trent	15. 4.1881	9.11.1949
Charles Edward Dench *1897–1902*	East Stoke	6. 9.1873	28. 6.1958
Hermon Walter Dexter *1902–1903*	Nottingham	3. 5.1877	31. 1.1961
Roy Evatt Dexter *1975–1981*	Nottingham	13. 4.1955	
Alfred John Day Diver *1858*	Cambridge	6. 7.1824	25. 3.1876
John Augur Dixon *1882–1905*	Grantham, Lincs	27. 5.1861	8. 6.1931
Bruce Dooland *1953–1957*	Cowandilla, Adelaide, S. Austr	1.11.1923	8. 9.1980
Dilip Rasiklal Doshi *1973–1978*	Rajkot, India	22.12.1947	
John Joseph Drury *1899–1902*	Kimberley	28. 5.1874	16.10.1919
Richard Berthell Earle *1861*	Driffield, Yorks	4.10.1827	2. 4.1884
Gordon Edwards *1973*	Glapthorn, Northants	17. 9.1947	
William Elliott *1871*	Bulwell	15.11.1842	
William Ellis *1948*	Blyth	16. 7.1868	7.10.1948
Henry Richard Nevile Ellison *1897*	Worksop	1. 6.1817	12. 7.1898
Michael Joseph Ellison *1852*	Meadows, Nottingham	6. 8.1857	23. 4.1901
Herbert William Emmitt *1888*	Hampstead	12. 9.1849	19. 9.1923
Henry Enfield *1869–1872*	Calverton	10. 9.1963	
Kevin Paul Evans *1984–1991*	Calverton	1.10.1965	
Russell John Evans *1987–1990*	Nottingham	16. 3.1924	
Bryan Henry Farr *1949–1951*	Sutton in Ashfield	28. 3.1835	22. 9.1916
Frank Henry Farrands *1871*	Newark	17.11.1960	
Mark Andrew Fell *1982–1983*	Beeston Fields	28. 3.1881	3. 2.1942
John Pulteney Fellows *1904–1905*	Basford	31. 8.1837	1. 4.1912
Alfred Fewkes *1864*	Mtarfa, Malta	23. 9.1964	
Michael Gwyn Field-Buss *1989–1991*	Nottingham	21. 1.1900	21. 9.1957
John D'Ewes Evelyn Firth *1919*	Nottingham	1818	16. 4.1852
Henry Flear *1843*			

Benjamin Flint *1919–1920*	Underwood	12. 1.1893	20. 7.1959
William Arthur Flint *1919–1929*	Underwood	21. 3.1890	5. 2.1955
Thomas Flowers *1894*	Daybrook	25.10.1868	26. 3.1939
Wilfred Flowers *1877–1896*	Calverton	7.12.1856	1.11.1926
George Savile Foljambe *1879–1881*	Osberton	10.10.1856	13. 9.1920
Carlton Forbes *1959–1973*	Cross Roads, Kingston, Jamaica	9. 8.1936	
Peter Ralph Forman *1959–1962*	West Bridgford	9. 3.1934	
William Foster *1889*	Beeston	8. 6.1859	1.11.1944
Frederick Isaac Fox *1890*	Nottingham	7.11.1863	21. 8.1935
John Foxcroft *1837–1840*	Nottingham	16.10.1806	26. 1.1853
Callum David Fraser-Darling *1984–1988*	Sheffield	30. 9.1963	
Bruce Nicholas French *1976–1991*	Warsop	13. 8.1959	
Graham Frost *1967–1973*	Old Basford	15. 1.1947	
George Gibson Galloway *1837*	Nottingham	1803	29. 8.1867
William Garrat *1835–1845*	Shrewsbury	21. 4.1805	
George Ogg Gauld *1913–1919*	Rubislaw, Aberdeen	21. 6.1873	16. 6.1950
John Gibson *1837–1842*	Nottingham	13. 3.1821	25. 9.1875
Robert Gibson *1855–1858*	Mansfield	7. 3.1816	22.11.1887
John Gilbert *1843–1845*	Chilwell	17.10.1919	
Ronald James Giles *1937–1959*	Underwood	5. 8.1940	
Alan Gill *1960–1965*	Crosland Moor, Huddersfield	8. 8.1934	
Keith Gillhouley *1963–1966*			
Bartholomew Good *1835–1843*	Market Rasen, Lincs	20. 1.1812	12. 3.1848
William Bennett Goodacre *1898–1903*	Nottingham	26. 2.1873	29. 6.1948
Harry Hornby Goodall *1902–1905*	Nottingham	17. 1.1877	20. 2.1961
Gamini Goonesena *1952–1964*	Colombo, Ceylon	16. 2.1931	
Christopher Robert Wellesley Grant *1968*	Lincoln	19.12.1935	
Benjamin Gregory – see B. B. Simpson			
John Thomas Griffiths *1891*	Long Eaton, Derbys	27. 1.1863	
George Jasper Groves *1899–1900*	Nottingham	19.10.1868	18. 2.1941
James Grundy *1851–1867*	New Radford	5. 3.1824	24.11.1873
George Gunn *1902–1932*	Hucknall Torkard	13. 6.1879	29.6.1958
George Vernon Gunn *1928–1950*	West Bridgford	21. 7.1905	15.10.1957
John Richmond Gunn *1896–1925*	Hucknall Torkard	19. 7.1876	21. 8.1963
William Gunn *1880–1904*	Nottingham	4.12.1858	29. 1.1921
Frank (Herbert) Guttridge *1889–1900*	Nottingham	12. 4.1866	13. 6.1918
Joseph Guy *1837–1854*	Nottingham	30. 7.1813	15. 4.1873
Peter John Hacker *1974–1981*	Lenton Abbey	16. 7.1952	
Richard John Hadlee *1978–1987*	St Alban's, Christ-church, NZ	3. 7.1951	
David John Halfyard *1968–1970*	Winchmore Hill	3. 4.1931	

Name	Years	Place	Birth	Death
John Bernard Hall	1935–1946	Worksop	17. 6.1903	27. 5.1979
Michael John Hall	1958–1959	Worksop	29. 5.1935	
Albert William Hallam	1901–1910	East Leake	12.11.1869	24. 7.1940
Alick Handford	1894–1898	Wilford	3. 5.1869	15.10.1935
Joseph Hardstaff sen.	1902–1924	Kirkby in Ashfield	9.11.1882	2. 4.1947
Joseph Hardstaff jun.	1930–1955	Nuncargate	3. 7.1911	1. 1.1990
Richard (Green) Hardstaff	1887–1899	Selston	12. 1.1863	18. 4.1932
Silas Hardy	1893–1895	Ilkeston, Derbys	30. 4.1867	27. 6.1905
William Henry Hare	1971–1977	Newark	29.11.1952	
Charles Bowmar Harris	1928–1951	Underwood	6.12.1907	8. 8.1954
Michael John Harris	1969–1982	St Just in Roseland, Corn	25. 5.1944	
William Harris	1886	Kimberley	17. 6.1864	18. 6.1949
Christopher Harrison	1878	Brandesburton, Yks	24. 3.1847	23. 2.1932
Isaac Marshall Harrison	1901	Calverton	8. 6.1880	25. 2.1909
Percy Harrison	1899	Mansfield Woodhouse	15.10.1878	11. 4.1935
Edward Samuel Evans Hartopp	1843	Thurnby, Leics	7. 9.1820	5.10.1894
Peter Fairfield Harvey	1947–1958	Linby	15. 1.1923	
Basharat Hassan	1966–1985	Nairobi, Kenya	24. 3.1944	
John Hatfield	1854	Southwell	2. 3.1831	1880
Frank Hawley	1897	Nottingham	19. 7.1877	23. 8.1913
Michael William Haynes	1959–1961	Sherwood	19. 5.1936	
James Gordon Rotherham Hayward	1951	Bridlington, Yks	31.12.1926	
George Frank Henry Heane	1927–1951	Worksop	2. 1.1904	24.10.1969
Thomas Heath	1835–1847	Sutton in Ashfield	10.12.1806	16.10.1872
Ralph Eustace Hemingway	1903–1905	Sutton, Cheshire	15.12.1877	15.10.1915
Edward Ernest Hemmings	1979–1991	Leamington, Warw	20. 2.1949	
Michael Hendrick	1982–1984	Darley Dale, Dbys	22.10.1948	
William Walker Henson	1897–1898	Lenton	7.12.1872	7. 9.1922
Mervyn Robert Howard Molyneux Herbert	1901–1902	Highclere Castle, Hants	27.11.1882	26. 5.1929
William Goodall Heymann	1905	West Bridgford	26.10.1885	27.11.1969
Maurice Hill	1953–1965	Scunthorpe, Lincs	14. 9.1935	
Norman William Hill	1953–1968	Holbeck	22. 8.1935	
John Hilton	1865	Mansfield	1838	8. 5.1910
Alfred Ernest Hind	1901	Preston, Lancs	7. 4.1878	21. 3.1947
Benjamin James Hind	1911	Nottingham	22.12.1882	1974
Samuel Hind	1877–1878	Calverton	14.12.1850	28. 3.1923
Harold Augustus Hodges	1911–1912	Mansfield Woodhouse	22. 1.1886	24. 3.1918
John Seymour Hodgkins	1938–1951	West Bridgford	2. 1.1916	16. 8.1988

317

John Hogg *1858–1861*	Woodborough	14. 2.1818	30.10.1885
William Holmes *1919*	Eastwood	29.10.1885	6.12.1951
James Horsley *1913*	Melbourne, Derbys	4. 1.1890	13. 2.1976
Norman Horsley *1947*	Leicester	20. 8.1922	
William Horsley *1862*	Southwell	6. 6.1835	
Richard Housley *1870*	Mansfield Woodhouse	8. 5.1849	23. 4.1881
John Stirling Howarth *1966–1967*	Stockport, Ches	26. 3.1945	
George Howitt *1866–1870*	Old Lenton	14. 3.1843	19.12.1881
Richard Holmes Howitt *1893–1901*	Farnsfield	21. 7.1864	10. 1.1951
Edward Arthur Howsin *1863*	North Muskham	26. 7.1838	27. 2.1921
Geoffrey Neville Bayley Huskinson *1922*	Locarno, Switz.	1. 2.1900	17. 6.1982
Nigel John Bartle Illingworth *1981–1983*	Chesterfield, Derbys	23.11.1960	
Albert Iremonger *1906–1910*	Wilford	15. 6.1884	9. 3.1958
James Iremonger *1899–1914*	Norton, Yorks	5. 3.1876	25. 3.1956
John Jackson *1855–1866*	Bungay, Suffolk	21. 5.1833	4.11.1901
William Jackson *1844–1848*	Basford	5. 8.1820	
Charles Cecil James *1906–1921*	New Basford	14. 9.1885	28. 7.1950
George Jarvis *1835–1841*	Radford	6. 7.1800	27. 3.1880
Arthur Jepson *1938–1959*	Selston	12. 7.1915	
(Anthony) Alexander Johnson *1963–1966*	Loughborough	30. 3.1944	
Isaac Johnson *1840–1843*		1808	5.10.1874
Paul Johnson *1982–1991*	Newark	24. 4.1965	
Peter David Johnson *1970–1977*	Sherwood, Nottingham	12.11.1949	
Arthur Owen Jones *1892–1914*	Shelton	16. 8.1872	21.12.1914
David Jones *1935–1939*	Hodthorpe, Derbys	9. 4.1914	
William Walter Keeton *1926–1952*	Shirebrook, Derbys	30. 4.1905	10.10.1980
John Kelly *1953–1957*	Conisbrough, Yks	15. 9.1930	
Robert Stuart Kelsall *1969*	Stockport, Ches	29. 6.1946	
John Kesteven *1876*	Sutton in Ashfield	8. 7.1849	
Lionel Kirk *1920–1929*	Sheffield	1.11.1884	27. 2.1953
William Kirk *1888*			
Joseph Knowles *1935–1946*	Nottingham	25. 3.1910	
Dean Ralph Laing *1990*	Durban, S. Africa	18. 9.1970	
George Lane *1881*	Kimberley	25. 7.1852	31. 7.1917
Harold Larwood *1924–1938*	Nuncargate	14.11.1904	
Amritt Harrichand (Harry) Latchman *1974–1976*	Kingston, Jam.	26. 7.1943	
Garnet Morley Lee *1910–1922*	Calverton	7. 6.1887	29. 2.1976
Benjamin Lilley *1921–1937*	Kimberley	11. 2.1894	4. 8.1950

Tinsley Lindley *1888*	Nottingham	27.10.1865	31. 3.1940
Cleveland Vincent Lindo *1960*	Bigwood, St Elizabeth, Jam.	6. 6.1936	
William (Henry) Lockwood *1886–1887*	Old Radford	25. 3.1868	26. 4.1932
Albert Longdon *1895*	Watnall Greasley	1.11.1865	13. 5.1937
Sam Lowe *1894*	Kirkby in Ashfield	1867	3.1947
Tom Lowe *1894*	Kirkby in Ashfield	25. 7.1859	29. 8.1934
Walter George Hassall Lowe *1895*	Bretby, Derbys	26. 8.1870	1935
Alexander William McDougall *1858*	Kingston, Jam.	19. 3.1837	1.11.1917
Martin McIntyre *1868–1877*	Eastwood	15. 8.1847	28. 2.1885
Michael McIntyre *1864*	St Anns, Nottingham	13.11.1839	9.10.1888
William McIntyre *1869–1871*	Eastwood	24. 5.1844	13. 9.1892
Kevin Scott Mackintosh *1978–1980*	Surbiton, Surrey	30. 8.1957	
Henry Maltby *1843*		1818	7. 4.1869
William Marriott *1880–1881*	Hucknall under Huthwaite	6. 1.1850	28. 8.1887
Bertie Marshall *1923–1929*	Sutton in Ashfield	5. 5.1902	5. 2.1991
Edwin Alfred Marshall *1937–1938*	Nottingham	21. 8.1904	28. 1.1970
Walter Marshall *1889–1891*	Hyson Green	27.10.1853	15. 1.1943
Eric James Martin *1949–1959*	Lambley	17. 8.1925	
George Need Martin *1870*	Nottingham	25. 7.1845	2. 9.1900
Duncan John Richardson Martindale *1985–1991*	Harrogate, Yorks	13.12.1963	
Percy Mason *1896–1901*	East Bridgford	19.11.1873	27.11.1952
Colin Matthews *1950–1959*	Worksop	17.10.1931	3.1990
Frank Cyril (Leonard) Matthews *1920–1927*	Willoughby on the Wolds	15. 8.1892	11. 1.1961
Cecil Reginald Napp Maxwell *1936–1939*	Paddington, London	21. 5.1913	25. 9.1973
Eric Alfred Meads *1939–1953*	Carrington, Nottingham	17. 8.1916	
Robert John Mee *1887–1896*	Shelford	25. 9.1867	6. 2.1941
Steven Robert Mee *1984*	Nottingham	6. 4.1965	
Gregory Wentworth Mike *1989–1990*	Nottingham	14. 7.1966	
Philip William Herbert Miles *1868–1877*	Bingham	7. 1.1848	4.12.1933
Keith Ross Miller *1959*	Sunshine, Australia	28.11.1919	
Geoffrey Millman *1957–1965*	Bedford	2.10.1934	
David James Millns *1988–1989*	Clipstone	27. 2.1965	
Edwin Mills *1878–1884*	Coddington	6. 3.1857	25. 1.1899
John Mills *1875–1881*	Coddington	28. 1.1855	27. 6.1932
Francis Moore *1862*	Nottingham	18. 7.1827	14. 1.1900
Harry Ian Moore *1962–1969*	Sleaford, Lincs	28. 2.1941	
Charles Morgan *1946*	Clay Cross, Derbys	7. 2.1917	

319

Michael Morgan *1957–1961*	Ynyshir, Glamorgan	21. 5.1936	
Frederick Morley *1872–1883*	Sutton in Ashfield	16.12.1850	28. 9.1884
Henry Morley *1884*	Edwinstowe	1852	16. 8.1924
Thomas Morley *1887*	Sutton in Ashfield	10. 3.1863	31.10.1919
Charles Richard Morris *1902–1904*	Nottingham	26. 8.1880	10. 8.1947
John Moss *1892*	Clifton	7. 2.1864	10. 7.1950
Deryck Lance Murray *1966–1969*	Port of Spain	20. 5.1943	
William Musters Musters *1845–1848*	Colwick	1. 1.1810	16.10.1870
Nirmal Nanan *1971–1980*	Preysal Village, Trinidad	19. 8.1951	
Joseph Stockley Need *1841–1855*	Nottingham	1819	25. 8.1892
Frank Needham *1890–1891*	Arnold	27. 8.1861	15.10.1923
Michael Newell *1984–1991*	Blackburn, Lancs	25. 2.1965	
Thomas Nixon *1841–1854*	Nottingham	4. 6.1815	20. 7.1877
Bernarr (Bill) Notley *1949*	Mapperley, Nottingham	31. 8.1918	
Francis Noyes *1842–1848*		1817	
Robert Patrick Oakden *1960–1961*	Kirkby in Ashfield	9. 5.1938	
Archer Williamson Oates *1931–1933*	Doncaster	9.12.1908	31.12.1968
Thomas William Oates *1897–1925*	Eastwood	9. 8.1875	18. 6.1949
William Coape Oates *1881–1882*	Besthorpe	7. 7.1862	20. 2.1942
Eric Oscroft *1950–1951*	Sutton in Ashfield	20. 4.1933	
John Oscroft *1842–1848*	Arnold	21. 7.1807	28. 9.1857
John Thomas Oscroft *1867–1874*	Arnold	24. 3.1846	15. 6.1885
Percy William Oscroft *1894–1900*	Nottingham	27.11.1872	8.12.1933
William Oscroft *1864–1882*	Arnold	16.12.1843	10.10.1905
William Padley *1876*	Moor Green	11. 4.1842	21. 7.1904
George Paling *1865–1867*	Nottingham	29.11.1836	18.12.1879
John Maurice Parkin *1966–1968*	Kimberley	16.10.1944	
Butler Parr *1835–1854*	Martin, Lincs	9.11.1810	16. 3.1872
George Parr *1844–1870*	Radcliffe on Trent	22. 5.1826	23. 6.1891
Henry John Parr *1856–1858*	Radcliffe on Trent	7. 1.1838	24. 4.1863
Samuel Parr *1840–1855*	Radcliffe on Trent	2. 5.1820	12. 5.1873
Edwin Patchitt *1840*	Nottingham	1808	6. 2.1888
Albert Ivan Payton *1922*	Stapleford	20. 1.1898	27. 9.1967
Wilfred Ernest Granville Payton *1935*	Beeston	27.12.1913	4. 9.1989
Wilfred Richard (Daniel) Payton *1905–1931*	Stapleford	13. 2.1882	2. 5.1943
Joseph Garside Pearson *1883*	Worksop	26. 3.1860	18. 1.1892
Philip John Sherwin Pearson-Gregory *1910–1914*	Harlaxton, Lincs	26. 3.1888	12. 6.1955
John Henry Pennington *1902–1905*	Sutton on Trent	24. 6.1881	2. 1.1942
Charles Pepper *1900–1901*		1875	13. 9.1917
Robert Andrew Pick *1983–1991*	Nottingham	19.11.1963	

Arthur Pike *1894–1899*	Keyworth	25.12.1862	15.11.1907
Peter John Plummer *1969–1972*	Nottingham	28. 1.1947	
Paul Raymond Pollard *1987–1991*	Nottingham	24. 9.1968	
Ian Leslie Pont *1982*	Brentwood, Essex	28. 8.1961	
Cyril John Poole *1948–1962*	Forest Town	13. 3.1921	
Kenneth John Poole *1955–1957*	Thurgarton	27. 4.1934	
Henry James Porter *1842–1843*	Nottingham	1810	
George Edward Power *1876*	Witchford, Cambs	16. 5.1849	29.10.1904
David Pratt *1962*	Watford, Herts	20. 7.1938	
Alfred Price *1887*	Ruddington	5. 1.1862	21. 3.1942
Walter Price *1869*	Ruddington	9.10.1834	4. 9.1894
David Anthony Pullan *1970–1974*	Farsley, Yorks	1. 5.1944	
Derek William Randall *1972–1991*	Retford	24. 2.1951	
Tom Bockenham Reddick *1946–1947*	Shanghai, China	17. 2.1912	1. 6.1982
John Reddish *1930*	Nottingham	22.12.1904	18.10.1989
Oliver Redgate *1889–1894*	Nottingham	16. 2.1863	11. 5.1913
Samuel Redgate *1835–1845*	Arnold	27. 7.1810	13. 4.1851
Thomas Blatherwick Redgate *1840*		1810	16. 2.1874
Henry Smith Reynolds *1872–1875*	Ollerton	6. 1.1844	21. 4.1894
Stuart Denzil Rhodes *1930–1935*	Sneinton	24. 3.1910	7. 1.1989
William Ernest Rhodes *1961–1964*	Bradford	5. 8.1936	
Clive Edward Butler Rice *1975–1987*	Johannesburg, S. Africa	23. 7.1949	
Allan Richardson *1949–1951*	Woodbeck	28.10.1926	
Henry Richardson *1887–1890*	Bulwell	4.10.1857	20. 3.1940
Stanley Hugh Richardson *1925*	Marston Green, Warw	2. 7.1890	24. 1.1958
Thomas Leonard Richmond *1912–1928*	Radcliffe on Trent	23. 6.1890	29.12.1957
James Riley *1898*	Kirkby in Ashfield	11.12.1860	8.11.1937
William Riley *1909–1914*	Newstead Colliery	11. 8.1888	9. 8.1917
George Lutha (or Luther) Robinson *1896*	Ruddington	22. 2.1873	8. 3.1930
George William Robinson *1930–1936*	Kirkby in Ashfield	15. 2.1908	16. 7.1967
Henry Robinson *1889*	Nottingham	13.11.1863	
John Sandford Robinson *1888–1896*	Arnold	5. 2.1868	21. 4.1898
Robert Timothy Robinson *1978–1991*	Skegby	21.11.1958	
George Rothera *1835–1837*	Nottingham	12.11.1809	31.10.1841
Edmund John Rowe *1949–1957*	Netherfield	21. 7.1920	17.12.1989
George Murray Royle *1871–1881*	Nottingham	9. 1.1843	26. 2.1910
Kevin Saxelby *1978–1990*	Worksop	23. 2.1959	
Mark Saxelby *1989–1991*	Worksop	4. 1.1969	
Christopher Wilmot Scott *1981–1991*	Thorpe on the Hill, Lancs	23. 1.1964	
William Henry Scotton *1875–1890*	Nottingham	15. 1.1856	9. 7.1893
John Seaton *1872*	Nottingham	15. 1.1844	14.10.1918
Richard Seddon *1845*	Leicester	11. 2.1825	13. 7.1884
John Selby *1870–1887*	Nottingham	1. 7.1849	11. 3.1894

William Ward Selby *1848*	Nottingham	1823	29. 1.1892
Francis Joseph Shacklock *1883–1893*	Crich, Derbys	22. 9.1861	3. 5.1937
John William Sharpe *1894*	Ruddington	9.12.1866	19. 6.1936
Samuel Sharpe *1868*	Ruddington	13. 1.1839	5.11.1924
Alfred Shaw *1864–1897*	Burton Joyce	29. 8.1842	16. 1.1907
James Coupe Shaw *1865–1875*	Sutton in Ashfield	11. 4.1836	7. 3.1888
William Shaw *1866*	Burton Joyce	5. 8.1827	2.1890
Mordecai Sherwin *1876–1896*	Kimberley	26. 2.1851	3. 7.1910
Frank William Shipston *1925–1933*	Bulwell	29. 7.1906	
Thomas Shooter *1881*	Hucknall Torkard	11. 3.1845	14. 7.1919
Charles Shore *1881–1885*	Sutton in Ashfield	21.11.1858	5. 6.1912
Arthur Shrewsbury *1875–1902*	New Lenton	11. 4.1856	19. 5.1903
Arthur Shrewsbury jun. *1892*	Nottingham	4. 7.1874	6.10.1917
William Shrewsbury *1875–1879*	New Lenton	30. 4.1854	14.11.1931
Anthony Siddons *1959–1960*	Lenton, Nottingham	29.12.1941	
William Arnold Sime *1935–1950*	Wepener, O.F.S.	8. 2.1909	5. 5.1983
Benjamin Bridge Simpson (aka Benjamin Gregory) *1895–1897*	Eastwood	6.10.1863	27. 1.1951
Reginald Thomas Simpson *1946–1963*	Sherwood Rise	27. 2.1920	
Thomas Simpson *1903–1905*	Keyworth	13. 8.1879	19.12.1961
Kenneth Smales *1951–1958*	Horsforth, Yorks	15. 9.1927	
Michael John Smedley *1964–1979*	Maltby, Yorks	28.10.1941	
Arthur Price Smith *1883*	Ruddington	3.12.1857	3. 6.1937
John Smith *1862–1863*	Gotham	12. 7.1834	
John Smith *1864*	Ruddington	8.11.1835	5.1889
Isaiah Smithurst *1946*	Hill Top, Eastwood	6.11.1920	
John Collis Snaith *1900*	Nottingham	24. 2.1876	
Garfield St Aubrun Sobers *1968–1974*	Bridgetown, Barbados	28. 7.1936	
Addil Somani *1987*	Kampala, Uganda	22.10.1967	
Walter John Speak *1905*	Ripon, Yorks	20. 2.1873	21. 6.1943
John Denis Springall *1955–1963*	Southwark, London	19. 9.1932	
Lord George Philip Cecil Arthur Stanhope *1860–1861*	Mayfair, London	29. 8.1831	1.12.1871
Arthur Staples *1924–1938*	Newstead Colliery	4. 2.1899	9. 9.1965
Samuel James Staples *1920–1934*	Newstead Colliery	18. 9.1892	4. 6.1950
James Stapleton *1899–1911*	Eastwood	8. 8.1879	10. 7.1944
Harvey Staunton *1903–1905*	Staunton	21.11.1870	14. 1.1918
Barry Stead *1962–1976*	Leeds	21. 6.1939	15. 4.1980
Franklyn Dacosta Stephenson *1988–1991*	Halls, St James, Barbados	8. 4.1959	

322

Frederick William Stinchcombe *1950–1951*	Barnby Moor	12. 3.1930	19. 9.1984
Frederick Wilfred Stocks *1946–1957*	Carcroft, Yorks	6.11.1918	
William Frederick Story *1878–1879*	Stockport, Ches.	3. 4.1852	1.12.1939
Peter Mark Such *1982–1986*	Helensburgh, Scotland	12. 6.1964	
Joseph Sulley *1887–1888*	Arnold	28. 5.1850	14. 2.1932
George Summers *1867–1870*	Nottingham	22. 6.1844	19. 6.1870
Cecil Alfred Leonard Sutton *1907*	Lambeth, London	1886	10. 2.1965
Roy Swetman *1966–1967*	Westminster	25.10.1933	
Benjamin (Williamson) Taylor *1902–1909*	Kimberley	16. 6.1873	24. 8.1938
John Taylor *1876*	Beeston	2. 7.1849	2. 3.1921
Michael Norman Somerset Taylor *1964–1972*	Amersham, Bucks	12.11.1942	
Paul Adrian Taylor *1958*	East Kirkby	9. 3.1939	
Ronald Alfred Taylor *1932–1935*	Meadows, Nottingham	25. 3.1909	29. 8.1986
William Taylor *1971–1977*	Manchester	24. 1.1947	
Francis Eastwood Tinley *1845–1856*	Southwell	3. 3.1819	2. 6.1889
Robert Crispin Tinley *1847–1869*	Southwell	25.10.1830	11.12.1900
Vincent Tinley *1864*	Southwell	26. 1.1828	19.11.1899
Paul Adrian Todd *1972–1982*	Morton, Southwell	12. 3.1953	
Robert Tolley *1871–1878*	Nottingham	14. 3.1849	2. 1.1901
John Richard Truswell *1868*	Farnsfield	14. 1.1841	6. 8.1892
Howard Trevor Tunnicliffe *1973–1980*	Derby	4. 3.1950	
Herbert Turland *1924*	Stapleford	29. 8.1894	
James Turner *1894*	Teversal	23. 7.1865	30. 1.1945
Noel Vernon Cyril Turner *1906–1909*	Langley Mill	12. 5.1887	13. 6.1941
Robert Harrison Tom Turner *1906–1927*	Langley Mill	26.10.1888	13. 9.1947
John Tye *1876–1881*	Bulwell	10. 7.1848	19.11.1905
Arthur Joseph Underwood *1949–1954*	Wiseton	21. 9.1927	
William Underwood *1881*	Ruddington	26. 2.1852	9. 5.1914
Patrick Vaulkhard *1934*	Nottingham	15. 9.1911	
William Voce *1927–1952*	Annesley Woodhouse	8. 8.1909	6. 6.1984
Roger Charles Vowles *1957–1961*	Grimsby, Lincs	5. 4.1932	
Alan Keith Walker *1954–1958*	Manly, New South Wales	4.10.1925	
George Arthur Walker *1937*	West Bridgford	25. 1.1919	
Willis Walker *1913–1937*	Gosforth, Northbld	24.11.1892	3.12.1991
Joseph Arthur Walters *1958–1959*	Bolsover, Derbys	12. 2.1940	
Jonas Bettinson Warwick *1843–1848*		1804	9. 8.1873
George Wass *1910*	Worksop	6. 2.1882	15. 6.1966
Thomas George Wass *1896–1920*	Sutton in Ashfield	26.12.1873	27.10.1953
Dennis Watkin *1937–1939*	Stapleford	28. 6.1912	23. 3.1983
William Kenneth Watson *1976–1980*	Port Elizabeth, S. Africa	21. 5.1955	

Peter David Watts *1967*	Henlow, Beds	31. 3.1938	
Neil Ivan Weightman *1981–1982*	Normanton on Trent	5.10.1960	
Bryan Douglas Wells *1960–1965*	Gloucester	27. 7.1930	
George Edward Wharmby *1891–1893*	Sutton in Ashfield	7.12.1870	15.11.1951
Arthur Bradley Wheat *1927–1939*	Halam	13. 5.1898	20. 5.1973
John Wheeler *1873–1877*	Sutton Bonington	9.12.1844	22. 9.1908
Alan Wheelhouse *1961*	Nottingham	4. 3.1934	
John William White *1902–1904*	Annesley	1. 8.1877	2.12.1958
Robert Arthur White *1966–1980*	Fulham, London	6.10.1936	
Norman Barrie Whittingham *1962–1966*	Silsden, Yorks	22.10.1940	
William Wilfrid Whysall *1910–1930*	Woodborough	31.10.1887	11.11.1930
Sam Weller Widdowson *1878*	Hucknall Torkard	16. 4.1851	9. 5.1927
Arthur Wilkinson *1894–1895*	Nottingham	28.12.1872	
Philip Alan Wilkinson *1971–1977*	Hucknall	23. 8.1951	
William Wilkinson *1892–1893*	Kimberley	5. 7.1859	6.10.1940
Guy Longfield Willatt *1939–1948*	The Park, Nottingham	7. 5.1918	
Philip Williams *1845*	Eton	7. 9.1824	18.11.1899
William Williams *1865–1875*	Arnold Grove	25.11.1844	12. 3.1885
Herbert Wilson *1911–1919*	Eastwood	22. 5.1892	3. 6.1972
Hugh Mervyn Winfield *1954–1966*	Gainsborough, Lincs	13. 6.1933	
Frederick Henry Winrow *1938–1951*	Manton	17. 1.1916	19. 8.1973
Robert Winrow *1932–1935*	Manton	30.12.1910	
Maurice Wood *1955*	Nottingham	6. 7.1933	18. 3.1978
Francis Gerald Woodhead *1934–1950*	Edwinstowe	30.10.1912	24. 5.1991
William Woodward *1835*	Radford	1812	4. 7.1862
George Wootton *1861–1871*	Clifton	16.10.1834	15. 6.1924
Charles William Wright *1882–1899*	Harewood, Yorks	27. 5.1863	10. 1.1936
Matthew William Wright *1889*	Keyworth	24. 7.1858	13. 5.1949
Thomas Wright *1868–1874*	Willington, Derbys	29. 4.1842	
Walter Wright *1879–1886*	Hucknall Torkard	29. 2.1856	22. 3.1940
Frederick Wyld (aka Wild) *1868–1881*	Eastwood	28. 8.1847	11. 2.1893
Walter Gerald Yates *1937–1938*	Warsop	18. 6.1919	

The following played for the First Eleven of the County, but only in a non–first-class match:

Edward Anthony *1879*	Arnold	1853	15. 4.1914
S. Bagguley *1843*			
James Barks *1885*	Basford	4.11.1861	
Abraham Bass *1843*	Burton on Trent	20.7.1804	15. 8.1882
George Bennett *1889*	Sutton in Ashfield	2.1867	10. 3.1918
Thomas Billyeald *1843*	East Retford	2. 3.1810	1874
Samuel Birmingham *1876*		7.10.1849	18. 6.1891

Name		Place		
Richard Gillies Bradshaw	*1895*	Retford	3. 1.1872	29. 8.1957
John Brown	*1842*	Nottingham	29. 3.1807	5. 6.1883
Frederick Aldis Charles	*1870*	Sheffield	1836	9. 1.1895
Francis Dixon	*1891*	Derby	31. 7.1855	20. 8.1943
Alvery Richard Dodsley-Flamsteed	*1864*	Lambley	1837	27.12.1901
George Freeman	*1876*	Ordsall	12. 9.1854	22.11.1931
Morton Handley	*1879*	Arnold	2.11.1844	14.11.1933
Frederick John Hingley	*1899*	St Anns, Nottingham	14.12.1867	19.10.1947
Maurice Linton Churchill Foster		Retreat, St Mary, Jamaica	9. 5.1943	
John Henry Hogg	*1880*	Burton Joyce	1.1858	
Nicholas Edward Hurst	*1842*	Nottingham	1815	
R. James	*1836*			
Walter James	*1896*			
Robert Jerram	*1837*			
John Johnson	*1848*	Nottingham	1809	5. 8.1877
Robert Byers Kerr	*1983*	Herston, Australia	16. 6.1961	
George McKenzie Kettle	*1843*	Overseal, Leics.	6. 8.1810	13.10.1887
Thomas F. King	*1871*			
James Lindley	*1874*	Sutton in Ashfield	18. 7.1844	15.10.1911
Richard Lowe	*1889*	Kirkby in Ashfield	18. 6.1869	3. 7.1946
John Orange	*1874*	Woodborough	27. 9.1848	24. 8.1907
Charles Henry Parr	*1897*			
Frederick Randon	*1871*	Stapleford	24. 6.1845	17. 2.1883
George Ratcliffe	*1896*	Ilkeston, Derbys	1856	7. 3.1928
Harold James Rhodes	*1970*	Hadfield, Glossop, Derbys	22. 7.1936	
Edward Mitford Hutton Riddell	*1873*	Carlton-on-Trent	31.10.1845	22.10.1898
Alfred Sears	*1867*	Carrington	9.11.1846	28. 4.1870
William Shelton	*1870*	Nottingham	31. 3.1848	31. 3.1883
Henry Slater	*1861*	Newark	15. 2.1839	4.11.1905
Alonzo Smith	*1876*	Nottingham	4. 5.1850	31.12.1881
Robert Posnett Smith	*1874*	Sawley, Derbys	1.11.1848	1. 5.1899
S. Thomas	*1896*			
Hubert Twells	*1900*	Newthorpe	17. 5.1874	3. 6.1924
Thomas Walker	*1870*	Eastwood	1845	11. 3.1871
Edward Cossall Weaver	*1895*	Sherwood, Nottingham	8.11.1874	
J. White	*1887*			
William Whitlock	*1895*			
Arthur Machin Wood	*1878*	Pye Bridge, Derbys	21. 2.1861	25. 8.1947
Peter George Wood	*1981*	Manchester	29. 9.1951	
George Woolley	*1892*	Lenton	1867	24.10.1938

CAREER RECORDS OF NOTTINGHAMSHIRE CRICKETERS, 1835–1991

Name	M	Inns	NO	Runs	HS	Avge	100s	Runs	Wkts	Avge	BB	5wI
Afford, J. A.	95	81	34	166	22★	3.53	0	8167	241	33.88	6/81	7
Allbrook, M. E.	12	10	5	42	13	8.40	0	937	16	58.56	4/106	0
Allen, E. G.	2	3	0	48	19	16.00	0					
Alletson, E. B.	118	177	6	3194	189	18.67	1	628	33	19.03	6/74	1
Anthony, A. F. O'C	3	6	0	14	11	2.33	0					
Anthony, G.	85	126	13	1721	89	15.23	0	2619	82	31.93	6/72	3
Anthony, H.	4	7	1	52	13★	8.66	0	81	2	40.50	1/15	0
Armitage, A. K.	5	8	1	160	43★	22.85	0					
Armstrong, T.	6	11	2	67	20★	7.44	0					
Ashwell, A. T.	2	2	0	0	0	0.00	0					
Atkinson, J.	7	12	4	40	19	5.00	0	236	10	23.60	4/22	0
Atkinson, T.	64	104	19	1127	48	13.25	0	5157	116	44.45	6/61	2
Attenburrow, H. C.	1	1	0	3	3	3.00	0		(10)			1
Attewell, T.	7	10	3	53	23★	7.57	0	12	0			
Attewell, Walter	1	2	10	0	0	0.00	0	10	0			
Attewell, William	283	419	37	5763	102	15.08	1	20226	1303	15.52	9/23	95
Bagguley, R.	45	72	12	661	110	11.01	1	875	38	23.02	6/74	3
Baker, D. W.	7	9	4	16	10	3.20	0	437	10	43.70	4/78	0
Banner, G.	1	1	0	5	5	5.00	0	33	2	16.50	2/33	0
Barber, T. D.	1	2	0	3	3	1.50	0					
Barber, W. D.	1	1	0	7	7	7.00	0					
Barker, T.	14	26	2	187	25	7.79	0	228	17(21)	13.41	5/46	3
Barnes, J. W.	3	5	0	19	12	3.80	0	105	2	52.50	1/30	0
Barnes, T.	5	6	0	65	33	10.83	0	23	2	11.50	2/23	0
Barnes, W.	257	399	34	8328	160	22.81	13	7926	436	18.17	8/64	17
Barnsdale, J. D.	1	2	0	10	10	5.00	0					
Barratt, F.	353	441	48	6101	139★	15.52	2	26299	1176	22.36	8/26	67
Batchelor, C.	3	6	2	27	13★	6.75	0					
Bateman, A.	1	2	0	63	63	31.50	0					
Bateman, E. L.	1	2	0	4	4	2.00	0					
Bates, A. J.	2	4	0	5	5	1.25	0					
Baxter, A. G.	13	22	1	314	98	14.95	0	8	0			
Bean, G.	5	7	1	68	27	11.33	0	65	0			
Beevor, J. G.	5	9	1	207	88	25.87	0					
Bembridge, H.	1	2	1	17	15★	17.00	0	34	0			
Bennett, A. R.	7	11	1	40	17	4.00	0	498	17	29.29	5/81	1
Beves, G.	9	15	0	141	42	9.40	0					
Bickley, J.	15	24	4	88	27	4.40	0	707	61	11.59	8/23	4
Biddulph, S.	76	118	17	983	54	9.73	0					
Bielby, S. R.	43	58	12	837	62	18.19	0	161	3	53.66	1/14	0
Bignall, T.	60	102	10	1895	116★	20.59	1	40	0			
Bilbie, A. R.	14	27	1	291	39	11.19	0					

Name	M	Inns	NO	Runs	HS	Avge	100s	Runs	Wkts	Avge	BB	5wI
Birch, J. D.	250	374	59	8673	125	27.53	6	2446	50	48.92	6/64	I
Birtle, T. W.	7	7	2	12	4*	2.40	0	593	8	74.12	2/68	0
Bishop, J. F.	3	4	2	21	15*	10.50	0					
Blackburn, B. F.	2	3	I	6	4*	3.00	0					
Blagg, E. A.	I		did not bat					20	0			
Bland, R. D. F.	33	39	14	240	20*	9.60	0	2697	73	36.94	5/61	I
Bolus, J. B.	269	482	47	15093	202*	34.69	25	400	8	50.00	2/24	0
Bond, J. D.	17	24	4	245	65*	12.25	0					
Bore, M. K.	85	80	31	393	27	8.02	0	6377	210	30.36	8/89	5
Bottom, D.	3	5	0	20	7	4.00	0	188	8	23.50	5/34	I
Bower, W.	I	I	0	0	0	0.00	0	51	I	51.00	1/31	0
Bradley, J.	9	8	3	30	13	6.00	0	781	19	41.10	4/116	0
Brampton, C.	36	64	4	1088	89	18.13	0	103	5(5)	20.60	3/25	0
Branston, G. T.	44	69	6	1178	106	18.69	I	955	24	39.79	5/43	I
Briggs, Joseph	6	10	0	20	9	2.00	0	168	14	12.00	5/34	2
Broad, B. C.	159	285	21	11346	227*	42.97	26	260	5	52.00	2/23	0
Broadley, V. J. P.	I	I	0	6	6	6.00	0	111	I	111.00	1/92	0
Brooks, A. J.	2	4	I	10	6	3.33	0	85	5	17.00	2/10	0
Brown, C.	25	43	5	320	36	8.42	0	46	3(3)	15.33	2/27	0
Brown, J.	3	6	2	33	24	8.25	0	15	0			
Brown, S.	14	17	2	194	40	12.93	0	1088	47	23.14	6/55	3
Brown, T.	4	7	0	118	74	16.85	0	42	0			
Buckland, T. G.	2	3	I	23	12	11.50	0	68	4	17.00	2/13	0
Burrows, A. D.	I	2	0	2	I	1.00	0	19	0			
Bury, W.	3	5	0	46	21	9.20	0					
Butler, F.	45	71	7	999	171	15.60	I	11				
Butler, G.	15	26	3	310	40	13.47	0	54	3(1)	18.00	3/54	0
Butler, H. J.	306	366	93	2870	62	10.51	0	22263	919	24.22	8/15	46
Butler, J.	6	8	I	111	56	15.85	0					
Butler, R.	7	12	0	120	60	10.00	0					
Buttery, J.	4	6	0	74	36	12.33	0	39	2(3)	19.50	1/13	0
Buxton, J. H.	I	I	0	6	6	6.00	0	90	I	90.00	1/54	0
Cairns, C. L.	10	13	2	246	58	22.36	0	817	28	29.17	4/70	0
Callaghan, D. J.	I	I	0	29	29	29.00	0	59	I	59.00	1/59	0
Carlin, J.	58	87	15	1344	85	18.66	0	99	4	24.75	3/25	0
Carr, A. W.	416	630	40	18855	206	31.95	43	1150	31	37.09	3/14	0
Carter, A. G.	2	3	I	16	13	8.00	0					
Cartwright, V. H.	7	8	0	60	22	7.50	0					
Castledine, S. W. T.	5	7	0	22	15	3.14	0	25	0			
Chambers, G. H. (1896)	3	4	2	25	16	12.50	0	235	6	39.16	3/44	0
Chambers, G. H. (1903)	4	6	I	58	30	11.60	0	54	0			
Chambers, M.	I	2	0	6	4	3.00	0	22	I	22.00	1/22	0
Champion de Crespigny, F. J.	I	I	I	20	20*	–	0	12	0			
Chapman, J.	8	12	4	133	41	16.62	0	83	4(2)	20.75	2/7	0
Charlton, T. B.	3	5	I	14	8	3.50	0					
Chatterton, J.	6	11	I	132	30	13.20	0		(1)			
Clarke, A.	25	41	4	394	57	10.64	0					
Clarke, W. (1835)	28	48	3	398	75	8.84	0	1256	134(6)	9.37	9/29	16

Name	M	Inns	NO	Runs	HS	Avge	100s	Runs	Wkts	Avge	BB	5wI
Clarke, W. (1876)	6	10	0	82	17	8.20	0	126	4	31.50	2/60	0
Clarke, W. (1874)	13	21	2	134	40	7.05	0	323	24	13.46	5/19	3
Clay, J. D.	236	400	17	9991	192	26.08	11	133	0			
Cleveley, A. B.	1	2	1	4	4★	4.00	0	107	3	35.66	3/63	0
Clifton, C.	9	16	2	163	45	11.64	0					
Clifton, C. C.	24	36	10	154	22	5.92	0	1334	50	26.68	4/25	0
Collins, T. H.	2	2	0	1	1	0.50	0	58	3	19.33	1/17	0
Cook, C. J.	2	2	1	1	1	1.00	0	105	1	105.00	1/50	0
Cooper, K. E.	270	279	67	2139	46	10.08	0	19241	705	27.29	8/44	25
Coote, D. E.	1	1	0	20	20	20.00	0					
Copley, S. H.	1	2	0	7	4	3.50	0	28	0			
Corran, A. J.	101	160	43	1829	75	15.63	0	8245	302	27.30	6/31	13
Cotton, J.	138	194	67	1047	58	8.24	0	10368	400	25.92	7/73	15
Cox, H. R.	23	30	6	268	64	11.16	0	1188	32	37.12	6/30	2
Crawford, A. B.	11	17	1	241	51	15.06	0	297	8	37.12	4/55	0
Crawley, M. A.	11	13	4	272	112	30.22	1	463	11	42.09	3/21	0
Creswell, C.	5	9	1	24	9	3.00	0					
Crook, H.	2	4	0	9	5	2.25	0					
Cursham, A. W.	12	20	0	208	67	10.40	0	49	1	49.00	1/39	0
Cursham, H. A.	2	3	1	41	25★	20.50	0	43	0			
Curzon, C. C.	17	21	4	255	45	15.00	0					
Curzon, J. T.	1	1	0	1	1	1.00	0	22	0			
Daft, C. F.	14	23	0	328	46	14.26	0					
Daft, H. (B)	190	293	34	4176	92★	16.12	0	2221	86	25.82	5/79	1
Daft, R.	157	261	35	6627	161	29.32	4	829	45	18.42	6/59	2
Daft, R. P.	1	1	0	5	5	5.00	0					
Dakin, S.	1	2	0	12	6	6.00	0		(1)			
Davis, T.	12	21	1	180	72	9.00	0					
Davison, I. J.	177	246	65	1641	60★	9.06	0	15562	540	28.81	7/28	22
Day, J.	2	4	0	13	7	3.25	0					
Day, J. W.	61	96	8	1233	88	14.01	0	950	27	35.18	5/50	1
Dench, C. E.	91	136	17	2660	88★	22.35	0	2191	78	28.08	7/28	4
Dexter, H. W.	10	17	6	223	38★	20.27	0	33	0			
Dexter, R. E.	22	36	6	464	57	15.46	0					
Diver, A. J. D.	1	2	0	74	46	37.00	0					
Dixon, J. A.	235	387	24	8956	268★	24.67	13	4777	172	27.77	5/28	2
Dooland, B.	140	213	18	4782	115★	24.52	1	14520	770	18.85	8/20	75
Doshi, D. R.	44	47	11	208	23	5.77	0	4589	157	29.22	6/33	3
Drury, J. J.	4	3	0	21	19	7.00	0	71	4	17.75	1/1	0
Earle, R. B.	1	2	0	16	15	8.00	0					
Edwards, G.	9	16	4	191	46★	15.91	0	224	12	18.66	5/44	1
Elliott, W.	2	2	0	8	5	4.00	0	41	1	41.00	1/18	0
Ellis, W.	2	1	0	29	29	29.00	0	77	1	77.00	1/49	0
Ellison, H. R. N.	1	2	0	5	3	2.50	0	5	0			
Ellison, M. J.	1	1	0	6	6	6.00	0					
Emmitt, H. W.	2	3	0	2	2	0.66	0					
Enfield, H.	2	4	0	6	4	1.50	0					
Evans, K. P.	70	99	26	1936	100★	26.52	1	4682	134	34.94	5/52	2
Evans, R. J.	6	9	3	112	50★	18.66	0	97	3	32.33	3/40	0
Farr, B. H.	6	10	2	127	37	15.87	0	485	10	48.50	5/96	1
Farrands, F. H.	2	3	1	19	11★	9.50	0	122	8	15.25	4/34	0
Fell, M. A.	15	27	0	408	108	15.11	1	157	1	157.00	1/20	0

328

Name	M	Inns	NO	Runs	HS	Avge	100s	Runs	Wkts	Avge BB	5wI
Fellows, J. F.	2	3	1	23	18*	11.50	0	36	1	36.00 1/3	0
Fewkes, A.	1	2	0	11	9	5.50	0				
Field-Buss, M. G.	8	7	1	53	25	8.83	0	414	11	37.63 4/33	0
Firth, J. d'E E.	2	2	0	3	2	1.50	0	161	4	40.25 2/71	0
Flear, H.	1	1	1	9	9*	–	0				
Flint, B.	13	13	4	81	36	9.00	0	564	19	29.68 3/28	0
Flint, W. A.	145	195	22	3345	103	19.33	3	6965	236	29.51 6/23	6
Flowers, T.	1	2	0	16	11	8.00	0	10	0		
Flowers, W.	281	436	28	8252	173	20.22	6	11712	714	16.40 8/22	33
Foljambe, G. S.	7	11	0	58	14	5.27	0				
Forbes, C.	244	319	69	3597	86	14.39	0	17914	706	25.37 7/19	23
Forman, P. R.	16	25	8	180	26	10.58	0	1291	40	32.27 5/73	1
Foster, W.	1	2	0	0	0	0.00	0				
Fox, F. I.	2	4	2	34	23	17.00	0				
Foxcroft, J.	3	5	2	37	12*	12.33	0				
Fraser-Darling, C. D.	11	12	2	242	61	24.20	0	876	17	51.52 5/84	1
French, B. N.	287	380	75	5788	105*	18.97	1	70	1	70.00 1/37	0
Frost, G.	102	165	17	3319	107	22.42	2	680	15	45.33 3/33	0
Galloway, G. G.	3	6	2	13	11	3.25	0				
Garrat, W.	11	18	2	183	39	11.43	0				
Gauld, G. O.	14	19	0	350	90	18.42	0	250	5	50.00 1/11	0
Gibson, J.	3	6	0	26	15	4.33	0				
Gibson, R.	3	5	1	46	17	11.50	0	85	3	28.33 2/39	0
Gilbert, J.	3	5	1	110	91	27.50	0				
Giles, R. J.	195	310	19	7639	142	26.25	9	1318	23	57.30 3/1	0
Gill, A.	53	98	7	1756	67	19.29	0	481	10	48.10 2/28	0
Gillhouley, K.	83	134	21	1709	75*	15.12	0	5107	170	30.04 6/95	4
Good, B.	10	19	3	153	24	9.56	0	38	2(1)	19.00 2/10	0
Goodacre, W. B.	43	66	4	1169	104*	18.85	1	440	12	36.66 3/30	0
Goodall, H. H.	5	7	1	92	26	15.33	0				
Goonesena, G.	94	146	17	2464	107*	19.10	1	7495	299	25.06 7/63	19
Grant, C. R. W.	3	6	0	125	48	20.83	0				
Griffiths, J. T.	1			did not bat							
Groves, G. J.	17	29	4	584	56*	23.36	0	6	0		
Grundy, J.	53	86	7	981	76*	12.41	0	2168	175(7)	12.45 9/19	12
Gunn, G.	583	959	74	31592	220	35.69	55	2183	61	35.78 5/50	1
Gunn, G. V.	264	391	43	10225	184	29.38	11	10026	281	35.67 7/44	9
Gunn, J. R.	489	769	94	23194	294	34.36	40	27336	1128	24.23 8/65	75
Gunn, W.	363	585	48	18295	273	34.06	34	1196	41	29.17 4/27	0
Guttridge, F. H.	58	86	15	1206	79	16.98	0	2543	70	36.32 6/61	4
Guy, J.	28	48	2	619	73*	13.45	0				
Hacker, P. J.	61	69	27	410	35	9.76	0	3979	126	31.57 6/35	2
Hadlee, R. J.	148	196	45	5854	210*	38.76	11	9031	622	14.51 8/41	38
Halfyard, D. J.	77	70	20	678	47*	13.56	0	5880	194	30.30 6/14	6
Hall, J. B.	5	10	0	67	24	6.70	0	316	10	31.60 4/90	0
Hall, M. J.	17	30	1	430	72	14.82	0				
Hallam, A. W.	194	261	73	1986	57	10.56	0	14565	767	18.98 8/67	51
Handford, A.	15	21	4	152	24*	8.94	0	1259	43	29.27 7/75	4
Hardstaff, J. sen.	340	560	70	15059	213*	30.73	22	2124	55	38.61 5/133	1
Hardstaff, J. jun.	408	632	73	24249	266	43.37	65	1635	28	58.39 4/43	0
Hardstaff, R. G.	30	41	10	252	60	8.12	0	1988	100	19.88 8/53	8

Name	M	Inns	NO	Runs	HS	Avge	100s	Runs	Wkts	Avge	BB	5wI
Hardy, S.	5	8	3	45	12*	9.00	0	274	4	68.50	2/100	0
Hare, W. H.	10	18	4	171	36	12.21	0	18	0			
Harris, C. B.	362	601	64	18823	239*	35.05	30	8395	196	42.83	8/80	3
Harris, M. J.	261	441	43	15308	201*	38.46	35	3374	77	43.81	4/16	0
Harris, W.	1	1	0	2	2	2.00	0					
Harrison, C.	1	2	0	3	3	1.50	0					
Harrison, I. M.	7	12	2	143	33	14.30	0					
Harrison, P.	1	2	0	13	11	6.50	0	25	0			
Hartopp, E. S. E.	1	2	0	6	6	3.00	0					
Harvey, P. F.	173	240	44	3632	150	18.53	2	11850	332	35.69	8/122	13
Hassan, B.	329	544	54	14355	182*	29.29	15	407	6	67.83	3/33	0
Hatfield, J.	1	2	0	4	3	2.00	0					
Hawley, F.	1	1	0	1	1	1.00	0	67	1	67.00	1/31	0
Haynes, M. W.	9	16	1	119	23	7.93	0					
Hayward, J. R. G.	1			did not bat				78	2	39.00	2/78	0
Heane, G. F. H.	172	241	24	5854	138	26.97	9	6532	201	32.49	6/52	4
Heath, T.	7	12	1	94	35	8.54	0					
Hemingway, R. E.	30	47	1	944	85	20.52	0	6	0			
Hemmings, E. E.	263	314	74	4234	127*	17.64	1	23079	832	27.73	7/23	43
Hendrick, M.	34	36	17	181	29	9.52	0	1681	100	16.81	6/17	6
Henson, W. W.	13	16	5	110	35*	10.00	0	835	24	34.79	4/82	0
Herbert, M. R. H. M.	6	8	0	112	65	14.00	0					
Heymann, W. G.	1			did not bat				48	2	24.00	2/37	0
Hill, M.	237	394	32	8977	137*	24.79	7	305	5	61.00	2/60	0
Hill, N. W.	280	513	32	14036	201*	29.18	22	261	2	130.50	1/28	0
Hilton, J. jun	1	1	0	7	7	7.00	0					
Hind, A. E.	1	2	0	5	3	2.50	0					
Hind, B. J.	1	2	0	28	23	14.00	0	42	0			
Hind, S. jun.	6	10	0	90	22	9.00	0	51	0			
Hodges, H. A.	3	4	1	141	62	47.00	0					
Hodgkins, J. S.	3	5	0	106	44	21.20	0	238	3	79.33	1/55	0
Hogg, J.	3	4	1	60	31	20.00	0					
Holmes, W.	2	2	0	33	19	16.50	0	105	4	26.25	2/50	0
Horsley, J.	3	5	2	18	8*	6.00	0	354	3	118.00	2/176	0
Horsley, N.	3	1	0	0	0	0.00	0	249	6	41.50	2/27	0
Horsley, W.	2	3	1	31	16	15.50	0					
Housley, R.	1	2	0	3	2	1.50	0					
Howarth, J. S.	13	7	3	0	0*	0.00	0	642	19	33.78	3/30	0
Howitt, G.	8	12	0	45	16	3.75	0	383	23	16.65	5/25	2
Howitt, R. H.	28	50	2	492	119	10.25	1	337	8	42.12	2/25	0
Howsin, E. A.	2	4	0	37	24	9.25	0					
Huskinson, G. N. B.	2	2	0	33	33	16.50	0					
Illingworth, N. J. B.	15	20	5	207	49	13.80	0	694	16	43.37	5/89	1
Iremonger, A.	14	19	3	261	60*	16.31	0	296	10	29.60	5/83	1
Iremonger, J.	315	507	60	16110	272	36.04	31	13350	596	22.39	8/21	34
Jackson, J.	33	52	5	719	100	15.29	1	1932	136(5)	14.20	9/49	10
Jackson, W.	2	4	2	4	2*	2.00	0	5	0			
James, C. C.	20	34	3	355	43	11.45	0					
Jarvis, G.	6	12	0	119	24	9.91	0	16	0			

Name	M	Inns	NO	Runs	HS	Avge	100s	Runs	Wkts	Avge	BB	5wI
Jepson, A.	390	531	88	6351	130	14.33	1	30510	1050	29.05	8/45	40
Johnson, A. A.	26	35	4	273	45	8.80	0	1582	49	32.28	4/13	0
Johnson, I.	2	4	2	6	4	3.00	0					
Johnson, P.	191	315	33	10095	165*	35.79	20	480	5	96.00	1/9	0
Johnson, P. D.	58	97	7	2306	106*	25.62	2	281	2	140.50	1/14	0
Jones, A. O.	397	648	35	20244	296	33.02	30	9449	294	32.13	8/71	7
Jones, D.	23	38	5	594	60	18.00	0	7	1	7.00	1/7	0
Keeton, W. W.	382	633	42	23744	312*	40.17	54	103	2	51.50	2/16	0
Kelly, J.	51	72	11	1303	113	21.36	1	1844	38	48.52	4/25	0
Kelsall, R. S.	1	1	1	8	8*	–	0	6	1	6.00	1/6	0
Kesteven, J.	3	4	0	24	12	6.00	0					
Kirk, L.	14	22	2	358	86	17.90	0	1	0			
Kirk, W.	1	1	0	4	4	4.00	0					
Knowles, J.	125	188	18	4194	114	24.67	2	1441	34	42.38	3/55	0
Laing, D. R.	1	1	0	2	2	2.00	0	21	0			
Lane, G.	3	6	3	28	19*	9.33	0	87	6	14.50	4/32	0
Larwood, H.	300	372	66	6137	102*	20.05	3	20253	1247	16.24	9/41	88
Latchman, A. H.	40	53	13	651	78	16.27	0	2339	81	28.87	7/65	4
Lee, G. M.	140	229	21	4976	200*	23.92	6	2629	73	36.01	6/68	1
Lilley, B.	369	507	79	10473	124	24.46	7	27	0			
Lindley, T.	4	6	0	64	40	10.66	0	11	1	11.00	1/11	0
Lindo, C. V.	1	2	0	42	24	21.00	0	74	0			
Lockwood, W.(H)	5	6	1	36	16*	5.14	0	279	6	46.50	4/69	0
Longdon, A.	2	4	1	28	20*	9.33	0					
Lowe, S.	1	2	0	8	8	4.00	0	19	0			
Lowe, T.	1	1	1	0	0*	–	0	41	0			
Lowe, W. G. H.	1	2	1	29	15*	29.00	0					
McDougall, A. W.	1	2	0	3	3	1.50	0					
McIntyre, Martin	45	73	3	1145	88*	16.35	0	1663	123	13.52	9/33	8
McIntyre, Michael	1	1	1	0	0*	–	0	6	0			
McIntyre, W.	14	23	3	405	99	20.25	0	825	43	19.18	8/36	3
Mackintosh, K. S.	19	21	8	186	23*	14.30	0	957	23	41.60	4/49	0
Maltby, H.	1	2	0	7	4	3.50	0					
Marriott, W.	2	3	0	27	14	9.00	0	10	2	5.00	2/10	0
Marshall, B.	4	5	1	61	36	15.25	0	203	5	40.60	2/39	0
Marshall, E. A.	4	5	0	19	13	3.80	0	167	3	55.66	2/43	0
Marshall, W.	3	4	0	42	26	10.50	0					
Martin, E. J.	125	199	20	4086	133*	22.82	3					
Martin, G. N.	1	2	0	15	14	7.50	0					
Martindale, D. J. R.	55	85	10	1861	138	24.81	4	8	0			
Mason, P.	43	64	10	879	80	16.27	0	402	10	40.20	2/20	0
Matthews, C. S.	84	102	36	474	41	7.18	0	5397	147	36.71	6/65	4
Matthews, F. C.	82	94	24	500	34	7.14	0	5331	261	20.42	9/50	14
Maxwell, C. R. N.	16	23	2	516	79	24.57	0					
Meads, E. A.	205	240	90	1475	56*	9.83	0	5	0			
Mee, R. J.	37	58	17	323	35	7.87	0	2844	126	22.57	9/54	4
Mee, S. R.	1		did not bat					63	2	31.50	2/44	0
Mike, G. W.	5	7	2	116	56*	23.20	0	370	4	92.50	2/62	0
Miles, P. W. H.	3	6	0	65	23	10.83	0	16	1	16.00	1/11	0
Miller, K. R.	1	2	1	164	102*	164.00	1	35	2	17.50	2/35	0
Millman, G.	257	440	48	7410	131*	18.90	3	32	0			
Millns, D. J.	15	15	6	36	9	4.00	0	1082	27	40.07	4/86	0

Name	M	Inns	NO	Runs	HS	Avge	100s	Runs	Wkts	Avge	BB	5wI
Mills, E.	29	43	3	616	74	15.40	0	1024	54	18.96	7/79	3
Mills, J.	11	16	2	116	24	8.28	0					
Moore, F.	1	2	2	12	8*	–	0					
Moore, H. I.	176	297	29	6735	206*	25.13	7	144	5	28.80	2/37	0
Morgan, C.	1	2	0	13	13	6.50	0	94	0			
Morgan, M.	61	86	16	488	56*	6.97	0	5287	146	36.21	6/50	3
Morley, F.	113	159	32	696	31	5.48	0	8168	666	12.26	8/26	64
Morley, H.	1	1	0	0	0	0.00	0	29	2	14.50	1/9	0
Morley, T.	1	2	0	17	12	8.50	0	5	0			
Morris, C. R.	5	8	1	63	24*	9.00	0					
Moss, J.	1	2	0	2	1	1.00	0					
Murray, D. L.	97	148	24	3873	166*	31.23	4	39	1	39.00	1/2	0
Musters, W. M.	3	4	1	78	51	26.00	0		(1)			
Nanan, N.	32	58	5	846	72	15.98	0	257	7	36.71	3/12	0
Need, J. S.	2	4	2	22	15*	11.00	0					
Needham, F.	5	10	2	33	13	4.12	0	234	16	14.62	4/28	0
Newell, M.	100	175	24	4561	203*	30.20	6	282	7	40.28	2/38	0
Nixon, T.	7	13	2	31	9	2.81	0	121	7(2)	17.28	3/33	0
Notley, B.	1	1	0	0	0	0.00	0	90	1	90.00	1/90	0
Noyes, F.	7	13	1	137	47	11.41	0					
Oakden, R. P.	8	10	3	68	24	9.71	0	728	17	42.82	4/78	0
Oates, A. W.	7	7	2	21	12	4.20	0	465	8	58.12	2/38	0
Oates, T. W.	420	559	106	5884	88	12.98	0	20	0			
Oates, W. C.	4	6	0	77	39	12.83	0					
Oscroft, E.	9	8	3	8	7*	1.60	0	707	13	54.38	4/88	0
Oscroft, J.	5	8	0	90	28	11.25	0		(2)			
Oscroft, J. T.	14	25	0	221	51	8.84	0	151	3	50.33	1/6	0
Oscroft, P. W.	18	31	2	409	40	14.10	0	37	2	18.50	1/10	0
Oscroft, W.	167	281	14	5237	140	19.61	2	1127	59	19.10	5/34	2
Padley, W.	1	2	1	15	10	15.00	0					
Paling, G.	7	12	3	123	41*	13.66	0					
Parkin, J. M.	28	39	8	349	53	11.25	0					
Parr, B.	18	30	0	260	36	8.66	0					
Parr, G.	54	89	7	1805	130	22.01	1					
Parr, H. J.	3	6	1	55	13	11.00	0					
Parr, S.	17	30	2	411	40*	14.67	0	18	1	18.00	1/18	0
Patchitt, E.	2	4	0	17	9	4.25	0					
Payton, A. I.	1	2	0	16	15	8.00	0					
Payton, W. E. G.	1	2	0	29	19	14.50	0					
Payton, W. R.	489	766	126	22079	169	34.49	39	68	1	68.00	1/18	0
Pearson, J. G.	1	1	0	1	1	1.00	0	1	3	0.33	3/1	0
Pearson-Gregory, P. J. S.	3	2	0	119	71	59.50	0					
Pennington, J. H.	18	24	8	89	18	5.56	0	1345	41	32.80	7/223	3
Pepper, C.	7	12	3	162	40*	18.00	0	72	3	24.00	3/23	0
Pick, R. A.	119	114	32	1311	63	15.98	0	9845	293	33.60	7/128	8
Pike, A.	65	99	20	1127	66	14.26	0					
Plummer, P. J.	33	37	7	386	46	12.86	0	2016	63	32.00	7/71	2
Pollard, P. R.	62	110	4	3156	153	29.77	6	80	1	80.00	1/46	0
Pont, I. L.	4	7	1	32	16	5.33	0	302	3	100.66	2/107	0
Poole, C. J.	366	615	40	18685	222*	32.49	24	259	2	129.50	1/11	0
Poole, K. J.	26	44	5	612	58	15.69	0	1361	21	64.80	2/10	0
Porter, H. J.	2	3	1	16	16	8.00	0					

Name	M	Inns	NO	Runs	HS	Avge	100s	Runs	Wkts	Avge	BB	5wI
Power, G. E.	1	1	0	3	3	3.00	0					
Pratt, D.	7	6	1	14	7	2.80	0	374	4	93.50	2/52	0
Price, A.	3	4	0	39	34	9.75	0					
Price, W.	5	8	1	165	57	23.57	0	26	0			
Pullan, D. A.	95	106	36	613	34	8.75	0					
Randall, D. W.	369	630	64	21907	237	38.70	39	368	12	30.66	3/15	0
Reddick, T. B.	50	80	10	2225	139	31.78	2	409	5	81.80	1/7	0
Reddish, J.	1	1	1	2	2★	–	0	125	0			
Redgate, O.	8	13	1	134	37	11.16	0	42	4	10.50	3/8	0
Redgate, S.	17	30	2	195	27	6.96	0	481	36(9)	13.36	5/36	2
Redgate, T. B.	2	4	1	2	1★	0.66	0					
Reynolds, H. S.	13	19	3	213	70★	13.31	0	16	0			
Rhodes, S. D.	19	23	3	452	70	22.60	0	57	0			
Rhodes, W. E.	36	66	6	1207	132	20.11	1	0	0			
Rice, C. E. B.	283	450	65	17053	246	44.29	37	11227	476	23.58	6/16	12
Richardson, A.	28	31	16	73	7★	4.86	0	1819	40	45.47	4/24	0
Richardson, H.	53	71	11	544	54★	9.06	0	1921	139	13.82	7/42	7
Richardson, S. H.	1	1	0	4	4	4.00	0					
Richmond, T. L.	245	268	112	1532	70	9.82	0	24184	1148	21.06	9/55	87
Riley, J.	2	1	0	3	3	3.00	0	49	0			
Riley, W.	80	110	24	740	48	8.60	0	5497	235	23.39	7/80	10
Robinson, G. L.	5	9	2	58	17	8.28	0	24	1	24.00	1/14	0
Robinson, G. W.	21	20	7	39	10	3.00	0	1196	46	26.00	4/54	0
Robinson, H.	1	2	0	0	0	0.00	0					
Robinson, J. S.	35	51	4	596	72	12.68	0					
Robinson, R. T.	242	423	58	15530	220★	42.54	34	235	3	78.33	1/22	0
Rothera, G.	4	8	2	23	8★	3.83	0					
Rowe, E. J.	103	122	68	295	16	5.46	0					
Royle, G. M.	3	5	0	52	45	10.40	0					
Saxelby, K.	136	137	42	1112	59★	11.70	0	9705	300	32.35	6/49	6
Saxelby, M.	16	27	6	520	73	24.76	0	743	9	82.55	3/41	0
Scott, C. W.	63	72	18	1263	78	23.38	0	10	0			
Scotton, W. H.	153	233	25	4144	110★	19.92	2	168	4	42.00	1/16	0
Seaton, J.	4	7	0	80	27	11.42	0	12	1	12.00	1/12	0
Seddon, R.	1	2	0	5	5	2.50	0					
Selby, J.	164	251	20	4287	128★	18.55	4	154	5	30.80	2/27	0
Selby, W. W.	1	1	0	28	28	28.00	0	23	0			
Shacklock, F. J.	117	164	18	1847	71	12.65	0	6747	360	18.74	8/32	27
Sharpe, J. W.	5	9	3	41	23★	6.83	0	284	10	28.40	2/22	0
Sharpe, S.	2	3	0	29	13	9.66	0					
Shaw, A.	193	269	53	3269	88	15.13	0	10342	899	11.50	8/25	82
Shaw, J. C.	69	101	38	244	11	3.87	0	5288	422	12.53	9/86	41
Shaw, W.	1	1	0	1	1	1.00	0					
Sherwin, M.	206	276	89	1444	35	7.72	0	42	5	8.40	2/7	0
Shipston, F. W.	49	72	8	1183	118★	18.48	2					
Shooter, T.	2	4	1	23	15★	7.66	0	57	0			
Shore, C.	10	16	7	70	24	7.77	0	724	31	23.35	5/36	2
Shrewsbury, A.	357	574	59	19409	267	37.68	44					
Shrewsbury, A. jun.	3	5	3	63	31★	31.50	0	31	0			
Shrewsbury, W.	9	13	2	77	34	7.00	0					
Siddons, A.	5	8	3	36	8	7.20	0	266	8	33.25	4/37	0
Sime, W. A.	91	131	14	2328	176★	19.89	1	2092	44	47.54	4/51	0

Name	M	Inns	NO	Runs	HS	Avge	100s	Runs	Wkts	Avge	BB	5wI
Simpson, B. B. (Gregory)	5	8	3	9	4*	1.80	0	321	9	35.66	4/48	0
Simpson, R. T.	366	630	42	23088	243*	37.26	48	2073	50	41.46	3/22	0
Simpson, T.	5	8	1	38	14	5.42	0	85	2	42.50	1/28	0
Smales, K.	148	210	52	2347	64	14.85	0	11179	367	30.46	10/66	18
Smedley, M. J.	357	599	74	16414	149	31.26	28	4	0			
Smith, A. P.	2	3	0	35	26	11.66	0					
Smith, J. (Gotham)	3	5	0	36	19	7.20	0					
Smith, J. (Ruddington)	2	4	0	30	27	7.50	0	21	1	21.00	1/21	0
Smithurst, I.	1	2	0	1	1	0.50	0	48	0			
Snaith, J. C.	1	1	0	21	21	21.00	0					
Sobers, G. St A.	107	174	30	7041	160	48.89	18	7202	281	25.62	7/69	9
Somani, A.	1	1	1	26	26*	–	0	7	2	3.50	2/7	0
Speak, W. J.	3	6	0	39	19	6.50	0	54	0			
Springall, J. D.	119	222	24	5097	107*	25.74	2	3287	80	41.08	6/43	2
Stanhope, Lord	2	4	0	30	14	7.50	0					
Staples, A.	353	505	57	12457	153*	27.80	12	18726	632	29.63	7/20	14
Staples, S. J.	368	457	91	6248	110	17.07	1	28874	1268	22.77	9/141	68
Stapleton, J.	10	15	2	152	21	11.69	0					
Staunton, H.	16	24	0	456	78	19.00	0	48	0			
Stead, B.	215	230	73	1938	58	12.34	0	16933	604	28.08	8/44	21
Stephenson, F. D.	82	127	17	2845	121	25.86	3	8124	349	23.27	8/47	23
Stinchcombe, F. W.	6	8	2	87	48	14.50	0	539	4	134.75	1/42	0
Stocks, F. W.	283	429	45	11378	171	29.63	13	9794	223	43.91	6/37	6
Story, W. F.	6	9	1	36	16	4.50	0					
Such, P. M.	52	50	17	72	16	2.18	0	4031	138	29.21	6/123	6
Sulley, J.	2	4	1	21	11	7.00	0	160	8	20.00	4/66	0
Summers, G.	18	33	1	579	57	18.09	0					
Sutton, C. A. L.	1	1	0	1	1	1.00	0	26	0			
Swetman, R.	56	90	16	1475	115	19.93	1	13	0			
Taylor, B.	31	41	11	379	54*	12.63	0	2790	85	32.82	6/109	3
Taylor, J.	1	2	0	2	2	1.00	0					
Taylor, P. A.	6	10	5	34	13	6.80	0	335	7	47.85	2/82	0
Taylor, M. N. S.	230	320	77	4385	105	18.04	1	14558	522	27.88	7/106	12
Taylor, R. A.	23	35	2	599	107	18.15	1	1	0			
Taylor, W.	95	97	39	374	26*	6.44	0	6291	211	29.81	6/42	6
Tinley, F. E.	12	20	5	126	22	8.40	0	356	35(2)	10.17	6/29	2
Tinley, R. C.	54	88	13	920	43	12.26	0	1902	127(11)	14.97	8/12	11
Tinley, V.	1	1	0	9	9	9.00	0					
Todd, P. A.	156	276	16	7168	178	27.56	8	3	0			
Tolley, R.	29	45	3	546	54	13.00	0	85	0			
Truswell, J. R.	2	4	0	18	9	4.50	0	51	6	8.50	5/45	1
Tunnicliffe, H. T.	65	110	27	2116	100*	25.49	1	1601	42	38.11	4/30	0
Turland, H.	1	2	0	29	29	14.50	0	14	0			
Turner, J.	2	3	0	30	26	10.00	0	72	1	72.00	1/11	0
Turner, N. V. C.	23	36	2	541	73*	15.91	0					
Turner, R. H. T.	26	48	6	755	84	17.97	0					
Tye, J.	17	27	7	175	48	8.75	0	941	43	21.88	5/41	2
Underwood, A. J.	14	12	2	98	39	9.80	0	789	8	98.63	2/72	0
Underwood, W.	1	1	0	10	10	10.00	0					
Vaulkhard, P.	9	13	1	169	40*	14.08	0	30	1	30.00	1/30	0
Voce, W.	345	418	96	6398	129	19.86	4	29207	1312	22.26	8/30	73

Name	M	Inns	NO	Runs	HS	Avge	100s	Runs	Wkts	Avge	BB	5wI
Vowles, R. C.	16	28	3	292	54	11.68	0	920	23	40.00	4/106	0
Walker, A. K.	49	73	15	1155	73	19.91	0	3049	93	32.78	7/56	3
Walker, G. A.	2	4	3	24	10*	24.00	0	176	1	176.00	1/98	0
Walker, W.	405	622	60	18242	165*	32.45	31	97	2	48.50	2/20	0
Walters, J. A.	5	9	8	64	21*	64.00	0	464	10	46.40	6/139	1
Warwick, J. B.	3	5	0	25	13	5.00	0					
Wass, G.	1	1	0	0	0	0.00	0	34	3	11.33	3/34	0
Wass, T. G.	308	388	97	2119	56	7.28	0	33619	1653	20.33	9/67	158
Watkin, D.	9	12	4	47	14	5.87	0	748	15	49.86	6/48	1
Watson, W. K.	22	24	11	234	44	18.00	0	1623	58	27.98	6/51	3
Watts, P. D.	23	35	9	436	50*	16.76	0	1466	30	48.86	4/39	0
Weightman, N. I.	4	6	0	175	105	29.16	1	4	0			
Wells, B. D.	151	217	59	1281	55	8.10	0	12052	429	28.09	7/34	17
Wharmby, G. E.	4	7	0	7	6	1.00	0	89	1	89.00	1/39	0
Wheat, A. B.	91	115	31	1127	52*	13.41	0					
Wheeler, J.	2	3	0	15	8	5.00	0					
Wheelhouse, A.	1	2	1	2	2	2.00	0	95	4	23.75	2/40	0
White, J. W.	3	6	1	43	14	8.60	0					
White, R. A.	298	448	80	8259	116*	22.44	3	21102	693	30.45	7/41	28
Whittingham, N. B.	77	141	7	2964	133	22.11	2	122	1	122.00	1/9	0
Whysall, W. W.	346	560	42	20376	248	39.33	50	191	6	31.83	3/49	0
Widdowson, S. W.	1	2	0	15	11	7.50	0					
Wilkinson, A.	19	35	5	293	62	9.76	0	926	33	28.06	5/56	1
Wilkinson, P. A.	92	117	38	949	77	12.01	0	6335	175	36.20	6/81	2
Wilkinson, W.	5	7	2	34	16*	6.80	0	133	5	26.60	3/41	0
Willatt, G. L.	22	38	4	844	131	24.82	2	9	0			
Williams, P.	2	3	0	17	14	5.66	0					
Williams, W.	9	16	1	111	31	7.40	0	8	0			
Wilson, H.	6	7	3	49	19	12.25	0	318	4	79.50	1/21	0
Winfield, H. M.	172	311	16	6799	134	23.04	7	5	0			
Winrow, F. H.	113	180	20	4769	204*	29.80	6	4009	95	42.20	6/56	3
Winrow, R.	5	6	1	173	137	34.60	1	76	1	76.00	1/27	0
Wood, M.	4	5	2	5	4	1.66	0	231	4	57.75	2/68	0
Woodhead, F. G.	141	174	44	1100	52*	8.46	0	10550	320	32.96	7/24	11
Woodward, W.	2	3	1	4	4	2.00	0					
Wootton, G.	52	82	16	701	60*	10.62	0	2832	180	15.73	7/33	11
Wright, C. W.	117	197	5	2565	99	13.35	0					
Wright, M. W.	1	2	0	6	6	3.00	0	7	0			
Wright, T.	9	15	0	138	25	9.20	0					
Wright, W.	72	100	24	979	127*	12.88	1	3422	193	17.73	8/53	8
Wyld, F. (Wild)	109	177	13	2726	104	16.62	1	93	7	13.29	4/33	0
Yates, W. G.	6	8	1	69	19	9.85	0	54	1	54.00	1/43	0

Notes:

1. The above figures include only Nottinghamshire matches listed as first-class in the Guides to First-Class Cricket published by the Association of Cricket Statisticians.

2. Wickets noted in parentheses were taken in matches where no bowling analyses can be found. These matches are: *v* Sussex (Brighton) 1835, (Brighton) 1837, (Brighton) 1840, (Trent Bridge) 1840, (Trent Bridge) 2nd inns 1843, (Brighton) 1848; *v* Kent (Town Malling) 1840, (Trent Bridge) 1841, (Canterbury) 1845; *v* England (Trent Bridge) 1842, (Trent Bridge) 1847, (Newark) 1856; *v* MCC (Lord's) 1843.

RESULTS OF ALL INTER-COUNTY FIRST-CLASS MATCHES 1835–1991

Year	CM	DY	EX	GM	GS	HT	KT	LA	LE	MX	NR	SM	SY	SX	WA	WO	YO	P	W	L	D	T
1835														WW				2	2	0	0	0
1837							-L							LL				3	0	3	0	0
1840							-W							LL				3	1	2	0	0
1841							L-											1	0	1	0	0
1843					WW									W				3	3	0	0	0
1845							WL											2	1	1	0	0
1848														DL				2	0	1	1	0
1851													-L					1	0	1	0	0
1852													WW					2	2	0	0	0
1853													-W	LW				3	2	1	0	0
1854													LL					2	0	2	0	0
1858													-L					1	0	1	0	0
1859													-W					1	1	0	0	0
1860													LW					2	1	1	0	0
1861													LL					2	0	2	0	0
1862	WW												WD					4	3	0	1	0
1863						DW											WL	4	2	1	1	0
1864	-L					WW											LW	7	3	4	0	0
1865	-W												WL	WW			WW	7	6	1	0	0
1866	DW							LD									WD	6	2	1	3	0
1867	LW							WW										4	3	1	0	0
1868							WW						WL				LW	6	4	2	0	0
1869							WW						WW				WL	6	5	1	0	0
1870							WW						LW				LD	6	3	2	1	0
1871					WD								WW				WL	6	4	1	1	0
1872					DD								DD				WWD	7	2	0	5	0
1873													WW	WW			WDL	7	5	1	1	0
1874								WW					WW	WL			LL	8	5	3	0	0
1875	WW				WD			WD					DW				LW	10	6	1	3	0
1876					LL		LW	DD					WW				DW	10	4	3	3	0
1877					LL		LW	WL		DW			WL				WD	12	5	5	2	0
1878	WW				DL		DW	WL		DD			WW				WL	14	7	3	4	0
1879	WW				DW		WW	DD		DD							DL	12	5	1	6	0
1880					DD		WW	WW					DW				WL	10	6	1	3	0
1881					DW			DL		DL			WL	WW			LD	12	4	4	4	
1882					WD			WD		DW			WW	WW			WL	12	8	1	3	
1883					WD			LD		DD			WD	WD			WD	12	4	1	7	
1884					WW					WW			WD	WW			WW	10	9	0	1	0
1885	DW				WW					DW			DD	WW			LD	12	6	1	5	0
1886					DD		WD	WD		DW			DW	WW			WD	14	7	0	7	0
1887					WW		WW	WL		DW			LL	WW			DD	14	8	3	3	0
1888					LW		LD	DD		DL			LL	WW			DL	14	3	6	5	0
1889					WW		WD			DW			WL	WW			DW	12	8	1	3	0
1890					LL		DD	DL		WL			WL	WW			DW	14	5	5	4	0
1891					LD		DD	WD		DL			LL	WW			WW	14	5	4	5	0
1892					WD		DW	WL		WW		WL	WW	WW			DD	16	10	2	4	0
1893					WW		DD	LW		LL		WL	LL	WD			LD	16	5	7	4	0
1894					WL		DW	WL		DL	WD	LL	DL	LD			LL	18	4	9	5	0
1895	DD				LL		DL	LL	WL	LL			LD	WW			DL	18	4	9	5	0
1896	WD				WL		DW	LD		DL			LL	WD			DW	16	5	5	6	0
1897	DD				LL		DD	DL		LD			DL	WW			DD	16	2	5	9	0
1898	DD				DD		WD	DL		LD			DD	DD			DD	16	1	2	13	0
1899	WD				DD		LD	DL		LW			DD	DD			LD	16	2	4	10	0
1900	WW		DW				WD	LL	WW	LW			LD	DD			DD	18	7	4	7	0
1901	WD	WD	DD				aD	DL	WL	DL			WW	LD			LL	19	5	6	8	0
1902	WW	DD	WD				DD	DW	DW	LD			DD	LW			DL	20	6	3	11	0
1903	WL	DW	WD				WW	DL	DD	DD			DW	DD			LL	20	6	4	10	0
1904	DW	DD	LW				DW	DD	DD	LW			WW	WL			LD	20	7	4	9	0

Year	CM	DY	EX	GM	GS	HT	KT	LA	LE	MX	NR	SM	SY	SX	WA	WO	YO	P	W	L	D	T
1905	WW	DW				DL	LW	DL	DD	DW			WL	LD			LL	20	6	7	7	0
1906	WW	DL	WD				DL	WW	WW	DW			LD	DL			DW	20	9	4	7	0
1907	WW	DW	WW				DW	WW	WW	WW			WD	WW			Da	19	15	0	4	0
1908	DL	WW	LW				LL	WD	LL	WD			DD	DW			DL	20	6	7	7	0
1909	Wa	DD	WW				WL	WL	DL	LL			WL	DL			DL	19	6	8	5	0
1910	DD	WW	DW				WL	WW	WD	DL			WL	WL			DD	20	9	4	7	0
1911	DW	DL	WW				DL	DW	WW	DW			WL	WD			LL	20	9	5	6	0
1912	WD		La				DL	DD	WW	DL			WD	WD			LL	17	5	5	7	0
1913	WL					WL	DD	WD	DW	WW	DL		WL	WD			DL	20	8	5	7	0
1914	WL					DW	DD	LW	DD	DW	LL		DD	WD			DL	20	5	5	10	0
1919	DW							DL	DW	DD			DD	WW			DW	14	5	1	8	0
1920	Wa					WW	DD	LL	WL	WL	WW		LW	WW			DL	19	10	6	3	0
1921	WL	DD				DW	LW	WD	WW	LL	DW		WD	WL	WL		LL	24	10	8	6	0
1922	WW	DW	WW			WD	DL	WL	WW	WL	WD		LD	WW	WD	WW	LW	28	17	5	6	0
1923	DD	WD	WW			WL	WW	WL	WW	DD	WW		WD	DL			DW	26	15	3	8	0
1924	WD	DD	WD			WL	WW	DD	WD	LD	DW		DD	DD	Wa	WD	DL	27	9	3	15	0
1925	WD			WW	WW	DD	LW	DD	WW	LW	WW		DD	WW		WW	DL	26	15	3	8	0
1926	DW	DW	WL	DW	DW	LL	LL	WW	WL	WW			DL	DW	WD	DW	Da	29	13	7	9	0
1927	DW	DW	WL	DW	DD	LL	DD	DW	DW	WD			WD	WW	WD	DW	DD	30	12	3	15	0
1928	DD	DD	WW	WD	DD	WW	DD	DW	DL	WW	WW		LD	LW	WD	DW	DD	32	13	3	16	0
1929	DD	WW	WW	WW		WD	DW	DD	WL	WW	WD	WD	DD	WW	WD		DL	30	16	2	12	0
1930	DD		WW			DL	WD	DD	WW	DD	WD	DD	WD	DD	DD	WW	DD	28	9	1	18	0
1931	DD	WD	WD	DL	WD	WL	DD	DD	DW	DD	WW	DW	DL	DD	WW		LD	32	10	4	18	0
1932	WL	WD	WD	WD	WW	WD	WL	WD	DW	WL	DD	DD				WW	DL	28	13	4	11	0
1933	WW				DD	DD	WD	DL	DD	DD	DW	WD	WD	DD	WL	DD	DL	28	7	3	18	0
1934	LL	DW				WL	WD	WL	LD	LW	WD	DD	LD	DD	WW	DD	DD	28	8	7	13	0
1935	WL	DD	WD	DD	WW	WL	WW	DD	WW	DD	DD	WL	DL				DD	28	10	3	15	0
1936	DW	WL	DD	WL	DW	DW	DW	DD	DL	DD			DW	DD	WD		DD	28	8	3	17	0
1937	DL	DL	DD	DL		DW	LD	WD	DW	DD	DW	WD	DD			DW	DD	28	6	4	18	0
1938	LL	LL	Da	DW	WW	DD	DD	LL	WW	LL	LD	LW				WD	DD	27	7	10	10	0
1939	DL	WL	DL	L-		WD	LW	LD	DD	LW			DW	WD	DD	DL	DD	27	6	8	13	0
1946	DD	-D	-D	LD	-W	WL	DL	L-	LD	W-	DD	DL	D-	WW	WL		DL	26	6	8	12	0
1947	DL	D-	D-	DL	D-	WD	DL	-L	LL	-W	DD	DW	-W	WD	DD		DW	26	6	6	14	0
1948	WL	DD	DL	-L	LW	-D	DL	DD	L-	DL	-L	WL	DW	W-	D-		DL	26	5	10	11	0
1949	DD	DL	DD	D-	WL	L-	DD	WL	-D	WL	D-	WD	WW	-D	-D		DL	26	6	5	15	0
1950	DW	DD	-D	-D	DD	DW	LL	DD	D-	DD	DL	LL	DD	DW	D-		LD	28	3	6	19	0
1951	DL	DD	D-	D-	WL	DD	DD	DD	-L	DD	LD	LD	DL	LL	-L		LL	28	1	11	16	0
1952	DL	D-	DL	DW	DL	-L	WL	-D	DD	LD	DD	LL	D-	WL	DD		LL	28	3	11	14	0
1953	WL	-W	LD	WD	WL	D-	LL	W-	DL	DD	WW	DL	-L	DL	WL		WD	28	9	10	9	0
1954	DD	WD	L-	-L	DW	WL	DD	WD	-L	WD	WL	DW	WD	W-			WD	28	10	6	12	0
1955	LD	LW	-D	L-	DW	WD	WW	WL	W-	DL	WW	LL	DL	WL	-L		DL	28	10	11	7	0
1956	WD	D-	DW	DL	DD	-D	DD	-W	LD	DD	WL	WD	D-	WD	WD		LD	28	7	4	17	0
1957	DD	-D	LL	LW	DL	L-	DD	-W	WL	DL	DL	DL	-L	WD	WD		DD	28	5	13	10	0
1958	LL	LD	L-	-D	WL	LD	DD	LW	-L	WL	LL	LL	LL	DD	D-		Da	27	3	15	9	0
1959	LL	LL	-D	D-	LW	LL	WL	WD	L-	DL	DL	DD	WL	-D			DL	28	4	14	10	0
1960	LL	L-	DW	-D	LD	L-	LW	DD	-L	DW	LW	LL	LL	DD	LL		LL	28	4	16	8	0
1961	DLD	-L	LL	L-	LL	-L	LL	DL	L-	WL	LW	WL	LL	WL	LL		LD	29	4	20	5	0
1962	DD	D-	DW	LL	LD	L-	WW	DD	-D	DW	DL	LD	LL	LL	LL		LD	28	4	12	12	0
1963	WD	L-	DL	LL	DD	-D	WW	-D	DL	DL	DD	WD	L-	LD	WW		DD	28	6	8	14	0
1964	DL	-D	LD	WW	DD	L-	WD	W-	LD	DL	LD	-L	DL	LL			LL	28	4	13	11	0
1965	LL	WD	L-	-D	LD	DL	DL	DL	-L	LL	DD	WD	DL	D-			LD	28	3	11	14	0
1966	LL	DL	-D	W-	DW	DD	DL	DL	D-	LW	LD	DD	DL	LD	-D		DL	28	3	11	14	0
1967	DD	-D	DL	DD	DD	D-	DL	D-	DD	DD	DD	-D	DL	DD			DL	28	0	4	24	0
1968	WW	D-	aW	WD	LD	-W	DW	-D	DL	DD	DW	DD	L-	DD	DD		DD	27	7	3	17	0
1969	DD	-L	D-	-D	DW	D-	DD	DD	-W	DD	-D	DD	D-	LL	-L		DW	24	6	2	16	0
1970	DW	D-	-W	W-	DD	-D	DD	DL	L-	DD	D-	LL	-L	WL	-L		DD	24	4	8	12	0
1971	DD	-D	DD	LL	D-	DD	DL	WD	WD	-L	-D	L-	D-	WL	D-		-L	24	3	7	14	0
1972	DD	D-	-D	-W	D-	D-	DD	LD	-D	-L	D-	-L	-D	LL	L-		D-	20	1	6	13	0
1973	DD	-L	L-	D-	-L	-L	WL	LD	D-	L-	-D	D-	-D	DL	-L		-D	20	1	8	11	0
1974	DD	L-	-D	-D	L-	W-	DL	DL	-D	L-	-D	-L	DL	L-	-L		L-	20	1	9	10	0
1975	DL	-D	D-	W-	-L	L-	DL	LL	D-	W-	-D	D-	W-	DL	-L		-L	20	3	9	8	0
1976	DD	D-	-W	-W	D-	D-	DL	LD	-L	-D	L-	-L	-W	D-	L-		WL	20	4	7	9	0
1977	DL	-L	D-	D-	-L	-L	LD	LD	LL	D-	-D	D-	L-	-D	LW		LD	22	1	11	10	0
1978	WL	L-	-D	-D	D-	D-	DD	DL	LL	-D	D-	-D	DL	L-	-D		WL	22	3	7	12	0
1979	Da	-L	W-	W-	-W	-L	DD	DL	Da	W-	-D	D-	D-	-W	LD		Wa	19	6	4	9	0
1980	WD	D-	-W	-D	W-	W-	DL	WD	DL	-D	D-	-W	-D	D-	LD		LL	22	6	5	11	0

Year	CM	DY	EX	GM	GS	HT	KT	LA	LE	MX	NR	SM	SY	SX	WA	WO	YO	P	W	L	D	T
1981	Wa	-D	W-	W-	-L	-D	WD	WL	LD	W-	-L	W-	D-	-W	WW	WD	WD	21	11	4	6	0
1982		DD	L-	-D	-W	W-	W-	DW	WL	LL	-D	L-	-L	-W	D-	WD	La	21	7	7	7	0
1983		LL	LL	-D	-D	DL	L-	WD	DL	D-	LD	D-	LL	-W	D-	-W	DD	24	3	10	11	0
1984		LD	-W	W-	W-	-W	-D	WW	DD	-W	W-	DL	W-	WD	WD	WD	DL	24	12	3	9	0
1985		WD	D-	LD	DD	D-	DW	DD	DD	LW	-D	-W	-D	D-	-D	D-	DD	24	4	2	18	0
1986		DD	DD	-W	-D	LD	W-	WD	WL	W-	DD	D-	WD	-D	D-	-D	WD	24	7	2	15	0
1987		DW	-D	W-	D-	-D	-W	DD	WD	-a	W-	WD	D-	WD	WD	DL	WD	23	9	1	13	0
1988		WD	-W	W-	L-	-D	-L	LW	DD	WL	W-	-D	L-	W-	-L	WL	LD	22	8	8	6	0
1989		WL	W-	-D	-W	D-	L-	LD	DL	DD	-L	W-	-D	-W	D-	LD	DW	22	6	6	10	0
1990		DD	-L	L-	D-	-L	-D	LL	DW	DL	W-	-D	D-	D-	-W	DL	LW	22	4	8	10	0
1991		LD	L-	-W	-D	D-	D-	WW	WD	LW	-W	D-	-D	-D	D-	WL	LD	22	7	5	10	0

Notes: CM = Cambridgeshire; T = Tied; a = abandoned without a ball being bowled (not included in results summary).

RESULTS OF ALL SUNDAY LEAGUE MATCHES 1969–1991

Year	DY	EX	GM	GS	HT	KT	LA	LE	MX	NR	SM	SY	SX	WA	WO	YK	P	W	L	T	NR
1969	W	L	L	W	L	T	L	L	NR	W	L	W	W	L	L	L	16	5	9	1	1
1970	L	L	L	W	W	L	L	W	L	W	W	L	W	L	L	W	16	7	9	0	0
1971	L	L	L	NR	L	W	W	L	L	L	W	L	L	W	W	W	16	6	9	0	1
1972	L	L	W	L	L	W	L	L	W	L	W	L	W	W	L	L	16	6	10	0	0
1973	L	NR	W	L	L	L	L	L	L	W	NR	W	W	L	W	L	16	5	9	0	2
1974	L	L	L	L	L	L	W	L	L	L	L	W	L	W	L	L	16	3	13	0	0
1975	W	L	W	L	L	L	L	W	W	L	W	L	W	W	W	L	16	9	7	0	0
1976	W	L	W	W	W	W	W	L	L	W	L	W	L	L	W	L	16	9	7	0	0
1977	W	L	L	L	W	L	L	L	W	W	L	W	L	W	L	NR	16	6	9	0	1
1978	W	NR	W	NR	L	NR	L	L	L	L	W	NR	NR	W	L	L	16	4	7	0	5
1979	L	NR	L	W	W	NR	NR	W	NR	L	L	W	L	W	W	L	16	6	6	0	4
1980	W	W	L	L	W	L	W	L	L	L	L	W	L	W	L	L	16	6	10	0	0
1981	NR	W	W	W	L	L	L	L	L	NR	L	L	W	L	W	W	16	6	8	0	2
1982	W	W	W	W	L	W	L	W	NR	W	L	L	L	W	L	T	16	8	6	1	1
1983	L	L	L	NR	L	L	L	L	W	W	L	NR	W	L	T	W	16	4	9	1	2
1984	NR	W	L	L	W	W	W	W	W	L	W	W	W	L	L	W	16	10	5	0	1
1985	L	L	W	L	L	L	L	NR	W	NR	L	W	W	L	W	W	16	6	8	0	2
1986	W	L	NR	W	W	L	W	W	W	W	W	W	L	L	W	L	16	10	5	0	1
1987	L	NR	W	L	W	W	NR	W	NR	L	NR	W	W	W	W	L	16	9	3	0	4
1988	L	L	L	L	L	NR	L	NR	L	L	W	W	L	W	L	L	16	3	11	0	2
1989	W	W	W	W	L	W	L	W	W	L	L	L	W	L	NR	L	16	9	6	0	1
1990	W	W	W	NR	L	L	L	W	W	W	L	W	W	W	L	W	16	10	5	0	1
1991	W	W	W	W	W	W	W	W	L	L	W	W	W	W	L	W	16	13	3	0	0

Notes: T = Tied; NR = No Result

338

RESULTS IN THE BENSON & HEDGES CUP COMPETITION 1972–1991

1972   *Group Matches:* Won *v* Minor Counties (N), *v* Derbyshire, *v* Yorkshire; Lost *v* Lancashire

1973   *Group Matches:* Won *v* Derbyshire, *v* Lancashire, *v* Minor Counties (N); Lost *v* Yorkshire; *Q/Final:* Lost *v* Worcestershire

1974   *Group Matches:* Won *v* Minor Counties (N); Lost *v* Derbyshire, *v* Lancashire, *v* Yorkshire

1975   *Group Matches:* Won *v* Minor Counties (N); Lost *v* Derbyshire, *v* Lancashire, *v* Yorkshire

1976   *Group Matches:* Won *v* Minor Counties (E), *v* Essex, *v* Middlesex, *v* Northants; *Q/Final:* Lost *v* Kent

1977   *Group Matches:* Won *v* Surrey, *v* Universities; Lost *v* Sussex, *v* Kent

1978   *Group Matches:* Won *v* Kent, *v* Yorkshire; Lost *v* Essex; Drawn *v* Surrey; *Q/Final:* Lost *v* Kent

1979   *Group Matches:* Won *v* Minor Counties (N), *v* Kent; Lost *v* Middlesex; Drawn *v* Yorkshire

1980   *Group Matches:* Won *v* Derbyshire, *v* Leicestershire, *v* Scotland; Lost *v* Lancashire; *Q/Final:* Lost *v* Northants

1981   *Group Matches:* Won *v* Northants, *v* Worcestershire, *v* Gloucestershire, *v* Leicestershire; *Q/Final:* Lost *v* Surrey

1982   *Group Matches:* Won *v* Northants, *v* Warwickshire, *v* Scotland, *v* Lancashire; *Q/Final:* Won *v* Leicestershire; *S/Final:* Won *v* Lancashire; *Final:* Lost *v* Somerset

1983   *Group Matches:* Won *v* Yorkshire, *v* Derbyshire; Lost *v* Lancashire; Drawn *v* Warwickshire

1984   *Group Matches:* Won *v* Worcestershire, *v* Derbyshire, *v* Minor Counties; Lost *v* Lancashire; *Q/Final:* Won *v* Surrey; *S/Final:* Lost *v* Lancashire

1985   *Group Matches:* Won *v* Scotland, *v* Derbyshire; Lost *v* Gloucestershire; Drawn *v* Northants

1986   *Group Matches:* Won *v* Yorkshire, *v* Scotland, *v* Lancashire; Lost *v* Worcestershire; *Q/Final:* Won *v* Essex; *S/Final:* Lost *v* Middlesex

1987   *Group Matches:* Won *v* Derbyshire, *v* Northants; Lost *v* Gloucestershire, *v* Leicestershire

1988   *Group Matches:* Won *v* Minor Counties, *v* Worcestershire; Lost *v* Northants; Drawn *v* Yorkshire; *Q/Final:* Lost *v* Glamorgan

1989   *Group Matches:* Won *v* Derbyshire, *v* Minor Counties, *v* Yorkshire; Lost *v* Somerset; *Q/Final:* Won *v* Gloucestershire; *S/Final:* Won *v* Kent; *Final:* Won *v* Essex

1990   *Group Matches:* Won *v* Leicestershire, *v* Scotland, *v* Northants; Lost *v* Essex; *Q/Final:* Won *v* Essex; *S/Final:* Lost *v* Worcestershire

1991   *Group Matches:* Won *v* Yorkshire, *v* Minor Counties; Lost *v* Hampshire, *v* Glamorgan

RESULTS OF ALL GILLETTE AND NATWEST TROPHY MATCHES
1963–1991

1963 Lost to Yorkshire
1964 Lost to Somerset
1965 Won *v* Wiltshire; Lost to Somerset
1966 Lost to Worcestershire
1967 Won *v* Durham; Lost to Northants
1968 Won *v* Lancashire, *v* Worcestershire; Lost to Gloucestershire
1969 Won *v* Middlesex, *v* Essex; Lost to Yorkshire
1970 Won *v* Warwickshire, *v* Leicestershire; Lost to Somerset
1971 Lost to Hampshire
1972 Lost to Hampshire
1973 Lost to Middlesex
1974 Won *v* Warwickshire; Lost to Worcestershire
1975 Won *v* Sussex, *v* Kent; Lost to Derbyshire
1976 Lost to Northants
1977 Lost to Hampshire
1978 Lost to Yorkshire
1979 Won *v* Warwickshire; Lost to Sussex
1980 Won *v* Durham; Lost to Middlesex
1981 Won *v* Kent; Lost to Derbyshire
1982 Won *v* Sussex; Lost to Gloucestershire
1983 Won *v* Worcestershire; Lost to Sussex
1984 Won *v* Glamorgan; Lost to Middlesex
1985 Won *v* Staffordshire, *v* Warwickshire, *v* Gloucestershire, *v* Worcestershire; Lost in final to Essex
1986 Won *v* Devon, *v* Kent; Lost to Surrey
1987 Won *v* Suffolk, *v* Middlesex, *v* Derbyshire, *v* Gloucestershire, in final *v* Northants
1988 Won *v* Devon; Lost to Worcestershire
1989 Won *v* Herts; Lost to Middlesex
1990 Won *v* Bucks; Lost to Northants
1991 Won *v* Lincolnshire, *v* Gloucestershire; Lost to Hampshire

TEAM RECORDS

(1) HIGHEST AND LOWEST SCORE FOR NOTTINGHAMSHIRE AGAINST EACH COUNTY IN FIRST-CLASS MATCHES

Opponents	Highest	Year	Lowest	Year
Derbyshire	661 at Derby	1901	53 at Derby	1983
Essex	662-8 dec at Trent Bridge	1947	58 at Southend	1931
Glamorgan	564-6 dec at Trent Bridge	1926	44 at Ebbw Vale	1963
Gloucestershire	607 at Bristol	1899	52 at Bristol	1896
Hampshire	511-8 dec at Trent Bridge	1930	42 at Southampton	1932
Kent	602 at Trent Bridge	1904	35 at Beckenham	1889
Lancashire	504-5 at Old Trafford	1949	35 at Trent Bridge	1895
Leicestershire	739-7 dec at Trent Bridge	1903	58 at Leicester	1974
			58 at Leicester	1986
Middlesex	596 at Trent Bridge	1887	40 at Lord's	1895
Northamptonshire	484 at Trent Bridge	1930	67 at Northampton	1974
			67 at Worksop	1975
Somerset	585-5 dec at Trent Bridge	1947	62 at Trent Bridge	1966
Surrey	548 at The Oval	1898	40 at The Oval	1955
Sussex	726 at Trent Bridge	1895	57 at Eastbourne	1962
Warwickshire	656-3 dec at Coventry	1928	34 at Nuneaton	1964
Worcestershire	540 at Worksop	1934	73 at Trent Bridge	1962
Yorkshire	492-5 dec at Bramall Lane	1949	13 at Trent Bridge	1901

(2) HIGHEST AND LOWEST SCORE AGAINST NOTTINGHAMSHIRE BY EACH COUNTY IN FIRST-CLASS MATCHES

Opponents	Highest	Year	Lowest	Year
Derbyshire	572-7 dec at Derby	1991	16 at Trent Bridge	1879
Essex	593-7 at Clacton	1951	44 at Trent Bridge	1910
Glamorgan	502 at Cardiff	1932	47 at Cardiff	1922
Gloucestershire	643-5 dec at Bristol	1946	44 at Gloucester	1909
Hampshire	507 at Southampton	1921	30 at Southampton	1932
Kent	507-6 at Trent Bridge	1953	36 at Town Malling	1878
Lancashire	627 at Trent Bridge	1905	37 at Liverpool	1907
Leicestershire	468-8 dec at Trent Bridge	1926	53 at Trent Bridge	1932
Middlesex	621-9 dec at Trent Bridge	1931	32 at Lord's	1882
Northants	521 at Northampton	1933	38 at Trent Bridge	1920
Somerset	459-4 dec at Trent Bridge	1986	62 at Bath	1931
			62 at Bath	1965
Surrey	706-4 dec at Trent Bridge	1947	16 at The Oval	1880
Sussex	562 at Trent Bridge	1959	19 at Hove	1873
Warwickshire	520 at Edgbaston	1930	49 at Edgbaston	1981
Worcestershire	486 at Dudley	1947	53 at Trent Bridge	1922
Yorkshire	562 at Bradford	1899	32 at Sheffield	1876

(3) HIGHEST SCORES IN LIMITED-OVERS COMPETITIONS

Competition	Score	Opponents and Venue	Year
For Nottinghamshire			
Sunday League	283-6	Yorkshire, Trent Bridge	1987
Benson & Hedges	296-6	Kent, Trent Bridge	1989
NatWest/Gillette	312-9	Buckinghamshire, Marlow	1990
Against Nottinghamshire			
Sunday League	306-2	Essex, Trent Bridge	1983
Benson & Hedges	288-5	Gloucestershire, Bristol	1985
NatWest/Gillette	296-8	Gloucestershire, Trent Bridge	1968

(4) LOWEST SCORES IN LIMITED-OVERS COMPETITIONS

Competition	Score	Opponents and Venue	Year
For Nottinghamshire			
Sunday League	66 (24.3 overs)	Yorkshire, Bradford	1969
Benson & Hedges	74 (32.4 overs)	Leicestershire, Leicester	1987
NatWest/Gillette	123 (50.5 overs)	Yorkshire, Scarborough	1969
Against Nottinghamshire			
Sunday League	43 (29.4 overs)	Northants, Northampton	1977
Benson & Hedges	67 (34.1 overs)	Minor Counties North, Newark	1975
NatWest/Gillette	82 (35.1 overs)	Gloucestershire, Bristol	1987

INDIVIDUAL BATTING RECORDS

(1) DOUBLE CENTURIES IN FIRST-CLASS MATCHES

Score	Player	Opponent	Venue	Year
312*	W. W. Keeton	Middlesex	The Oval	1939
296	A. O. Jones	Gloucestershire	Trent Bridge	1903
294	J. R. Gunn	Leicestershire	Trent Bridge	1903
274	A. O. Jones	Essex	Leyton	1905
273	W. Gunn	Derbyshire	Derby	1901
272	J. Iremonger	Kent	Trent Bridge	1904
268*	J. A. Dixon	Sussex	Trent Bridge	1897
267	A. Shrewsbury	Middlesex	Trent Bridge	1887
267	A. Shrewsbury	Sussex	Trent Bridge	1890
266	J. Hardstaff jun	Leicestershire	Leicester	1937
261	W. W. Keeton	Gloucestershire	Trent Bridge	1934
250	A. O. Jones	Gloucestershire	Bristol	1899
249	A. O. Jones	Sussex	Hove	1901
248	W. W. Whysall	Northamptonshire	Trent Bridge	1930
247	J. Hardstaff jun	Northamptonshire	Trent Bridge	1951
246	C. E. B. Rice	Sussex	Hove	1976
244	W. W. Whysall	Gloucestershire	Trent Bridge	1929
243	J. Hardstaff jun	Middlesex	Trent Bridge	1937
243*	R. T. Simpson	Worcestershire	Trent Bridge	1950
242	W. W. Keeton	Glamorgan	Trent Bridge	1932
239	J. Iremonger	Essex	Trent Bridge	1905
239*	C. B. Harris	Hampshire	Trent Bridge	1950
238	R. T. Simpson	Lancashire	Old Trafford	1949
237	D. W. Randall	Derbyshire	Trent Bridge	1988
236*	W. Gunn	Surrey	The Oval	1898
234	C. B. Harris	Middlesex	Trent Bridge	1933
230	W. Gunn	Derbyshire	Trent Bridge	1897
230*	R. T. Simpson	Glamorgan	Swansea	1950
227*	A. Shrewsbury	Gloucestershire	Moreton in Marsh	1886
227*	B. C. Broad	Kent	Tunbridge Wells	1990
224*	A. Shrewsbury	Middlesex	Lord's	1885
222*	C. J. Poole	Indians	Trent Bridge	1952
223	W. W. Keeton	Worcestershire	Worksop	1934
221*	J. Hardstaff jun	Warwickshire	Trent Bridge	1947
220	G. Gunn	Derbyshire	Trent Bridge	1923
220*	R. T. Robinson	Yorkshire	Trent Bridge	1990
219	W. Gunn	Sussex	Trent Bridge	1895
219	C. J. Poole	Derbyshire	Ilkeston	1952
216	R. T. Simpson	Sussex	Trent Bridge	1952
214*	J. Hardstaff jun	Somerset	Trent Bridge	1937
213*	J. Hardstaff sen	Sussex	Hove	1914
213*	C. E. B. Rice	Lancashire	Trent Bridge	1978
213	C. E. B. Rice	Glamorgan	Swansea	1978
212	A. Shrewsbury	Middlesex	Lord's	1892
212	R. T. Simpson	Essex	Clacton	1951
210	J. Iremonger	Kent	Trent Bridge	1903

210	W. W. Keeton	Yorkshire	Bramall Lane	1949
210*	R. J. Hadlee	Middlesex	Lord's	1984
209	A. Shrewsbury	Sussex	Hove	1884
209	W. W. Whysall	Essex	Leyton	1926
209	D. W. Randall	Middlesex	Trent Bridge	1979
208	W. W. Keeton	Glamorgan	Trent Bridge	1949
207	A. Shrewsbury	Surrey	The Oval	1882
207*	W. Gunn	Derbyshire	Derby	1896
207	R. T. Robinson	Warwickshire	Trent Bridge	1983
206	A. W. Carr	Leicestershire	Leicester	1925
206*	H. I. Moore	Indians	Trent Bridge	1967
205*	W. Gunn	Sussex	Trent Bridge	1887
204	A. W. Carr	Essex	Leyton	1921
204*	F. H. Winrow	Derbyshire	Trent Bridge	1947
204*	D. W. Randall	Somerset	Trent Bridge	1976
203*	M. Newell	Derbyshire	Derby	1987
202	J. Hardstaff jun	Worcestershire	Dudley	1947
202*	J. B. Bolus	Glamorgan	Trent Bridge	1963
201	R. T. Simpson	Warwickshire	Trent Bridge	1946
201	R. T. Simpson	Oxford University	The Parks	1951
201*	N. W. Hill	Sussex	Shireoaks	1961
201*	M. J. Harris	Glamorgan	Trent Bridge	1973
200*	J. Iremonger	Gloucestershire	Trent Bridge	1906
200*	G. M. Lee	Leicestershire	Trent Bridge	1913
200*	W. W. Keeton	Cambridge University	Fenner's	1932
200*	J. Hardstaff jun	Somerset	Trent Bridge	1947
200*	R. T. Simpson	Surrey	Trent Bridge	1949
200	R. T. Simpson	Warwickshire	Trent Bridge	1952

(2) CENTURIES IN LIMITED-OVERS MATCHES
a) Sunday League (John Player/Refuge Assurance)

Score	Batsman	Opponents	Venue	Year
123	D. W. Randall	Yorkshire	Trent Bridge	1987
123*	P. R. Pollard	Surrey	The Oval	1989
120*	C. E. B. Rice	Glamorgan	Swansea	1978
120*	B. Hassan	Warwickshire	Edgbaston	1981
117	C. E. B. Rice	Northamptonshire	Trent Bridge	1982
116*	G. St A. Sobers	Worcestershire	Newark	1971
116	C. E. B. Rice	Lancashire	Old Trafford	1977
116	R. T. Robinson	Derbyshire	Derby	1990
114	P. Johnson	Warwickshire	Edgbaston	1990
111	B. Hassan	Surrey	The Oval	1977
109*	M. Newell	Essex	Southend	1990
108	B. Hassan	Warwickshire	Edgbaston	1979
108	B. C. Broad	Glamorgan	Cardiff	1991
107*	D. W. Randall	Middlesex	Lord's	1976
107	D. W. Randall	Essex	Trent Bridge	1983
107*	R. T. Robinson	Glamorgan	Trent Bridge	1990
106*	B. C. Broad	Surrey	Trent Bridge	1990
105	C. E. B. Rice	Middlesex	Trent Bridge	1981

104*	M. J. Harris	Hampshire	JP Ground, Nottm	1970
104*	B. C. Broad	Derbyshire	Trent Bridge	1986
104	P. Johnson	Sussex	Trent Bridge	1990
103	C. E. B. Rice	Gloucestershire	Trent Bridge	1977
101	C. E. B. Rice	Leicestershire	Leicester	1981
100*	B. Hassan	Warwickshire	Trent Bridge	1980
100*	R. J. Hadlee	Gloucestershire	Cheltenham	1982
100*	B. C. Broad	Somerset	Bath	1986
100	R. T. Robinson	Surrey	Trent Bridge	1988
100	P. R. Pollard	Kent	Trent Bridge	1989
100	P. Johnson	Middlesex	Lord's	1990
100*	B. C. Broad	Lancashire	Old Trafford	1991

b) Gillette/Natwest Trophy

Score	Batsman	Opponents	Venue	Year
149*	D. W. Randall	Devon	Torquay	1988
139	R. T. Robinson	Worcestershire	Worcester	1985
124	R. T. Robinson	Lincolnshire	Trent Bridge	1991
115	B. C. Broad	Buckinghamshire	Marlow	1990
107	M. Hill	Somerset	Taunton	1964
105	P. A. Todd	Warwickshire	Edgbaston	1979
101	M. J. Harris	Somerset	Trent Bridge	1970
101*	P. Johnson	Staffordshire	Trent Bridge	1985
100*	J. B. Bolus	Yorkshire	Middlesbrough	1963

c) Benson & Hedges Cup

Score	Batsman	Opponents	Venue	Year
130*	C. E. B. Rice	Scotland	Glasgow	1982
122	B. C. Broad	Derbyshire	Derby	1984
120	R. T. Robinson	Scotland	Glasgow	1985
116	R. T. Robinson	Glamorgan	Cardiff	1991
108*	B. C. Broad	Yorkshire	Trent Bridge	1991
106	B. C. Broad	Gloucestershire	Bristol	1989
106*	R. T. Robinson	Northamptonshire	Trent Bridge	1990
104*	P. Johnson	Essex	Chelmsford	1990
103*	D. W. Randall	Minor Counties (N)	Trent Bridge	1979
103*	D. W. Randall	Surrey	Trent Bridge	1984
102*	P. Johnson	Minor Counties	Trent Bridge	1991
101	M. J. Harris	Yorkshire	Hull	1973

(3) MOST RUNS IN A SEASON

Scorers of 2,000 runs or more in a season in First-Class Nottinghamshire matches

Player	Year	M	I	NO	Runs	HS	Avge	100s
W. W. Whysall	1929	34	52	3	2620	244	53.46	7
W. W. Whysall	1928	34	51	2	2573	166	52.51	9
J. Hardstaff jun	1947	25	39	6	2272	221*	68.84	7

M. J. Harris	1971	26	45	1	2238	177	50.86	9
B. C. Broad	1990	22	43	2	2226	227★	54.29	9
N. W. Hill	1961	30	58	4	2185	201★	40.46	6
W. W. Whysall	1930	29	45	3	2151	248	51.21	8
D. W. Randall	1985	25	47	7	2151	117	53.77	5
N. W. Hill	1959	30	57	2	2129	167	38.70	6
W. W. Keeton	1933	28	49	3	2112	168	45.91	6
J. B. Bolus	1970	25	49	9	2073	147★	51.82	2
W. W. Keeton	1949	24	38	1	2049	210	55.37	6
R. T. Simpson	1959	30	55	5	2033	132	40.66	5
R. T. Robinson	1984	27	47	7	2032	171	50.80	5
W. W. Whysall	1927	31	48	5	2028	184	47.16	5
R. T. Simpson	1950	19	30	6	2010	243★	83.75	7
J. Hardstaff jun	1949	22	36	8	2005	162★	71.60	7
W. W. Keeton	1937	30	52	8	2004	136	45.54	4

(4) CENTURY ON FIRST-CLASS DEBUT

Player	Score	Opponents	Venue	Year
F. W. Stocks	114	Kent	Trent Bridge	1946
★P. F. Harvey	125★	Derbyshire	Trent Bridge	1947
K. R. Miller	102★	Cambridge U	Trent Bridge	1959
B. C. Broad	108★	Oxford U	The Parks	1984
M. A. Crawley	112	Oxford U	The Parks	1991

★This was Harvey's second match, but he did not bat in his first

(5) CENTURY IN EACH INNINGS IN A FIRST-CLASS MATCH

Batsman	Scores	Opponents	Venue	Year
J. B. Bolus	147 and 101	Northants	Trent Bridge	1969
B. C. Broad	132 and 113	Glamorgan	Cardiff	1989
G. Gunn	132 and 109★	Yorkshire	Trent Bridge	1913
	169 and 185★	Surrey	Trent Bridge	1919
	100 and 110	Warwickshire	Trent Bridge	1927
J. Hardstaff sen	118 and 106★	Derbyshire	Trent Bridge	1911
J. Hardstaff jun	100★ and 114★	Northants	Trent Bridge	1949
M. J. Harris	118 and 123	Leicestershire	Leicester	1971
	107 and 131★	Essex	Chelmsford	1971
	133★ and 132	Northants	Trent Bridge	1979
N. W. Hill	101 and 102	Lancashire	Trent Bridge	1959
A. O. Jones	137 and 100	Lancashire	Trent Bridge	1903
D. W. Randall	209 and 146	Middlesex	Trent Bridge	1979
C. E. B. Rice	131★ and 114★	Somerset	Trent Bridge	1980
R. T. Robinson	103 and 130★	Glamorgan	Swansea	1985
	128 and 146★	Kent	Trent Bridge	1989
A. Shrewsbury	101 and 127★	Gloucestershire	Trent Bridge	1902
R. T. Simpson	143 and 102★	Leicestershire	Trent Bridge	1949
M. J. Smedley	109 and 119	Lancashire	Old Trafford	1971
G. S. Sobers	160 and 103★	Surrey	Oval	1970

346

F. D. Stephenson	111 and 117	Yorkshire	Trent Bridge	1988
W. W. Whysall	100 and 167★	Gloucestershire	Trent Bridge	1926
	117 and 101★	Hampshire	Trent Bridge	1930

(6) BATSMEN TO CARRY THEIR BAT THROUGH A COMPLETED INNINGS

Batsman	Score	Opponents	Venue	Year
W. Oscroft	53★	Surrey	Trent Bridge	1865
R. Daft	12★	Lancashire	Trent Bridge	1877
W. Wright	127★	Gloucestershire	Trent Bridge	1883
A. Shrewsbury	224★	Middlesex	Lord's	1885
W. H. Scotton	110★	Surrey	Trent Bridge	1886
A. Shrewsbury	227★	Gloucestershire	Moreton in Marsh	1886
W. H. Scotton	35★	Lancashire	Old Trafford	1887
W. H. Scotton	17★	Yorkshire	Bramall Lane	1888
A. Shrewsbury	111★	Kent	Canterbury	1892
A. Shrewsbury	125★	Gloucestershire	Trent Bridge	1896
H. B. Daft	77★	Surrey	The Oval	1896
J. Iremonger	189★	Middlesex	Lord's	1904
A. O. Jones	125★	Australians	Trent Bridge	1909
G. Gunn	91★	Yorkshire	Trent Bridge	1909
G. Gunn	52★	Essex	Leyton	1911
G. Gunn	64★	Middlesex	Lord's	1913
G. Gunn	62★	Yorkshire	Dewsbury	1913
G. Gunn	117★	Middlesex	Lord's	1921
W. W. Whysall	109★	Kent	Canterbury	1924
W. W. Whysall	111★	Essex	Trent Bridge	1929
G. Gunn	109★	Sussex	Eastbourne	1929
G. Gunn	67★	Gloucestershire	Cheltenham	1926
G. Gunn	85★	Kent	Trent Bridge	1931
C. B. Harris	117★	Yorkshire	Headingley	1934
W. W. Keeton	99★	Kent	Trent Bridge	1937
R. T. Simpson	230★	Glamorgan	Swansea	1950
C. B. Harris	239★	Hampshire	Trent Bridge	1950
N. W. Hill	23★	Sussex	Eastbourne	1962
J. B. Bolus	136★	Derbyshire	Trent Bridge	1963
M. Newell	10★	Warwickshire	Edgbaston	1988

INDIVIDUAL BOWLING RECORDS

(1) FOUR WICKETS WITH CONSECUTIVE BALLS IN FIRST-CLASS MATCHES

Bowler	Opponents	Venue	Year
F. Shacklock	Somerset	Trent Bridge	1893
A. K. Walker	Leicestershire	Leicester	1956

Note: Walker took a wicket with the last ball of the first innings and then achieved a hat-trick with the first three deliveries of the second innings, a feat unique in first-class cricket.

(2) HAT-TRICKS (EXCLUDING 4 IN 4) IN FIRST-CLASS MATCHES

Bowler	Opponents	Venue	Year
H. J. Butler	Leicestershire	Worksop	1937
	Surrey	Trent Bridge	1937
	Hampshire	Trent Bridge	1939
C. E. Dench	Gloucestershire	Bristol	1899
J. A. Dixon	Lancashire	Trent Bridge	1887
W. Flowers	Kent	Maidstone	1888
J. R. Gunn	Middlesex	Lord's	1899
	Derbyshire	Chesterfield	1904
A. W. Hallam	Leicestershire	Trent Bridge	1907
R. J. Hadlee	Kent	Canterbury	1987
E. E. Hemmings	Northants	Trent Bridge	1984
H. Larwood	Cambridge University	Fenner's	1926
	Glamorgan	Trent Bridge	1931
T. L. Richmond	Lancashire	Trent Bridge	1926
A. Shaw	Derbyshire	Derby	1875
	Gloucestershire	Trent Bridge	1884
K. Smales	Lancashire	Trent Bridge	1955
B. Stead	Somerset	Trent Bridge	1972
M. N. S. Taylor	Kent	Dover	1965
T. G. Wass	Essex	Trent Bridge	1908

Note: A. Shaw achieved a hat-trick in each innings in the 1884 Gloucestershire match at Trent Bridge.

(3) 125 WICKETS IN A SEASON IN FIRST-CLASS MATCHES

Bowler	Year	Overs	Mdns	Runs	Wkts	Avge
B. Dooland	1954	1197.4	393	2708	181	14.96
T. L. Richmond	1922	862.2	209	2279	169	13.48
T. G. Wass	1907	885	218	2328	163	14.28
B. Dooland	1953	1151.3	444	2613	160	16.33

A. W. Hallam	1907	857	280	1901	156	12.18
T. L. Richmond	1926	978.1	149	3156	149	21.18
H. Larwood	1932	725.4	179	1702	149	11.42
T. L. Richmond	1920	928.4	158	2884	148	19.48
B. Dooland	1955	1198.3	325	3263	147	22.19
B. Dooland	1956	1198.4	400	2883	146	19.74
T. G. Wass	1902	803.2	188	2225	140	15.89
W. Voce	1935	1973.4	224	3000	139	21.58
B. Dooland	1957	1293	415	3053	136	22.45
W. Voce	1936	1100.1	262	2655	135	18.66
T. G. Wass	1908	837.5	165	2379	130	18.30
H. Larwood	1931	634.3	142	1506	128	11.76
W. Voce	1934	1044	214	2822	128	22.04
S. J. Staples	1927	1264.4	376	2837	127	22.33
F. Morley	1878	1142.2	637	1250	126	9.92
T. L. Richmond	1921	990.3	157	3272	125	26.17

Since the reduction in Championship matches in 1969, three bowlers have taken 100 wickets in a season for Notts:

R. J. Hadlee	1981	708.4	231	1564	105	14.89
R. J. Hadlee	1984	772.2	248	1645	117	14.06
K. E. Cooper	1988	816	220	2179	101	21.57
F. D. Stephenson	1988	819.1	196	2289	125	18.31

(4) TEN AND NINE WICKETS IN AN INNINGS FOR NOTTINGHAMSHIRE

Analysis	Bowler	Opponents	Venue	Year
10-20	J. C. Shaw	England	Eastwood Hall	1870
10-66	K. Smales	Gloucestershire	Stroud	1956
9-19	J. Grundy	Kent	Trent Bridge	1864
9-21	T. L. Richmond	Hampshire	Trent Bridge	1922
9-23	Wm. Attewell	Sussex	Trent Bridge	1886
9-29	W. Clarke	Kent	Trent Bridge	1845
9-33	Mart. McIntyre	Surrey	Oval	1872
9-41	H. Larwood	Kent	Trent Bridge	1931
9-49	J. Jackson	Surrey	Oval	1860
9-50	F. C. Matthews	Northants	Trent Bridge	1923
9-54	R. J. Mee	Sussex	Trent Bridge	1893
9-55	T. L. Richmond	Northants	Trent Bridge	1925
9-67	T. G. Wass	Derbyshire	Blackwell	1911
9-84	J. C. Shaw	Gloucestershire	Trent Bridge	1871
9-91	T. G. Wass	Surrey	Oval	1902
9-141	S. J. Staples	Kent	Canterbury	1927
9-?	W. Clarke	Kent	Town Malling	1840

Notes: (1) J. C. Shaw's performance in 1870 is not regarded as strictly first-class, since Notts fielded 16 men against 11 of England.

(2) W. Clarke took 9 wickets *v* Leicester in 1845 at Trent Bridge; this was not however a county match, the Notts team being Nottingham Amateurs.

(5) FIFTEEN WICKETS IN A MATCH FOR NOTTINGHAMSHIRE

Analysis	Bowler	Opponents	Venue	Year
17-89	F. C. Matthews	Northants	Trent Bridge	1923
16-69	W. Clarke	Kent	Trent Bridge	1845
16-69	T. G. Wass	Lancashire	Liverpool	1906
16-83	B. Dooland	Essex	Trent Bridge	1954
16-103	T. G. Wass	Essex	Trent Bridge	1908
15-35	F. Morley	Kent	Town Malling	1878
15-73	J. Jackson	Surrey	Oval	1860
15-78	R. C. Tinley	Cambridgeshire	Trent Bridge	1862
15-106	F. D. Stephenson	Essex	Trent Bridge	1989
15-193	B. Dooland	Kent	Gravesend	1956

(6) BEST BOWLING PERFORMANCES IN LIMITED-OVERS MATCHES
(a) Sunday League

Analysis	Bowler	Opponents	Venue	Year
6-12	R. J. Hadlee	Lancashire	Trent Bridge	1980
6-16	P. J. Hacker	Essex	Chelmsford	1980
6-20	K. Saxelby	Leicestershire	Leicester	1989

Note: K. Saxelby took 5 wickets in four consecutive innings in 1989, a League record. He is also the only Notts bowler to take a hat-trick (*v* Worcestershire, Trent Bridge, 1987).

(b) Benson & Hedges Cup

Analysis	Bowler	Opponents	Venue	Year
6-22	M. K. Bore	Leicestershire	Leicester	1980
6-22	C. E. B. Rice	Northamptonshire	Northampton	1981
6-33	M. Hendrick	Northamptonshire	Northampton	1982

(c) Gillette/Natwest Trophy

Analysis	Bowler	Opponents	Venue	Year
6-18	C. E. B. Rice	Sussex	Hove	1982
5-17	R. J. Hadlee	Surrey	The Oval	1986
5-22	R. A. Pick	Gloucestershire	Bristol	1987
5-44	B. Stead	Worcestershire	Worcester	1974

(7) ONLY TWO BOWLERS USED THROUGHOUT A COMPLETED MATCH

Bowlers	Opponents	Venue	Year
J. Jackson, J. Grundy	Kent	Cranbrook	1863
A. Shaw, F. Morley	Australians	Trent Bridge	1878
	Surrey	Trent Bridge	1878
	Yorkshire	Trent Bridge	1878
	Kent	Town Malling	1878
	Derbyshire	Trent Bridge	1879
	Derbyshire	Derby	1879
A. Shaw, Wm. Attewell	Gloucestershire	Trent Bridge	1884
T. G. Wass, A. W. Hallam	Northants	Northampton	1907
	Derbyshire	Chesterfield	1907
	Essex	Trent Bridge	1908
	Derbyshire	Trent Bridge	1909
T. G. Wass, J. Iremonger	Derbyshire	Chesterfield	1913
H. Larwood, W. Voce	Leicestershire	Trent Bridge	1932

ALL-ROUND RECORDS

(1) THE DOUBLE

Player	Year	Runs	Avge	Wkts	Avge
J. R. Gunn	1903	1517	45.97	108	18.47
J. R. Gunn	1904	1086	36.20	106	24.93
J. R. Gunn	1906	1312	37.49	110	20.72
F. Barratt	1928	1070	29.72	109	24.64
B. Dooland	1957	1517	29.17	136	22.44
R. J. Hadlee	1984	1179	51.26	117	14.05
F. D. Stephenson	1988	1018	29.08	125	18.31

FIELDING RECORDS

(1) MOST CATCHES IN A FIRST-CLASS MATCH

Player	Catches	Opponents	Venue	Year
A. O. Jones	7	Gloucestershire	Trent Bridge	1908
W. Voce	7	Glamorgan	Pontypridd	1929
A. Shrewsbury	6	Middlesex	Trent Bridge	1880
A. O. Jones	6	Philadelphians	Trent Bridge	1903
A. O. Jones	6	Northants	Northampton	1906
A. O. Jones	6	Sussex	Hove	1907
A. O. Jones	6	Yorkshire	Trent Bridge	1908

G. M. Lee	6	Hampshire	Southampton	1913
W. W. Whysall	6	Worcestershire	Trent Bridge	1929
A. W. Carr	6	Leicester	Trent Bridge	1933
J. D. Clay	6	Derbyshire	Trent Bridge	1957
N. W. Hill	6	Northants	Trent Bridge	1958
M. N. S. Taylor	6	Surrey	Oval	1965
D. W. Randall	6	Yorkshire	Trent Bridge	1987

Notes: (1) J. D. Clay took all his catches in a single innings, a record for the County.

(2) The most by a fieldsman in a season for Notts is 44 by W. W. Whysall in 1929; S. J. Staples took 39 in 1926 and A. O. Jones 37 in 1908.

WICKETKEEPING RECORDS

(1) MOST DISMISSALS BY A WICKET-KEEPER IN A FIRST-CLASS MATCH

Keeper	Total	Ct	St	Opponents	Venue	Year
T. W. Oates	10	9	1	Middlesex	Trent Bridge	1906
B. N. French	10	7	3	Oxford University	The Parks	1984
C. W. Scott	10	10	0	Derbyshire	Derby	1988
B. Lilley	9	9	0	Somerset	Taunton	1932
G. Millman	9	8	1	Warwickshire	Trent Bridge	1964
M. Sherwin	8	5	3	Gloucestershire	Trent Bridge	1889
T. W. Oates	8	7	1	Leicestershire	Leicester	1907
T. W. Oates	8	8	0	Kent	Dover	1923
D. L. Murray	8	7	1	Warwickshire	Trent Bridge	1969
B. N. French	8	8	0	Lancashire	Trent Bridge	1981
B. N. French	8	6	2	Somerset	Taunton	1984
C. W. Scott	8	7	1	Derbyshire	Derby	1986

Notes: (1) On nine occasions wicket-keepers have made 6 dismissals in an innings. B. N. French has achieved the distinction on three occasions, and E. A. Meads and T. W. Oates have achieved the distinction twice each and B. Lilley and G. Millman once each.

(2) The most dismissals in a season for Notts are 87 by B. N. French in 1984, 85 by G. Millman in 1961, 80 by B. Lilley in 1926.

RECORD WICKET PARTNERSHIP

(1) IN FIRST-CLASS MATCHES

FIRST WICKET

391	A. O. Jones *and* A. Shrewsbury *v* Gloucestershire (Bristol)	1899
318	R. T. Simpson *and* W. W. Keeton *v* Lancashire (Old Trafford)	1949
303	A. O. Jones *and* J. Iremonger *v* Gloucestershire (Trent Bridge)	1904
284	R. T. Simpson *and* R. J. Giles *v* Oxford University (The Parks)	1951
282	P. R. Pollard *and* R. T. Robinson *v* Kent (Trent Bridge)	1989
277	W. W. Keeton *and* C. B. Harris *v* Middlesex (Trent Bridge)	1933
269	R. T. Simpson *and* W. W. Keeton *v* Kent (Trent Bridge)	1951
252	G. Gunn *and* W. W. Whysall *v* Kent (Trent Bridge)	1924

SECOND WICKET

398	W. Gunn *and* A. Shrewsbury *v* Sussex (Trent Bridge)	1890
333	A. W. Carr *and* G. M. Lee *v* Leicestershire (Trent Bridge)	1913
312	W. Gunn *and* A. Shrewsbury *v* Sussex (Hove)	1891
289	A. Shrewsbury *and* W. Barnes *v* Surrey (Oval)	1882
274	W. Gunn *and* A. Shrewsbury *v* Sussex (Hove)	1893
265	G. Gunn *and* W. Walker *v* Hampshire (Bournemouth)	1928
265	R. T. Robinson *and* D. W. Randall *v* Yorkshire (Trent Bridge)	1984
265	P. R. Pollard *and* R. T. Robinson *v* Derbyshire (Derby)	1991
261	N. W. Hill *and* J. D. Clay *v* Yorkshire (Trent Bridge)	1959
256	W. W. Whysall *and* W. Walker *v* Hampshire (Trent Bridge)	1930
251★	R. T. Simpson *and* C. J. Poole *v* Leicestershire (Trent Bridge)	1949

THIRD WICKET

369	W. Gunn *and* J. R. Gunn *v* Leicestershire (Trent Bridge)	1903
270	D. W. Randall *and* C. E. B. Rice *v* Yorkshire (Harrogate)	1980
266	C. B. Harris *and* J. Hardstaff jun *v* Gloucestershire (Trent Bridge)	1936
263	D. W. Randall *and* C. E. B. Rice *v* Yorkshire (Trent Bridge)	1981
260	W. W. Keeton *and* J. Hardstaff jun *v* Yorkshire (Bramall Lane)	1949
256	W. W. Whysall *and* A. W. Carr *v* Leicestershire (Leicester)	1928

FOURTH WICKET

361	A. O. Jones *and* J. R. Gunn *v* Essex (Leyton)	1905
345	M. Newell *and* D. W. Randall *v* Derbyshire (Trent Bridge)	1988
323	A. W. Carr *and* W. R. D. Payton *v* Kent (Trent Bridge)	1923
285	B. C. Broad *and* D. W. Randall *v* Kent (Tunbridge Wells)	1990
266★	W. R. D. Payton *and* J. R. Gunn *v* Gloucestershire (Trent Bridge)	1911
263	J. Hardstaff jun *and* F. W. Stocks *v* Northants (Trent Bridge)	1951
260	C. E. B. Rice *and* P. Johnson *v* Kent (Folkestone)	1984
251	H. I. Moore *and* D. L. Murray *v* Indians (Trent Bridge)	1967

FIFTH WICKET

266	A. Shrewsbury *and* W. Gunn *v* Sussex (Hove)	1884
247	J. Hardstaff jun *and* A. Staples *v* Middlesex (Trent Bridge)	1937
246★	M. J. Smedley *and* G. S. Sobers *v* Glamorgan (Swansea)	1971
244	F. H. Winrow *and* T. B. Reddick *v* Kent (Trent Bridge)	1947
236	W. W. Keeton *and* A. W. Carr *v* Essex (Trent Bridge)	1932
229★	C. E. B. Rice *and* M. J. Smedley *v* Lancashire (Trent Bridge)	1978
228	J. Hardstaff jun *and* F. W. Stocks *v* Northants (Northampton)	1952
205	W. Barnes *and* W. Gunn *v* Sussex (Trent Bridge)	1887

SIXTH WICKET

303*	F. H. Winrow *and* P. F. Harvey *v* Derbyshire (Trent Bridge)	1947
270	R. T. Simpson *and* A. Jepson *v* Worcestershire (Trent Bridge)	1950
247*	W. R. Payton *and* W. A. Flint *v* Northants (Trent Bridge)	1927
208	C. E. B. Rice *and* H. T. Tunnicliffe *v* Glamorgan (Swansea)	1978
206*	J. D. Birch *and* R. J. Hadlee *v* Somerset (Trent Bridge)	1986
201	A. W. Carr *and* W. Walker *v* Leicestershire (Leicester)	1925
200	W. R. D. Payton *and* S. J. Staples *v* Surrey (Oval)	1923

(P. F. Harvey was batting in only his second innings in First Class cricket when he helped to create the present record)

SEVENTH WICKET

204	M. J. Smedley *and* R. A. White *v* Surrey (Oval)	1967
201	R. H. Howitt *and* R. Bagguley *v* Sussex (Trent Bridge)	1895
178	W. Walker *and* W. A. Flint *v* Surrey (Oval)	1924
177	A. Shrewsbury *and* Wm. Attewell *v* Middlesex (Lord's)	1885
169	C. J. Poole *and* B. Dooland *v* Somerset (Trent Bridge)	1953
166	J. Hardstaff jun *and* B. Lilley *v* Warwickshire (Trent Bridge)	1936
159	W. Gunn *and* Wm. Attewell *v* Middlesex (Trent Bridge)	1884
159	B. Hassan *and* S. R. Bielby *v* Somerset (Taunton)	1969
158	D. L. Murray *and* M. N. S. Taylor *v* Surrey (Oval)	1966

EIGHTH WICKET

220	G. F. H. Heane *and* R. Winrow *v* Somerset (Trent Bridge)	1935
195	W. R. Payton *and* T. W. Oates *v* Kent (Trent Bridge)	1920
167	A. Staples *and* F. Barratt *v* Surrey (Trent Bridge)	1928
163	D. W. Randall *and* E. E. Hemmings *v* Leicestershire (Leicester)	1990
151	W. R. D. Payton *and* H. Larwood *v* Northants (Trent Bridge)	1925

NINTH WICKET

165	W. McIntyre *and* G. Wootton *v* Kent (Trent Bridge)	1869

TENTH WICKET

152	E. B. Alletson *and* W. Riley *v* Sussex (Hove)	1911
140	S. J. Staples *and* T. L. Richmond *v* Derbyshire (Worksop)	1922
136	H. Larwood *and* W. Voce *v* Sussex (Trent Bridge)	1931
123	B. Dooland *and* A. K. Walker *v* Somerset (Trent Bridge)	1956
111	J. R. Gunn *and* W. A. Flint *v* Middlesex (Trent Bridge)	1919
110*	F. W. Stocks *and* E. A. Meads *v* Worcestershire (Trent Bridge)	1946
109	W. Gunn *and* R. G. Hardstaff *v* Derbyshire (Derby)	1896
103	S. J. Staples *and* W. Voce *v* Leicestershire (Leicester)	1933
101	W. W. Whysall *and* W. Voce *v* Gloucestershire (Trent Bridge)	1929
100	W. A. Sime *and* W. Voce *v* Cambridge University (Fenner's)	1935

(2) IN LIMITED-OVERS MATCHES
(a) Sunday League (John Player/Refuge Assurance)

1st	188	D. W. Randall *and* B. Hassan *v* Warwickshire (Edgbaston)	1981
2nd	200*	R. T. Robinson *and* C. E. B. Rice *v* Worcestershire (Worcester)	1984
3rd	169	P. Johnson *and* R. T. Robinson *v* Warwickshire (Edgbaston)	1990
4th	127	D. W. Randall *and* C. E. B. Rice *v* Lancashire (Trent Bridge)	1986
5th	111	D. J. R. Martindale *and* F. D. Stephenson *v* Hampshire (Trent Bridge)	1989
6th	114	S. R. Bielby *and* M. N. S. Taylor *v* Derbyshire (Chesterfield)	1971
7th	76	J. D. Birch *and* B. N. French *v* Gloucestershire (Bristol)	1985

8th	51	B. N. French *and* E. E. Hemmings *v* Hampshire (Trent Bridge)	1985
9th	46*	M. Newell *and* E. E. Hemmings *v* Hampshire (Southampton)	1990
10th	50*	E. E. Hemmings *and* M. K. Bore *v* Northants (Northampton)	1979

(b) Gillette/Natwest Trophy

1st	146	B. C. Broad *and* R. T. Robinson *v* Gloucestershire (Bristol)	1985
2nd	118	B. C. Broad *and* M. Newell *v* Derbyshire (Derby)	1987
3rd	89	B. C. Broad *and* D. J. R. Martindale *v* Hertfordshire (Hitchin)	1989
4th	205*	D. W. Randall *and* J. D. Birch *v* Devon (Torquay)	1988
5th	92	G. St A. Sobers *and* D. L. Murray *v* Worcestershire (Worcester)	1968
	92	R. T. Robinson *and* R. J. Hadlee *v* Warwickshire (Trent Bridge)	1985
6th	105	G. St A. Sobers *and* R. A. White *v* Worcestershire (Worcester)	1974
7th	119	P. Johnson *and* B. N. French *v* Stafford (Trent Bridge)	1985
8th	53*	P. Johnson *and* E. E. Hemmings *v* Stafford (Trent Bridge)	1985
9th	80	P. A. Wilkinson *and* W. Taylor *v* Sussex (Trent Bridge)	1975
10th	24	P. D. Watts *and* J. S. Howarth *v* Northamptonshire (Northampton)	1967

(c) Benson & Hedges Cup

1st	199	M. J. Harris *and* B. Hassan *v* Yorkshire (Hull)	1973
2nd	179	J. D. Birch *and* D. W. Randall *v* Minor Counties (North) (Trent Bridge)	1979
3rd	164	D. W. Randall *and* C. E. B. Rice *v* Surrey (Trent Bridge)	1984
4th	147	R. T. Robinson *and* M. A. Crawley *v* Glamorgan (Cardiff)	1991
5th	125	B. Hassan *and* R. J. Hadlee *v* Warwickshire (Trent Bridge)	1982
6th	98	J. D. Birch *and* R. J. Hadlee *v* Lancashire (Liverpool)	1986
7th	85	B. Hassan *and* B. N. French *v* Worcestershire (Trent Bridge)	1984
	85	R. T. Robinson *and* E. E. Hemmings *v* Scotland (Titwood)	1985
8th	50	H. T. Tunnicliffe *and* P. A. Wilkinson *v* Northamptonshire (Northampton)	1976
9th	49*	J. D. Birch *and* E. E. Hemmings *v* Middlesex (Lord's)	1986
10th	44*	B. N. French *and* R. A. Pick *v* Hampshire (Southampton)	1991

(3) OPENING CENTURY STAND IN BOTH INNINGS IN FIRST-CLASS MATCH

134 *and* 144*	A. O. Jones *and* J. Iremonger *v* Surrey (Oval)	1901
102 *and* 303	A. O. Jones *and* J. Iremonger *v* Gloucestershire (Trent Bridge)	1904
125 *and* 128	W. W. Keeton *and* C. B. Harris *v* Kent (Trent Bridge)	1933
122 *and* 151*	W. W. Keeton *and* C. B. Harris *v* Northamptonshire (Northampton)	1950
172 *and* 154	J. B. Bolus *and* M. J. Harris *v* Lancashire (Trent Bridge)	1970
161 *and* 220*	B. C. Broad *and* R. T. Robinson *v* Oxford University (The Parks)	1984
222 *and* 282	R. T. Robinson *and* P. R. Pollard *v* Kent (Trent Bridge)	1989

NOTTINGHAMSHIRE CAPTAINS

1834–1855	W. Clarke	1947–1950	Mr W. A. Sime
1856–1870	G. Parr	1951–1960	Mr R. T. Simpson
1871–1880	R. Daft	1961	J. D. Clay
1881–1882	W. Oscroft	1962	Mr A. J. Corran
1883–1886	A. Shaw	1963–1965	G. Millman
1887–1888	M. Sherwin	1966–1967	N. W. Hill
1889–1899	Mr J. A. Dixon	1968–1973	G. St A. Sobers
1900–1914	Mr A. O. Jones	*(Sobers resigned in May 1972 and*	
	(during 1913 Dr G. O. Gauld	*J. B. Bolus was appointed, but resigned*	
	acted as Captain due to A. O.	*at the close of 1972)*	
	Jones' illness)	1974	J. D. Bond
1919–1934	Mr A. W. Carr	1975–1979	M. J. Smedley
1935	Mr G. F. H. Heane	1979–1987	C. E. B. Rice
	and Mr S. D. Rhodes	*(Rice was appointed on 16 July 1979)*	
1936–1946	Mr G. F. H. Heane	1988–	R. T. Robinson

NOTTINGHAMSHIRE PLAYERS' TEST RECORDS

Player	Country	Test dates	M	Runs	Avge	Wkts	Avge
Wm. Attewell	England	1884/5–1891/2	10	150	16.66	27	23.18
W. Barnes	England	1880–1890	21	725	23.38	51	15.54
F. Barratt	England	1929–1929/30	5	28	9.33	5	47.00
G. Bean	England	1891/2	3	92	18.40	–	
J. B. Bolus	England	1963–1963/4	7	496	41.33	0	
B. C. Broad	England	1984–1989	25	1661	39.54	0	
H. J. Butler	England	1947–1947/8	2	15	15.00	12	17.91
C. L. Cairns	New Zealand						
A. W. Carr	England	1922/3–1929	11	237	19.75	–	
B. Dooland	Australia	1946/7–1947/8	3	76	19.00	9	46.55
D. R. Doshi	India	1979/80–1983/4	33	129	4.60	114	30.71
W. Flowers	England	1884/5–1893	8	254	18.14	14	21.14
B. N. French	England	1986–1987/8	16	308	18.11	–	
G. Gunn	England	1907/8–1929/30	15	1120	40.00	0	
J. R. Gunn	England	1901/2–1905	6	85	10.62	18	21.50
W. Gunn	England	1886/7–1899	11	392	21.77	–	
R. J. Hadlee	New Zealand	1972/3–1990	86	3124	27.16	431	22.29
J. Hardstaff sen	England	1907/8	5	311	31.10	–	
J. Hardstaff jun	England	1935–1948	23	1636	46.74	–	
E. E. Hemmings	England	1982–1990	16				
M. Hendrick	England	1974–1981	30	128	6.40	87	25.83
A. O. Jones	England	1899–1909	12	291	13.85	3	44.33
W. W. Keeton	England	1934–1939	2	57	14.25	–	
H. Larwood	England	1926–1932/3	21	485	19.40	78	28.35
W. H. Lockwood	England	1893–1902	12	231	17.76	43	20.55
K. R. Miller	Australia	1946/7–1956/7	55	2958	36.97	170	22.97

G. Millman	England	1961/2–1962	6	60	12.00	–	
F. Morley	England	1880–1882/3	4	6	1.50	16	18.50
D. L. Murray	West Indies	1963–1980	62	1993	22.90	–	
C. J. Poole	England	1951/2	3	161	40.25	0	
D. W. Randall	England	1976/7–1984	47	2470	33.37	0	
H. J. Rhodes	England	1959	2	0	–	9	27.11
T. L. Richmond	England	1921	1	6	3.00	2	43.00
R. T. Robinson	England	1985–1989	29	1601	36.38	0	
W. H. Scotton	England	1881/2–1886/7	15	510	22.17	0	
J. Selby	England	1876/7–1881/2	6	256	23.27	–	
J. W. Sharpe	England	1890–1891/2	3	44	22.00	11	27.72
A. Shaw	England	1876/7–1881/2	7	111	10.09	12	23.75
M. Sherwin	England	1886/7–1888	3	30	15.00	0	
A. Shrewsbury	England	1881/2–1893	23	1277	35.47	0	
R. T. Simpson	England	1948/9–1954/5	27	1401	33.35	2	11.00
G. St A. Sobers	West Indies	1953/4–1973/4	93	8032	57.78	235	34.03
S. J. Staples	England	1927/8	3	65	13.00	15	29.00
R. Swetman	England	1958/9–1959/60	11	254	16.93	–	
W. Voce	England	1929/30–1946/7	27	308	13.39	98	27.88
W. W. Whysall	England	1924/5–1930	4	209	29.85	0	
C. W. Wright	England	1895/6	3	125	31.25	–	

Notes:
(1) G. St A. Sobers played in 31 Tests whilst registered as a Notts player, and R. J. Hadlee played in 50 Tests whilst registered as a Notts player.
(2) W. H. Lockwood and G. Bean had left Notts and were playing with Surrey and Sussex respectively during their Test careers.
(3) J. W. Sharpe, though Notts born, made his Notts debut after playing for England.
(4) B. Dooland and K. R. Miller played for Australia before appearing for Notts.
(5) D. L. Murray played in five Tests whilst registered as a Notts player.
(6) D. R. Doshi played for India after leaving Notts.
(7) R. Swetman, H. J. Rhodes and M. Hendrick played for England prior to joining Notts.

NOTTINGHAMSHIRE CRICKET GROUNDS

1. *The Forest, Nottingham.* First first-class inter-county match *v* Sussex, 7, 8, 9 September 1835. Last first-class inter-county match *v* Sussex 21, 22, 23, 24 August 1837. The site of these two matches, inside the oval racecourse on the Forest, was first used for cricket in 1814. Cricket was played on the site until 1979. It is now an informal play area.

2. *Trent Bridge, Nottingham.* First first-class inter-county match *v* Sussex, 27, 28 July 1840. This is the headquarters of the County Club and has been in use continuously since it was laid out in 1838 by William Clarke, the then captain of the County side.

3. *Brackenhurst, Southwell.* Only first-class match *v* England, 27, 28 August 1846. The ground is used by Southwell Cricket Club at the present time and the first definite reference to cricket on the site was in about 1830.

4. *Kelham Road, Newark.* Only first-class match *v* England, 21, 22, 23 August 1856. The ground is used by Newark Cricket Club at the present time and has been used for cricket since at least 1823.

5. *Welbeck Abbey.* First first-class match *v* Derbyshire, 12, 13, 14 August 1901. Last first-class match *v* Derbyshire, 28, 29, 30 July 1904. The ground was laid out by the 6th Duke of Portland adjacent to Welbeck Abbey in the 1880s. It is now used by the pupils of the Army Public School which occupies the Abbey at the present time.

6. *Steetley Company Ground, Shireoaks.* Only first-class match *v* Sussex, 5, 6, 7 July 1961. The ground was laid out by the Company in 1951 and is still in use by the Company Cricket Club, playing in the Bassetlaw League.

7. *Central Avenue, Worksop.* First first-class match *v* Derbyshire, 20, 21, 22 July 1921. The ground was laid out for Worksop Cricket Club and first used in 1901. It is still in use both for County matches and by the local club who play in the Bassetlaw League.

8. *Elm Avenue, Newark.* First first-class match *v* Lancashire, 6, 7, 8 July 1966. Last first-class match *v* Worcestershire, 18, 19, 20 May 1978. The ground was laid out in 1930 by Ransome & Marles Ltd for their works team and is still in use by RHP Ltd (formerly Ransome & Marles).

9. *Aspley Lane, Nottingham.* Four Sunday League county matches, between 1970 and 1974, have been played on the ground. The ground was laid out in 1904 by the John Player Company and has been used by the company employees since that date.

10. *Chichester Road, Cleethorpes.* First first-class match *v* Worcestershire, 20, 21, 22 August 1980. The ground was laid out in 1930 and is used by Cleethorpes Cricket Club at the present time.

Two other grounds worthy of note are West Park, West Bridgford, used by Sir Julien Cahn's Team 1926 to 1939 and Meadow Road, Beeston, used by Gentlemen of Nottinghamshire 1866 to c.1900.

BIBLIOGRAPHY

F. S. Ashley-Cooper: Nottinghamshire Cricket and Cricketers (Saxton) Nottingham, 1923

E. Browne: A Short History of Nottinghamshire Cricket (G. Richards) Nottingham, 1887

C. H. Richards: Nottinghamshire Cricket Scores & Biographies Vol 1 & 2 (Richards) Nottingham, various years

F. G. Spybey: Nottinghamshire County Cricket Matches 1865–1877 (Spybey) Nottingham, 1878

F. G. Spybey: Annual Register of Nottingham County Matches (Spybey) Nottingham, various years

P. Wynne-Thomas: Nottinghamshire Cricketers 1821–1914 (Author) Retford, 1971

P. Wynne-Thomas: Nottinghamshire Cricketers 1919–1939 (Notts CCC) Nottingham, 1980

P. Wynne-Thomas: Trent Bridge (Notts CCC) Nottingham, 1987

J. F. Sutton: Nottingham Cricket Matches 1771–1865 (Sutton) Nottingham, 1865

Association of Cricket Statisticians: Nottinghamshire Cricketers 1835–1978 (ACS) Nottingham, 1979

Notts CCC: Yearbooks 1947 to date (Notts CCC) Nottingham, various years

A. W. Carr: Cricket With The Lid Off (Hutchinson) London, 1935

R. Daft: Kings of Cricket (Arrowsmith) Bristol, 1893

R. Daft: A Cricketer's Yarns (Chapman & Hall) London, 1926

H. Larwood: Bodyline? (Matthews & Marrot) London, 1933

P. Wynne-Thomas: Give Me Arthur (Arthur Barker) London, 1986

A. W. Pullin: Alfred Shaw – Cricketer (Cassell) London, 1902

The following periodicals were also used extensively:

Wisden Cricketers' Almanack 1864 to 1991; *Cricket* 1882 to 1913; *World of Cricket* 1914; *The Cricketer* 1921 to date; *Playfair Cricket Monthly* 1960 to 1973; *Wisden Cricket Monthly* 1979 to date; *Playfair Cricket Annual* 1948 to date; *The Cricket Statistician* 1973 to date; *The Cricket Quarterly* 1963 to 1970.

ACKNOWLEDGEMENTS

The author would like to thank Philip Thorn for his work on the biographical details of players, Philip Bailey for checking the career records; Michael and John Goulder for checking the record section in general; the county scorers Len Beaumont and Gordon Stringfellow for providing various details; Brian Robson for reading through the manuscript and providing corrections; the staff at the Notts County Library, Angel Row, for their help over many years.

INDEX